D1216260

BUCK OWENS

The Biography

EILEEN SISK

CHICAGO
REVIEW
PRESS

An A Cappella Book

Copyright © 2010 by Eileen Sisk
All rights reserved
First hardcover edition published 2010
First paperback edition published 2012
Published by Chicago Review Press, Incorporated
814 North Franklin Street
Chicago, Illinois 60610

ISBN 978-1-61374-335-5

The Library of Congress has cataloged the hardcover edition as follows:
Sisk, Eileen.
Buck Owens : the biography / Eileen Sisk. — 1st ed.
p. cm.
Includes bibliographical references and index.
ISBN 978-1-55652-768-5
1. Owens, Buck, 1929–2006. 2. Country musicians—United States—Biography. I. Title.
ML420.O945S57 2010
782.421642092—dc22
[B]
2010017642

Cover and interior design: Scott Rattray
Front cover photo: GAB Archive/Redferns

Printed in the United States of America
5 4 3 2 1

FOR BUCK OWENS AND HIS BUCKAROOS.
AND FOR MY FATHER, HUGH ALBERT SISK,
A TRUE OKIE FROM MUSKOGEE AND DUST BOWLER
WHO INSTILLED IN ME A STRONG WORK ETHIC
AND A LOVE FOR THE BAKERSFIELD SOUND.

"IT AIN'T SLANDER IF IT'S TRUE."

—Buck Owens

CONTENTS

ACKNOWLEDGMENTS

It would be impossible to write a nonfiction book without the help of many people, but first I would like to thank Buck Owens. Buck read my first book and told me, "I couldn't put it down—the continuity and style of your writing suggest mucho talent." He said he was getting older and warming to the idea of putting his "life down on paper," and after a few friendly letters he invited me to Bakersfield to discuss writing his autobiography. When I met with the country icon at 4 P.M. on April 4, 1997, in his office above the Crystal Palace, he launched into details about his marriages, sex life, lawsuits, health, and more. For some reason, though, he did not want to talk about his music. He said, "If I write a book, I want it to be entertaining. I don't want people getting bored."

Thus began an exchange of letters—all but one written in Buck's own hand—over the course of almost three years. Then one day his spokesman Jim Shaw called and left a message saying Buck did not want to get involved and that "he's going to be treating this as an unauthorized biography. I'm not sure if that means he's going to be uncooperative or ask other people to be uncooperative, but it will be unauthorized."

After a three-year time investment, I wasn't about to abandon the project. I joined forces with Buckaroo bass player Doyle Holly, whom I'd met at the Continental Club in August 1997. Doyle set about enlisting people to go on the record for the unauthorized version.

Writing a book about such a complex man has been like assembling a difficult thousand-piece puzzle, dark on one end and light on the other, with varying shades of gray in between. Each person interviewed supplied one or more of the pieces; some of those pieces were essential, while some didn't fit and had to be left out. As a journalist, it is my responsibility to be fair and listen with a keen ear and a sensitive heart to all voices, large and small; give voice to the voiceless; weigh conflicting statements with an open mind; and verify and present facts so readers can decide for themselves what is and isn't true. "Print the truth," singer-songwriter Gene Price told me. "That will shake people up."

Among those who played key roles are God; my agent, Jim Fitzgerald; my editor, Yuval Taylor; Devon Freeny, Mary Kravenas, Scott Rattray, and the entire staff at Chicago Review Press; and many of the folks who knew Buck Owens well, including Larry Adamson, Kris Black, Jerry Brightman, Jackson Brumley, Rolene Brumley, Tom Brumley, Willie Cantu, Doyle Holly, Ronnie Jackson, Jana Jae, Bill Mack, Jay Dee Maness, Jo McFadden, and Marlane Ulrich-Dunivent.

Extra-special thanks goes to my transcription tag team: Jeanie Freeburg, Susan Kuyrkendall, Julie Lloyd, Kendra Mellar, Mikal Rankin, Doug Tetreault, and Jeff Tetreault. Special recognition goes to Dennis Payne and Pete Pittman, who shared interviews they did with Tommy Collins and Gary Paxton that otherwise would not have seen print; Pamela Coyle, Bradley Hartman, and Bill Mack for being my extra set of eyes; Frank Frantik for compiling the discography; Joann Barr for genealogical access; and Clinton Erb and Russ Varnell for carrying the torch.

My gratitude also goes to all the others who shared generously of their time, expertise, and/or memories, especially: Kay Adams, Lisa Aguilar, Cheryl Albers, Charlie C. Allen, Earl Poole Ball Jr., Richard Bennett, Tony Booth, Maxine Brown, Wayne Roland Brown, Jann Browne, Susan Buckles, Ray Burdett, Bob Burke, John Cappello, Mark Carlile, Shirley Carlile, Bill Casey, Liz Cavanaugh, Roy Clark, the Country Music Foundation, Patsi Bale Cox, Mary Lou Cushman, Don Cusic, Mary Davis, Jimmy Dean, Frank Delaney, George Ducas, Mary Ellen Duerr, Steve Duncan, Wayne Durham, Ralph Emery, Jim Foglesong, Sandy Fox, Vic Fusco, Dave Gant, Barbara Gasta, Jim Hager, Jon Hager, Norm Hamlet, Stacy Harris, Chuck Harter, Linda Hicks, J. C. High Eagle, Wes Holcomb, Janette Jones, Kay Johnson, Loretta Johnson, Loudilla Johnson, Sharon Kite, Steve LaNore, Sandy Liles, John Lomax III, Sam Lovullo, Robert Marlowe, Jean Marris, Bryce Martin,

Marvin Mason, James P. McCarty, Cameron McCurdy, Joe McFadden, Barbara McGee, Don Menzel, Eugene Moles, Cathy Nakos, Kevin Nimmo, Mayf Nutter, Dawn Oberg, Cathy O'Brien, Patrick John O'Connor, Michael Paladini, Wade Pepper, Mark Phillips, Jim Pierce, Neil Pond, Wil Potts, Gene Price, Ronnie Pugh, James Pyle, Leigh Ray, Bill Rick, Smiley Roberts, Thomas Rockwell, Nancy Wilburn Rodriguez, Dan Rogers, Lulu Roman, Johnny Russell, the San Luis Obispo Sheriff's Office, Anthony Scarlati, Billy Sipes, Sirius XM Satellite Radio, Billy Mack Smith, Cindy Mack Smith, LaWanda Lindsey Smith, Lee Allen Smith, Mark J. Smith, Sandra Smith, Gus Snijdewind, Chuck Snow, Walt Spearman, Sue Spencer, Daryl Stogner, Viola Stogner, Alan Stoker, Terri Lynn Clark Thomson, Porter Wagoner, Ruth Lance Wester, Jim White, Tex Whitson, Alf Wigen, Jerry Wiggins, Susan Raye Wiggins, and Whip Wilson. I'd also like to thank "Luanne," a former OMAC employee, and the former military police officer, who requested and were granted anonymity.

No doubt, there will be gaps in this story because many people have died and others opted to remain silent. For instance, Ken Nelson told me I would be able to find whatever I needed in his self-published book, *My First 90 Years Plus 3*, because he was "all talked out about Buck Owens." In addition, I want to thank Jan Howard and Del Reeves, who agreed to do interviews, but because of poor health were unable to follow through. Del told me, "I'll give you an interview only if you promise to print the truth." I promised, but he died January 1, 2007.

PREFACE

"Little girl, you're staring into the faces of Hell," singer-songwriter Gene Price said. "Do you know what kind of book you will write? Well, I'll tell you what kind of book you'll write. You'll write a book about a very bad man who made very good music."

Thus began this Ballad of Buck.

Imagine Buck Owens's and Don Rich's twanging Telecasters and Tom Brumley's crying steel guitar making musical statements while Doyle Holly's thumping bass and Willie Cantu's beating drums punctuate every phrase. A chorus of voices, both big and small, join together to sing the high, low, and in-between notes. Make no mistake, this is no overly arranged Nashville tune with session players, strings, and singers with perfect pitch. Rather, it is a rough-and-tumble story-song riddled with good times, hard times, and heartaches by the number. It is a cheatin'-hurtin'-drinkin' song all rolled into one, worthy of any honky-tonk jukebox.

So quiet yourself and listen. Listen with your heart as well as your ears to the message within. Hear the soft and the loud voices, the smooth and the coarse voices, as they gain momentum, driven along by the surging "freight-train" sound generated by Bakersfield's finest. The melody may not always be easy on the ears, but its passion and raw honesty beg to be heard. For the verses in this story-song compose a character study in the round of a country music superstar, by people who knew him, worked with him, loved him, and, yes, even hated him.

You'll hear of an American dream come true, as Buck Owens rises from poverty, the son of a tenant farmer, to become one of the nation's best-loved country entertainers and a multimillionaire. You'll watch as his rhinestone-studded layers are peeled off, and you'll look beyond the facade to see a regular guy with real hopes and dreams as well as real fears and character flaws. You will learn that Buck was a complicated and perhaps conflicted man, not to mention vulnerable, sad, and lonely, who wanted nothing more than money, love, and acceptance, which he succeeded in finding but did not know how to embrace.

And every now and again, you might hear Don Rich's fuzztone guitar licks blurring aspects of Buck's life—especially the parts he'd sooner forget.

So turn up the volume and listen. One of the most intriguing story-songs is about to begin.

SON OF A TENANT FARMER

Sherman, Texas, is a city of mood swings. One minute, all is calm and peaceful, a bucolic backdrop of parched prairie and Prussian blue, and the next, a screaming blue norther—the mother of all north Texas storms—rolls in without warning like a bipolar on a rant. Stratus clouds seemingly boil up out of nowhere, thick shades of blue and gray, a foreshadowing of things to come: a drastic drop in temperature that can transform a blast-furnace summer into an ice-cold winter in an instant. Sherman is no place for sissies; it's the stuff of survivors.

In the years leading up to the Great Depression, area farms were failing by the hundreds as myriad Texans joined a surge of Dust Bowlers from Arkansas, Oklahoma, Kansas, and Missouri escaping a dry, windswept land that offered little to no hope of earning a living. Although times were tough all over north Texas, Sherman, which lies fifteen miles south of the Red River and the Oklahoma border, held promise and hope for at least one young tenant farmer from nearby Bonham. A tall, salt-of-the-earth teenager, Alvis Edgar Owens was a simple guy with hangdog looks and workingman's hands. He was young and tough, and not afraid to do an honest day's work.

Alvis was fifteen with a seventh-grade education when he met Maicie Azel Ellington, a busty, short brunette, at a church social. Although he was two years younger, his Model T Ford gave him an edge over the other boys in winning Maicie's affections. They began dating, which consisted of attending the Southern Baptist Church and various church functions. Alvis persisted in asking Maicie's father for permission to marry his daughter, but Micheal Ellington (whose first name was not spelled the conventional way, although it was pronounced the same) put the boy off, saying first that they could marry after the crops were planted, then after they were harvested, and so on. Alvis was impatient, though, so in January 1926 he and Maicie eloped. They married in a snowstorm, sitting in Alvis's Model T with the preacher standing outside the car window conducting the ceremony while Maicie's uncle and the preacher's wife served as witnesses. Alvis was sixteen and Maicie was eighteen.

The young couple set up housekeeping three miles from the heart of Sherman—a large town square and courthouse surrounded by shade trees and red brick streets—in a tenant farmer's house at the old Ashland Dairy Farm, according to Texas kin. Alvis worked split shifts at the dairy, getting up at either 2 or 3 A.M. to milk cows, only to do it again twelve hours later. Maicie would rise with him and prepare breakfast so her husband could start the day right. In between dairy shifts, Alvis would pick up work at surrounding farms. The work and schedule were grueling, but he was able to provide for Maicie and their daughter, Mary Ethel, who was born October 6, 1927.

In August 1929, a brutal heat wave engulfed Sherman. The unrelenting sun bore down on the town, which saw temperatures soar to at least 100 degrees Fahrenheit or higher for twenty days. No rain was recorded, and on the twelfth day, the mercury was a blistering 99 degrees when the Owenses welcomed their second child and firstborn son, Alvis Edgar Jr., into the world.

All odds were against Alvis Jr., who made his debut on the cusp of the Great Depression. Not only was he born into a dirt-poor family, but also he weighed a puny five pounds and had two congenital birth defects—only one functioning kidney and a cleft palate. Lord knows, his young parents had enough worries to shoulder for a family of four in a failing economy without having to scrape up cash for reconstructive surgery for their infant son, but they managed to get it done. Years later, Buckaroo Doyle Holly recalled, Buck had a scar on the left side of his upper lip and drank out of a straw because cold liquids bothered him.

The Owenses didn't stay in Sherman long, because as a tenant farmer, Alvis Sr. was forced to follow the work. By 1931, the family had moved to Van Alstyne, about twenty miles south of Sherman, where their second son, Melvin Leo, was born on July 20. It wasn't too long thereafter that Alvis Jr., by then a precocious two-year-old, insisted that he be called "Buck," after the family mule and dog. Many published accounts say Buck was either three or four when he affected his nickname, but his mother said he was two. Thus, the sandy-haired, blue-eyed boy began rewriting his life story. His new name turned out to be a fitting moniker for someone who bucked convention all his life and grew to worship the almighty dollar.

Although Buck would later speak of his family's privation, he seemed to dwell on what they didn't have as opposed to what they did. The Owenses did not have an easy life, but few did back then, and their situation was much better than others who got only oatmeal to eat three times a day. As Gospel singer-songwriter Albert E. Brumley, father of future Buckaroo Tom Brumley, put it, "Those were hard times back then, and poor people didn't have any times at all." In Texas, Buck's family always had shelter, food on the table, plenty of milk to drink, a car, a mule, and even a radio. The radio opened up a brand-new world for young Buck, who became mesmerized by the music emitted by its tinny speakers. Not knowing any better, the boy believed that miniature people lived inside the box and made the music. He would hide and peek at the radio every now and again to see whether any small folks would venture out, but they never did.

By the time their fourth and last child, Dorothy Juanita, was born on January 12, 1934, the family had moved a few miles north to Howe. When Dorothy was eleven months old, she and Buck both contracted pneumonia. Then, on December 14, 1934, Maicie's father died. One of Buck's most vivid memories of childhood was when he and Dorothy were recuperating and Maicie held them up to the window to watch their grandfather's funeral procession pass by their house.

Although Buck was a Texan by birth, his family roots were tangled deep in the South and in Appalachia. His great-grandparents had begun the slow migration westward from as far east as North Carolina, and subsequent generations slowly migrated westward with stops in Tennessee, Alabama, Arkansas, Illinois, Ohio, Indian Territory (now Oklahoma), and ultimately Texas.

Buck's father was the third of six children born to Carl Lee Owens and Carmenia "Minnie" Alzada Wattenbarger (pronounced "Vattenbarger"). Carl Lee was born in Whistler, Alabama, and Minnie in Sweetwater, Tennessee. They were living in Bonham, Texas, when Alvis Edgar Sr. was born May 26, 1909. He had two brothers and three sisters. Carl Lee switched his name at some point so he wouldn't be confused with another man of the same name; he became known as Lee Carl Owens. They eventually settled in Sherman, where Lee Carl and Minnie lived until their deaths.

Buck's mother was also one of six children—three brothers and two sisters—born to Micheal Monroe Ellington Jr. and Mary Myrtle Curliss. Micheal and Mary Myrtle were both born in Arkansas and married in Indian Territory, and Maicie was born December 4, 1907, in Okolona, Arkansas. When she was a year old, the family moved back to Indian Territory, which by then had become Oklahoma, and later to Grayson County, Texas, of which Sherman is the county seat.

Growing up, Buck ate his share of country "vittles" home-cooked in cast iron. Diet staples included fried bread, biscuits and gravy, cornbread and milk, banana pudding, and "poke salet," a wild green much like Swiss chard or spinach in flavor. He remembered catching crawdads in a creek as a boy in Texas, and taking them home to his mother, who would bread them in flour and fry them for supper. It made him feel like a man to help put food on the family table. He also helped his mother do the laundry, which entailed boiling dirty clothes in a pot over a fire and half-heartedly agitating the load with a long stick before they were hung out to dry.

Like all families, the Owenses were dysfunctional in their own special way. Maicie doted on her oldest son and felt he could do no wrong, while Alvis Sr. set high standards for the boy and felt he could do no right. When it came to punishing the "young uns," Alvis Sr. lived by the maxim of the time, "Spare the rod and spoil the child," and would plant several firm blows on Buck's backside with a razor strop. Such ardor in discipline caused Buck to harbor a lifelong resentment toward his father. Maicie, on the other hand, was more lenient. She would tell the errant child to go outside, cut a switch, and bring it to her, and then she would mete out a few quick stings on the back of the legs, which were more easily forgiven and forgotten than his father's blows from the strop.

When Buck was growing up, it was the norm for a man to discipline his wife as well as his children, and the pressures and stress of providing for a family under harsh economic conditions took their toll. Alvis Sr. would strike Maicie, which upset young Buck and moved him to defend her. Maicie adored her firstborn son and Buck had an unnatural attachment to his mother, whom he worshipped. According to Kris Black, former national promotion director of Buck Owens Enterprises, "Buck had emotional incest with his mother, possibly because he'd seen his dad hit his mother and he took over as her protector." Whippings aside, the hard times brought the family closer together, and there was never a question that they loved and remained loyal to one another.

Although he was a bit on the homely side, Buck's spunky personality, bright eyes, and easy smile endeared him to the womenfolk. Not only did his mother put him on a pedestal, but his younger sister Dorothy and his Grandma Ellington did, too. Mary Myrtle doted on her grandson and told him when he was about eight that when he grew up she would come keep house for him because he didn't need any of those "pissy-tailed girls" hanging around him. As a result of this female adoration, young Buck came to believe that he was truly special.

When he wasn't in school, Buck said, he worked in the fields four months out of the year, picking cotton, potatoes, peaches, and more, and hoeing land to contribute to the support of the family. Buck's father explained to him about tenant farming, or "farming on the halves," as it was called, which was a notch above sharecropping. "Halves" meant the tenant farmer furnished the mules and sometimes the seed, while the owner provided the housing and the land, "and at the end of a year, you split with the owner fifty-fifty," Buck said. Sharecropping, on the other hand, meant the sharecropper often lived in a house owned by the landlord, who furnished the land, seed, farm equipment, house, animals, and so forth—basically, the farmer worked not only for a roof over his head but also for credit and food on the table. Nevertheless, the boy made no distinction between the two, and sharecropping was a vocation he despised and vowed never to do. Someday, somehow, he would escape the life of a dirt farmer. He would see to it because he was bet-ter than that.

At some point, after the birth of Dorothy, the Owenses left Howe and moved to Garland, Texas. On November 30, 1936, when Buck was seven years old, his father applied for a Social Security card. His application indicated a general delivery mailing address in Garland, on the outskirts of Dallas, where he was working split shifts at Dieterich Certified Farms on Dairy Road. One day, Buck was walking home from school for lunch and passed by the house of his father's brother. His Uncle Vincent was out in the yard and told the boy he'd best not bother going home and to come in and eat at his place. Not knowing what his uncle was talking about, Buck proceeded on his way, only to arrive at a burned-out shell of a house. Their home had caught fire while his mother was preparing lunch. It was then that the Owenses, who had already uprooted several times in Texas, were faced with deciding whether to stay in a drought-stricken land or follow other kin who had gone west-ward. They decided to go.

★ 2 ★

THE EXODUS

The Owenses' exodus from Texas occurred midway through a four-year span in which up to half a million Dust Bowl migrants fled Louisiana, Texas, Arkansas, Oklahoma, and Missouri. Alvis Sr. had heard there was plenty of work in California, so they decided to go there. He built a two-wheel trailer to hitch to the back of their 1933 Ford sedan, and loaded it with what was left of their belongings. On November 8, 1937, the whole family shoehorned themselves into the Ford and headed west: Alvis Sr., Maicie, their four children, Maicie's mother, Maicie's brother Vernon Ellington, his wife, Lucille, and their son, Jimmy. Transporting ten passengers and hauling a heavy load slowed them so considerably that they were lucky if they traveled two hundred miles in a day. They would stop to buy gasoline, bologna, and bread, and camp out by the roadside at night, eating a supper of either fried bread or biscuits and water gravy prepared over an open fire. A week after they started their journey, the trailer hitch on the Ford broke in Phoenix, Arizona, so they looked up relatives in nearby Mesa and decided to stay a while before going on to California.

Buck wasn't impressed with Arizona. It was hot and dusty just like Texas. Times were lean for the Owenses, but not as lean as they had been in Texas. At least the Arizona climate was consistent, warm year-round. The family, like most Southwestern migrants, may have been poor as puppy's piss, but they were prideful folk and always worked for what they got in life. They would sooner die than go on the relief. No task was too small or too menial as long as it brought in money. Alvis Sr. worked at local dairy and fruit farms and got paid in milk and produce. He drove trucks and dug ditches. He did it all.

Buck would recall a poverty-stricken childhood of picking cotton, cold nights, twine for belts, reinforced shoe soles of cardboard, hunger, and more—but photographs of his family's life in Arizona tell a different story. They had Sunday-best clothing, hats, shoes, shirts, socks, leather belts, bicycles, musical instruments for Buck and his siblings, and even a piano for Maicie. On Saturdays, the family would clean up and drive into town, where Buck got a dime to see a picture show, a nickel for popcorn, and a nickel for a drink. On occasion, Maicie would serve Buck's favorite, banana pudding, for dessert.

The family lived in Arizona from 1937 until 1951. Buck recalled having to change schools often because the family had to follow the work. He talked of how the family moved from house to house, living in Gilbert, Higley, Mesa, Scottsdale, Tempe, and Valley of the Sun—although he never mentioned how the family moved Maicie's piano during all those moves.

In addition, Buck said, he left school two weeks early and started two weeks late every year so he could live the life of a nomad, traveling with his family to the San Joaquin Valley in California to stay in federal labor camps and pick cotton, fruit, and vegetables. It was a great environment for him, he said, because after a hard day's work, the laborers would gather around a campfire to pick and sing music. It makes for a good story, but it doesn't exactly jibe with the historical timeline. Buck's parents bore the brunt of the Great Depression more than their children did; by the time the Owenses left Texas in 1937, the nation was on the rebound from the Depression, which ended in 1939.

Buck said he assigned no romance to being poor, yet he compared his family's travails and migration westward with those of the fictional Joad family, who fled Oklahoma for California during the Great Depression in John Steinbeck's American classic *The Grapes of Wrath*. In 1940, the novel was made into a movie, starring Henry Fonda, which became a favorite of Buck's. Although Buck was a Texan by birth, he seemed to have a bad case of Okie envy and played the Okie card whenever it was convenient. "I was part of the *Grapes of Wrath* migration west," Buck said, and over the years he referred to himself as an "Okie by default," because his birthplace was near the state border, his maternal grandparents had lived there, he had married at least two

Okies, and most migrants were referred to as Okies no matter where they came from.

A few years after settling in Arizona, Buck experienced what he called "the darkest moment" of his childhood either at age nine or eleven, depending on the account. He contracted what the locals called "brain fever," and spent more than two months in South Side Hospital in Mesa with his mother at his side. The condition, which today might be diagnosed as either meningitis or encephalitis, occurs when the lining of the brain or the brain itself becomes infected by a virus or bacteria. If left untreated, serious mental problems can occur. When Buck was released from the hospital, he couldn't remember much of what he had been taught over the years; he had to relearn his ABCs and more. In addition, he wasn't as agile as he'd been before his illness, and his younger brother could outrun him after that.

Despite these setbacks, Buck remained a quick learner. He may have been born a simple country boy, but he was no simpleton. He possessed a photographic memory, and like his father, he excelled at math. He was often picked to be head of the mathematics team and took pride in showing off his skills. He also loved to read and was a good speller. His sixth-grade teacher would read books to the class to interest the students in literature and then give them a choice either to write an essay on the book or perform a skit. Being the show-off he was, Buck always opted for the latter. He soaked up praise and adulation like soppin' bread in gravy. Also, he was gregarious and outgoing and got along well with his peers. Buck liked going to school in Arizona, even though he hated everything about the classroom, especially the authority and the structure.

At home, Buck's mama raised him well, teaching him to be a gentleman to the ladies and to write thank-you notes. Both were lessons well-learned that worked to his advantage as an adult and in business. The women loved the way he opened doors, and a personal thank-you note written in his own hand always made a good impression on folks. Buck also attended church regularly as a boy—but, he later admitted, he had a real problem with the Scripture that said, "It is more blessed to give than to receive." He simply could not fathom how that could be, and when he grew older would give to charity not so much out of generosity as for the tax deductions he would reap from giving.

Buck was a cocky little cuss, a boyhood trait that carried over to adulthood and served him well when he was watching out for number one. If someone told him something couldn't be done, by Ned, he'd set out to prove that person wrong. Buck would develop a propensity for making up tales and embellishing the truth, and even though he spent little time in California as a boy, he dwelled on the time he did spend there. One story he like to tell was about how he had gone to a store there to buy candy and a sign in the window said, "No Okies." He marched inside and surveyed the goods. The shopkeeper took one look at him and asked him if he had seen the sign. Buck told him, "I saw it, but I ain't no Okie; I'm a Texan." He said the man admired his spunk, sold him his candy bar, and took an immediate liking to the boy.

In the summer of 1941, Buck turned twelve, but at six feet tall he looked to be a grown man. He was lean and lanky, all muscle and sinew. Alvis had a steady job driving truck, and the Owenses moved to a house on the outskirts of Mesa. It was a memorable event for young Buck, because it was the family's first house with indoor plumbing, even though the toilet didn't work. There was an outhouse on the premises, however. The house also had electricity and wood floors, so things were looking up.

Music was an integral part of the Owens household. Maicie Owens was an accomplished pianist and, in Buck's words, she "could shred a piano." Other musically inclined kin included Buck's father, who played harmonica, and two uncles and a cousin, Mary Lee Bounds, who played guitar. All of the Owens children were encouraged to be musical, but Buck was clearly the star. His sister Dorothy told of a game they used to play where either she or Maicie would strike a key on the piano and Buck would guess which note it was. He was right every time.

In 1942, Buck's parents gave him a mandolin for his thirteenth birthday and he got his first job playing it on the radio. (Buck later told *Guitar Player* he was twelve when his parents bought him the mandolin.) Somewhere between 1943 and 1945, Buck's father gave him a Regal resonator guitar. According to Dorothy, their mother showed Buck a few chords on the guitar and he took it from there. He was a quick study and taught himself to play several other instruments, including steel guitar. Alvis Sr. adapted an old radio as an amplifier for his son's electric steel. Buck said a musician friend taught him about "diminished and augmented chords. It spun my head around, learning there were more to music than just strumming."

Buck also ingested a steady diet of music each day over his parents' battery-operated radio. He remembered his father taking out the car battery, grounding it on a pipe, and tuning into megawatt "X" stations that broadcast across the U.S.-Mexican border. Buck acquired a taste for such artists as Bob Wills, Merle Travis, and Moon Mullican. He continued his musical education at the Southern Baptist Church, where his mother played piano and where he was exposed to gospel music and learned to harmonize. Buck was naturally gifted, and his genius came in spurts when the spirit moved him. He never wrote down songs; rather, he'd play them on his guitar and memorize the notes for later.

If Buck was something of a spitfire as a child, he became even more so during puberty, when he began to assert his independence. In addition to the mandolin, he took up smoking and sex at age thirteen. After finishing eighth grade in 1942, Buck said, he was able to find work because so many men were fighting in World War II and he was big for his age. He said that he saved the money he earned, but that it all was spent within a couple of months after he entered ninth grade that fall. The teen had had a taste of what it was like to earn and spend his own money, and he liked it and wanted more. So he dropped out of school.

He promised his mother he would finish someday, but he never did. Maicie was disappointed, because she always thought that out of all her children, Buck would be the one to exceed her tenth-grade education. In fact, it was Dorothy who advanced the farthest of the Owens brood; she graduated from high school and attended business college. Mary Ethel went as far as her junior year in high school before dropping out and getting married. Melvin, the poorest student of them all, barely made passing marks and didn't go past eighth grade, but he was an excellent mechanic who could fix anything.

After quitting school, Buck said, he worked various jobs: Western Union messenger, car washer, fruit truck driver, and more. He claimed he worked to help support his family, whom he referred to as "sharecroppers," "dirt people," "fruit tramps," and "fruit gypsies." When he was fourteen, although he was not particularly religious, he got baptized on a whim in the Salt River in Chandler, Arizona.

As "fooling around" with girls became a priority for Buck, it would naturally follow that he wanted his own car. So he squirreled away his money until he had saved $130, enough for an old blue 1933 Ford coupe with nonworking fog lights. Because he was underage, he had to have his father buy the car for him. Buck drove the coupe with pride—and without either instruction or a license. Whenever he was stopped for traffic infractions, he'd make up a story that sounded important, such as being late for work, and the officers would give him a warning and let him go on his way. Thus, Buck became adept at talking his way out of tight spots and creating stories as he went along.

The ability to tell tales in a believable fashion carried over into Buck's adult life as well, and it was a trait that endeared him to many. Years later, as his mother worked in her son's office, she was reviewing a country music biography of her son and discovered several inaccuracies. On Buck's letterhead, she wrote the following letter dated January 26, 1966, to Thurston Moore of Heather Publications, Inc.:

Dear Thurston:

After reading your attached article on Buck I thought you would like to know that part of it is not true.

Buck did not have to drop out of school to help support his family. His Dad supported the entire family.

Buck never drove a fruit truck or any truck at any time or any place.

He has been called "Buck" since he was about two years old and using the name ever since that time. Buck is a nick name and he has never changed his name—he is still Alvis E. Owens, Jr.

He has played music since he was thirteen. His first job was playing mandolin on the radio. His second job on the steel guitar on radio. Both these were in Arizona before moving to California in 1951.

He was a singer and had written several songs before 1955.

He had several record releases on the Pep label before he recorded on the Capitol label.

I though [sic] you would like to have the true facts instead of untruths and half-truths.

Sincerely,
Mrs. Maicie Owens

Thurston Moore replied the following day in a letter that said, in part:

I was quite chagrined to hear from you that the biography on Buck that has been included in our Programming Service is erroneous. I certainly appreciate your writing and telling us of this, since we don't wish to publish prevarications and false information.

This does make me wonder a bit about the reliability of some of our sources of information, since the information you mentioned was obtained from the enclosed copy of a biography from Capitol Records. We have several of these biographies, and every single one of them mentions that he drove a fruit truck and dropped out of school in his teens, plus the other things mentioned in our biography.

Buck himself had filled out the application for Heather Publications, listing his pet peeve as "people who try to be something they are not." He also provided Capitol Records with the biographical material to which Moore referred. A master of promotion, Buck realized early on that it made a much more interesting back story if he were to create a hardscrabble Tom Joad boyhood for himself as a sharecropper's son who grew up picking cotton, fruit, and driving truck when in reality his first job was playing mandolin on the radio. He may have dropped out of school, but he did not do so to earn money for his family.

Buck admittedly stretched the truth. Always. Buck once told author Nicholas Dawidoff, "I'll do my best to lie to you, but I'll tell you I'm lying." Believing that is a mistake, however, because, as future Buckaroo Doyle Holly learned, "With Buck, everything is 50 percent bullshit and 50 percent truth."

★ 3 ★

BONNIE

When Buck was fifteen, he ran away from home and went to Bakersfield, California. He wasn't particularly impressed with the city—just as Arizona had failed to impress him when he landed there—so he turned around and went back to Mesa. Looking back, he wouldn't be able to recall why he ran away, but perhaps he simply wanted to find out whether he could. He probably wanted to make his own decisions, he said, even though he wasn't ready to yet.

Shortly after returning home, Buck met Bonnie Morine Campbell at the Mazona Roller Rink in Mesa. She was just his type, a sweet, petite brunette with a nice smile and a button nose, and Buck, in his words, "fell in lust." Bonnie's family were also Dust Bowlers, who had relocated to Gilbert, Arizona, from Blanchard, Oklahoma. Bonnie was born October 1, 1929, to a Works Progress Administration laborer, Wallace Jefferson Campbell, and his wife, Davis Campbell (nee McKinney). Bonnie was one of eleven children, which included twins two years older who had died at birth.

By the time Buck and Bonnie met, the strapping man-child already had two years of experience with the opposite sex, enough time for him to make a distinction between girls he fooled around with and girls he dated—as Buck said, you didn't "have sex with your best girl." It was the respectful thing to do. Bonnie fell into the dating category.

He continued to fool around with other girls, though, and it wasn't long before the teenage lothario discovered that this behavior carried consequences. When he was sixteen, in either the latter part of 1945 or the early part of 1946, he had to marry another girl. His first wife was a beautiful young woman who bore him a daughter. She didn't stay long and left with the baby. It was then that Buck developed a pattern of blocking out things he'd sooner forget. Even though he was devastated by his young wife's departure, he pretended the marriage had never happened. Whenever the issue of that marriage was brought up, Buck would brush it off with a terse "That one doesn't count" and change the subject.

Around this same time, Buck got a regular gig playing music on the radio and at a local club as part of the duo "Buck and Britt" with Theryl Ray Britten, who was nineteen. The duo had a daily fifteen-minute radio show playing for free on KTYL in Mesa. The studio had a twenty-five-foot-long plate glass window that faced the parking lot, and fans would drive in and tune in the station on their car radios and watch the show. Buck and Britt also played in various clubs and added a trumpet player known only as Kelly, who was stationed at a nearby air base. The trio then got a regular job playing at the Romo Buffet for $10 a night, which they divided three ways.

In 1947, shortly after the breakup of his marriage, Buck met a service station owner named Mac McAtee, who played an hour of recorded country music at his gas station over a public address system that was simulcast on a local radio station. Mac decided to assemble a live seven-piece band called Mac's Skillet Lickers for his show and asked Buck to play lap steel. One day, Buck showed up for rehearsal and was surprised to see Bonnie. "What're you doin' here?" he asked, thinking she was there to see him. She informed him that she was auditioning as a singer; he didn't know she could sing. As it happened, she was a yodeler, too, and a damn good one at that. She was hired as the girl singer for the group. In addition to Mac, Bonnie, and Buck, there was a saxophonist, a fiddle player, a drummer, and a guitarist.

It is not known whether Bonnie was aware of Buck's marriage, but they continued to date. Although Buck initially said he didn't have sex with her out of respect, he later said they were afraid of getting pregnant so they waited to do "it" until his eighteenth birthday, when Bonnie was still seventeen. Then Buck had to get married again, when he and Bonnie were both eighteen and she was four and a half months pregnant. On January 13, 1948, Buck's father and Bonnie's mother accompanied the teens as they got their marriage license, and they were wed that night. Buck's parents thought Bonnie was the sweetest girl in the world, so kind and helpful. They were thrilled to have her in the family. The young couple's first son, Alan Edgar, was born May 22,

1948. Buddy, as he has been known all his life, physically resembled his father but inherited his mother's even temper.

Their second son, Michael Lynn Owens, was born March 8, 1950. Mike was shorter and prettier than his older brother but inherited his father's business acumen and mercurial personality. Buck later claimed that at this point he was forced to find work picking oranges and driving a truck to supplement his meager honky-tonk earnings, but it is likely that he was stretching the truth once again. About this time, the musician struck up a friendship with a trucker-turned-musician named Martin David Robinson, better known as Marty Robbins.

In late 1950, Alvis Sr. and Maicie figured they'd had enough of Arizona and that it was time to venture on to California. Son Melvin, daughter Dorothy, Maicie's mother, Mary Myrtle, and Maicie's brother Vernon and his wife, Lucille, and their son, Jimmy, went with them. By then, Mary Ethel had a family of her own, as did Buck, so they stayed behind.

Buck had been married to Bonnie only a couple of years when the responsibilities of being a husband and a father began to weigh heavily on him. Being a family man was not his idea of a good time. Music and women were his priorities, and as he got more club dates, he also got more dates. With all the attention he had gotten growing up from his mother, his maternal grandmother, and his sisters, he saw nothing out of the ordinary when women paid attention to him. Buck was used to being the center of the universe.

Buck worked during the day and played the 'tonks at night, and sometimes he disappeared for two days at a time with nary an explanation to his wife. Bonnie could not bear the strain of caring for two young children while her husband philandered and thought only of himself. They had married too young and their life had become an endless disagreement. By early 1951, she did as his first wife had done. She packed up and left for California with Buddy and Mike in tow. When she arrived in Bakersfield, she stayed with Lucille and Vernon Ellington, Buck's favorite aunt and uncle, and got a job as a carhop at Mooney's Drive-In, a hamburger joint on the corner of South Union and Truxtun avenues, while Lucille looked after the boys.

If Bonnie hadn't split with the boys, it's possible Buck might have remained in Arizona indefinitely, but now there was no reason for him to stay. So a dozen years after the Great Depression, Buck, too, headed to California. In May 1951, he arrived in Bakersfield solo, driving a beat-up red 1941 Chevrolet coupe with his guitar and no more than $20 in his pocket. He slept in his car to make his money stretch, even though he could have stayed with his folks or gotten a room for two or three bucks a night. When his money ran out, he hocked his electrified Gibson L-7 archtop for $10 at a pawnshop on Nineteenth Street and was told he had two weeks to retrieve it.

Buck had always been an affable guy, and he made friends easily in his new hometown. He met a stocky, dark-haired steel player named Dusty Rhodes and moved out of his car and onto Dusty's sofa. Dusty gave him a job in his four-piece band at the Round Up out on Highway 99. The pay was $8 a night—a whopping $40 a week, the most money Buck had ever made up to this point. The only problem was that he had nothing to wear—and no guitar, since his was still in hock. Oscar Whittington, a fiddle player, lent him a shirt, and Billy Mize, who played steel at the Hurry Back Inn over in Weedpatch, heard of Buck's plight and lent him a guitar. The three men's acts of generosity were kindnesses Buck would never forget. When he finally went to the pawnshop to get his guitar, more than two weeks had passed and it was too late to get it back.

Fate may have stepped in, however, when Lewis Talley sold him his used white Fender Telecaster for $35. It was probably the best purchase Buck ever made. That guitar became instrumental in creating the so-called Bakersfield Sound, a surging freight-train rhythm with a rock edge, unlike Nashville's smooth, homogenized productions. Buck used to lean the guitar up against the wall during band breaks and one night it fell, breaking the piece that held the top string in place. Fiddle player J. R. "Jelly" Sanders came to his rescue and Okie-rigged it by cutting a groove in a piece of Buck's comb with his pocketknife, then soaking it in brandy to "glue" it in place; it stuck. Buck never had the guitar repaired and it remains that way to this day.

It didn't take long for a talented guitarist such as Buck to be noticed, and in September 1951 another expatriate Texan, Bill Woods from Denison, wooed the twenty-two-year-old guitarist away from Dusty and the Round Up over to the city's hottest new nightspot, the Blackboard. The move was a big step up for Buck, with a $4.50-a-night raise in pay. He started at $12.50 a night playing lead guitar for the house band, Bill Woods and the Orange Blossom Playboys. Buck recalled that at that juncture, the band consisted of Bill, Buck, Billy Mize, Red Simpson, and Tommy Collins, though in actuality Tommy didn't hit town until the following year. The Playboys were a dance band that played everything from country to sambas to polkas to rumbas.

Now that he had a steady job, Buck tried to make things right with Bonnie. He rented a small house for his estranged family in Oildale, an unincorporated, dilapidated working-class neighborhood north of the Kern River, populated mostly by Okies. They set up house together, but Buck's attempt to reconcile was short-lived, mostly because he hadn't changed his errant ways. Unlike his mother, Bonnie wasn't so willing to overlook Buck's bad behavior. After all, she deserved a little fun in life, too. It wasn't all about him, and there were plenty of guys interested in a good-looking gal such as herself.

In the spring of 1952, a year after Buck moved to Bakersfield, Bonnie and Buck legally separated. On November 12, Bonnie filed for divorce. According to her divorce petition, she was a twenty-three-year-old single mother living at 115 East McCord in Oildale. She had full custody of their sons— Buddy, then four and a half, and Mike, two and a half—and was paying $50 a month in rent. Bonnie said that she and Buck had no community property and that Buck earned $90 a week to her $30. She listed her financial net worth as "none" and Buck's as "unknown." Her previous year's net income was roughly $2,100 compared with Buck's $4,680. Not only did she ask the court to be "awarded the care, custody and control of the minor children," but she also requested a court-appointed lawyer because of her paltry income. She said she had the ability to pay only $100 a month for the support and maintenance of the minor children, and $150 for her attorney's fees and costs. In addition, her petition claimed that ever since she and Buck had married, he had treated her "with extreme cruelty" and had "wrongfully inflicted upon her grievous mental suffering."

Buck's and Bonnie's divorce was granted January 13, 1953, on what would have been their fifth wedding anniversary. Buck had no one to blame but himself. He had behaved like a feral tomcat prowling for pussycats in heat. "The most trouble I've ever gotten into in my whole life was when I had too many women at the same time that weren't mine," Buck told an A&E televi-

sion special in 2000. "Bonnie didn't like it and divorced me in 1953." Over
the years, Buck had maintained that he and Bonnie remained legally married
at least until 1955 because they couldn't afford a divorce. It wasn't until the
A&E appearance that he admitted they had divorced two years earlier.

After the divorce, Bonnie, who earned little money, bounced around
among rented houses and relatives' homes and moved at least twenty times
until Buddy and Mike were in high school. Buck moved back in with his folks.
Alvis Sr. had a steady job as a tank truck driver for Biggs Oil and Gas Company, and life was better than it ever had been for Maicie and him. Life was
better for Buck, too. He was making good money and had no responsibilities
to tie him down. So he concentrated on teaching himself the saxophone and
the drums, and played both the clubs and the women. His parents, however,
held Buck responsible for his divorce from Bonnie, whom they had loved as
their own child. Once when he brought a woman home with him, Maicie
gave her an ice-cold reception. As Buck put it, she was "downright rude" to
his date.

Buck's parents, who were staunch Southern Baptists, also disapproved of
their son making a living in honky-tonks. As Alvis Sr. told his son, "Ain't
nothin' good ever come out of a honky-tonk." Buck, of course, set out to prove
his father wrong.

★ 4 ★

THE PROMISED LAND

The allure of California's Central Valley to Dust Bowlers was undeniable. With its blue skies, temperate climate, fertile valleys, and vast petroleum reserves, the region beckoned like a beautiful, fecund woman, ripe with the promise that life could—and would—go on. There was infinite work in the area's orchards, fields, and oil fields for the thousands of transplants willing to do it. Buck Owens, however, was not one of the willing. Nothing about the thought of hard labor thrilled him. He had higher aspirations in life than to pick fruit; he wanted to pick guitars.

Fortunately, Bakersfield, the county seat of Kern County with a population of 45,497 in 1951, was the Promised Land for pickers of either stripe. Honky-tonks, all with live music nightly, were as abundant as the crops in the fields. In addition to the Round Up and the Blackboard, other popular Bakersfield nightspots of the early 1950s included Bob's Lucky Spot, Tex's Barrel House, Club 409, Hacienda, High Pockets, Rainbow Gardens, Rhythm Rancho, Jimbo's, Doc's Club, the Green Door, and the Funny Farm. And the surrounding area was home not only to the Hurry Back Inn in Weedpatch but also to the Clover Club in Arvin, the Pumpkin Center Barn Dance in Pumpkin Center, Beardsley Ballroom and Trout's Cocktail Lounge in Oildale, and the Big Fresno Barn near Fresno. Dust Bowlers survived the long, hot workdays by looking forward to sipping a cold one while playing, listening to, and dancing to the white man's blues.

There were distinctive musical styles within the region, and music lovers could tell where a picker was from just by the way he played guitar. For example, Bakersfield pickers, including Buck, used the open-chord style of strumming versus the closed style preferred in Fresno. When singer-songwriter, sometime preacher, and sometime Electrolux hawker Tommy Collins moved to Bakersfield from Oklahoma in 1952 with his then-girlfriend and future rockabilly queen Wanda Jackson and her family, he found that Bakersfield offered the "truest form of country music," compared with either Fresno or Los Angeles.

In Buck's short time in Bakersfield, he had had a taste of the good life doing what he loved most, playing music in an air-conditioned club, making better money than he ever could have hoped to earn in the fields. There was no turning back now.

When Buck was hired at the Blackboard, it was a far different place than it had been when its owners, Joe Limi, an Italian, and Frank Zabaleta, a California-born Basque, bought it in 1949. Tommy's Place, as it was called then, was a blue-collar cafe frequented by truckers and oil field workers. It specialized in breakfast and greasy road food. The cafe had a blackboard wall at the entrance on which customers could scrawl messages for each other. So when Limi and Zabaleta knocked down the old termite-ridden structure and rebuilt it into a bar and dance hall, they renamed it the Blackboard. The club reopened in 1951 at 3601 Chester Street, a few blocks up from where Buck would later begin his business empire.

The 'Board had a brick front with an awning, two sets of double doors with portholes, and glass-block windows on either side of the doors. Inside, there was a low ceiling, mirrors behind the bar, a jukebox, a wooden dance floor, and a shuffleboard table. When the band was on a break, Buck liked to challenge trumpet and saxophone player Don Markham to a game of shuffleboard. The Blackboard was the city's largest nightclub, with a capacity of five hundred and live music and dancing six nights a week. It also was the most expensive club in town: bottled beer cost 75 cents as opposed to the 25 cents other clubs charged, though draft beer could be had for 40 cents. The brand-spanking-new club was the "in" place to be, and welfare mothers hung out there in hopes of snagging a man with money. Patrons often would fill up on beer at less expensive clubs before ending up at the 'Board fueled and ready for action.

The Blackboard was a honky-tonk of the first order, with pickled eggs at the bar, the loudest band, the most music, the most dancing, the most smoking, the most drinking, the most cussing, and, of course, the most brawling. It was immortalized in the song "Dim Lights, Thick Smoke (and Loud Loud Music)," which Joe Maphis wrote after playing his first gig there in 1952. Tommy Collins, who played at the club and later performed with Elvis, was the biggest star Bakersfield had seen in the early 1950s. Tommy said he had never heard women talk as vulgarly as they did at the Blackboard. Customers there, Bonnie Owens remembered, would "fight and drink, in that order."

House band leader Bill Woods didn't seem to care how much people fought or how crude the women talked, because he spent most of his time onstage flirting and smoking his pipe while Billy Mize sang and the band played. Buck would be "working his ass off, getting a menial wage," Buck's future song-writing partner Harlan Howard recalled. Buck didn't seem to mind. It wasn't long before Billy Mize left to pursue a solo career and Buck was drafted to do vocals. At this point in his life, however, Buck had no great desire to sing, because it made him feel vulnerable and exposed. He considered himself more of an instrumentalist than a singer, and even though the crowd would chant "More Buck! More Buck!" and females swarmed to him like flies on a watermelon on a hot day, he was insecure about his rough-cut looks. The thought never entered his mind that women might like him for the whole package he offered: a sexy, charming, witty, smart, energetic, talented gentleman with a soft twang in his voice.

There are two versions of the story about how Buck came to be the lead singer of the Orange Blossom Playboys. In the first, told by Buck himself, one of the owners called him into his office and told him, "The people like your singing. The waitresses like your singing. So you're now the singer." Buck asked, "OK, how much am I gonna get?" and the owner replied, "You're gonna get to keep the job you got!" In the second version, according to Bill Woods, Woods told Buck he was going to have to sing, which Buck didn't want to do. Buck didn't want to lose the best-paying job he'd ever had, so he reluctantly agreed to fill in, Bill said, but only until Billy Mize came back. After a show, Buck would fume about having to sing, but he sang nevertheless.

Billy never did return. He moved to Los Angeles, where he appeared on such television shows as *Town Hall Party* and Gene Autry's *Melody Ranch*, then moved back to Bakersfield and hosted *The Billy Mize Show* in the mid-to-late 1960s. Mize never became a national artist, but he was well known in Southern and Central California.

Buck performed at the Blackboard from September 1951 to May 1958. Although the work was steady, Buck also appeared as a guest on local television shows such as Herb Henson's *Cousin Herb's Trading Post Gang* and Dave Stogner's *KLYD's Kountry Korner*. In addition, the owners of the Blackboard allowed him to take time off to do shows throughout the Central Valley and in Northern California. When Buck made his early appearances upstate, he stayed with Larry Adamson, a handsome businessman who was born and still resides in Northern California. Larry owned the Robin Club in Rocklin, California, where Buck often played. Rocklin is near Sacramento and Placerville and is about five miles from Roseville, where Buck's future manager, Jack McFadden, had graduated from high school. As it happened, Larry and Jack were good friends, although Buck didn't know it at the time. "I knew Buck when he was nobody, really nobody," Larry said.

During Buck's Blackboard stint, he hooked up with a twenty-year-old brunette from Placerville named Marjorie. She had a year-old daughter from a previous liaison and then, in 1956, another daughter with Buck. Buck may have married Marjorie, though he only admitted to being married three times in his life; Jack said Buck had married at least seven times. One of Buck's nieces, Mary Agee, daughter of his sister Mary Ethel, insists her uncle neither married Marjorie nor had a child by her—"There have been many people claiming relationship or knowledge of our family who are just trying to jump on Buck's bandwagon." Mary was only nine when Buck's second daughter was born and was probably unaware that Maicie Owens babysat the girl until she was six. Marjorie had a son in 1958 by another man, whom she later married. She married three more times and adopted another son in the 1980s. For many years, she lived in Pierce City, Missouri, and she died in Aurora, Missouri, on April 1, 2009.

Back in Bakersfield, Buck's ex-wife was getting on with her own social life and career. Bonnie would sneak onstage at the Clover Club to sing with Fuzzy Owen, a sometime boyfriend of hers, and his cousin, Lewis Talley, also a sometime boyfriend. Back then, Bakersfield was a hotbed of iniquity, and everybody had someone else on the side. After Buck, Bonnie dated Roy Nichols for awhile, then Lewis Talley, and then she was Fuzzy's girl.

One day, Thurman Billings, the owner of the Clover Club, and his wife went to the drive-in where Bonnie worked. They knew her from the club and told her if she came to work for them as a waitress, she could sing anytime she wanted. It took her no time at all to make the switch from carhop to cocktail waitress. She worked as a relief waitress at both the Clover Club and the Blackboard, where her sister Betty Campbell was a regular cocktail waitress. Bonnie was allowed to sing for a buck a song at both clubs, and she often scribbled song lyrics on a cocktail napkin when inspiration struck. In 1953, she first saw her future husband Merle Haggard, when Lefty Frizzell was headlining at Rainbow Gardens and called Merle onstage to sing. Curiously, she never met Merle at the Clover Club, although he played there before he played bass for Buck—as did another of Buck's bassists, Doyle Holly.

Opportunity knocked for Buck as well, thanks to Merle Haggard's close friend and fishing buddy Tommy Collins. Back then, all the Bakersfield musicians not only drank and played together but also fished and hung out together. Tommy was a good-looking, chain-smoking good old boy who had the good fortune of snagging a Capitol Records recording contract within a year after moving to Bakersfield. Tommy also was a friend and former housemate of Ferlin Husky, another Capitol recording artist, who also recorded under the names Terry Preston and Simon Crum. Husky had helped Tommy get signed to the label, and he played guitar on Tommy's first Capitol session. Shortly thereafter, however, Ferlin scored his first #1 with "A Dear John Letter," a duet he sang with Jean Shepard. Ferlin's career took off, and Tommy was left without a guitarist, so Ferlin, who knew Buck from the Bakersfield club circuit, called Buck and asked him to give Tommy a hand. On September 8, 1953, Buck played guitar on Tommy's second release, "You Better Not Do That," to which he gave a raunchy, intricate intro that catapulted the song to #2 upon its January 1954 release.

Tommy was preparing for his first national tour and wanted to take Buck on the road as his guitarist. "He'd put a little style to my music," Tommy said. So one Sunday afternoon in late 1953, he had his booking agent, Jack McFadden, go with him to the Blackboard to see Buck in action. Jack was impressed with Buck's stage presence and the way he worked a crowd. "Buck Owens had that something," Jack said. "He was gonna be a star." Jack wasn't the only one who became acquainted with Buck through Tommy; Capitol Records producer Ken Nelson did, too. Tommy insisted on Buck playing guitar in his Capitol sessions, and Ken was impressed enough with Buck's fancy fretwork that he started calling him in on sessions with other Capitol artists.

Years later, Tommy would admit that even though he was a little jealous of Buck at times, he acquired a lot of respect for him because he had gone so far from such a meager beginning. He also had one of the most exciting shows around.

Singer Porter Wagoner, who shared a birthday with Buck but was two years older, said he met Buck for the first time around 1953, before either of them had a recording contract. They were on the same bill at a show in Wichita Falls, Texas, and Buck was playing his used Telecaster, which "looked like it had been through a damn war," Porter said. He said Buck had a great sound and an original way of playing. At the hotel the afternoon before the show, Buck and Porter were noodling on guitar and singing. Buck was playing the lick he had played on Tommy Collins's "You Gotta Have a License." "Man, that's a real original lick," Porter said. Buck replied, "Hell, I got all kinds of original stuff."

Porter didn't know Buck sang, either. "Man, you don't sound like anybody I ever heard," Porter said. Buck joked, "A lot of people told me that," and Porter tried to reassure him: "No, I mean that in a great way, because you sound really great."

After the show, the musicians got together to jam in somebody's room, and after hearing Buck sing to the group, Porter said, "Hell, you are the one who ought to be singing, Buck! You really sing great." Buck said, "I am going to sometime, I just don't feel like I can have a career. I'm just too damned ugly."

Even though Buck had made the statement in a joking manner, Porter was shocked; he knew that deep down, Buck was serious. "Hell, I know a lot of people, man, that ain't pretty that's in the music business," Porter said. "Hell, you just look like a tough old cowboy that's been around the bars." Buck seemed to like that, and said, "Well, I hope someday I can make some records." Porter had no doubt: "I bet you do."

As the years passed, Porter would kid Buck, telling him that he hoped he would live a long time, because as long as Buck and former WSM disc jockey and *Grand Ole Opry Live* host Keith Bilbrey were alive, Porter would "never be the ugliest man in the world." Porter said he always admired what Buck had accomplished in his career. Buck had a real problem with his looks, but he overcame his hang-up to attain the fame for which he had always hungered.

When royalties started pouring in for "You Better Not Do That," the first thing Tommy Collins did was buy a brand-new Cadillac. In 1954, he was asked to sing at the *Grand Ole Opry* and he insisted on driving to Nashville in the Caddy. Of course, Buck had to go, because nobody else could play the intro the way he could. They invited Ken Nelson to go, too. It was a memorable trip for them all, especially for Buck. He met and had his picture taken with legendary guitar guru Chet Atkins and *Grand Ole Opry* stalwart Roy Acuff.

It also was the first time Buck ever played at the *Opry*'s Ryman Auditorium, the so-called mother church of country music. He recalled that the *Opry* wouldn't allow Tommy to use drums, and that *Opry* sound technicians controlled the amplifiers. Buck had never played anywhere where he couldn't control the volume or tone, and it bothered him. He wanted to be in command of his own sound.

Something else that bothered him was when some Nashville naysayer told him he was a pretty good guitarist but he'd never make it as a singer. It may have been that single statement that put Buck at odds with Music City and spurred him to prove the establishment wrong. "My problem with Nashville was simple," he told the *Bakersfield Californian* in later years. "I don't like the way they do talent and I don't like the way they cut records." So he did what only he could do so well: he bucked the system.

CAPITOL

In the early-to-mid 1950s, Ken Nelson said, he used Buck in every Capitol recording session for which Ken had to line up the musicians. In addition to Tommy, Buck played for Sonny James, Faron Young, Gene Vincent, Stan Freberg, Wanda Jackson, and others. Buck's session work wasn't lucrative—for example, he earned $41 playing rhythm guitar on Wanda's "Silver Threads and Golden Needles" in September 1956—but it was more than he made in the 'tonks. Not only did it help pay the bills, but also it gave him needed exposure. Guitarist Richard Bennett, who would play for many years with Neil Diamond and Mark Knopfler, cited Buck's session work with Tommy Collins and Stan Freberg as his finest, especially his work on Freberg's version of the Elvis standard "Heartbreak Hotel."

Tommy wrote a song titled "You're for Me," though Buck was listed as a cowriter and later claimed sole writing credit. Tommy recorded the song in 1954, and from Buck's half of the royalties, he was able to put $500 down on a small two-bedroom house, the first he'd ever owned, which cost $5,000. Years later, he sold it for eleven times his investment.

Buck scored another coup in 1954 when he played and sang harmony on Terry Fell's trucker anthem "Truck Driving Man." The record was cut at Lewis Talley's Lu-Tal Studio in Bakersfield but was released on RCA's "X" label. Terry tried to get Buck signed to "X," but couldn't sell the studio chiefs on him.

At the same time, Buck was trying to get himself signed to Capitol. After many of the sessions with Ken Nelson, Buck often drove Ken home. Ken didn't know how to drive after living in Chicago for years and taking the elevated trains wherever he needed to go. The producer said he really liked Buck, except for his constant pestering to audition him as a singer. Ken's attitude was, "Get away from me, boy; you bother me."

In spite of his busy work schedule, Buck still found time for an active social life. He set his sights on a striking brunette carhop who worked at the Little Sweden drive-in at South Union and Kentucky streets. Phyllis Irene Buford was a young widow working to support her two young children, Theresa and Jacky. Like Bonnie, Phyllis was an Okie, born August 3, 1930, in Hooker, Oklahoma, to Alvin Phillip Buford and Mildred Irene Fornas. Kern County records indicate that Phyllis was using her maiden name when she and Buck married in 1955. On May 9, 1956, Buck and Phyllis had a son of their own, John Dale, better known as Johnny.

In March 1955, Bill Woods left his tenure as leader of the house band at the Blackboard to open a honky-tonk on South Union called Bill Woods Corral. The Blackboard owners knew Buck was responsible in part for the club's phenomenal success, so Joe Limi asked him to take over for Woods. When it came to his music, Buck had a strong work ethic; he was reliable and always showed up on time, not to mention playing loud, proud, and almost nonstop. And even if he did show up with unkempt hair and shabby clothes, the women loved him. The more women in a club, the more men; the more men, the more drinks they bought for the women, and so on. So Buck Owens and the Schoolhouse Playboys became the Blackboard's new house band. It consisted of Buck on guitar, Lawrence Williams on piano, Junior Stonebarger on steel guitar, and Ray Heath on drums.

The next year at the Blackboard, Wynn Stewart, who had fronted the band at the Round Up in Bakersfield at one time but was now based in Los Angeles, introduced Buck to songwriter Harlan Howard. It wasn't long after the two met that Harlan was heading to Bakersfield on the weekends to visit Buck and craft songs. Harlan wrote the lyrics and Buck set them to music. Harlan called Buck his "starvation buddy," because they were both scraping by waiting for a big break. He stayed at Buck's house, where he slept in a broken bunk bed—Buck's rough-housing sons had knocked off a leg during one of their visits, so Buck replaced it with a cinder block.

At the time, Harlan had a publishing deal with Central Songs, which was co-owned by Ken Nelson, Cliffie Stone, and Lee Gillette. Buck realized early on that in exchange for managing the copyright process, the publisher keeps most of the money. Buck thought if he wrote and published the songs himself, he could earn twice as much. So he and Harlan set up Blue Book Music, the publishing company that started Buck on the road to financial security.

Buck also had a desire to stretch himself musically. Inspired by genre-bending singers such as Little Richard and Elvis Presley, in 1956 he released two rockabilly numbers, "Hot Dog" and "Rhythm and Booze," under the pseudonym "Corky Jones" so as not to upset his country fans. (Coincidentally, Corky Jones was the nickname of a songwriter Buck knew named Charles Lee Jones. Buck had Marjorie put "Corky Jones" as the father on their daughter's birth certificate that year.) They were among ten songs he recorded for Pep Records, an independent label owned by Claude Caviness. Claude, a baker from Pico Rivera, California, had been introduced to Buck that same year by Terry Fell. The Corky Jones tunes did well on a local level but lacked national distribution and fizzled. Buck said in 1989 that "Hot Dog" had been influenced by both Elvis Presley and Gene Vincent and "Rhythm and Booze" by Elvis. Oddly enough, Elvis released a different song titled "Hot Dog" in 1957. In 1999, however, Buck contradicted himself and told the *Bakersfield Californian* that he had not been influenced by Elvis at all when he cut his 1956 rockabilly recordings.

Buck continued to get word-of-mouth referrals for sessions at Lu-Tal for Lewis Talley and at Capitol Records in Los Angeles for Ken Nelson. In 1957, Bill Woods returned to the Blackboard after his honky-tonk went out of business, and Buck went back to playing and singing in Bill's band. Buck also recorded a single on the Chesterfield label, "Country Girl (Leavin' Dirty Tracks)" with "Honeysuckle" on the flip side.

The year 1957 marked a turning point for Buck. Not only was he getting steady session work at Capitol, but also he was gaining respect as a songwriter.

The Farmer Boys, another Central Valley act, asked Buck to give them some songs for a recording session at Capitol. This vocal duo, Bobby Adamson and Woody Wayne Murray, performed fruit-picker music at its best. They were edgy for the day, combining western swing and honky-tonk to kick open the door to the Bakersfield Sound. They had toured with several *Grand Ole Opry* stars and, like Tommy Collins, had performed with Elvis. The duo worked in Northern and Central California, and their stage outfits, decorated with pictures of hay bales and overalled farmers carrying water buckets, had been designed by Nudie Cohn, the famed Russian immigrant who was the so-called "rodeo tailor to the stars." Various musicians backed the Farmer Boys, including Cliffie Stone on stand-up bass and Buck on guitar. Buck would play rhythm guitar during their upcoming session, on an open-holed Martin.

Ken Nelson thought of the duo as a novelty act, but they wanted to be taken seriously and sought more sophisticated fare. So they approached Buck, who gave them one song he had written, "Yearning, Burning Heart," and three he had cowritten, "Flash, Crash and Thunder," with Rollie Weber; "No One," with Dusty Rhodes and Rollie Weber; and "Someone to Love," with Joe "Red" Simpson. Despite their up-tempo beats, Buck's songs were all hurtin' songs about serious heartbreak. After discovering what Buck had done, Ken became angry; he, too, had given Bobby and Woody four songs, and they had chosen Buck's offerings over his. Buck said Ken told him, "I don't appreciate people slugging my artists with songs." It wasn't until the February 21, 1957, recording session that Ken got over the blow to his ego and complimented Buck on his song picks.

Buck would recall that it was because of his picks that Ken finally warmed to the idea of signing him to Capitol. Terry Fell and Claude Caviness had implored the producer to sign him, Buck said, and Ken had brought up the possibility halfway through the Farmer Boys' session. According to Buck, he told Ken that he was in negotiations with Columbia Records, and Ken presented him with a contract on the spot. Buck said that two Columbia artists, Johnny Bond and Joe Maphis, had sent a demo of Buck singing to Columbia's legendary A&R man Don Law, and that Law had wired Bond and Maphis telling them to "hold Buck for me."

Ken, on the other hand, claimed that he signed the singer out of "self-defense" because Buck was hounding him so badly. Finally, Ken acquiesced and auditioned him. Buck hadn't completed the first thirty-two bars of a song when Ken stopped him. Buck came out of the booth looking downcast when Ken told him, "Buck, you've got a contract!"

As for the Farmer Boys, the February 21 session would turn out to be their last for Capitol. The duo wanted to sing more ballads, but Ken felt the novelty tunes were selling and took the if-it-ain't-broke-don't-fix-it mentality. Thus, Capitol Records did not renew the Farmer Boys' contract, ending their national recording career.

According to Ken Nelson, Capitol signed only three artists in 1957: Del Reeves, Ray Stevens, and Buck Owens. After about two years, Ray's and Del's albums had gotten neither airplay nor sales, so they were released from their contracts. After Ray left Capitol, he became known for his novelty songs and went on to become a crossover success. "I missed the boat with Ray," Ken said, "but I hit the jackpot with Buck Owens!"

Of course, even if he didn't say so, Ken missed the boat with Del, too. When Buck recorded his first four songs for Capitol on August 30, 1957, Ken put a Nashville spin on the tunes; they were recorded with "doo-wahs," Buck said, and were "kinda pop country." His first single was "Come Back," released on October 21, 1957, with "I Know What It Means" on its flip side. Both songs bombed. The Nashville sound didn't cut it where Buck was popular out West—where people liked to dance to music more than to sit and listen. Buck wrote to Ken offering to relinquish his Capitol contract, but Ken would hear nothing of it. He sent the letter back to Buck with a message on the back: "I still want to record you, and I still like what you do." However, if Buck's future recordings were to succeed, Ken would need to find a different approach.

6

WASHINGTON

Long before Kurt Cobain and Courtney Love made Seattle famous for grunge rock, the Pacific Northwest's country music scene rivaled that of Central California. Both Washington and Oregon drew their share of singers, musicians, dancers, and fruit pickers to their fertile valleys. Unlike Central California, the Pacific Northwest would never be known for a distinctive local sound, but it was home to honky-tonks and bands aplenty, and more record labels than in Bakersfield. Various radio and television variety shows featured live music. Even Hank Williams and Willie Nelson found their way to the area in the 1950s—as did Buck Owens.

In January 1958, Dusty Rhodes, the musician who had offered Buck his first job in Bakersfield and cowrote "No One" with him, persuaded Buck to join him in Washington. Dusty had moved there the previous year and found work at a small radio station in Puyallup, as well as club gigs as a steel player. He argued that Buck, too, should take advantage of the thriving country music scene in the Pacific Northwest. "Come Back" and "I Know What It Means" had flopped, so Buck figured, what the heck, it wasn't happening in California—he may as well head north. He uprooted his new wife, Phyllis, their son, and his two stepchildren, and left the Blackboard and Bakersfield.

When they arrived in Washington, Buck bought one-third interest in KAYE, a 250-watt radio station in Tacoma (not to be confused with KAYO in Seattle). He joked that with a good radio, the station signal could be picked up in the parking lot. At KAYE, Buck learned the radio business hands-on; he served not only as a station owner but also as a drive-time disc jockey, a media buyer, and an ad salesman. He earned 40 percent commission on his ad sales, which brought in more money than he had ever made playing music. Still, he could not give up performing. In spite of his workload at the station, he got a regular gig playing at the Britannia Tavern in Tacoma for $5.50 an hour. He also promoted and played a big dance on Saturday nights out at Bresemann Park near Spanaway Lake in Pierce County.

At the Britannia, he judged a couple of talent contests. The winner both times was a teenage housewife named Loretta Lynn. She won a couple of cheap watches, which quit working after three days. When she complained, Buck told her, "Hell, what do you expect? They only cost $3!" Thus began a lifelong friendship between the two artists.

The next couple of years proved to be busy ones for Buck. He divided his time between working in Washington and recording in California. After Buck's first two Capitol songs flopped, Ken Nelson changed the way he produced Buck's tracks, allowing the artist to make his own stylistic decisions. "Buck produced his own sessions, basically," future Buckaroo Tom Brumley recalled, "and I think that's what an artist should do. An artist should know what he wants to do, and know what songs he wants to do and do 'em. If the artist don't know what he wants, what happens when he changes producers?" Ken became very hands-off, preferring to doodle Xs and pipe up once in a while to call for a new take, comment on the sound quality ("Don, I think your E string's a little flat"), or make technical adjustments ("OK, four thousand forward and twelve, cut one or cut two"). Buck, meanwhile, practiced what he called "head management." That is, there were no rehearsals or arrangements. Everybody came in and brainstormed on a song and let it unfold in the studio spontaneously.

On April 7, 1958, Capitol released the remaining tracks from his initial recording session, "Sweet Thing" and "I Only Know That I Love You." Later that year, on October 9, he recorded four ballads, including "Second Fiddle" and "My Everlasting Love." On November 10, "I'll Take a Chance on Loving You" and "Walk the Floor" were released. Finally, on March 23, 1959, Buck had his first big chart success with the single release of "Second Fiddle," which reached #24 on *Billboard*.

Buck returned to Hollywood on June 16, 1959, to record "Under Your Spell Again" and "Tired of Livin'," which were released July 13, 1959. "Under Your

Spell Again" charted at #4 that fall and became Buck's first entry into the top ten. Buck was credited as the sole writer of the song and even won a song-writing award for it from the music licensing organization BMI. Buck said he got the idea for the song from an R&B tune he'd heard that had a line about "castin' my spell on you," and he went home and wrote the song just like that. The truth is that the song came easy for Buck because Dusty Rhodes bought "Under Your Spell Again" from somebody in either Washington or Oregon for $20 and Buck put his name on it.

After he broke into the top ten, Buck's recording fortunes were on a definite upswing. The dean of Nashville disc jockeys, Ralph Emery, said he believed he was the first DJ in the United States to start playing Buck's records. He remembered "Under Your Spell Again" as the song that kick-started Buck's career, and he saved a picture postcard Buck sent him thanking him for his support.

George French and Jim Pierce alternated playing piano on most of Buck's early Capitol hits. After George and Buck had a spat, Jim recalled, he would be called in to play for a while until Buck and George patched things up again. Jim had first met Buck back when Buck was playing lead guitar for Tommy Collins and didn't sing much. It came as a surprise to those who knew Buck then, he said, when a few years later Buck was cutting hit records as a vocalist for Capitol. Buck had a good ear for songs, though, Jim recalled, and the songs he wrote were simple and to the point, not to mention commercial.

As he actually worked with Buck for the first time, however, what impressed Jim most was that Buck was the first artist with whom he had played who actually knew what he wanted. Buck was very emphatic about his sound. For example, he knew at that time that one key to his sound was the steel guitar of the now-legendary Ralph Mooney, so he would go to Ralph to bolster his playing: "Play it a little bit higher. That's it. Now put it over here." Mooney was already a driving instrumentalist, Jim recalled, but he loved the encouragement, because Buck was pushing him to go beyond his best.

At home in Washington, Buck scored another job, as host of a half-hour TV show, *The Bar-K Jamboree,* which aired every Saturday night on Tacoma's channel 11, KTNT. The program was simulcast on radio; Buck and Dusty joked that this meant it was broadcast in "stereo." The house band was the Bar-K Gang. At various times it included "Shot Gun" Red Hildreth on upright bass; Dusty Rhodes on steel; Rollie Weber (another of Buck's cowriters on the Farmer Boys songs), Don Markham, and Nokie Edwards (whom Buck called "a great thumbpicker") on guitar; and Howie Johnson on drums. It also featured a couple of girl singers, Gail Harris and Barbara Vogel.

Buck had persuaded Don Markham, whom he'd known at the Blackboard as a saxophone and trumpet player (he also played piano), both to take up the electric bass and to join them in Washington. Don and his wife, Wanda, stayed for only about six months before returning to Bakersfield. Eventually, he would play saxophone and horns for Merle Haggard's Strangers. Fellow Bar-K Gang members Howie and Nokie would play drums and guitar, respectively, for the Ventures.

The Bar-K Gang cut several records on local labels, but they lacked a fiddle player. So Dusty set out to find one.

7

DANGEROUS DON

Marlane Lydia Schindler, who grew up in the small mountain town of Morton, Washington, recalled first seeing her future husband, Donald Eugene Ulrich, playing for the Tex Mitchell Band at the Plaquato Ballroom in Chehalis, and again at Steve's Gay '90s in Tacoma. She was smitten by his good looks, blue eyes, and ready smile, but friends advised her to keep a distance, because he had an overprotective mother. "I don't want to mess with his mother," she thought. So Marlane, a mere slip of a girl with a dry wit, steered clear for the time being.

Professionally, however, the young man was attracting less cautious admirers. One day in mid-1958, Dusty Rhodes announced to Buck that he had found the band a fiddle player: a dynamo who was only sixteen. "You *what*?" Buck responded. He didn't want to babysit some pimply-faced kid! After hearing the kid play, however, Buck lost any reservations he may have had about hiring a teenager—he was amazing. Don became the first of many teens Buck would hire over the years. "I would drive from the Tacoma-Puyallup area over to Tumwater to pick up Don from high school to rehearse," said Buck.

For stage purposes, Buck shortened Don's surname from "Ulrich" to "Rich." And unsurprisingly for the man who had dubbed himself "Buck" at age two, he had an affinity for nicknaming other people. He favored alliterative adjectives that fit each person's name and personality, so he began introducing Don as "dandy, dangerous Don Rich"—an ironic reference to the fact that Don wouldn't harm a fly. Behind the scenes, Buck just called him "Dangerous."

Don was born on August 15, 1941, in Olympia, Washington, and grew up in nearby Tumwater, in strawberry country not far from where they make beer.

He was raised by William Walter Ulrich and Anna M. Jackson Ulrich—Bill and Ann to those who knew them—who were fifty-five and fifty-two when the boy was born. Everybody, including Buck, said Don was always aware that he was adopted. It nagged at him, the thought that his birth parents didn't want him. But according to singer Kay Adams, Don dearly loved his adoptive mother and talked about her a lot.

Kay said Jack McFadden had told her that Don never knew it, but his adoptive father was actually his biological father. "I don't know if he had had an affair," Kay said. "I don't know what happened." Marlane, however, said she didn't think anyone knew for sure what the real story was. She said many Ulriches in Missouri claimed that Bill was Don's birth father, although Don's Aunt Juanita, who was friends with Don's biological mother, said that was untrue. According to Juanita, Don's birth father had been killed in World War II, which left his pregnant mother in a predicament. Single and alone, the young woman was ill-equipped to care for a newborn by herself. So she looked for a family for her son and found Ann and Bill. She lived with them during her pregnancy, and when she delivered, Ann and Bill's names were put on the birth certificate; there was no adoption per se. Still, some Ulrich cousins in Missouri resemble Don and maintain that Bill was his biological father.

In any case, Bill and Don shared an undeniable affinity for music. When Don was growing up, his father was a barber with a one-chair shop on the property where they lived. But during the Depression, several years before Don came into their lives, Ann and Bill had lived in a migrant camp near Taft, California. They picked the crops and hunted cotton-field rabbits to eat for food. Years later, when they went to Bakersfield to visit their son, they showed Don and his family where they lived in the tents. The only things they wanted their son to pick, however, were string instruments, and they did everything in their power to make that happen.

When Don was only two, Bill made him a tiny hand-carved violin. Ann was very strict and made Don practice music when he would rather have been outside playing with other boys his age. He was forbidden to join in sports because it might injure his hands and therefore hurt his ability to play music. Once, when Don was in junior high, there was a heat wave that threatened the local strawberry harvest. The school excused the students from class and sent them into the fields so they could pick strawberries. They were paid for their efforts, but Don was a poor picker and only made 35 cents. When he told his parents where he'd been, they got angry at him and at the school for risking his future as a musician.

All his practicing paid off, however. By three and a half, Don was singing and playing guitar. At age five, the musical boy wonder was performing on the radio. Formal violin lessons followed at six and he was playing lead guitar at eight. In 1952, eleven-year-old Don won a talent contest and a two-week trip to Hollywood. By high school, he was playing violin in the school symphony and had his own rock band, which played regularly at Steve's Gay '90s. He also played guitar in a jazz band at the Hofbrau restaurant in Seattle. At fifteen, he graduated to playing lead guitar for the Tex Mitchell Band.

If Ken Nelson had hit the jackpot with Buck Owens, the same could be said about Buck with Don Rich. Their partnership would become unparalleled in country music history. Much has been written about the duo's near-telepathic ability to anticipate each other's song choices and follow each other's licks. Sometimes Buck would change a lick to see if he could throw Don, but he never did. Entertainer Roy Clark knew Buck and Don in the early days of their partnership, and characterized the way they worked like this: "Buck could think it and Don could do it." They bolstered each other. If one was having an off-day, the other stepped in and covered. "He could read my mind, and I could read his. We were on the same wavelength," Buck said. That is how many others viewed their relationship as well. "Don and Buck shared the same soul," said Jon Hager, another adopted young man whom Buck would befriend in later years. "Buck could do anything as long as Don was at his side." The soul connection was there, the energy was there, and the vocal harmony was there—which meant the music was there.

In the fall of 1959, Don entered Centralia College, a community college in Centralia, Washington, as a music major. There, he again crossed paths with Marlane. She was getting an associate of arts degree in business and was required to take a couple of music courses, which landed her in some of the same classes as Don. Although Marlane was interested in him, she ended up dating his best friend. She soon realized that Don was hanging around more than his friend was, so she and Don started going to lunch together. Because she was on a tight budget, she told her grandfather, "I am doing OK. I have a new boyfriend taking me out to lunch. I'm saving money!" It wasn't long before she and Don were sweethearts. On weekends, Don would play music with Buck while Marlane, who was raised by her grandparents, would go home to Morton to help her blind grandfather at his business as a judge and justice of the peace. It was an arrangement that worked out well for all involved.

On his first winter break, Don traveled to Los Angeles and went into the Capitol studio to record with Buck for the first time. He took over fiddle-playing duties from J. R. "Jelly" Sanders, who had fiddled for Buck on many of his earlier recordings. On December 23, 1959, they recorded "Above and Beyond," by Buck's old friend and business partner Harlan Howard. Wynn Stewart had recorded Harlan's song earlier in the year, and when Buck heard it, he wanted to cut his own version.

In the same session, Buck also recorded "Take Me Back Again," "Till These Dreams Come True," and "Excuse Me (I Think I've Got a Heartache)." Harlan conceived "Excuse Me" after he and Wynn Stewart visited their disc jockey friend "Texas" Bill Strength while his wife was in the process of moving out. It was awkward for Harlan and Wynn to be present during the marital drama, and Bill wasn't much in the mood for visitors. Bill said, "Well, you guys'll have to excuse me—I think I've got a heartache." After they left, Harlan told Wynn, "That's a hell of a song title." He went to work writing the lyrics, while Buck composed the music.

As Buck's musical partnership with Don was beginning, his publishing partnership with Harlan reached what Buck characterized as an amicable end. In 1959, Harlan moved to Nashville to be with his wife, Jan Howard, who was a rising star. According to Buck, Harlan decided to let him take over his share in their publishing company, Blue Book Music. Buck became sole owner, which was one of the most lucrative business deals he ever clinched.

Buck and Don began playing as a duo at various venues in the Pacific Northwest. In the beginning, it was just Buck and Don traveling the region in Buck's yellow 1959 Ford Fairlane Skyliner. (Buck told *Guitar Player* that the car was a 1960 hardtop convertible Ford Skyliner, but Ford produced its last Skyliner in 1959.) They would load their instruments in the car and set the Fender Bassman amplifier atop the luggage rack. Buck had an old tweed Bassman amp with four ten-inch speakers that they used on all their records for years. The two of them would plug their instruments into the same amp, Buck on guitar and Don on fiddle, and it was able to carry both instruments without distortion. The Bassman is the Holy Grail of amplifiers and a very sought-after piece of equipment, according to amp expert Dave Gant. Back when Buck was plugging into his Bassman, Dave said, the amp cost around $329, but the same one today sells in the $8,000 to $10,000 range. Years later, Buck would try to persuade Tom Brumley to give him his Bassman amp to put in his mini-museum at the Crystal Palace, but Tom refused because he still used it. The Bassmans are that good.

The duo hired freelance musicians and used various house bands to back them along the way. One steel player, Neil Livingston, who with his twin brother backed the duo for two weeks, recalled that Buck paid them only with bologna, white bread, and water. Buck and Don's venues included the Belfair Barn, "the home of Bill Griffith and the Jackpine Ramblers," over in Mason County. The Belfair was an actual barn, which had been converted into a Saturday night dance hall. They also played at Bresemann Park with musicians such as bass player Gary Paxton of Skip & Flip fame, who later formed the Hollywood Argyles.

By teaming up with Buck, Don came into his own musically. Don's ability to hit the high notes when he harmonized caused singer Jimmy Dean to call him "a tenor-singing son-of-a-gun," while International Fan Club Organization president Loudilla Johnson said, "Don was just as much a part of the Buck Owens sound as Luther Perkins was to Johnny Cash." At first on fiddle and then later on guitar, Don clinched Buck's trademark sound with his "chicken pickin'" style of playing, which many musicians say originated with an earlier Capitol recording artist, guitar legend Jimmy Bryant, whose instrumental "Pickin' the Chicken" was recorded in a 1951 session but wasn't released until 1954. Buck cited Jimmy Bryant as one of his musical heroes and said he played sessions with him.

In addition to being a primo musician, Don was an all-around nice guy with an infectious personality and compassion for his fellow man; he endeared himself to almost everybody he met and even men referred to him as a "sweetheart." "There was never a person that met Don Rich that did not like him," Jon Hager's twin brother, Jim, pronounced. Don hated injustice and befriended outcasts and underdogs, always seeking to make everybody feel comfortable and at ease. One way he did this was through his humor, which is why so many of his associates remember him as being funny, fun-loving, gregarious—and somewhat reckless. Latter-day Buckaroo Ronnie Jackson called him "the Will Rogers of country music." Don was truly a man of excess. Not only was he excessively talented, excessively good-natured, and excessively good-looking, but also he ate and drank like a horse and had the sex drive of a stallion—or, as Doyle Holly so indelicately put it, "Don loved to fuck."

But Don's charismatic and unrestrained nature overshadowed a quiet, serious side to which only a handful of people were privy. Humor, in part, was a defense mechanism to conceal the pain he felt over never knowing his birth parents. Over the years, *Hee Haw* producer Sam Lovullo, singer Kay Adams, and Buck's national promotion director Kris Black, were among the sensitive few who saw the behind-the-scenes Don. As with most cut-ups and class clowns, Don had a fragile heart and used humor to mask his true feelings.

8

BAKERSFIELD REDUX

In Don Rich, Buck had found the perfect musical partner, but his personal life was not so harmonious. Not only was life with Phyllis rocky, but on February 25, 1959, Bonnie sued him for back child support. According to Buck, the couple shared custody of Buddy and Mike, but Bonnie's petition indicated that the boys lived with her in Oildale, outside Bakersfield, while Buck lived in Puyallup, Washington, with his new family. According to both Buddy and Bonnie's future husband Merle Haggard, Bonnie raised the boys single-handedly while they were young.

Bonnie noted that her monthly earnings were $162 and that Buck had paid her only $70 in December 1958, $20 in January 1959, and $20 on February 2, 1959. It was barely enough for a young mother with two growing boys to survive on. "Previous payments have never been regular or correct amount," she said in her motion. It wasn't that he couldn't pay, because he was earning at least $400 or $500 a week at the time. Buck was just watching out for number one, that's all. If he could weasel out of paying, he would. If Bonnie wanted the money, well, then she was going to have to put some effort into getting it.

Later in 1959, just as Marlane and Don were getting serious, Buck's short marriage to Phyllis ended in divorce. It came as no surprise, because he was rarely home and he did as he pleased while she was raising three small children. Buck decided the breakup was cause for celebration, so he took Marlane and Don out to Steve's Gay '90s. It didn't much matter to him that either his third or fourth marriage in roughly fifteen years had disintegrated, or that seven kids (including Phyllis's two by her late first husband) were the fallout from his philandering. Hell, no. He was unencumbered once again, and Marlane and Don soon found themselves providing a personal taxi service for

Buck by driving women from Buck's apartment back home after he had finished having his way with them.

Buck could also celebrate the fact that his professional life had never been
better. Buck and Don continued to play at various clubs with house bands
backing them. He still hosted *The Bar-K Jamboree*, and in 1960 he booked
his good friend Loretta Lynn as one of the guests. On February 1 of that year,
"Above and Beyond"/"Till These Dreams Come True" was released as a single. It peaked at #3.

With his recording career on the upswing, Buck divested his interests in
KAYE. In June, he moved back to Bakersfield. Don was still in school, so he
stayed behind in Washington. At some point Phyllis also moved back to California, and soon she and Buck were living together again with her three children in a two-bedroom house.

To the casual observer, it may seem odd that Buck would divorce, celebrate,
and then move back in with his ex-wife a few months later, but that was Buck's
way. He ran hot and cold; one minute he did and said one thing, and the next
he did the complete opposite. As for why Buck chose only to live with Phyllis
instead of remarrying her right away, that remains a mystery, although
finances probably played a role for both of them. Friends say Phyllis truly loved
Buck, and it is likely she also loved the security of knowing that her and her
children's needs were met, because it would have been difficult for her to support three children on a carhop's pay. Buck, on the other hand, did not like to
be alone, and it was cheaper for him to support one household instead of two,
particularly if he could remain legally unencumbered.

Upon his return to California, Buck took over the Big Fresno Barn dance
hall—or so he said. The Barn was a huge, rambling structure about five miles
outside the Fresno city limits and 90 miles north of Bakersfield, four miles
west of Highway 99. The family dance hall gained prominence when Bob Wills
played there in the 1940s. In the 1950s, Dave Stogner and his western swing
band, the Western Rhythmaires, were synonymous with the Big Fresno Barn.
They were the house band, and Dave was responsible for booking acts, including Hank Williams and Marty Robbins, at the Barn until 1962. Buck claimed

that beginning in 1960, he also performed and booked bands at the Barn. But Viola Stogner, Dave's widow, and Daryl Stogner, Dave's son and Viola's step-son, did not recall Buck having been involved in the booking process. "I think I would have heard Dad talking about that somewhere along the way," Daryl said. "He might have played there, as it was rented out for weekends for a while." The only other person Daryl knew of who booked acts there besides his father was the owner, Izette Davis, who lived in a house behind the Barn. Daryl said the venue did well financially until his father left in 1962. After that, he said, Mrs. Davis tried to keep the Barn afloat, but it began to sink and was rented out to various bands, including rock groups.

On August 1, 1960, "Excuse Me (I Think I've Got a Heartache)"/"I've Got a Right to Know" broke out as a single and peaked at #2 on both the *Billboard* and the *Cashbox* charts. The success of "Excuse Me" spawned even more acclaim for Buck; he was invited to make his second appearance and his solo debut at the *Grand Ole Opry* in Nashville.

On December 3, Buck recorded "Foolin' Around" and "High as the Mountains," with Jelly Sanders back on fiddle. Harlan Howard wrote the lyrics to "Foolin' Around," and as he often did, he gave the lyrics to Buck and told him to put some "Owens hydromatic" to them. "Foolin' Around" was released as a single on January 2, 1961. It spent eight weeks at #2 on the *Billboard* chart and was Buck's first #1 on *Cashbox*.

Buck was on his way to the top, and Don Rich wanted to be there alongside him. Don knew he wanted to spend the rest of his life making music with Buck, so he didn't see much sense in continuing his college education. He wrote to Buck, telling him the last two years had spoiled him and he wanted a job. Buck told him college was important; he wanted to make sure Don was making the right decision. Don insisted he was, so Buck offered him $75 a week and a roof over his head. In addition, as a condition of his employment, if Don earned any money from outside jobs, he had to turn it over to Buck. Don agreed, and after the first semester of his sophomore year, in December 1960, he dropped out of Centralia College and moved to Bakersfield. He moved in with Buck and Phyllis. Almost everybody who knew the two men described their relationship as a cross between big brother/little brother and father/son.

The reunited duo performed at clubs such as the Blackboard, where Buck now introduced Don as "Pecos Pete." Because they played venues where alcoholic beverages were served, the underage Don used a fake ID to get in. Singer-songwriter Johnny Russell recalled a night in early January 1961 when he, Don, Buck, and KUZZ-AM disc jockey Eddie Briggs went clubbing. Johnny was about a year and a half older than Don, but unlike Don, he didn't have a fake ID. Even though Johnny was about to turn twenty-one, he still couldn't get into the clubs. He said that Don, ever the diplomat, would not go inside, opting to sit in the car with him while Buck and Eddie partied.

Not long after Don moved in with Buck and his family, Buck bought a twenty-acre ranch in Edison on the edge of Bakersfield. He stocked it with a small herd of black angus and a couple of horses and referred to it as "Buck's Black Angus Cattle Place." It would be the Owenses' home for several years; his parents even moved into a house on the ranch next to the corral.

Meanwhile, Don was trying to decide what to do about his girlfriend back home in Washington. He missed Marlane and kept calling and proposing to her. "OK, pack up. I'm going to get married." Then he would call back an hour later and say, "Oh, I changed my mind." Marlane was getting weary of the emotional roller coaster, and she confessed her frustration to Buck. Once, when the duo had a gig in the Pacific Northwest, Don went ahead to set up and Marlane and Buck joined him later, sharing a cab. On the way, Buck told Marlane he, too, was sick and tired of Don's indecision. "You ought to just break up with him and tell him you want to start going out. Just break it off and see what he does. And I'll bet you . . . he will call and say, 'I am on my way.'" Buck had been around, so Marlane did as he suggested.

Just as Buck had predicted, Don soon called his sweetheart and said, "I am on my way." He arrived in Washington within fifteen hours. At the time, people had to be either twenty-one or have parental consent to marry. Marlane and Don both knew his parents would never give their only son permission to marry an "older woman," so they eloped to Las Vegas. It took them a couple of tries because Don had to present his fake ID at the courthouse, and the people on duty wouldn't accept it. So they waited until the shift changed and finally succeeded. They were married on April 21, 1961.

After their nuptials, the young couple briefly lived with Buck and his family. Marlane got a job as an accountant for a group of architects, but Don was jealous of her being in an office full of men. He wanted her to work for Buck instead, so Buck hired her at Blue Book for 75 cents an hour. She later took a $5-a-week cut in pay when she signed on as Buck's secretary with a weekly salary of $25.

January 1961 saw the release of Buck's first Capitol LP, *Buck Owens*. (It was later released as *Under Your Spell Again*, because Buck had a different LP titled *Buck Owens* released on the obscure La Brea label the same year.) On January 16, he recorded "Mental Cruelty"/"Loose Talk," both duets with Rose Maddox, who had been a successful recording artist since the late 1940s and was also Buck's sometime lover. The single was released April 10. "Mental Cruelty," written by Larry and Dixie Davis and Buck, peaked at #8, and "Loose Talk," written by Freddie Hart and Ann Lucas, at #4; both held the distinction of being in the top ten with "Foolin' Around" simultaneously. On July 24, "Under the Influence of Love," another Harlan and Buck collaboration, with "Bad Bad Dream" on the flip side, was released as a single and peaked at #2. Buck's second Capitol LP, *Buck Owens Sings Harlan Howard*, was released August 28.

On September 26, 1961, Buck returned to the Capitol studio to rerecord "You're for Me," the song Tommy Collins had released seven years earlier; Buck had also recorded it six years earlier for Lu-Tal. Instead of being Buck's usual shuffle, "You're for Me" was the start of the freight-train sound and suggested a hint of rock 'n' roll. Buck's new version of "You're for Me" was first released October 1, 1962, on the LP of the same name. Other tracks included "Under the Influence of Love" and "Bad Bad Dream." The song wasn't released as a single until about a month later, November 5, 1962. It peaked at #10.

Buck recorded "Kickin' Our Hearts Around," on December 6, 1961. Tommy Collins's former girlfriend, Wanda Jackson, wrote the song especially for Buck. On August 20, 1962, "Kickin' Our Hearts Around"/"I Can't Stop

(My Lovin' You)" was released as a single. It peaked at #8. On April 18, Buck recorded the Drifters' rock 'n' roll hit "Save the Last Dance for Me," which was released as a single on May 21 and peaked at #11.

As Buck's career gained momentum, he helped young Don and his new wife settle into a place of their own for a monthly rent of $35, which was deducted from Don's pay. When Buck was on the road, Marlane spent a lot of time at his ranch, looking after the Owenses' kids so Phyllis could travel with her ex-husband.

On January 11, 1963, Marlane gave birth to their first son, Vance Owen, named for their boss and benefactor. Their second son, Victor Walter, named for Don's father, was born on October 19, 1964. Don was really enjoying his life and was proud of his family. He especially loved being a dad and doted on his sons. Although his hectic work schedule kept him away from home for long periods, he called home, took photographs, and wrote letters so his family could be part of the road experience. He may have been gone, but he was at home in spirit.

★ **9** ★

GENERAL JACK

As Buck Owens's songs got more airplay and he began to get more club dates, Buck thought it also might be time to hire a booking manager to line up regional gigs and otherwise take care of business so he could focus on playing music. He offered the job to Larry Adamson, with whom he stayed whenever he played at Larry's club, the Robin Club, in Rocklin, California. But Larry didn't want to manage Buck, because he didn't like the way Buck conducted his affairs, business and otherwise. Instead, he suggested that Buck approach his longtime friend Jack McFadden, who was working either as a used car salesman or as a radio advertising manager for Sacramento's KRAK and wanted a full-time gig managing a major country star.

Jack had become a part-time booking agent in the early 1950s, while working as a salesman in a Stockton, California, shoe store. One day, Jack recalled, country singer Clyde Easley came into the shop looking for a pair of black boots. There weren't any in his size, so Jack sold him white ones instead, along with a dozen pair of socks and four bottles of white shoe polish. The singer left the store, but returned a few moments later. He figured that anyone who could sell him on white boots when he wanted black ones just might have a future in show business, so he asked Jack, "Hey, boy, you want to be my manager?" The young salesman took the singer up on his offer, and began booking regional acts on the side.

Larry felt that his friend had a higher tolerance for bullshit than he did, and the ability to focus on what was good about an artist while overlooking some of the more unsavory aspects of the artist's personality. Moreover, Jack had aspired to manage someone who might hit it big, and ever since he and

Tommy Collins saw Buck perform at the Blackboard in 1953, Jack truly believed Buck was going places.

When Larry spurned Buck's offer to become his manager, Buck did what he did so well with people he felt didn't deserve any more of his time and attention: He erased Larry from his personal memory chip. In Buck's mind, Larry simply ceased to exist. Then Buck did as Larry had suggested and asked Jack to book a few dates for him.

Buck was already scheduled for a couple of dates in Washington and Oregon, and he asked Jack if he could book him a few more so he could make it a ten-day tour. At this point, Buck was still thinking of himself only as a West Coast act. He was making fairly good money playing clubs, but he wasn't looking at the big picture. Jack, on the other hand, had a vision for Buck that extended beyond the moment. He came back to his client not with a few additional gigs but with sixteen dates that paid more money than Buck had ever dreamed. Later that day, Jack called Buck and the subject of Jack handling Buck exclusively came up. Buck then invited Jack to go to Las Vegas with him so they could discuss the details.

As the two men were riding along in Buck's car discussing an exclusive management deal, Jack said to Buck: "I want to make you a million dollars."

Buck slammed on the brakes and said, "A million dollars! What's in it for you?"

"A hundred thousand."

Suddenly, Jack had Buck's full attention; he was speaking his language. Jack's take was 10 percent of all the deals he negotiated for Buck. They shook hands and the agreement was sealed. Although Buck was usually a stickler for contracts, in this case he figured a handshake would suffice. If the deal went south, well, no one had done any paperwork, and it would be easy enough to walk away.

Jack, it seems, was less equivocal. Like Larry, pianist Jim Pierce knew Jack when he was selling used cars at a Chevrolet dealership in Sacramento. Jim was in Las Vegas playing piano for Wynn Stewart at the Nashville Nevada Club, east of town on the Boulder Highway, when Jack walked in "all smiles and happiness." He went over to the piano and said to Jim, "Guess what? I've just become Buck Owens's manager!" Jim said, "Man, that's great!" Jack waited for Jim to finish his shift, and then the two of them went out and partied all night, celebrating Jack's new job.

Thus began Buck's relationship with the man he would nickname "the General," in an obvious attempt to outrank Elvis Presley's legendary manager, Colonel Tom Parker. Despite Buck's initial ambivalence, it turned out to be a partnership from which both men prospered for the next three decades. Their motto became "Whatever it takes."

Jack McFadden was born in St. Louis, Missouri, on January 9, 1927, to Louie A. McFadden and Lillie Mae Gulley McFadden. His family moved to Northern California when he was a boy. After graduating from high school, he served in the U.S. Navy during World War II in the Pacific Theater of Operations. When he got out of the navy in either 1945 or 1946, he married Peggy Featherstone, with whom he had three children, Joe, Jack Jr., and Lana.

Jack was a hardworking, honest, and warm man who was respected by almost everyone with whom he had dealings. "We all liked Jack," Jim recalled. Disc jockey Bill Mack said he liked Jack because he was a sincere friend who "filled him in on lots of secrets." Jon Hager said, "Jack was always up-front." He also was a true believer in country music and Buck Owens. After years of booking acts on the side, he had made many contacts and was able to open doors for Buck that the artist might otherwise have walked past. Many people credited Jack with Buck's overwhelming success. Others, however, felt that Buck would have made it anyway, just not as soon. Sam Lovullo recalled that they made a good team, because Jack would make the moves and Buck would take it from there.

Even though Jack was Buck's manager, Buck still had to sign off on everything Jack arranged. Jack once complained to Jim, "I can't really make any decisions except superficial ones. All the important decisions that a manager might make, I have to go to Buck for his approval."

Jim said he saw Jack several times after he went to work for Buck and that "Jack had been drinking quite a bit, and he would express regret that he didn't have a bit more of a say when he knew some of the best paths for him to take, but everything had to be approved by Buck. Of course, Buck was wildly successful, so who's to say that's wrong? Actually, Jack was manager in name only. He didn't really make decisions for Buck. Buck made his own decisions."

Not everyone got good vibes from Jack, however. Singers Kay Adams and LaWanda Lindsey both felt Jack could be rather harsh, but it was not beyond Buck to set up an underling like Jack to take a fall so as to cast himself in a better light. Former Capitol Records field vice president Wade Pepper liked Jack personally but didn't think he was as dependable as Buck. "Buck's word was good as gold," Wade said. "If Buck made a commitment—I represented the label back at the time—I could bank on it. He was one of the few artists on that roster that was that type. Jack nurses you, a sweet guy, but didn't have the dependability." Naturally, Buck would aim to please a higher-up on his record label and follow through on commitments, because he was nothing if not professional—that is what kept the money flowing in.

Jo McFadden, on the other hand, was certain that her husband earned every nickel he made. "I'm sure it was not given to him," she said. "He worked his ass off for it. He more than paid his dues, in more ways than one."

Tom Brumley agreed, characterizing Jack as "a teddy bear acting like a lion." When Jack took over and Buck's hits started rolling in, nobody had to tell Jack what to do. He went for it. "He just kept pushing it and pushing it and pushing it farther," Tom said. "He'd make 'em mad the first time, then they just couldn't do a show without Buck. Buck just had to be there. He was the number one act, the hottest thing in America, and they had to have him. Buck had the respect for what Jack was doing. I know Jack was doing a heck of a job. Jack stayed with him till he died, I guess. Thirty years, you know, and so I know the only manager he ever had was Jack. There must have been a pretty good relationship or it wouldn't have lasted that long. I know it was a good financial relationship for both of 'em."

★ 10 ★

UNCLE DOROTHY

In addition to Jack McFadden, Buck Owens relied heavily on the business acumen of his younger sister Dorothy. In 1963 he established Buck Owens Enterprises, his personal business corporation, and named Dorothy vice president and business manager. She stayed with the company until her dying day. Together she, Buck, and Jack were the triad, the holy trinity of Buck Owens Enterprises.

Dorothy was an attractive blonde with a strong jaw and a fondness for redheads and bowling shirts. Her brother was the idea man, and she took care of the logistics and tracked every dime. Whenever he left home, she gave him self-addressed, stamped envelopes for each day he was gone so all he had to do was put his receipts in and send them back to her. She took care of the rest. Of course, Buck was good about turning everything in, but without Dorothy he never would have been able to tell where the money had been spent. No matter how many people credit Buck for running a tight ship, more people say Dorothy ran a tighter one. She was the one who drew up the contracts and ruled with an iron hand. "God bless her and everything like that," Jon Hager said, "but she could've run a Nazi concentration camp."

Dorothy was always nice as she could be to people, but protecting Buck's interests was her first priority. She was loyal and dedicated to her brother and reported every word she heard back to him. Basically, she was nice on the surface but could betray someone in a heartbeat if it put her in good stead with Buck. Dorothy was slick and had her own agenda, and over the years she would use people such as Kris Black for her own benefit. "She was so touched, she would do anything for Buck, and, God knows, sometimes she had to," said Kris, who later reported to Dorothy in her job as Buck Owens

Enterprises' national promotion director. Dorothy was Kris's favorite business mentor. "She ran the business like she was Buck's wife, but I adored Dorothy and she adored me." It is possible Kris might have changed her mind about that had she been privy to some of the sly remarks and innuendoes Jo McFadden said Buck's sister made behind Kris's back; Dorothy might utter a sarcastic "Well, what would you expect?" when Kris was out of the room, then turn around and brag on her to her face. Kay Adams said that Dorothy had gone out of her way to help her a couple of times and had been "really, really, really good" to her. "She must have really liked me a lot," Kay said.

Although Buck didn't adopt his "all-American" image until a few years after he brought his sister onboard, he sought to keep her sexual preferences quiet. But she was an out-of-the-closet lesbian who lived with a woman at a time when that wasn't an everyday occurrence. She and her partner, who had a young son, bought a house together, and lived as wife and wife. People talked, though. Buck had nicknamed his baby sister "Toots," while behind her back others called her "Uncle Dorothy," which was Doyle Holly's favorite way of referring to her. Singer-songwriter Dennis Payne preferred "Unkie Dorothy."

11

"Act Naturally"

At the same time that Buck Owens was establishing the core of his business empire, he was also assembling the musical family that would help propel him to country music stardom. He began to hire full-time band members and paid them $75 a week to join him and Don onstage. Steel guitarist Jay McDonald was his first hire. The band's stage apparel was off-the-rack basic: white shirts, skinny ties, and dark pants.

Then, in early 1961, Buck added drummer Wayne "Moose" Stone, who earned his nickname because the guys thought "he looked like a moose in heat." Moose played on early recording sessions for Buck's next LP, *On the Bandstand*. Next, Buck hired two young brothers, bassist Kenny Pierce and guitarist Alan Pierce. Alan was only with the band briefly and did not play on any sessions. Buck also enlisted another drummer, Ken Presley; it is not known why his and Moose's tenures overlapped. By this time, the group had graduated to wearing fringed black leather jackets with black-and-white cowhide insets across the chest, white shirts with black scarf ties, and either black or red pants.

Buck and the band performed nonstop with few if any breaks, and each song seemingly rolled into the next. In the early days, Buck usually gave audiences their money's worth; he was an engaging entertainer who drew people in with his folksy, down-to-earth style and slight drawl. By 1962, Buck and his musicians were traveling to gigs not by car but in a full-size camper on a 1960 or 1961 Chevrolet pickup. In fact, over the next couple of years they went through *two* campers, the first borrowed from Bakersfield television host Cousin Herb Henson, and the second purchased by Buck.

By 1963, they were traveling to the Capitol studio as well, to participate in further recording sessions for *On the Bandstand*. Ken Nelson allowed the entire band to play on the album, which was released April 29, 1963, and they are even featured on the cover, dressed in their leather jackets. Buck, though, is wearing the first outfit he ever bought from designer Nudie Cohn, a tailored, watermelon-colored suit. Although both of Buck's drummers contributed to the album, only Ken Presley is pictured on the LP cover.

Kenny Pierce's picture doesn't appear on the cover, either, because he quit the band on the way to the March 1963 photo shoot. In the camper halfway between Bakersfield and Los Angeles, he came to the conclusion that the guys in the cab of the truck were talking about him behind his back about something involving a gambling debt. Kenny made them stop and let him out so he could hitchhike back to Bakersfield.

The new band also joined Buck for the recording of his first *Billboard* #1. "Act Naturally" was recorded on February 12, 1963, and released March 11. It was the first hit on which Don took over lead guitar duties from Buck, who would later claim that Don had little prior experience with the guitar. Buck told *Guitar Player* magazine that "Don was a fiddle player who knew little to nothing about guitar . . . but superseded me completely." The two were so close, it is hard to fathom that Buck was unaware that Don had been playing guitar since age three and a half. "Act Naturally" was on the chart for twenty-eight weeks before it hit the top spot, and it stayed there for four weeks. "Love's Gonna Live Here" would pick up where "Act Naturally" left off; released August 19 of the same year, it would hold the top spot for sixteen weeks and become Buck's biggest career hit. So began a streak in which Buck monopolized the *Billboard* country chart with fifteen consecutive #1 singles.

"Act Naturally" in particular was so good that even the Beatles recorded it. The Beatles were huge fans of Buck Owens and his band, and vice versa. "We were big Beatles fans," Buck said. "I loved the Beatles. If Don Rich were here today, he'd tell you the same thing." Ken Nelson recalled having to send all Buck's records to the Beatles as soon as they were released so they could listen to them. Ringo Starr picked "Act Naturally" for his cut on *Help!* and the Beatles recorded it on June 17, 1965.

"Hell, I made Buck Owens!" said Johnny Russell, the writer of "Act Naturally." At the same time, it was Buck's chart-topping rendition that established the twenty-three-year-old Johnny as a serious tunesmith. He wrote the song in 1961 after he had to break a movie date with a girl because he'd been called to a last-minute Saturday-night recording session in Los Angeles with Dave Stogner and some visiting musicians. When his date asked why he couldn't make it, Johnny told her, "They are going to put me in the movies and make a big star out of me." They laughed over his remark, and as Johnny rode to L.A. in the back of Dave's station wagon, "Act Naturally" came to him.

Johnny shopped the song to various artists for a couple of years, he said, but it was rejected everywhere he went. He couldn't understand why, because he thought he had a twist on a love song that had never been done before. Eventually he played it for Voni Morrison, his songwriting partner at the time, with whom he had a deal to share credit on songs they each had written individually, a practice not uncommon in the music business. She loved "Act Naturally" and thought it would be perfect for Buck.

As was Buck's habit, he floated several fictitious scenarios to explain how the song came to his attention. In a 1969 interview with the *Nashville Banner*, Buck told how Johnny had brought him tapes of five songs. After listening to four, Buck said he couldn't use any of them. Johnny told Buck he knew he wouldn't like the last song and started to leave. "I insisted I hear it," Buck said. "It was 'Act Naturally' and became a million-plus seller. It was a song for me."

Buck told a different story in his Rhino Records CD booklet. This time he said that it was Voni Morrison who brought a demo disc to him and Don Rich. Voni supposedly told them that she doubted they wanted the final song, but Don wanted to hear it anyway. "I wanted it right then," Buck said. "I looked at Don, he looked at me, and I said, 'We'll take it.'"

Johnny, however, told yet another story. He said that Voni was indeed the one who pitched the song, since she did a lot of work with Buck. She took him the song, along with four others she and Johnny had written, to see if he wanted any of them. Weeks later, Voni broke the news to Johnny that "Act Naturally" was the song Buck had liked the least of the five she'd played for him. Don Rich, however, had liked it best; he kept humming and singing the tune over and over. Buck finally called Johnny and told him he was interested in recording the song—provided that Johnny agreed to his terms, which gave Buck all the publishing rights. Of course, Johnny wanted the song cut, so he agreed.

What Johnny didn't know, though, was that Buck had already recorded the song. He was just holding out for 100 percent of the publishing. In other words, he flat-out screwed Johnny and Voni out of any share of the song. Pianist Jim Pierce called it "a typical Buckism." Throughout the 1960s, Buck insisted on obtaining at least 50 percent of the publishing rights for the songs he recorded. Since the unknown songwriters did benefit from his high profile, it was only fair that he get *some* share of their profit, though 15 to 20 percent would seem a more reasonable cut. If Buck didn't get what he wanted, though, he refused to record a song. Many writers went along with Buck's terms, because it meant guaranteed royalties, no matter how small. Otherwise, as singer-songwriter Mayf Nutter said, the songs "never would have been heard by anybody but Grandma."

But it wasn't just the legal rights to "Act Naturally" that Buck wanted to claim for himself; he also tried to pass off the composition as his own. When the Beatles' 45 was released, Buck's name was on the label as the sole writer. He told a *San Diego Union TV Week* editor in 1970: "I never hardly ever dream up a tune in short order. I have to let a tune work at me a while. I can't force it out. I have to nurture it until it comes out at its own pace. On the other hand, in '63 I wrote 'Act Naturally'—a song the Beatles recorded, by the way—in five minutes, which I guess was its proper gestation time."

Johnny remembered being backstage one night and hearing Buck say onstage, "Here's a song I wrote." He didn't think much about it until he realized Buck was launching into "Act Naturally." Of course, Johnny was pissing mad. He went to Jack McFadden and said, "I'm either gonna whip his ass or sue him!" Jack told him, "Well, whip him. That don't cost us no money."

Ultimately, Johnny and Voni did take Buck to court, where they won full credit and retroactive royalties for the song. Basically, Buck had taken the same tack with them as he had with Bonnie when she sued him for back child support. He wasn't going to make it easy for anyone to get what was rightfully his or hers. In addition, he knew most people didn't have the time, the money, and/or the fight to go up against somebody as powerful or as selfish as him. It was like a game to Buck, one that he took great pleasure in playing—and usually won.

12

MERLE AND THE MOOSE MEDICINE

In the early days, musicians in Buck Owens's band seemed to quit as quickly as they were hired. Often, what drove them off was not so much the low pay but the way Buck overworked people. Even though the group was poised to become the top country band of the day, their leader had a way of extracting whatever he could and then some from his musicians, including having them pull double and triple duty as chauffeurs and roadies, all in the name of saving a buck or two. No one was exempt from pulling extra duty; Buck, too, did his share of the driving and the loading and unloading.

After bassist Kenny Pierce left, Buck hired Merle Haggard to replace him in the latter part of March 1963. Merle had gained a following on the Bakersfield club circuit by working at three local clubs seven nights a week—two at Bob's Lucky Spot, four at High Pockets, and a Sunday-night gig at Tex's Barrel House. During that period, Merle also played bass for Larry Adamson's wife, Rusty Wood. Even though playing bass wasn't Merle's forte, Buck told him to fake it.

Merle soon discovered what it was like to work for Buck. He found himself performing nonstop at night, driving a truck and camper hundreds of miles each day, and earning only half as much pay as he had in the clubs, where he'd pulled in $150 a week. "Had I known about the pay, I might have stayed home," Merle said. Buck's attitude was that it was worth the $75 a week in lost income for the privilege of playing in his band. Merle, like all of Buck's musicians, more than earned his pay during his time with Buck. He also did something that Buck himself had failed to do. He named the band: the Buckaroos.

Buck would later maintain that the Buckaroos were clean-cut all-Americans who only drank socially and never took anything stronger than No-Doz, and for the most part, they were. But because they worked such long hours, many of the band members took pills to stay awake on the road. They didn't associate taking uppers such as Benzedrine, a prescription medication, with "doing drugs." Even so, according to Kay Adams, who later became Don's lover, Don kept his habit quiet except to a select few, because he didn't want Buck to know he was taking pills.

As for Buck himself, few people ever saw him popping uppers, though future Buckaroo Doyle Holly did recall seeing him take a "white cross bennie," or Benzedrine, once around three o'clock in the morning. There Buck sat, wide awake, yapping in pig latin nonstop: "En-whay is is-thay ill-pay oing-gay o-tay ake-tay effect-ay?" Doyle and the others tried to suppress their laughter so Buck wouldn't get mad at them. Don's wife, Marlane, later recalled from her time as Buck's secretary that Buck would speak in pig latin if he didn't want somebody to know what he was talking about, especially when the wives were present. When he took the bennie, she theorized, "I guess he got to talking pig latin and after he did that he couldn't talk normal."

Buck regularly took other prescription drugs, though, including Valium in the early years and OxyContin in later years for pain. Those around him did not consider him to be drug-dependent, though; they just thought of him as being a hypochondriac, because he worried that he had every new illness that came along. He had any number of doctors he could call who would write prescriptions for him in a heartbeat, and he was never without his "shaving kit."

He also liked to smoke, because it relaxed him. He'd started with cigarettes as a teenager before graduating to a pipe and occasional cigars. He used a Meerschaum pipe with Black Diamond tobacco, not "behavior blend," as Jim Hager put it. Although Buck emphasized to the press that he was a teetotaler, he drank; he just didn't do it publicly, nor did he drink to the point of drunkenness, perhaps because he was born with only one working kidney. He was a closet drinker and his favorite drink was a margarita. Most of the people he worked with never saw him drink anything more than water, Coca-Cola, and iced tea—but, then, he only drank around people he knew wouldn't broadcast it. He also liked a couple of glasses of wine with dinner now and then.

Near the end of March 1963, the band's camper was pulled over in either Washington or Oregon for speeding. Back in those days, a highway patrolman could search a vehicle without permission, and this one did. The officer found a bottle of drummer Moose Stone's white cross bennies in the glove box of the truck and pulled it out.

"What's this?" he asked.

"Oh, that's Moose medicine," a quick-thinking Merle said.

The patrolman, believing that they were hunters, put the pills back in the glove box and said, "OK, you guys slow down. Be careful."

After either two short weeks if you go by Merle's account, or three if you go by Buck's, it was Merle's turn to quit; he was on the cusp of making it as a solo act. Evidently Buck convinced his previous bassist, Kenny Pierce, to rejoin the group as Merle's replacement.

In mid-April 1963, Moose Stone left as well. Two months later, on June 16, 1963, Buck's remaining drummer, Ken Presley, was killed in a car accident. Buck hired Mel King to take up sole drumming duties. Then in July, Kenny Pierce quit again. For the third time, Buck was faced with the arduous task of trying to find a replacement bass player willing to work for low pay.

Merle Haggard eventually superseded Buck's career milestones by racking up more awards and thirty-eight #1s to Buck's twenty-one on the *Billboard* country chart.

★ 13 ★

DASHING DOYLE

The third time was the charm for Buck when he hired twenty-seven-year-old Doyle Holly to replace Kenny Pierce on bass. Aside from Don Rich, Doyle was the Buckaroo from the early years with the most staying power. He joined the band on August 12, 1963 (Buck's thirty-fourth birthday), and except for a nine-month split in 1966–1967, he remained with the group until 1971.

Doyle was five foot ten and a half inches tall with sandy blond hair, a trim physique, killer blues, dimples, a ready smile, and a great sense of humor. Buck nicknamed him "Dashing Doyle," and dashing he was; groupies flocked to him in droves. Nevertheless, Doyle thought he had acquired his nickname because he was always dashing off to do something for Buck—being a gofer was part of the job description for most all of the Buckaroos. Doyle would get annoyed with his errand-boy status. "I'd dash through the snow. I'd dash to get Buck a sandwich," he remembered.

If somebody truly needed help, though, Doyle was there. Others remembered him as a good person and friend, and he would become an older brother figure to many of the younger musicians who later toured with Buck, such as his son Buddy Alan and the Hager twins.

Doyle was a funny guy, always hamming it up. He'd get all over Buddy, kissing on him, or he'd mangle people's names, referring to Jim and Jon Hager as Jim and Jon "Hagers." Onstage, too, he was the comedian of the group, known for classic comedy interludes such as "Vanish" and "Ugly Finder." Doyle recalled the latter: "That's the ugly one of the band, the ugly one of the group, that's a cue to do the 'whoop, whoop, whoop' joke." It was a running gag used in many of the band's shows. Doyle would point at Buck and say, "Whoop, whoop,

whoop" and Buck would say, "Why you doing that to me for?" Doyle would reply, "That's my ugly finder—whoop, whoop, whoop—and it's working."

Buck Owens also liked to rib his musicians, but Doyle sensed that his banter often had an underlying cutting edge. "Buck liked to humiliate people," said Doyle, who not only was better-looking than his boss but also had a better voice and was seven years younger. Buck would say, "Doyle suffers from a LOT disease—Lack Of Talent." Buck also made pointed jabs about Doyle being an Okie, the Bakersfield equivalent of being Polish. It was comments such as these that made Doyle feel like less of a person.

Though Don joined in on some of Buck's ribbing—they both used to say, "Doyle has a lot of class. It's all third, but he has a lot of it"—Doyle didn't hold it against him. In fact, he said of his early years with the Buckaroos that "Don Rich was my best friend. We would get on our motorcycles and go up in the hills of Bakersfield and we'd go rabbit hunting. We'd go shooting groundhogs or ground squirrels or whatever you want to call them. And we rode our motorcycles just about every day that we had off."

As with Don, Doyle's knife-sharp wit was a defense mechanism that concealed the hurt he had experienced as a boy. If Buck thought he had been born into abject poverty, he had nothing on his bass player, who was the seventh of ten children of an impoverished wildcatter, or oil prospector, Burt Hendricks, and his stay-at-home wife, Arvie Houston Hendricks. He was born Doyle Floyd Hendricks on June 30, 1936, in the tiny Oklahoma farming town of Perkins. His father went from place to place in search of oil, so the family rarely lived in a town for more than four to six months. They moved from state to state as well, with stops in Texas and Louisiana. One childhood memory he never forgot was wrapping up empty boxes and bricks in newspapers so they would have something to put under the Christmas tree and open come Christmas morning. "You can't miss something you never had," he said.

The saddest moment of his life, however, occurred when he was about ten years old: his mother left the family. He remembered her saying that when the youngest child was weaned she was going to leave. Then one day, rail-thin Arvie packed a suitcase and headed out to the main highway. She stood out on the road, thumb out, waiting for somebody, anybody, to pick her up and take her away. "I wanted to run after her and beg her to stay, but I didn't," Doyle said. "I just stood there and cried. She didn't look back."

As a boy, Doyle learned to play guitar and washboard bass. He credited his older brothers Art and Bob with influencing him to make country music his career. The three brothers had a band called the Hollys and they worked the rodeo circuit. After his mother left, he went to live with Bob in Caldwell, Kansas, and at thirteen, Doyle began working in the oil fields there. He continued this back-breaking labor until he joined the U.S. Army in 1953.

Just as Buck didn't have anything on Doyle when it came to being a poor boy, Doyle had a love life that paralleled Buck's in personal drama. He married young to his first wife, Rose Marie Thibodeaux, and they were husband and wife just three months when nineteen-year-old Rose ran off with a sixty-year-old man. He met his next wife, Letha, when he was a staff sergeant at Fort Benning, Georgia, and she was a specialist third class. Originally from Norfolk, Virginia, Letha was a young, skinny brunette with an equine face and a killer wit. They had four children in rapid succession—Letha Joanne, Robert Doyle, Billy Wynn, and Tamzin "Tammy" Lee.

Doyle did tours of duty in Korea and Okinawa. After he was discharged from the Army in 1957, he moved to Bakersfield. By 1962, he had a day job working for Standard Oil in Taft, just outside of Bakersfield, and he worked nights playing bass and singing in Dusty Rhodes's band.

That same year he met his future employer, when he and Dusty went to Las Vegas to see Buck, who was appearing at the Golden Nugget on Fremont Street for the first time. They took off in Dusty's Volkswagen with only $9 between them. Nine bucks bought them a tank of gas to get there and a six-pack of beer—but then they had no money to get home. So they picked up three days of work at the County Line Club, where Red Simpson was playing. He, too, was flat broke—but he was one of Buck's writers at Blue Book Music. So the men met with Buck, who was dressed in a tailored western suit, and Red talked him into lending him $18 in silver dollars. From it, he gave Dusty gas money for the trip back to Bakersfield.

The next year, it was one of Buck's people who needed a favor from Doyle. He was playing in Fuzzy Owen's band at Bob's Lucky Spot when Don came in to ask for Doyle's guitar. Doyle was playing an old Fender Telecaster that had been in a trailer house fire; he had scraped the burnt spot off the guitar with a knife. It was a ratty-looking instrument, but one Don needed. Buck was about to start endorsing Fender products, but to do so he had to turn in old guitars to be replaced by Fender. Don said to Doyle, "Let me take your guitar so they'll give us a new one, because I don't have a Fender guitar that I want to turn in to the company." Doyle gave it to him. A week later Don returned and asked Doyle if he was interested in going on the road with Buck Owens as the Buckaroos' new bass player.

At the time, Doyle was also working for Joe and Rose Lee Maphis. They were doing tours with Jack Lord, who had a television series about a rodeo star called *Stoney Burke*. Doyle asked Joe whether he should join Buck, despite the low pay. Joe said, "Yeah, I think Buck is gonna amount to something. It might be a good job for you later on."

When Doyle went to work for Buck in August 1963, there was no interview, no rehearsal, no nothing, but he started with a bang. For his first gig, he returned to the Golden Nugget in Las Vegas, along with Buck, Don, Jay McDonald on steel, and Mel King on drums. Though Doyle had played bass with other groups, he considered himself more of a singer and a rhythm guitarist. "Buck and Don more or less taught me how to play bass," he said. Buck concurred: "I'm sure there were better studio musicians, as far as maybe a bass player, but Doyle Holly never represented himself as a bass player; he was a guitar player. I told him, 'Well, now you're a bass player.'"

As far as Doyle could recall, everyone in the band had a different deal with Buck, but to begin with he was earning Buck's standard $75 a week. He also got $10 a day for expenses. Later, his salary doubled to $150 a week; Buck had given him a choice of either that or $30 a day, but only for the days they worked. He said if he had known they were going to work 300 to 320 days a year, he would have taken the $30 a day instead. When he quit the Buckaroos in 1971, he was still making the same base pay, which added up to $7,800 a year.

By the time Doyle joined, the band had instituted a policy regarding the camper they took to gigs: a musician had to be with the group anywhere from six months to a year before he could be trusted to drive it. The first year Doyle was with the band, only Buck, Don, and Jay were allowed to drive. It frustrated Doyle to be stuck in an enclosed camper while the driver was up front in the pickup enjoying the scenery. Fortunately, the rear window of the pickup had been removed and there was an opening between it and the camper so the passengers were able to crawl through either to sit up front or to lie down and sleep in the back.

Despite their precautionary policy, shortly after Doyle's arrival the band had its first wreck, when the camper hit a Greyhound bus near San Francisco. Doyle was in the top bed over the cab with Mel King, and Buck was lying down in the back bed. Jay McDonald was driving and Don was in the pickup's passenger seat. It was foggy out and the bus pulled out in front of the pickup and Jay hit it. Buck's ribs got bruised and the rest of the guys had minor bruises and abrasions. But Buck's little 000-18 Martin guitar was in the corner of the bed next to where Doyle was sleeping—right where the bus hit. Either Buck's mother or grandmother had bought the guitar for him, Doyle recalled, so it held sentimental value. The instrument was broken into a hundred pieces.

That night they were playing a small club near San Francisco, "the Golden Cockroach or something," Doyle said, when a Greyhound representative came in and settled up with everybody. He gave each band member $100 to sign a release saying they would not sue Greyhound. Everybody signed except for Buck. Doyle didn't know what kind of settlement Buck was holding out for, but he got one. He eventually had his 000-18 glued back together.

On another occasion, when the band got lost in the desert of New Mexico around three o'clock in the morning, Doyle almost got left behind. Buck wasn't riding with them on that trip, but Don and Jay were in the pickup and Doyle and Mel were back in the camper. Don and Jay stopped, turned on the dome light, and studied the map to figure out where they were. Doyle decided to take advantage of the stop and got out to relieve himself, but he failed to tell anyone what he was doing. As he stood there, pants unzipped, midstream, he noticed the camper slowly pulling back onto the road and driving away. He quickly picked up some rocks and started pelting the camper. The guys soon realized somebody was missing and turned around and went back for him.

Not only did the band members have to put in their time before they could drive the camper, but also they had to prove themselves before Buck would allow them to sell concessions after a concert. It was a venture Buck had devised so the musicians could earn extra income via commission. During the show, Buck would plug various items for sale such as photographs and songbooks, and afterward the band would sign autographs and hawk souvenirs. Buck would stay out there until the last person left the auditorium. Whether it was to give everyone a chance to meet him or just because he wanted to sell the last album and make a few more dollars, no one knew for sure, but Buck was definitely loyal to his fans, and often posed for snapshots with them.

The guys, meanwhile, would either check out or be assigned the number of albums Buck felt they would be able to sell on a tour. For example, if it was a one-day tour, Doyle would take a box of twenty-five albums, twenty-five songbooks, and twenty-five pictures. The photographs sold for 25 cents in the beginning, then went up to 50 cents and eventually $1 for an eight-by-ten black-and-white glossy. Songbooks sold for $1.50 or $2. Albums cost $5. Sometimes, Doyle would average as much as $75 to $100 extra a day on commissions. The most he ever made in one day was $180, which was more than he made in a week as a Buckaroo.

By 1963, Doyle's marriage to Letha was tenuous at best. Still in her early twenties, Letha was looking raggedy from having to raise four kids by herself, and took to drinking and smoking too much. Rolene Brumley, wife of soon-to-be Buckaroo Tom Brumley, noted that Letha was losing her teeth at a young age, and that Doyle didn't take care of her very well. "Even with a wife and four kids, I still wasn't worried about making money," Doyle admitted. "I was worried about having fun." He recalled trying to reconcile with her on the telephone in his hotel room when Buck barged in, took the receiver from his hand, slammed it down, and said, "Let's go!" Doyle failed to convince Letha that it was Buck who had hung up on her, not him. They got divorced in Mexico—or so they thought.

After Buck himself, Doyle was probably the biggest womanizer of the group. He took full advantage of his popularity with the ladies by sleeping with women both known and unknown. One of Doyle's more famous lovers would be June Carter, whom he nicknamed "Long Legs" because hers were longer than his thirty-inch inseams. He remembered June telling him that she didn't write "Ring of Fire," but that Johnny Cash, whom she married in 1968, had written it with Merle Kilgore in 1963 while Johnny was still married to his first wife. Johnny supposedly put June's name on it instead of his so he wouldn't lose the royalties when he finally divorced Vivian Liberto Cash and married June. Two of Doyle's unknown conquests included a pretty brunette, with whom he was in love and saw as often as possible, and Virginia Mae Driskill, a blonde he had seen fleetingly while driving the band through her hometown of Spearfish, South Dakota in 1966. At the time, Doyle had no clue the petite blonde would become his third, fourth, and last wife. To him, she was just another pretty face in the crowd.

"The first part of the '60s was probably the happiest years that I ever spent in the Buck Owens organization," Doyle recalled. But tensions with Buck sometimes boiled over into full-blown confrontations: "Me and Buck had a love-hate relationship. He'd fire me a couple of times a month, and I'd quit a couple of times a month," Doyle said. One particularly significant showdown occurred after Doyle bought Buck's old Ford Fairlane Skyliner in 1963 or '64. The 1959 Skyliner, the one in which Buck and Don had traveled in the early days, had ninety thousand miles on it. Buck agreed to sell it to Doyle for $900 and worked out a payment plan by which Doyle would pay him compound interest on the purchase price. Doyle did not understand the concept of compound interest, let alone how Buck's payment plan worked, so he was upset to discover that after making payments for the better part of a year, he still owed Buck $900.

While on tour in Washington State, he got into it with Buck over something, "or maybe I just got tired of the band." So he went to Buck's motel room and gave him notice that he was quitting the group. Buck talked with Don and Jack McFadden, who evidently told Buck how he could sidestep the problem of replacing yet another bass player. Buck summoned Doyle back to his room and said, "If you take back your notice and stay with the band, I'll give you the car." Doyle finally owned the Skyliner free and clear, and he stayed with the group.

★ 14 ★

TIMID TOM

The year 1963 proved to be a pivotal one for Buck Owens. He assembled his award-winning band, scored his first *Billboard* #1, and even made his first appearance on national television, on ABC's *The Jimmy Dean Show*. He was Bakersfield's resident celebrity, and with his growing fame came money, control, flashy stage costumes, and fans. The adulation of thousands—male and female, big and small—fed his already considerable ego. To those close to him, he proclaimed himself the King of Country. Larry Adamson said, "Buck kind of changed personalities. He thought he was the King."

Nineteen sixty-three was also the year Buck brought his ex-wife Bonnie onboard to sing backup. Band members recalled that she was like a mom to them on the road, always offering to do their laundry, iron their shirts for them, and such—she would do anything they asked of her. Bonnie was also completely loyal to Buck, and she and Buck got along great on the road. There was never any friction or any hint that there had ever been a relationship between them. But Bonnie would only stay with the group until 1964, when she left to join the road show of her future husband Merle Haggard.

Turnover among Buck's musicians continued as well, and the next to leave was Jay McDonald. The remaining band members considered Jay to be such a great steel player that they drove nails into and ripped strings off his Fender 1000 steel guitar so no one else would be able to play the instrument. But someone had to take over for him, and the musician Buck chose was Tom Brumley, whom he had first met in 1961 when Tom went to California to record with his older brother Albert E. Brumley Jr. Tom had just gotten married to Rolene Spencer and the trip was their honeymoon. Buck and Don were in the Capitol studio both days Tom was there with Al, and Tom met and talked with them. Buck was impressed with Tom's finesse on the steel guitar and remembered him.

When Tom got the call in November 1963 to work for Buck, he and his family had recently moved to Texas, where he was working as a builder for his father-in-law, Rollie Spencer. The Brumleys had just built a house but did not yet have telephone service. One day, his father-in-law came over and said, "Tom, do you know a fellow named Buck Owens?"

"Well, sure I do. Why?"

"Well, he called here."

"Ah, you're kiddin'!"

"No, he called. I forgot to give you this," Rollie said, reaching into his shirt pocket and handing Tom a message.

Buck had called the Anchor Restaurant over in Marble Falls, Texas, and asked the owner, "Do you know Tom Brumley?" The owner replied, "Yeah, I do." Buck said, "This is Buck Owens, would you have him call me?" The restaurant owner took Buck's number and passed on the message to Rollie, who had carried it around a couple of days before remembering to give it to his son-in-law. So Tom called Buck, who offered him $125 a week to play steel for him.

"I'm making good money. I can't do it for that, Buck. I mean, I'm glad to work with you, but I can't afford to give this up right now."

"Well, you think about it two or three days and call me back," Buck said.

Tom had been around enough entertainers to know how some of them mistreated musicians, and he was no masochist. So he wrote out a list of conditions. "One thing about Buck is, you have to go after what you want. He's not going to give it to you," Tom said. "I told him things like 'I play the steel guitar, and I don't drive, I don't shine boots, I don't run errands. You're payin' me to play steel guitar and that's what I do, and nothin' else.'" Tom also told Buck that he wanted a room to himself on the road. But the biggest thing Tom insisted upon was that he always would deal directly with Buck—Buck was the one calling and hiring him, so he didn't want to answer to anyone but him. Tom told himself if Buck agreed to his terms, then he would go to work for him, and if he didn't, he would be fine. So Tom called Buck back and told him what he wanted.

To his amazement, Buck agreed to all of his demands. "Something else I'll throw in," Buck said, "if you don't like the job I'll move you back to Texas."

"OK, I am on my way," Tom said.

Tom became a Buckaroo on December 26, 1963, just fifteen days after he turned twenty-five. Of course, it was easy for Buck to say yes to everything on Tom's list, because he knew he was going to do things his way anyway. If Tom didn't like it, well, then, he'd have to call him on it. "That first check I got, I think he had shorted me some because he started it on a different pay period on a different day than what it was supposed to start," Tom said. "I went to see Buck when I went to work that day and he fixed that. And that was fine. But I was so worried. You had to bird-dog him a little. That's what you had to do. If you stayed on top of your deal and made him stay on top of it, well, he did. If you didn't make a deal, then you had nothing to go by."

To know Tom Brumley, one must go back to his roots. He was born December 11, 1938, in Stella, Missouri, to Goldie Edith Schell Brumley and Gospel songwriter Albert E. Brumley. Like his famous father, who had penned such standards as "I'll Fly Away" and "Turn Your Radio On," Tom was a musical genius, although both father and son were too humble to admit it.

Albert saw to it when his children were young that they were grounded and well-rounded. He made sure they ate well, played baseball, and worked in the family business assembling songbooks in Powell, Missouri. In addition, all six of his children had musical instruments and they played and sang in the Brumley Brothers Band—even little sister Betty. When it came to music, Albert was of the sink-or-swim mentality, so Tom had to teach himself how to play steel guitar, which is not an easy instrument to learn even with instruction. "We were on our own," Tom said. "Nobody showed me how to play the steel guitar. It's kinda like anybody who does, like my Dad writin' those songs. He only had an eighth-grade education, but he taught himself because he loved it so much. If you really love it, you'll go do whatever is necessary and spend the time." So Tom would go to concerts and visit with the steel players and try to learn from them. He would study their techniques, talk to them, and try to figure out how they did what they did.

When there were no concerts to attend, Tom would listen to the radio and try to re-create what he had heard.

Unlike Buck and Doyle Holly, Tom married only once and it was for keeps. He fell for Rolene, a beautiful blonde, when he was twenty and she was only fifteen. She was selling concessions at the local movie theater, and he would go there and buy popcorn and orange soda just so he could see her. However, he waited until he was out of the army and she was eighteen before courting her. The couple married on June 9, 1961, and went on to have three children, Tom Jr., Todd, and Tracie.

Shortly after their honeymoon in California, Tom and Rolene moved from Missouri to Ohio. They stayed a while, until Tom decided to make a go of playing music for a living. Instead of going to Nashville, he returned to Southern California, where he spent about eight months playing at the Palomino and Rag Doll clubs, which were both on the same street in North Hollywood. Tom made many friends, including Elvis Presley's guitarist, James Burton, but he never enjoyed working in the clubs, he said. The Brumleys moved to Texas, along with Tom's mother, and soon thereafter came the job offer from Buck.

About a week before Tom started playing for Buck, Tom called him and said, "Buck, do you want to rehearse?" Buck said, "No, I don't think so." Tom had to adjust quickly to the fact that the Buckaroos never rehearsed one minute. Sometimes Buck and the band would talk about changing a joke or another element of the show, but to sit down and do a practice run through the play list was out of the question. Buck preferred to let the band go onstage cold to see where his muse would take them.

So Tom flew out and said, "Buck, where's the steel guitar that you said that you had for me?" Tom had left all of his at home because Buck had told him he had one for him. "I don't know," Buck said. "Don't worry about it." As his first gig with the Buckaroos approached, Tom was getting antsy; he persisted in asking Buck where the steel was. Buck's standard response was, "Ah, don't worry about it." An hour before the gig, Tom finally saw the steel guitar Buck had for him. It was the Fender 1000 that Jay McDonald had left behind, the one the other band members had mangled in Jay's honor so that no one else could play it. (Tom, however, thought Jay had destroyed it.) Strings were ripped off, string holders pulled off, the changer pulled loose, and a pedal broken off, and all the cables were loose.

Tom was frantic—he couldn't play an instrument in that condition. Buck didn't seem to be fazed in the least by Tom's dilemma; it wasn't his problem, it was Tom's. Tom and Don Rich quickly put new strings on it, tightened the cables, and got two pedals working before the show started. "I'll tell you, that was one way to start a job," Tom said. "You know, we hadn't rehearsed with Buck, not for one second. No, and I am glad. 'Cause what happened was, I did that job and Buck gave me a raise after that first night. He liked what he heard and gave me a raise, come over and complimented me." Tom said the other Buckaroos were unaware that he had gotten a raise after the very first show and was then earning $180 a week to their paltry $75, although he felt they suspected something was up. He would get another raise after only three months with the band.

A few days after his first gig, on January 6, 1964, the Buckaroos went into the studio to record "Louisiana Man," "Abilene," "A Maiden's Prayer," and "Bud's Bounce," the last of which was an instrumental featuring Tom on steel. Tom got the same steel guitar—with the same set of problems and only two pedals—to play his first session. Three of the songs from that midday session—"Louisiana Man," "Abilene," and "Bud's Bounce"—would appear on the *I Don't Care* LP, released later that year.

The musicians developed an unspoken rule in the studio that Don would play the fills on guitar for the up-tempo numbers and Tom would play the fills on steel for the slow songs; for any given song, one instrument or the other would do the fills all the way through. Tom said that in the studio Buck never told him or Don what to play. "We just played what we felt." But when the Buckaroos played live, Don found it hard to sing and fill at the same time, so Buck had Tom do all the fills, which is what you hear on the band's live albums—even on the up-tempo numbers such as "Tiger by the Tail." To produce those Don Rich licks, Tom had to put an E string on the bottom of his steel guitar, which he did by having Zane Beck of ZB Custom Steels build him a custom model with an eleventh string in addition to the usual ten.

⌘⊗⊙

Singer Kay Adams remembered Tom as the least outgoing of all the Bucka-roos. He kept to himself, but she always thought of him as "closet rowdy," someone who probably could have cut loose if only he'd let himself. By his own admission, Tom was always shy onstage and something of a loner, but "I wanted to play so bad." He liked nothing more than to blend into the back-ground and get lost in the music; he was happy just to be himself. Appropri-ately, Buck nicknamed him "Timid Tom," but onstage he referred to him as "Tender Tom" and "the skinny one of the group." Buck called attention to the steel player's gaunt physique, saying that his concave chest looked "like the inside of a teaspoon."

Tom's physical condition can be attributed in part to the band's grueling schedule, which was particularly hard on him. While on the road for long periods, he wasn't eating right and couldn't rest; he was living on nothing but coffee and cigarettes. The six-foot-tall steel player dropped from 150 to 132 pounds. He ended up developing ulcers that required three operations. "All the time I was with Buck, those things just killed me," he said. "I was so puny. I got pictures of me—wow, what in the world? All you see is teeth and hair."

Rolene Brumley remembered the time her husband spent as a Buckaroo as "the worst five years of my life." It was hard enough raising children on her own without having to worry about her husband's behavior on the road. Because the band was gone so much of the time, there was a great deal of worry and speculation among the Buckaroo wives about their husbands' escapades. The women talked "all the time," Rolene said. "They all knew Kay Adams and Don Rich were carrying on, and they knew Doyle Holly was hav-ing an affair with anybody and everybody." Rolene didn't think Tom was step-ping out on her, but if he was, she didn't want to know. What's more, the other wives thought Tom was the one coming home and telling Rolene what was happening, which is why the women—except for Don's wife, Marlane, and Buck's once and future wife Phyllis—treated her like dirt.

Tom recalled how hard it was being on the road in the beginning. "That's not my fun thing to be out on the road for three weeks with the kids and wife at home," he said. Sometimes he'd be on the verge of quitting and would call

Rolene and tell her he was on his way home. He'd tell Don, "I just can't take this road. I just don't want this road," and Don would reassure him: "Just hang in there, buddy. Things will get better" or "No, no, you think about this. It's all right. It's gonna get better."

"Don always talked me back," Tom remembered. "He made me realize that this was what I really wanted to do. If I quit, what else would I do? We're number one right now. Ride it out, and when it's over, then you can always say, 'I've done that.'"

★ 15 ★

THE PEACEMAKERS

As Buck's bandleader, Don Rich often assumed the role of friend and supporter, offering encouragement whenever anyone was frustrated with either Buck or the road. He was a born peacemaker, and he also took it upon himself to quell Buck's storms of temper as evenly and as quickly as possible.

Those who knew Buck said he projected a different persona publicly than he did in private, so fans never knew that he was prone to drastic mood swings not unlike the north Texas weather. He could be good-hearted, but then he could turn in a nanosecond and become contrary and temperamental to everybody around him. When he was irritated or mad, his nostrils flared and his lips quivered. He had a demon mean streak and either would lash out instantly or would plan a sneak attack in an underhanded, passive-aggressive way. Buck was the kind of guy who if somebody sat there and took what he dished out, he would pile on even more to see how much he or she would endure. It was like a game that he took a perverse pleasure in playing, hence people both loved him and hated him.

Everyone felt safer when Don was around to even things out. He looked up to Buck, never said anything bad about him publicly, and never spoke "out of school." Buck's every wish was Don's command, and he carried out every order Buck gave him efficiently, almost to the point of subservience—and Buck appreciated it. But Don also knew what he wanted to achieve in the studio and would stand up to Buck if he felt it was necessary. He knew just how far he could go with Buck. When his boss's temper turned ugly, he could simply say, "Come on, Chief, let's go talk," and everything would be calm within five minutes. (The Buckaroos nicknamed Buck "Chief" after he acquired a show costume from singer Ray Price, whose band, the Cherokee Cowboys, called Ray the Chief.)

Nonetheless, because Don used conciliation to defuse Buck's temper, he often bore the brunt of Buck's abuse himself. Buck treated him much like a stray dog he had befriended and had every right to kick around.

Tom Brumley would ask Don, "Why do you let him talk to you like that?" but Don would always laugh it off: "Well, he don't mean it." Tom would counter, "No matter whether he means it or not, you are due that respect. If he is in a bad mood, that don't give him the right to chew you out because he feels bad." Tom felt that Buck was all bark and not so much bite, and if people gave him a legitimate reason to leave them alone, he would. When Tom stood up to him, Buck would sound off and back off; he never really came down hard on Tom or took advantage of him. Don, on the other hand, "never did do anything," Tom said. "Buck just used him for a punching bag."

Kay Adams recalled that Don turned to alcohol to help him cope—but according to Tom, it never affected his personality. "Don never acted any different than he did when he was Don," he said. "With or without bennies or with and without booze, he was the same Don. His attitude never changed."

Jack McFadden also discovered that working for Buck Owens did not come without a price. As Buck's manager, he was a go-between who had to carry out the most unpleasant of his boss's orders. He was the bearer of bad news to promoters, radio stations, fans, and employees. According to Kris Black, "Jack handled all the tough stuff."

For instance, Kris recalled a situation from her time as promotion director for Buck Owens Enterprises in which Jack had to break some bad news to one of Buck's fans. A certain radio station had refused to play any of Buck's records for years because somebody there "had gotten cross-ways with Buck," and Kris and Jack were brainstorming how they could get the station to start playing Buck's records again. As it happened, the station in question was talking a lot about a local cancer victim who was in pain and heavily medicated, and had but one wish in her miserable life: to have lunch with Buck Owens so she could die a happy woman. Buck hated to be around sick people and hospitals—it upset him—but Jack finally persuaded Buck to agree to have lunch with the sick woman so they could smooth over relations with the station. "Oh, fine," Buck said. Upon hearing the news, the radio station began playing Buck's tunes again. Everything was moving along as planned for the lunch, and the ill woman had been taken off most of her medications so she would be aware of her special date. Then Buck decided not to go, and somebody had to call and break the bad news to the station.

"Krissy, can you do this?" Jack asked.

"Jack, I just can't do it. I just can't do it," she said.

"Don't worry, Krissy, I will take care of it," he said.

This was but one example in a pattern Buck had of standing people up— also known in the music business as "getting Bucked." Stacy Harris, a Nashville music journalist, recalled her attempts to interview Buck for a 1978 feature in *Country Song Roundup*; she had to reschedule at least three times before he finally sat down with her. Another time, a couple of country music fans had traveled to see Buck, but he ducked out the back door because he wasn't in the mood to glad-hand. He was known to set lunch and dinner meetings and never show up. Sometimes, when he didn't want to talk to someone on the telephone, he would sit and listen without saying a word and/or slam the telephone receiver down as hard as he could.

Jack's job placed him under extreme pressure, but he worked very hard and did well. Even so, Buck was especially short-tempered with him. He was forever raising his voice and yelling, "Jack!" to get his attention and then barking out orders such as "Take care of this, Jack!" or "Do that, Jack!" or "You didn't do that, Jack!" When Buck dressed him down, his manager would take it in stride. "An artist with that kind of pressure on him has to blow steam," Jack would say, "and he can blow steam at me anytime he likes." Jack's second wife, Jo McFadden, explained that growing up, Jack had had so many people disappoint him and be unkind to him that he had gotten to the point that nothing like that could faze him; "I'd rather it be me than another innocent person over there," he'd say.

He also had to put up with Buck's personal insults. In addition to the public designation of "the General," Buck bestowed upon Jack a private nickname: "Pony Boy." It was a reference not only to his height—Jack was a considerably handsome man, but smaller in stature than his boss—but also to the size of his penis. It was of normal proportions, but Buck considered it inferior to his abnormally large member, which the Hager twins would later dub the *real* Buck Owens Empire. "Some people have to feel bigger than life and more important, and if it makes them feel good to put somebody else down, then that's them," Jo said. "The people that are standing and watching, they know who the ugly person in the bunch is."

Although Jack put up a good front, Buck's ill treatment bothered him. Like Don, Jack took comfort in the bottle; he preferred stingers, a cocktail made with brandy and white crème de menthe. He would also corner Tom Brumley and say, "Let's go for a ride, somewhere we can talk," and as they drove along, Jack would vent about how frustrated and fed up he was. Tom would boost Jack's self-esteem by saying, "You're the best manager in the world, you don't have to put up with that stuff. You get no respect. Look what you've done. Look what you're doin'." Tom, in turn, would vent to Jack about being tired of the road and wanting to quit. In effect, they were a support group of two.

Everybody in Buck's organization knew that being Buck meant never having to say he was sorry. "He'd choke somebody and then five minutes later pat them on the back as if nothing happened," said Jo. Doyle Holly, who felt Buck's wrath often, said his boss "would cuss and rave then thirty minutes later take you out to dinner," which was his way of apologizing.

Future Buckaroo Ronnie Jackson agreed. Once Buck fired him only to call and rehire him. "The boys tell me you want to come back," he said to Ronnie. No apology, no nothing. "Yeah, well, I didn't want to leave, Buck," Ronnie replied.

Why Buck was so temperamental and had such drastic mood swings will probably remain a mystery. His behavior could have stemmed from the brain fever he had as a boy, but some family members believe he suffered from manic-depressive disorder, which runs in the family. Buck's oldest sister Mary Ethel was institutionalized for bipolar disorder type I, which is current medical terminology for the condition. Mary Ethel is a topic the family chose not to discuss, much like the Kennedys chose not to discuss the lobotomy and institutionalization of JFK's sister Rosemary.

Kris Black, who is herself bipolar and is an active member of the National Association of Mental Illness, said there is no doubt in her mind that Buck suffered from manic-depressive disorder, as evidenced by his drastic mood swings and hypersexuality. Kris said his moods would change instantly and without warning. She recalled a business meeting during which Buck "changed personalities no less than eighteen times." Jana Jae, one of Buck's later wives, said he was "mentally ill and was at the time we were married" and was "completely erratic," and Kay Adams noted, "A psychiatrist would have a field day with this person. He was so big in his own mind." In fact, his sister Dorothy sought to get her brother psychiatric help, but he refused.

Nevertheless, many bipolar people, including Frank Sinatra, Ernest Hemingway, and Patty Duke, have achieved great things in spite of their mood extremes. Buck Owens was no different.

16

DENNIS PAYNE

For all his demons, Buck was basically a nurturer at heart. He took young artists under his wing, especially those who had been either orphaned or adopted, and did his best to help them gain a foothold in the business. This arrangement was beneficial to Buck as well, since young musicians appealed to a younger fan base, had more stamina, worked for less money, and were easier to manipulate.

In 1963, Buck sought to expand his business by drawing more songwriters into the Blue Book Music fold. He watched the local music variety television shows searching for promising writers he could publish. That is how he came to know Dennis Payne, a young performer on Dave Stogner's *KLYD's Kountry Korner*. Dennis, like Buck, was a musical prodigy, all of fourteen years old. He was a second cousin of the famed Leon Payne, who played for Bob Wills and the Texas Playboys. His father, Charles Payne, was one of the Light Crust Dough Boys. Dennis appeared on Dave's TV show and met and worked with the likes of Buck, Doyle Holly, and Red Simpson.

Buck took a special interest in Dennis, who had never known his father up to that point, and signed him to Blue Book as a songwriter. (In addition, Buck would sign him to his next business venture, the booking agency OMAC.) He was really good to Dennis, allowing him to produce his own records, which he never let anybody do. He also let the boy use other musicians besides the Buckaroos on his recordings. Naturally, Buck didn't want to spend any money to help market and sell Dennis's records, but he still let Dennis do whatever he wanted in the studio. "I was on Capitol, but it was only through him," Dennis said. "It was the only way you could be on Capitol."

According to Dennis, not long after he signed his first contract with Buck, Dorothy Owens called the boy into her office and said, "You know, Buck's been watching you for a long time. He never misses the TV show you're on. He watches this show and he always watches you. He's been watching you for years. He's got a lot of big plans for you. Buck's gonna make you a big star."

"Dorothy, I don't know if I want to be a big star," Dennis said. "I feel more like I want to be an artist—I think there is a difference. I can't really explain it, but I know Buck's a big star, and that's neat and all, but I am not sure that's it." Dorothy went back to Buck and repeated their conversation to him.

"I don't know if that disappointed him or pissed him off or whatever," Dennis said. "He may have taken that wrong." Indeed, if there was one thing Buck couldn't tolerate, it was someone who lacked the same hunger he possessed for making it big. He didn't seem to realize that the musician he was dealing with was just a kid who might not know what he wanted to do yet. And perhaps he was envious of the handsome young performer, who was big for his age, six-foot-five.

Whatever the reason, Buck's demons reemerged. Dennis was still a teenager when Buck set out to teach him a lesson during a show at the Civic Auditorium in Bakersfield. Various local dignitaries were in attendance and several different acts were on the bill, but Buck decided to throw Dennis a curve. Buck did his own set, then turned to Dennis, and said, "All right, you're on" and went out and introduced the boy—he forced the unsuspecting teen to follow his act. Poor Dennis wanted to disappear. He was mortified but went out and sang anyway. It baffled the boy as to why a star as big as Buck would go onstage first. He felt so humiliated that he went home and cried for a couple of weeks.

17

THE FIRING OF MEL KING

Drummer Mel King was a tall guy with a baby face and curly blond hair and blue eyes. He had worked as a drummer for Fuzzy Owen at Bob's Lucky Spot in the early 1960s. By 1964, he had been with Buck for at least seven months and had some quirky ways about him. For example, he smoked in both the bathtub and the shower. Then at every meal, Mel would eat chicken fried steak. "I never seen him eat anything but chicken fried steak," Doyle Holly said. "His middle name should be Mel 'Chicken Fried Steak' King." Mel was also chronically tardy, and he didn't pull his weight in the band. He would stall in the bar while the other guys loaded his drums into the camper for him. One rainy night in El Paso, the other Buckaroos had had enough; they left Mel sitting inside at the bar and his drums sitting outside in the rain while they drove on to the next town.

They had also had enough of traveling by camper. The band had worn out one and were halfway through the second when they graduated to the Green Goose—or Pregnant Goose, as Doyle called it—a big green Winnebago. Buck acquired it from Cal Worthington, a Southern California car dealer known for his zany advertisements featuring Cal and his "dog Spot," which was usually a tiger or some other exotic animal. Cal also had a television show broadcast out of Los Angeles, *Cal's Country Caravan*, on which Buck appeared.

In early January 1964, the Buckaroos were traveling in the Green Goose to a performance at the Albuquerque Coliseum. Glen Campbell, Willie Nelson, and Carl Perkins were also on the bill, and the show was to be broadcast on the television show *Hullabaloo*. But it would end up being more noteworthy because it was the night Don Rich fired Mel King.

Don never lorded his status as bandleader over the other Buckaroos. Only once did he pull rank, and it was that night in Albuquerque. The auditorium was filling up, and behind the curtains, the Buckaroos were setting up onstage. The lineup was supposed to be, from left to right, Doyle, Don, Buck, and Tom, with Mel in the back between Buck and Don. Instead, Mel started setting up his drum kit on the front line. As Tom recalled, it was "a ridiculous move on Mel's part. He was holding up the show." Don asked him what he was doing.

"I want to be up there just like the rest of you. I want to be noticed," Mel said.

"If you don't move your drums back, I'll have to fire you."

"You didn't hire me, you're not going to fire me."

"You're fired!" Don shot back.

Mel ignored him and continued setting up his drums. Don told Doyle to go backstage and tell Buck what was happening. Upon hearing the news, Buck stormed onstage, lips a-quivering, wearing nothing but a pair of pants and a robe. Out in the auditorium, probably five thousand to six thousand people sat waiting, unaware.

"Don, what's Mel's drums doing sitting up on the front?" Buck asked, livid.

"He wouldn't move 'em, so I fired him."

"I'll move 'em!" Buck replied.

He proceeded to throw the drums off the side of the stage, brass clang-banging away. Glen Campbell whispered to Tom, "What's going to happen to him? What's happening!" When Buck finished ridding the stage of Mel's drums, he turned and went back to his dressing room to get ready for the show.

Mel went to find Buck to raise holy hell with his former boss. Buck was ready for him, though, and the minute the drummer stormed into his dressing room, Doyle recalled, Buck "knocked the shit out of him," breaking Mel's tooth.

That night, the band did the show with a young pickup drummer from the union who tried to fill in the best he could. The kid was scared to death, playing for the great Buck Owens, whom he had never listened to and didn't know much about until he was briefed on the star before the show. About thirty minutes into the performance, a county sheriff arrived and waved Buck offstage. "There's a warrant for your arrest," the officer said. "Come on, we'll get you out of the city."

Buck was whisked away, and the band played one more song and ended the show. The people were upset that the show had been cut short, but it would not be the last time a Buck Owens concert would end too soon. The band tore down as quickly as possible, loaded up the motor home, and headed for Bakersfield. They got as far as Gallup, New Mexico, when a city cop stopped them and wanted to know if Buck was onboard. The guys said, "No, he's in Albuquerque" and the officer told them, "Well, you've got to come down to the station." So they started following him, until he stopped his patrol car and got out. He told them, "Buck surrendered himself in Albuquerque, so you guys can go on." Buck had to pay a $25 fine and agreed to pay for Mel's dental work.

Buck could embroider a story better than an expert needlecrafter at a stitch-and-bitch club, though. When he told the *Bakersfield Californian* about the incident years later, his version of the story included several embellishments. He correctly recalled that the band was doing a series of package shows with Glen Campbell and Willie Nelson, but he also said Roger Miller was on the bill, not Carl Perkins. Buck said he only hit Mel once in the face but fretted that it hadn't been hard enough. "All I remember," Buck said, "is him running out of the dressing room, saying, 'Law! Law! Law! He attacked me! Law!' He ran out of the hall and I didn't see him no more." Buck said the pickup drummer they hired that night was a nice old gentleman—not a kid—who looked like an aspiring drummer for Lawrence Welk and played in the old "boom-chuck, boom-chuck" style.

His account of the Buckaroos being stopped in Gallup was embellished, too. He said they were on the band's tour bus (not the motor home they drove at the time) when state troopers (not a city cop) stopped them and ordered them to remove all the amplifiers, guitars, and suitcases from the bus. Then he told how the troopers went onboard and tapped on the paneling and ordered the band members to unlatch the hump cover next to the driver's seat, supposedly to search the engine for Buck. Also, in Buck's version, the judge said, "Mr. King, you've failed to prove anything. Case dismissed."

Buck said that after Mel left the band he still played with them off and on until 1965, but Doyle didn't remember that. "I heard Mel was playing some small jobs around Bakersfield for about a year. After that, I don't know what happened to him."

★ 18 ★

WILLING WILLIE

Doyle Holly and Don Rich had discovered seventeen-year-old drummer Willie Cantu in November 1963, when the young musician was playing in the house band at the Maverick Club in Corpus Christi, Texas. Doyle and Don were so taken by Willie's skills that they brought Buck and the rest of the band to the Gulf Coast burlesque club the next night—November 22, 1963, the day President John F. Kennedy was assassinated in Dallas. Although they were shocked about the day's events, they quickly set aside the death of the president as they focused on Willie's finesse on the drums. "Man, that guy is fast!" Don said. So Doyle approached Willie after the show and got his phone number.

"Even Mel King couldn't play 'Orange Blossom Special' as fast as Don played it, and Willie could," Doyle said. "Willie's got real fast hands. So that convinced Don to get Willie."

"Just that I could play fast, is that any qualification?" Willie replied with a laugh.

"If you can play fast you can play slow, I think that was our philosophy," Doyle said, "and I'm sure it didn't just come down to playing that one fast song."

After Mel King was let go, Mel Taylor, who later replaced *Bar-K Jamboree* alumnus Howie Johnson as the drummer for the Ventures, sat in on most of Buck's recording sessions for the better part of 1964. But Buck needed a drummer for his shows as well, so Don and Doyle gave Buck Willie's phone number and he placed a call to Corpus Christi. Willie told him, "I am going to have to talk to my parents about this," because he still lived at home.

Willie said his parents didn't know who Buck Owens was at the time. They didn't know that their only son would have to live on Buck's Edison ranch, nor any of the other details. They only knew Willie had been offered a job and he felt good about it. They trusted him to make the right decision. So Willie called Buck the next day and told him he would take the job. Buck either wired him money or sent him a ticket, and off he went.

"He said we'd do some recording, go on the road, do this, do that," Willie recalled. "He never really said, 'We're going be on the road 325 days or close to that a year.' I had no clue what I was in for."

When Willie arrived at Bakersfield Airport on January 28, 1964, he was met by Rolene Brumley and Phyllis. "I was surprised and I thought, 'Where's the band? Where's Buck?'" Willie said. As it happened, Buck and his Buckaroos were in the studio that day recording "My Heart Skips a Beat"/"Together Again."

Phyllis and Rolene took Willie back to the ranch so he could get settled. Phyllis told him that Buck had said he could share a room—and a bunk bed— with her son Jacky. Here was Willie, seventeen and living away from home for the first time, and he had a preteen boy for a roommate. It wasn't exactly his idea of striking out on his own. There was a separate two-room place behind the main house at Buck's ranch where Willie used to set up his drums and practice. He holed up in there most of the time to escape and have some privacy.

As if sharing a room with a boy several years younger wasn't strange enough, Willie also had to deal with the culture shock of moving from Texas to California. He had been born Guillermo Cantu in a Tex-Mex household in Corpus Christi on May 26, 1946. His mother, Trinidad Parra, was a housekeeper, and his father, Manuel Jose Cantu, was a jack-of-all-trades. He had a younger sister, Susie, his only sibling. "Just to be in an all-white kind of environment was a big change for me," he said. "Mine's a heavy Tex-Mex background, and so going from that to Bakersfield, California, and living in a home with all Anglos where everybody just speaks English and that's it, it was a totally different environment."

Willie recalled sitting down at the dinner table with Buck and his family for the first time. "There we were with all this lovely looking food, but I didn't like it. Biscuits and gravy, I had never seen that before in my life. I remember Buck saying, 'Go on, have some gravy.' I tried it, but I did not—to this day I can't—

eat it. I don't. Especially white gravy. I like chicken fried steak and I can eat white gravy with chicken fried steak, but with biscuits, forget it. There was a lot of other things I liked, but the biscuits and gravy, that always stood out."

It was also a different environment musically for Willie. He had grown up with Tejano music, and once he started learning drums and playing in the school band, he gravitated toward jazz, which a lot of his friends in the school band were listening to, and which he found exciting and stimulating. When he joined the Buckaroos, he was not a country music fan, but he said it "grew on me to where I loved it."

Because Willie had learned his trade in a house of burlesque, he knew how to punctuate musical phrasing. "If somebody farted, Willie would cue it," Doyle said. Tom Brumley agreed: "If you moved something, you said something, he'd get you: boom, boom. He had recovery, boy, and that was never rehearsed." As Willie explained it, "I always wanted to play in a circus band. Vaudeville. Sound effects. You punctuate the obvious. I played burlesque, not only bump-and-grind strippers. I can sense 'when.'"

Willie was the youngest member of the band, and because he was so young, Buck aged him by three years in fan club publications by printing his birth year as 1943 instead of 1946. The other Buckaroos knew Willie had never been on the road before, and they took full advantage of that knowledge. They joked with him, called him "the kid," and used to tell the girls that he was Indian instead of Mexican. "They couldn't tell if I was Indian or Spanish," Willie said. "You know, I couldn't make up my mind at that time which one was the better of the two. You will have to realize at that time coming from South Texas, being Mexican wasn't necessarily the greatest thing. I grew up with an inferiority complex because of that."

The first gig Willie played with the band was in Redding, California. Willie was nervous because, of course, they had never practiced. Buck never told him what to play or what not to play; Willie didn't even get to talk to him until they were getting ready to perform. Then Buck told him, "If there's anything I don't like, I'll let you know. Just play." Buck added, "One thing to remember is that we all play on top of the beat." Poor Willie had no clue as to what Buck meant by that; he had to listen and figure it out for himself. Doyle recalled another idiosyncrasy of the band that no one was ever told about ahead of time: they always tuned their instruments a half-step lower than the standard.

However, Willie said that "my biggest complaint about the band, especially in the early years, was about my friend here, Doyle Holly." Willie had heard the Buckaroos play at a club in Texas before he came on board, and he'd never heard a band with such clarity, or an electric bass that sounded as good as Doyle's. After joining the band, though, he found that Doyle would focus on other things than playing at the top of his ability. "He would occupy his time onstage not playing the bass but being a funny man and being off to the side flirting with the girls." As a result, the beat used to go different directions, which Willie found frustrating.

Another beef Willie had with the band was their stage outfits. Willie was a fastidious dresser who had learned to iron his own clothes at an early age. When Don handed him his uniform, he was appalled by what he saw: a yellow suit the color of French's mustard. "I don't want to wear this. They're awful!" he said. What's more, the pants were too short; he'd always hated high-water pants, even as a preteen. Then there was the jacket. It was uncomfortable and huge, "big enough for an elephant," he recalled. Willie had first-night jitters as it was, and to have to go onstage in a roomy jacket with short pants added to his anxiety. He didn't know how he could go out there and feel good about playing when he didn't feel good about the way he looked.

Fortunately, as soon as they got home from their long stretch on the road, Buck did something about the ill-fitting suits. He and Phyllis measured Willie to find out his proper size, and the whole band had new outfits in time for the November 2 release of the *I Don't Care* LP, which was Willie's first album cover. The new costumes consisted of gold lamé jackets, white shirts, black ties, and black pants. "Those clothes were made to measure. So I was a lot happier then," he said.

There was no doubt that Willie was dedicated to his craft. As they drove down the highway, Willie passed the time practicing and doing wrist exercises, eight hours a day. As Doyle put it, "Willie's drums, or brains, just leaked out his fingers."

Willie also passed the time on the road by assembling small drum sets, using wire coat hangers to create the accessories. "I made bass drum pedals so I could make a sound out of the little parade drum," he said. "I'd make stick holders and things like that." Later, in the late 1970s or early 1980s, he would actually start making his own drums.

Willie was the deep thinker of the group, and when he wasn't practicing, he was either reading or studying. Kay Adams said, "Willie's deep. I don't know how else to say except he thinks probably too much. He's always analyzing and thinking and dissecting things and wanting to know what makes them tick and wanting to learn things. He once said, 'The definition of time is the distance between birth and death.'"

Tom Brumley also thought highly of his fellow Buckaroo. "He just looked so good back there. Cutie, boy, I mean, he looked good onstage and he conducted himself in just a spotless manner. Buck could not ever say anything to Willie, because Willie did not require it. Willie, I can say nothing but good stuff about him. Willie was the greatest kid, seventeen years old out there doin' stuff, and just playin' so good. So unique in the way he played, and he just loves his drummin'. He wanted to do more and better."

Onstage, Buck referred to his drummer as "Wonderful Willie" Cantu, but offstage his nickname was "Willing Willie." The source of the latter nickname is a mystery, but Willie thinks he got it because he hated waiting for things to happen when the group was on the road. "For example, we were in Tokyo or in Frankfurt, Germany, I always would take off, even if I didn't speak the language, and go exploring by myself. I've always been like that, ever since I was a little baby. They'd really have to keep me under a leash to keep me put, you know, so the 'willing' part, it's like I was willing to—I was the explorer of the band."

★ 19 ★

Road Stories

With the addition of Willie Cantu, the band that the world would forever identify as *the* Buckaroos was complete. Backed by Willie, Don Rich, Doyle Holly, and Tom Brumley, Buck rose to a level of artistic success he had never before achieved—and would never again equal once his current band members began to move on. As Larry Adamson said, "Buck wasn't that good of a singer, but he had one hell of a band." Singer Jimmy Dean concurred, recalling an incident in which Jack McFadden booked Buck on Jimmy's show in New York but failed to book the Buckaroos. Since all the allotted money had gone to pay for Buck and his expenses, Jimmy paid out of his own pocket to fly the band in and put them up in a hotel so they could appear on the show. "Everybody knew Buck without the Buckaroos was nothing," he said.

Buck had a hell of a band, all right, and the guys had one hell of a time. To provide comic relief on the road, they played practical jokes on one another. More often than not, mild-mannered Tom Brumley was the instigator. Like his father, Albert E. Brumley, Tom loved to play jokes on people. So shortly after Willie Cantu signed on as a Buckaroo, Tom orchestrated a plan with the other guys to initiate the young man into the group.

They were somewhere in the mountains of Oregon, and Tom was at the wheel of the Green Goose; Buck wasn't along for the ride. (Tom, who had told Buck in the beginning he did not want to drive, had been allowed in the driver's seat before Doyle, who wouldn't get his turn until either February or March 1964—in the middle of San Diego rush-hour traffic.) Tom drove around until he found a convenience store, then circled the store three or four times, mumbling to Don and Doyle, "Is this OK? We could hit this one all right. But somebody's gotta tell Willie what's goin' on, 'cause he's got to know.

He's got to know. We've got to let him know." He turned to Willie himself and said, "Now look, we're gone from home an awful lot as you know, and we don't make a lot of money. We've got families back home that need to be taken care of, and sometimes we'll knock off a 7-Eleven or somethin'. You know, pick up some extra money. Nobody would ever suspect the Buckaroos for this kind of stuff."

"Oh, shit, you guys!" Willie said, tears welling up in his eyes.

Doyle carried a starter pistol that shot blanks, and he stuck it in his belt for Willie to see. He said, "We can't make it on the money that Buck pays, so we're going to stop on top of the ridge up here and rob this little store." Tom stopped the motor home and Doyle rose to get off.

"No, I can't do that, man. I'm not gonna rob no store!" Willie said. He didn't know what to believe; his fellow Buckaroos didn't seem like the type of people who would rob a store.

"OK," Don said, "then you stay and be the lookout man."

Doyle, Don, and Tom went inside and got some snacks and came back out. Willie was standing outside nervously guarding the motor home. The guys got back on the Green Goose and went on their way.

Another bit of horseplay the Buckaroos didn't find so amusing. It was early 1964, shortly after Willie joined the band, and they were on a package tour in Canada along with George Jones and Buck Owens's future *Hee Haw* cohost, Roy Clark. They were in some Canadian town, Tom remembered, when Roy and George decided to see who could do away with the most $100 bills the quickest. Roy would eat one, then George would flush one down the toilet, then Roy would eat another one, and George would flush another one down the toilet. Being grossly underpaid, the Buckaroos yelled, "Hey, give those to us! Don't throw those things away!" Tom figured they got rid of about $500 apiece, just eating and flushing bills. For the Buckaroos, it was pure heartbreak.

On February 24, 1963, "My Heart Skips a Beat"/"Together Again" was released as a single. Although the songs were recorded while Willie was settling in at Buck's ranch, "My Heart Skips a Beat" featured a prominent drum part, played by Ventures drummer Mel Taylor, to simulate the sound of a heart skipping a beat. At the time, drums were not prominent in country music, and one irate fan wrote to Buck and told him to stop it with the drums or he was going to quit buying his records. Nonetheless, "My Heart Skips a Beat" stayed at #1 on *Cashbox* for seven weeks until its flip side, "Together Again," pushed it to #2. Doyle said the latter song was written by two unknown writers from Washington State, but that Buck took full credit for writing the song himself. Buck claimed the inspiration for the song had come to him in a dream. The two songs switched #1 positions twice on *Billboard*.

"Together Again" drew raves from critics, fans, and other artists for Tom Brumley's emotional steel guitar solo. One can almost hear tears sliding off the strings as Tom deftly glides his steel slide over them. In fact, the licks he did for "Together Again" were one of a kind, and they helped establish Buck as a new kind of country artist. Tom said that after the song came out, he got calls from Nashville to come do sessions, but that was not his thing; he didn't want to be forced to try to replicate his licks for every song coming out of Nashville. "I never wanted to be a session player," he said, "because you gotta do so many different things and there are things that don't really feel good to you. Playing's gotta be fun. If you're a session player, you have to play like all those different people that they ask you to because they are paying you to do this."

On June 1, a little more than a year after Buck's first #1, Capitol released his first "best of" LP, *The Best of Buck Owens*. He recorded "Hello Trouble" and "A-11," on June 10, followed by "I Don't Care (Just As Long As You Love Me)" and "Buck's Polka" on July 8. The *Together Again/My Heart Skips a Beat* LP was released July 20. "I Don't Care (Just As Long As You Love Me)"/"Don't Let Her Know" was released as a single on August 3 and peaked at #1, with the *I Don't Care* LP released on November 2.

Buck scored another #1 with "I've Got a Tiger by the Tail," which was recorded during an afternoon session on December 1, 1964, and released as a single on December 28. Buck said he got the idea for the song after seeing promotional billboards for Esso gasoline that said, "Put a tiger in your tank," when he was driving to a show in Amarillo, Texas with his songwriting part- ner, Harlan Howard, and Harlan's wife, Jan. He told the songwriter about his idea and Harlan jotted down twelve lines for Buck to look over. "I looked at it, started singing it, and we never changed a note," Buck said. Harlan figured that because it was a novelty song, it would sit at the bottom of the chart. He was surprised when he saw it at #8, because he had never had a song of his "hit so fast or jump so high."

Surprisingly, the flip side of "I've Got a Tiger by the Tail," "Cryin' Time," failed to do much on the chart. Buck took full credit for writing "Cryin' Time," saying the idea came to him when he was speeding down a highway in Madison, Wisconsin, trying to get to the airport to catch a flight home. In reality, Doyle said, he, Tom, Don, and Bonnie helped write it while they were traveling down the road one day—although Tom said, "I certainly didn't contribute enough that I'd want some of the writers' credit." Tom said the melody of the song always sounded like "Vaya Con Dios" to him.

Buck recorded his last track of 1964, "Gonna Have Love," on December 29.

Now that Buck Owens had a cohesive band and was dominating the top of the country chart, it was only natural that he branch out to other things. In April 1964 Buck made his first foray into film in a plotless 95-minute Embassy Pictures musical titled *Country Music on Broadway*. The movie had an all-star cast of country music luminaries of the day such as George Jones, Ferlin Husky, Porter Wagoner, and Ralph Emery. It was shot in a theater on New York's 42nd Street made to look like Nashville's *Grand Ole Opry* set.

In May, Buck Owens and his Buckaroos headlined the first country music extravaganza at Madison Square Garden in New York City. The show was so popular among New Yorkers that it was held over for three additional performances, each of which was a sellout. Also on the bill were George Jones, Ernest Tubb, Webb Pierce, Bill Monroe, Stonewall Jackson, "Whisperin'" Bill Anderson, Porter Wagoner, Leon McAuliffe, and Skeeter Davis, whose then-husband, Ralph Emery, was the emcee of the show. Buck was the closing act, but he got upstaged the first night by George Jones, who refused to sing the allotted two numbers and sang five instead. Monroe and a band member literally had to carry George offstage so Buck and his band could set up, sing their two songs, and close the concert on time, or else the promoters would have to pay overtime to the union-scale workers involved in putting on the show.

As Buck gained in popularity, he became a big draw in Las Vegas, where one year he worked eighteen weeks at the Golden Nugget. Buck quickly reneged on his promise to provide Tom Brumley a room of his own; Tom recalled that when the band played there in 1964, he and Don roomed together. Because they were going to be there for such a long stretch, they stocked the refrigerator in their room with snacks, peanut butter, hot dogs, condiments, and so forth. Right before checkout time, Don piled all the leftovers on his plate like a pile of garbage, then squirted mustard and ketchup on it and downed it. Tom said, "Don! That stuff is disgusting!" Don replied, "Mmmm. Boy, that's good!"

It didn't matter what Don did, the word moderation was not in his vocabulary. Tom recalled that "Don could drink more, take more pills, and eat more than anyone I've ever seen. He'd take a big old steak and make it white with salt, then black with pepper, and red with ketchup. I'd say, 'Don, you might as well as had bologna.' 'Hmmm? Oh, no, that's good! That's good stuff.'"

As much fun and as much success as the band had on the road, Tom was always eager to get home. Once, when they headed back to Bakersfield after several weeks away, Don ran the Green Goose off a snowy road somewhere in North Dakota. Tom couldn't bear to wait around, so he volunteered to get to a phone and call a wrecker. While they were waiting on the wrecker to arrive, Doyle said, "I think I can get it out of here."

"Doyle, leave it alone," Tom said. "We got a wrecker comin'. We got a wreck in hell to nowhere and if you break something, we're stuck!"

Doyle ignored him, got under the hood, and tore out the transmission. It was an automatic and Doyle shoved it from forward to reverse and snapped it. Then the wrecker showed up. Tom was hopping mad. "We would've been on the road in ten minutes if he'd just left it alone, but he knew he could get it out of there." They ended up having to wait for a bus to the next town, where they caught a plane back to Bakersfield. It added another day to their trip. "Who wants to wait another whole day when you're goin' home?" Tom said. "I could've wrung his neck!"

For Willie, Buck's ranch was home for about a year, until he met his first wife, Jeraldine. He moved out after the two got married, around Christmastime, when Willie was just eighteen. "When I lived in his home," Willie said of Buck, "I could do whatever I wanted. He was somewhat of a father figure without really being a father figure." Buck was very good to Willie from beginning to end. "Even though he could be very hard with people, I never had any bad dealings with Buck," he remembered. "It just turned out that way."

Willie's good relationship with Buck may have had a lot to do with his youth and the fact that he was low-maintenance, compared with the older guys who had families. Buck could be the older and more mature mentor, who guided him the few times Willie needed to make a major decision—such as whether to get married.

Buck also offered his advice when Willie was weighing another job offer, from Roger Miller. At the time, Roger's band included Thumbs Carlille and Bobby Dyson, who were jazz players like Willie. They had gotten together with the drummer to jam, and they asked Willie to leave Buck's band for Roger's so they could have a cool little trio. Willie was on the fence; he had never considered leaving, but "I would get to be around these other musicians who loved to play like I do." Willie first talked to Don about the possibility, but Don said, "Go talk to Buck." Buck talked to him calmly about it and told him to make sure he weighed the pros and cons, and in the end, Willie decided to stay.

"Buck can manipulate people," Doyle said.

"Well, maybe he did," Willie said, "but in my mind I wasn't sure that I really wanted to leave."

★ 20 ★

BUCK'S PLEDGE

On March 1, 1965, Buck Owens ran a controversial ad in Nashville's *Music City News* that expressed his commitment to country music and its fans. His infamous "Pledge to Country Music" read:

> I shall sing no song that is not a country song. I shall make no record that is not a country record. I refuse to be known as anything but a country singer. I am proud to be associated with country music. Country music and country music fans made me what I am today. And I shall not forget it. Buck Owens.

On the very same day, however, Capitol Records released Buck's album *I've Got a Tiger by the Tail*—which included Buck's take on Chuck Berry's classic rock song "Memphis."

Despite his promise of musical purity, there was no neat little box in which Buck's brand of twang would fit. Buck loved rock 'n' roll, and his Telecaster-and-drums-infused music was more in line with Memphis's rockabilly than with the syrup-and-strings pop that Nashville was churning out. Both lead guitarist Don Rich and steel player Tom Brumley, in large part, were responsible for helping Buck blaze a new trail. Ken Nelson produced and mixed the tunes through small speakers with less bass and more high-end treble so they would transmit best over an AM radio in a moving car. And Buck turned up the volume and let 'er rip, which he was accustomed to doing in honky-tonks to drown out the fighting and the din.

Buck credited his success with songs such as "My Heart Skips a Beat," "I Don't Care (Just as Long as You Love Me)," and "I've Got a Tiger by the Tail" to his own hit-making formula, by which he varied chord progressions just a bit and sold them to the public "over and over again." But clearly the fans welcomed the change from Nashville's "countrypolitan" sound of the day. Thus, the Bakersfield Sound solidified, and widened the schism between Bakersfield and Music City. Buck began referring to Nashville dismissively as "Bakersfield East."

Buck's Nashville disestablishmentarianism may have been in part why he never became a member of the venerable *Grand Ole Opry*. He certainly met *Opry* membership requirements, but it is not known whether Buck was invited to join; the *Opry* doesn't keep records on either invitations or the number of times an artist appeared on its stage. Former WSM disc jockey and *Grand Ole Opry Live* host Keith Bilbrey, who was a friend of Buck's, thinks that it may have been Buck's choice not to join; to meet the *Opry*'s stringent performance requirements, he would have had to travel to play for free, which would have interfered with his rigorous touring schedule that made him big bucks. "Buck had his Bakersfield empire and was quite self-sufficient as an artist, and I'm sure would not have wanted to give up any control of his career to anyone," Keith said. "Buck also admitted to me that he never was good at playing Nashville politics, and that would have been required to be a member of the *Opry*. The same was true of Merle Haggard. There was also that tension between the West Coast and Nashville music centers."

The Bakersfield singer was certainly welcome on the *Opry* stage, however, as long as he played by *Opry* rules, and he did appear there at least four times. After appearing with Tommy Collins in 1954 and in his solo debut in 1960, he returned to the *Opry* in 1964 and 1974 with his Buckaroos. Tom Brumley recalled that playing the *Opry*'s Ryman Auditorium in 1964 was one of the highlights of his career.

From the other side of the country came recognition of a different sort. Buck, his band, and even his manager began racking up awards from the brand-new Los Angeles–based Academy of Country and Western Music, founded in 1965. Buck was voted top male vocalist in 1965 and best bandleader from 1965 to 1967. Tom Brumley tied for best steel player in 1966 with Ralph

Mooney, and the Buckaroos were named touring band of the year from 1965 to 1968. In 1965 and 1966, Jack McFadden was voted best talent manager and booking agent.

Buck was also a popular artist overseas and had a big international fan base. His first tour abroad was to Bermuda in 1965. It was followed the same year by a European tour to England, Ireland, Scotland, France, the Netherlands, Belgium, Denmark, Germany, and Switzerland. He would visit Europe many times, and his itinerary eventually included Norway, Sweden, and Czechoslovakia as well.

His discography for 1965 was impressive. In addition to the release of the album *I've Got a Tiger by the Tail*, "Before You Go"/"(I Want) No One But You" was recorded March 25 and released as a single on April 19; it peaked at #1. The *Before You Go/No One but You* LP was released July 26. On May 4, he cut "Only You (Can Break My Heart)," which was released as a single on July 5 and peaked at #1. Its flip side, "Gonna Have Love" peaked at #10. On May 5, the band recorded "Buckaroo."

"Buckaroo," an instrumental composed by Bob Morris, would become Buck's signature song, but it only got recorded that day because the band finished the afternoon session with fifteen minutes to spare. Ken Nelson asked if anybody had anything else they wanted to record and Bob, who was one of Capitol's preferred house bass players during that period and who played on that session, piped up and said he had something. (In addition to Bob, Allen Williams and Bobby Austin also played bass for Buck in Capitol sessions, though none of them were considered Buckaroos.) The working title of the piece was "Paris," but it was quickly changed to "Buckaroo." It was not released as a single until October 11, with "If You Want a Love" on the flip side, and it peaked at #1.

On June 14, the *Four by Buck Owens* EP was released, followed by *The Instrumental Hits of Buck Owens and His Buckaroos* LP on July 26. Buck and the band were back in the studio recording "Sam's Place" on August 23. "Sam's Place"/"Don't Ever Tell Me Goodbye" would not be released as a single for almost two years, however, until March 3, 1967; it, too, hit #1. On August 24, they recorded "Waitin' in Your Welfare Line," which Nat Stuckey wrote, but Buck and Don changed a few things and took top billing on the writing credits.

On November 8, "Santa Looked a Lot Like Daddy"/"All I Want for Christmas, Dear, Is You" was released as a single. Buck and Don cowrote "Santa Looked a Lot Like Daddy," and years later, Garth Brooks, whom Buck advised, recorded it. When Don's wife, Marlane, got a royalty check for $30,000 in the mail, she was shocked.

Buck wrapped up recording for the year on November 11, with "Dust on Mother's Bible," which he wrote for his beloved maternal grandmother.

21

THE BARON OF BUCKERSFIELD

In 1965, Buck Owens and his Buckaroos spent 302 days touring, and he ranked third in Capitol sales behind the Beatles and the Beach Boys. His earnings for the year were $600,000. Buck was on top of the world, and he damn well was going to make sure he stayed there.

As a child, Buck had abhorred the fact that his father was a tenant farmer and had to turn over half of what he produced to the landowner. His fear of poverty drove him to succeed beyond the average Dust Bowler's dreams. Despite being a ninth-grade dropout, Buck caught on quickly to the inner workings of the music business—which, ironically, weren't too different from sharecropping. He reinvested his earnings to create a vast music and media business empire, centered in his adopted hometown of Bakersfield. The city's residents loved him for the influx of jobs, cash, tourists, and notoriety he brought to their otherwise flat and boring Central Valley burg. People even called him "the Baron of Buckersfield." But to some of those who saw behind his carefully crafted public image, he had a slightly different name: "the *Robber* Baron of Buckersfield."

In 1965, Buck partnered with Jack McFadden to establish the booking agency Owens McFadden Artist Corporation. OMAC, as it was known, began as a high-dollar operation run on a shoestring budget out of a shabby office on Truxtun Avenue. Jack was its president, and for the first year he and an assistant composed the entire operating team. Artists in OMAC's early talent pool of fourteen acts included all the Buckaroos; Merle Haggard, whom

Jack managed from 1965 to 1971; Kay Adams; Dick Curless; Freddie Hart; Joe and Rosalie Maphis; Bonnie Owens; and Wynn Stewart. Later, the OMAC flock grew to include Bobby Austin, Tony Booth, David Frizzell, Eddie Fukano, the Hager twins, Kenni Huskey, LaWanda Lindsey, Darrell McCall, Mayf Nutter, Jeanie O'Neal, Susan Raye, Wynn Stewart, Mona Vary, Sheb Wooley, and many others. In fact, the Hagers nicknamed Buck "Geese" because he had "a flock of goslings."

In April 1966, Tom Brumley's younger brother Jackson was offered a job at the fledgling agency. Jackson was fresh out of the U.S. Army and was working in the advertising department at a Neosho, Missouri, newspaper when Buck offered him a base salary of $300 a month plus commission to come work for him as a booking agent. Jackson turned him down, but when Buck raised the offer to $400 a month plus commission, he reconsidered. He hit town on a Friday and started work the following Monday. The younger Brumley recalled being shown a desk, a telephone, a Rolodex, and photos on the walls of artists he would be booking. The next day, Buck and Jack left town and Jackson was immediately thrown into the job.

For the most part, OMAC was now Jackson and the assistant, because Jack and Buck were on the road all the time. A few months after Jackson started working at the agency, it moved from its office on Truxtun to one on Chester Street. At one point, Jack's son Joe McFadden, who was about twenty at the time, joined the agency, and it fell to Jackson to train him. (Joe went on to become an executive at Capitol Records.)

With the stress and the workload, it didn't take long for Jackson to develop bleeding ulcers just like his older brother. Because of them, he was out of work for five or six days in December 1966. When he went to pick up his paycheck, Dorothy told him he would have to talk to Buck first; Buck, of course, was out of town at the time. When Buck returned, he informed Jackson that he was going to dock his pay. "How can you dock my pay out of money I've already earned?" he asked. "That was money I earned on commission." Jackson finally got his money, but like his brother, he had to fight for what was rightfully his. Jackson stayed three years at OMAC before leaving in 1968. Jackson said it wasn't easy working for Buck and "there were times it wasn't easy working for Jack."

Not all went smoothly between the principal partners of OMAC, either. Buck and Jack were always arguing over how the business should be run. Buck would say to Jack, "If you don't like the way I'm doing business, why don't you just buy me out? Give me $10,000 and you can just take over OMAC." Jack started carrying a blank check with him at all times; he told Doyle Holly that the next time Buck asked him "Why don't you just buy me out?" Jack was going to whip out the check and do just that. Nevertheless, the partnership survived, and by 1969, OMAC was the third-largest country music booking agency in the United States.

Meanwhile, Buck's personal business corporation, Buck Owens Enterprises, was growing as well. As the years progressed, it became an umbrella corporation that covered several cottage industries, including the Buck Owens Guitar Method Course, the *Buck Owens Chord Book*, and the Buck Owens fanzine *All American*. In addition to Buck Owens Enterprises, OMAC, and Blue Book Music, Buck had myriad business ventures ranging from almond and cattle ranches to a chain of drive-ins called Buck-O's.

Radio stations in Bakersfield and Phoenix made up a large portion of Buck's business empire. In March 1966, he bought KUZZ-AM and a year later, he bought KBBY-FM, both in Bakersfield. Buck Owens Production Co., Inc., was the parent company for his Bakersfield radio operations until they moved under the umbrella of Owens One Company. Like the names of Buck's businesses, the stations' call letters changed often. For example, he quickly changed KBBY's call letters to KZIN, and it became KKXX in 1977. KUZZ is the area's premier country radio station and has won numerous Country Music Association awards for best country station. KKXX was Bakersfield's number one rock-'n'-roll station for at least a decade.

In 1967, Buck purchased KTUF-AM in Phoenix for $350,000. The next year he bought the city's KNIX-AM/FM for $75,000, supposedly as a tax write-off. Like KUZZ in Bakersfield, KNIX repeatedly took home the CMA award for best country station. The Phoenix stations' parent company, which was actually based in Tempe, went through several incarnations: Thunderbird Broadcasting merged into Buck Owens Broadcasting, LLC, then Owens

One Company, Inc., before the stations were sold in 1998 and Buck parlayed a $450,000 investment into a cool $142 million. Upon the sale of the stations to Jacor Communications, Inc., Buck rewarded longtime KNIX program director Larry Daniels and his sons Buddy and Mike bonuses of $15 million each. Mike and Larry, in particular, were credited for turning the flagging stations into profitable and award-winning ventures.

One of the secrets to Buck's business success was that he surrounded himself with good people, both personally and professionally. "You're as good as the people around you," he would tell future wife Jana Jae. Many people contributed, in many different ways, to make him the towering figure he became—most notably his family members.

Unlike many employers, Buck had no problem with nepotism. He knew and trusted his relatives more than anybody, so he enlisted them to help run his businesses. Not only was his sister Dorothy the vice president and business manager of Buck Owens Enterprises, but also his father, Alvis Owens Sr., was put in charge of his ranching operations and his mother, Maicie Owens, worked in his office and ran his fan club. His brother, Mel Owens Sr., and later his nephew Mel Owens Jr., managed his Bakersfield radio stations. His son Mike started out learning the radio business in Bakersfield, too, before Buck put him in charge of the Arizona radio operations. His other son Buddy later joined him in Phoenix after retiring as a singer.

In addition to his family, Jack McFadden, and Don Rich, Buck's inner circle would eventually include Larry Daniels and latter-day Buckaroos Jim Shaw and Terry Christofferson. Also among Buck's close associates was a lesser-known Bakersfield resident named Jimmy Tapps, a beefy guy who was a barber by day and a bouncer and a drummer by night, though he was not actively involved in running any of Buck's businesses. Tom Brumley remembered him as a nice guy who would eighty-six offensive barflies with a smile—and with such efficiency that they never knew they were out the door. But he agreed with singer-songwriter Gene Price that Jimmy could also be "one mean sonofabitch" with "an extremely hot temper." He had such a legendary reputation as a badass that tough guys would drive to Bakersfield from as far away as Los Angeles just to see if they could whip him, but nobody ever did. Jimmy sometimes cut Buck's and some of the Buckaroos' hair, and Doyle Holly said that Jimmy "loved Buck so much he would've killed anybody for $250 and a plane ticket."

Buck was always on the lookout for new talent to draw into the OMAC fold, and he would buy out the contracts of other labels and/or agencies with whom they were signed. He was very shrewd and made sure to get someone for the lowest possible price. For example, when Buck asked his later duet partner LaWanda Lindsey to sign with him, she said yes but told him she was working with an attorney to get out of an existing deal with Chart Records. Buck said that he could buy out her contract, but if the label knew he was interested it might cost him $100,000. If LaWanda bought it herself, the label would settle for a lot less. So Buck wrote her a check for $2,500 and LaWanda wrote a check to Chart Records for the same amount. She remembered her father saying what a trustworthy person Buck must have been to write her such a large check when he didn't really know her. "To my family that was a lot of money," LaWanda said. "To Buck, it would probably be 'Oh, well.'"

Buck was a stickler for contracts. At some point, almost everybody he hired had to sign at least one, which was always slanted in Buck's favor. He tried to underpay everybody. Even at the top of his career, Don Rich only made $39,000 a year in take-home pay. Royalties and session work for other artists bumped it up to around $50,000 a year, but "it was hard to make ends meet," Don's wife, Marlane, noted.

In his immediate circle, Jack McFadden was the only person known to have just a verbal agreement with Buck. Initially, Tom Brumley worked under the terms he'd presented to Buck over the phone, but soon enough Buck asked him to sign a written agreement. Tom knew Buck had broken their original deal many times over; he'd made notes of dates and times just in case. He took the new contract to his attorney, who told him it would never hold up in court—which is the only reason Tom signed it. "Otherwise I would never have changed my original deal, not ever."

Doyle Holly recalled having to sign several contracts, including a labor contract, a recording contract, a management contract, a personal management contract, and a songwriter's contract. Doyle didn't know at the time, but a lawyer later told him that it was illegal for one artist to have another under contract because of conflict of interest. "As smart as Buck is," Doyle said, "it's hard to believe that he didn't know it was illegal. But back in those days I was young. I didn't care. I wasn't in it for the money and fame or anything. I was in it for the fun."

Of course, if the other party failed to question an agreement, it was all the better for Buck. Either he or Jack would press artists to sign their contracts without reading them. Even the Hagers, who adored Buck, got the short end. As Jon Hager said, "He had a contract figured out for us, and Buck was going to be getting the benefits." Jack presented the Hagers with their contract after Dusty Rhodes brought them to Buck's attention, and told them, "Don't worry about it, just sign it."

The artists Buck signed to OMAC all had different deals depending on what they were able to work out with Buck. Often they would be sent on the road for long stretches to unheard-of places and work every night, and never be paid anything extra. "I was so young and stupid," Dennis Payne said. "When I was signed with Buck and Jack, Jack would send me on just stupid shit. It would cost me $600 for airplane flights and rent-a-cars and I'd go make a hundred bucks and then go pay him his 15 percent and they'd have a big laugh about it. They'd all sit around and laugh, 'These stupid kids!'" Jo McFadden, however, said that Jack didn't approve of the way Buck treated Dennis.

Many of Buck's musicians were paid only a flat rate with small incremental raises; if they collected any royalties or outside earnings, Buck kept that money for himself. "Extra checks that were made out to us, we had to sign those back over," said Buck's later wife and the first Buckarette, Jana Jae. "Sometimes it was very hard to do that. We were under contract, so I suppose legally, that's right."

It could be costly to sever a deal with Buck, too. Kay Adams, Dick Curless, Joe and Rose Lee Maphis, and Rusty Wood all paid dearly for having signed to Blue Book Music and/or OMAC. OMAC owed Kay $1,900 or $2,000, and she had to relinquish that money before she was released. Dick Curless fell behind in money he owed OMAC for booking percentages, so Buck put a lien against Dick's late-model Chevrolet until the commission was paid. The move nearly caused Dick to have a nervous breakdown. Joe and Rose Lee Maphis fared much worse, however. OMAC put a lien against their house for commissions. As for Larry Adamson's then-wife Rusty Wood, Buck flat-out refused to release her from her contract to take a deal with Capitol Records unless he got 50 percent of the deal. She stayed with Buck, which was the end of her career. In addition, Buck often insisted that artists sign an exit agreement when they left his employ—a requirement that Tom and Doyle would both have problems with when they quit the Buckaroos.

Buck Owens was not an easy boss to work for. He could be insensitive to his underlings, and expected and demanded their loyalty. He subscribed to the theory of management by fear—when he said, "Jump!" people jumped, or else. Buck was very hands-on, sometimes to the point of being a control freak, because he simply wasn't wired to delegate responsibility. He had to have his stamp on every little thing, every second of every day. He couldn't function otherwise. As Jo McFadden put it, "He liked to be lord of the coop."

Buck also let it be known that his people were not to talk to one another about anything. He didn't want them to compare notes because he usually told them each different stories. It was all part of his way of creating a sort of managed chaos so only he knew what was going on. In addition, he could not and would not tolerate a "no" man. As Tom Brumley said, "It's 100 percent 'yes' or nothing," which led the steel player, who got along well with Buck, to conclude: "Buck doesn't have any friends, only people he can buy."

Buck would blame anyone but himself if the slightest thing went wrong, and he was known to fire people for the smallest infractions, even on holidays. Jo recalled a man named Dennis—not Dennis Payne, but another Dennis—who was let go on Christmas Eve. Technically Dorothy did the firing, but "it was through chain of command, I suppose," Jo said. Fortunately, the man went on to be very successful without Buck; he and a partner started a business and then sold it for what Jo called "a shit-pot full of money."

Not everyone Buck worked with had a bad experience, however. Singer-songwriter Mayf Nutter said that Buck had fun but didn't waste time fooling around. "People who didn't like Buck were those who didn't have the end in mind or want to trample over the bushes to get there," said Mayf, whom colleagues also described as aggressive. "I used to get alone with Buck, sing songs I'd written, and he'd say, 'I don't know how that'll work in the studio, but if anyone does, you will.' Buck was always open to new stuff. I went to him with some pretty far-out ideas." Buck never asked for writing credit on any of his songs, Mayf said, and Buck gave him ownership of his own masters. "Buck told me, 'Son, one of these days you're gonna break out in a rash of hits.'" But that never happened; instead, all his songs went to Blue Book and weren't pitched to other performers. The same thing happened to young Dennis Payne. Mayf saw that as a good thing, though, since it kept his songs from going to someone else before he himself had a chance to record them. In reality, it was Buck's way of keeping the competition in its place—well behind him.

Jon Hager also spoke highly of his time with Buck, and felt he was exceptionally good to his employees. He didn't see Buck as one of those people for whom "money and everything is the goal—how many toys can I get, how many people can I step on to get up to where I want to get, and everything else like that. Buck didn't do that. Buck took care of his people. Always took care of his people."

Kris Black, however, compared Buck to "a mafia character, where they do great good for their family, and then they do these horrific things to other people. He had a terrible mean streak." She said her experience of working for Buck was "pretty bad. He would cuss and yell at everybody, but he never did at me." She recalled one incident in which Buck got angry at public relations executive Sandy Friedman and said, "Hitler was right! He should've killed all you goddamn Jews!" Kris was horrified and pulled Sandy into her office afterward and apologized to him for her boss's bad behavior, but Sandy blew it off saying, "Oh, Buck was just blowing steam."

This was an isolated incident, however, because Buck admired Jewish people, if primarily for their reputation for handling money well. When someone asked him the secret to his success, he would say, "Get yourself a Jewish lawyer that hates his mother; he'll get blood." Over the years, he retained many Jewish lawyers. According to Larry Adamson, Buck even had an affair with the wife of one of them, and fathered a daughter by her; he supposedly ended up supporting her and their daughter in exchange for their silence.

Even though Buck could be manipulative, childish, and downright mean in his business dealings, Kris always believed there was an underlying goodness, a real caring and kindness, in Buck. "He had a spiritual side and a good side," she said. "He was at war with that more than anything else. You've got to remember, even the meanest bullies have feelings." Still, Kris was thankful that Jack understood the stress she was under, and that he cared. He would walk by her office and say, "God save the queen!"

Other associates also saw a positive side of Buck the businessman. People such as *Hee Haw*'s Lulu Roman called him "the consummate professional," and Bill Mack and Jimmy Dean remembered him as being all business all the time. "You know, it's funny," Jimmy said, "I usually remember at least one funny story about somebody, but I don't remember anything about Buck that was loaded down with humor."

Wade Pepper, former field vice president for Capitol Records, called Buck a hard-driven businessman, one of the most efficient he had ever encountered, but he also remembered Buck's penchant for having fun. Buck worked hard and played hard, and he liked to start his day with either a game of tennis or a round of golf. On the road, he played golf with the likes of Tom Brumley and Bill Mack and tennis with LaWanda Lindsey. Wade was also a tennis fanatic, and during the *Hee Haw* years, Buck would often hook up with his old friend to play. Once, Buck invited him out to Reno, where he was performing. When Wade's plane arrived, the pilot made an announcement: "Will Mr. Pepper please wait and leave the plane last when the plane lands." When Wade got off the plane, Buck had arranged for a band to play, welcoming him to Reno. People turned and stared as if thinking, "Who is this nonentity getting off the airplane?" Wade was embarrassed and wanted to crawl away and hide somewhere, though he was somewhat flattered that Buck would go to all that trouble for him. From the airport, they went to the tennis club to play a few sets. At the club, Buck introduced Wade to a fellow wearing blue jeans and said, "Why don't you play him?" Wade got the impression that the guy didn't have much experience playing tennis at all; he seemed to barely know how to hold the racquet. So they went out on the court and hit a few balls. Wade was being very solicitous, telling the man, "Hey, that was a good shot! You are doing better." Then all of a sudden, the jeans guy was lobbing shots over Wade's left shoulder like a pro—which, of course, he was. Buck had set him up and was on the sidelines doubled up, dying of laughter.

"We were that kind of friends," Wade said, "always playing practical jokes on each other. The guy was a good actor. Buck got a good laugh out of it. We went ahead and played doubles the rest of the afternoon. He was a fun guy—and businesslike."

Most everybody gave Buck high marks for putting his money to work for him and not squandering it as many of his contemporaries did. According to Wade, "He was much tighter with the buck than Merle Haggard and other artists that are free and fancy with their money that ended up with none. Buck ended up with all of his."

To his family and longtime, loyal associates, Buck could be surprisingly generous, but with others he could be staggeringly chintzy. "He was one of the most selfish people I've ever met," Jo McFadden declared. To his latter-day disciple Dwight Yoakam, he once gave a Cadillac. On the other hand, when LaWanda Lindsey married businessman Billy Smith in 1976, Buck's wedding gift was a cheap peanut butter maker. He was also known to give people his signature red, white, and blue Gibson acoustic guitars—the design of which he patented on November 28, 1972. He sold the instruments for $1,000 apiece, but they wholesaled for only $17. Once, when Wayne Newton gave him an Arabian horse, Buck reciprocated by giving Wayne one of these guitars.

Buck was willing to provide his employees with loans against their paychecks—but these, too, were often not what they appeared to be. "If we needed money, which everybody did, we'd make a draw from Buck," Doyle remembered. "He would ask you to make a draw slip—an IOU, so to speak. Foolish me, along with the rest of them, we wouldn't date the receipts. We would just say '$20.'" When payday arrived, Doyle said, Buck would deduct the owed amount—but claim that he had thrown away the draw slip. At the end of the next pay period, however, he would produce the IOU as if it were a new one, and withhold another $20. Doyle caught on after a while; "It was just Buck," he said.

To be sure, Buck was money-conscious at all times. If he could save a buck, he would. On one occasion, he approached Dennis Payne to see if his new father-in-law, who owned a chain of meat markets, could get Buck a discount on steaks for the office Christmas party. Dennis was happy to make it happen—but when he got to the party, he found that Buck was charging everybody $15 a head to attend the steak dinner. "Buck's a little bit on the tight end there," Dennis said. "It's the only Christmas party I got invited to where I had to pay."

"I told him he had respect for the dollar," Doyle Holly added.

"No kidding, and everybody else's dollar!" Dennis said.

"Yeah, you gotta tell it like it is," Doyle said. "Buck was cheap."

"Yep, he was cheap," Dennis agreed.

To Wade Pepper, Buck "gave me the impression that he was brought up in poverty and that was why he was obsessed with the dollar and did a very good job of it. He worshipped the dollar, he did. I think he was the most business-minded of the artists that I worked with at Capitol, there is no question about that. Over a period of time, I began to think that he was more of a great businessman than possibly a true artist." But Wade added, "That's not fair either, because he wrote some awfully good songs earlier in his career."

Needless to say, with Buck's focus always on the money, he was adept at finding tax loopholes. One year in the mid-1960s, Buck had to find additional tax deductions or he was going to have to cough up more funds to pay his federal income tax. So Buck gave Don money and sent him out to buy tax-deductible gifts for people. Some of the items Don purchased included a Jeep for Buck's ranch in Edison, and a pool table, entertainment centers, and television sets for Buck's uncles. All the purchases sat in either Buck's house or his garage, however, because he was too stingy to give them to the people for whom they were purchased. One tax-deductible gift did reach its intended recipients, however: Buck gave each of the Buckaroos their only Christmas bonus that year.

In addition, Buck involved himself in charitable endeavors, which not only won him accolades from the press and the people of Bakersfield but also provided him with tax shelters. As Jo McFadden pointed out, Buck did not like to give unless it benefited him in some way. Over the years, Buck sponsored Toys for Tots drives; an annual Buck Owens Celebrity Golf for Cancer tournament he hosted from 1970 to 1973, with Jack McFadden as executive director; and fundraisers for the Kern County Cancer Society, which Jack was director of from 1970 to 1972. In addition, he set up at least three nonprofits over the years: Buck Owens Charities, Inc., Buck Owens Health & Research Organization of Kern County, and the Buck Owens American Music Foundation.

Jimmy Dean, who made a fortune in the sausage business, recalled Buck giving him tax advice once, and shortly thereafter, "Buck got in a bit of tax trouble." Jimmy doesn't recall what year that was, though on March 30, 1998, the state of California filed a $150 state tax lien against Buck Owens Production Co. Inc. By April 30, it had been classified as "filed in error," and it was released by May 29.

Buck also kept an eye out for other legal loopholes. For example, in 1988, Dorothy started an independent television station in Bakersfield, KDOB-TV, then filed for bankruptcy and sold the station to Buck two years later. Tom Brumley said that Buck had Dorothy start the station so he could sidestep the FCC rules against media monopolies, which at the time would have prohibited him from founding the station himself when he owned radio stations in the same city. If his sister filed for bankruptcy, Buck could snap it up and avoid the conflict of interest.

As for Buck's total net worth, the truth may never be known. Buck's businesses were not publicly traded, and his family isn't talking, so one can only look at the few available figures to get a sense of the balance sheets: In 1974, Buck performed just two country shows at Madison Square Garden in New York, and grossed more than $31,500. In 1995, operating revenues from his Bakersfield radio and TV stations reached $17 million. A Securities and Exchange Commission quarterly report showed that on October 16, 1997,

Buck sold his television station in Bakersfield, by then renamed KUZZ-TV, for approximately $14 million. And, of course, there's the $600,000 he earned in 1965, and the $142 million he took in from the sale of his Phoenix radio stations in 1998.

By any estimate, Buck Owens was loaded. As his former starvation buddy, Harlan Howard, told author Nicholas Dawidoff, "Shit! He's rich."

22

PHYLLIS

One way that Buck took advantage of his growing wealth was to exert financial control over his ex-wife Phyllis, who by 1965 had once again become his current wife. After five years of cohabitation, the couple remarried on December 28 in Las Vegas. Curiously, Phyllis used the name "Phyllis Irene Wall" on marriage records, although her maiden name was Buford; perhaps Wall was the surname of her first husband. Buck found that he could keep his wife at his mercy simply by not giving her access to the bank accounts. When she needed to buy groceries or clothes for her three young children, he forced her to grovel to Dorothy for money. Buck knew Phyllis couldn't survive and provide for her family on a carhop's pay, so she'd stay with him and take whatever he dished out.

And he dished out plenty. Like his father before him, Buck used his wife as a punching bag. He was verbally and physically abusive; her good friend Rolene Brumley said, "She had a black eye a time or two. She had a rough life." Once, Buck even whacked Phyllis in the face with a golf club and broke her jaw because he thought she was having an affair with one of the Buckaroos, which her friends say was untrue. Rolene denied that Phyllis had ever stepped out on her husband. "She loved Buck. I mean, she was so good and faithful to him. She loved him. I don't know how she could, but she did."

Phyllis was a quiet, gentle, artistic woman who preferred to stay in the background. She was very much a homebody; she loved taking care of her home and raising the children. Her friends remembered her as a hard worker with a generous spirit who wanted to do something for everybody. Not only did

Phyllis attend to the needs of Buck and her own kids, but also she took care of the ranch and the extended Owens brood, including Buddy and Mike. Buck's sons with Bonnie had not spent much time with their father until they were older and Phyllis was in the picture. Bonnie loved her sons more than anything and genuinely appreciated Phyllis looking after them while she was on the road with either Buck or Merle. Phyllis and Bonnie were friends and there was neither animosity nor jealousy between the two women. Phyllis also briefly looked after the children of Buck's brother, Mel, after he died on June 14, 1971.

Phyllis liked to do ceramics as a hobby and be with friends so she could be herself and laugh in spite of the pain her husband subjected her to. She had a fun nature and loved to play games. Once a month, Phyllis would get together with the Buckaroo wives and a few other women for "the Bunco Club," a party in which everyone would bring their kids and play a dice game called Bunco. Rose Lee Maphis started the club, and singer Barbara Mandrell was among the women who took turns hosting. It was an inexpensive way to amuse themselves while their men were on the road. As Don Rich's wife, Marlane, said, "It was a lonely life, but all of us seemed to band together to give each other support."

Tom Brumley appreciated Phyllis for being such a good friend to his wife and looking after her while he was on the road with Buck. "Phyllis was pretty quiet, but she had a really good personality," Tom said. "Rolene and I both just loved her to death. She was really a good lady." Still, he was not the only person to wonder how she—or anyone in her right mind—could stay in a marriage as toxic as the two she had with Buck.

Doyle Holly went further, calling Phyllis "the dumbest person in the world" for failing to recognize that Buck was unfaithful. Once, he said, Phyllis walked in on Buck and found him in bed with another woman. Buck had a motto: "Never admit to anything." So he told his wife, "I don't know how she got here; she was just in my bed." Doyle said Phyllis believed him, but Phyllis was not stupid. If anything, she was one step ahead of her philandering husband. In the later years of their second marriage, her friend Rolene recalled, she would go through his billfold and find papers with women's names and phone numbers on them. She called and confronted a few of them as to who they were and what they wanted with her man. As a result, Phyllis was eaten up by Buck's infidelity and became very depressed. According to Rolene, "She wanted to not see what she was seeing."

Even to people who were unaware of how badly Buck treated his wife, he and Phyllis sometimes seemed like an ill-matched pair. Buck's longtime friend and business associate Wade Pepper thought that "a housewife reclusive" such as Phyllis was an unlikely spouse for the extroverted Buck. Both he and *Hee Haw* producer Sam Lovullo thought Buck was more compatible with his ex-wife Bonnie, who was outgoing and personable and knew the music business. Sam saw Bonnie as "the backbone of Buck's career," and Wade said, "My wife used to say, 'If you want to be a country star you should marry Bonnie Owens.'" They were overlooking the fact that Bonnie didn't want Buck anymore. Unlike Phyllis, Bonnie wasn't going to tolerate his crap.

Buck's ego had to have been bruised, both personally and professionally, when Bonnie got together with Merle Haggard and left Buck's road show for his. Merle and Bonnie married in Tijuana, Mexico, on June 28, 1965—six months to the day before Buck and Phyllis tied the knot for a second time.

23

PROFESSIONAL JEALOUSY

By 1965, Merle Haggard was not only husband to Buck's ex-wife but also one of his main competitors on the charts. Even though Merle was signed to Buck as a songwriter and an artist and they were on friendly enough terms at the time, Buck couldn't help but envy him. Dennis Payne and Doyle Holly both recalled that Buck once chased Merle down the road in a fit of rage, gun in hand, threatening to kill him. Another time, Merle got a standing ovation in Milwaukee and Buck, who was headlining the show, didn't get one. "Buck was jealous, and it showed," Merle recalled. Shortly thereafter, he received a call from Buck saying he wanted to record "Swinging Doors," which Merle had penned. Merle decided that if Buck wanted it, it had to be good, so he kept it for himself. He recorded it in December 1965 and released it in April 1966. The song became Merle's first top ten hit for Capitol Records.

"Swinging Doors" wasn't the only song of Merle's that Buck coveted, however. A couple of years later, Buck also wanted "Sing Me Back Home," which Merle had published with Blue Book Music and had already recorded in 1968. He asked Buck for a $15,000 advance so he could repay some gambling debts to Benny Binion, who owned the Horseshoe in downtown Las Vegas. Buck laughed at him, but Merle knew a song like "Sing Me Back Home" would earn back its advance and then some. Buck reveled in watching Merle squirm; he told him he wasn't a loan company, then proceeded to offer him the advance only if Buck got half-ownership of the song. Out of desperation, Merle agreed. Unbeknownst to Merle, his song had already earned $35,000 and Buck had the check for that amount in his desk drawer. Buck already knew the song was a moneymaker and pulled a fast one on Merle, who had to sue Buck to regain full rights to the song.

The ordeal soured the two men's working relationship, and for about ten years, Merle would refuse to be a guest on *Hee Haw*. Still, he saw the incident as part of his education in the music business. "If I hadn't learned it from Buck," he wrote, "I would've learned it from somebody else."

Buck Owens was the jealous type, and he was resentful of anyone he saw as a threat to his chart success. Other artists he envied included Tony Booth, Bobby Durham, George Jones, Elvis Presley, Hank Thompson—and even the Buckaroos. Tom Brumley said Buck was possessive and never gave any of the Buckaroos credit for anything. "He just didn't do it," Tom said. "He was afraid to give us credit for too much."

Doyle Holly remembered Buck as being jealous of George Jones the most, because at one point Buck held the #1 and #3 spots on the *Billboard* country chart and George held the #2 spot with "Love Bug." That song had been written for Buck, but he had turned it down. George was a sad reminder for Buck of what could have been: holding the top three chart positions simultaneously.

24

THE FLEX BUS

As Buck Owens became more successful, his modes of transportation improved as well. After the Ford Fairlane, the two campers, and the motor home came the Flex bus, which was in service from 1966 to 1968.

Tom Brumley shamed Buck into buying the bus after a tour back East in 1965. The Green Goose was broken down and instead of renting another Winnebago, Buck borrowed his father's old truck and camper. On the last day of the tour, the band pulled up to the venue in Philadelphia and started unloading, when Tom overheard someone say, "Who is in that awful old thing!" He went over and told them in no uncertain terms that it was the great Buck Owens. There they were, the number one country band in the nation, surrounded by big fancy tour buses and traveling in a beat-up truck and camper. Tom was so embarrassed that he decided to do something about it. After the show that night, he went to his boss.

"Buck, now on the way back home you're gonna fly home and we're gonna take the camper, but we're gonna stop and have the name painted on that camper," Tom said.

"No, you're not! Nooooo, you're not!" Buck said.

"Now, what's the matter, Buck, are you ashamed of us that you don't want people to know who we are? There's people out there who've got their names on their buses and we should have the name on the camper. One way or the other when I get to Bakersfield if I have to stop and get a can of red spray paint I am going to put 'Buck Owens and his Buckaroos' on that camper."

"No, you're not! No, you're not!"

"Yes, I am, too, Buck!"

Tom was mad, but Buck was madder. After they returned to Bakersfield, Tom failed to get his customary early morning phone call from Buck to play golf. This went on for three days. Finally, Jack McFadden called from a pay phone out on the highway and said, "Tom, Buck wants to talk to you just a minute."

Buck got on the phone and said, "Tom!"

"Yeah?"

"Go get a bus!"

"Well, what kind of bus?"

"I don't care! Just go get a bus! Bye." Buck hung up.

So Tom called Dorothy Owens and asked her to get him a plane ticket to Columbus, Ohio. He flew out to the factory where the Flex tour buses were built and picked one out by himself. He put a lot of thought into the purchase. Since he knew it had to be something all the guys could drive, he decided against a diesel engine because the guys might ruin it and they'd be stuck. He opted for a 1966 model with underneath loading, a 534-cubic-inch Ford V8 industrial engine, and a six-speed Allison transmission. Inside were bunks where band members could stretch out and go to sleep. There were four beds in the middle, and in the rear lounge were two couches that folded out into four more bunks (although the band would never once unfold them). It was a good, solid rig, and it cost $60,000 brand-new.

When the bus was ready, Tom and Don Rich flew to Ohio to drive it back to Bakersfield. On the way home, they stopped in Powell, Missouri, to visit Tom's folks and show off their new wheels. Tom also made sure that they were almost out of gas when they got to Powell so they could fuel up at his old friend Dynamite's service station, because he wouldn't be able to sell that much gas in a month.

The guys in the band couldn't have been any prouder of that vehicle had they owned it themselves. To them, it said they had arrived. No longer did they have to endure ridicule by showing up packed inside a motor home or a ratty camper like sardines in a tin. Finally, they could get the respect they deserved among their fans and peers.

Tom and Doyle Holly were put in charge of ensuring that the bus was kept in running order and repaired and serviced regularly. All the band members took turns driving the bus, but Tom recalled that Don had a lead foot. "I had that bus designed myself and that bus would run at 120 miles an hour, and I had to put a governor at 82 so it wouldn't go over 82 miles an hour. And Don would put it on the floor and keep it there. I'd see a cop crouching down with the radar and Don would be yakking, his foot up on the dash, and drivin'. He wouldn't even see it and I'd say, 'Don, there's a ticket.' 'Where? Where? Where?' By that time, he'd already been got.

"Actually, they let us go. They were really good about letting us go. They really were. And the speed limits were higher then, too. The speed limit's about seventy-five and you're doing eighty-two—they wouldn't really bother us over speeding. But he'd speed it up several times."

Doyle remembered another time when Don was driving and a car pulled out unexpectedly and caused him to slam on the brakes. Behind him, Doyle and Buck were playing a game of chess for a dollar a game. Doyle's back was to Don because Buck couldn't stand facing backward. Doyle was within two moves of a checkmate; he had a king and a queen to Buck's knight and a king. When Doyle turned to see what was going on, Buck moved the pieces so Doyle couldn't checkmate him.

While on the road, Buck made the most of every penny, not only by curtailing the number of stops but also by scrimping on food and lodging. Each band member got $10 a day for meals, but in the early days he paid for only two rooms: one for himself and the other for the band, thus putting two Buckaroos to a bed. As he became more successful, however, he reserved more rooms for his entourage, including two rooms instead of just one for the band. Even then, they always had a roommate—though that didn't mean the roommate was always there.

As far as accommodations were concerned, Tom said that Buck never showed any favoritism to specific band members. He said Buck hung around them most of the time, and one night Don and Tom would share a room and the next night it might be Tom and Willie. But in general, Tom bunked with

Willie and Doyle bunked with Don. "I guess that's the way it just sort of fell into place," Doyle said. Perhaps because Tom and Willie were the quiet ones and Doyle and Don "liked to roar," Willie said. Tom didn't go out and party and Willie was underage, so he and Tom ended up staying in the motel room. Many times other steel players would stop by to visit Tom, and Willie would listen to records. "Willie drinking Coke and Tom drinking Maalox," Doyle joked.

Buck may have been cheap, but he wasn't shy, and Willie said he used to get annoyed with the way Buck loved to draw attention to the band in public places. "There was a reason for it, I'm sure. He wanted to let everyone know that we were there," Willie said. "He's got to be aware he had a big ego. It used to bother me, because I was quiet. I just wanted to be left alone and go on the trip and not be recognized."

Loudilla Johnson of the International Fan Club Organization never thought of Buck as being egotistical, though. He talked fairly loud, but she thought that may have been because, like many musicians, he'd developed hearing problems working with loud music and amplifiers. Buck also had confidence in his ability to do things, which may have contributed to people thinking he was full of himself. "He never came across that way to me," she said.

Tom Brumley had still not agreed that driving the band to and from gigs was part of his job description. The only time he drove was when he wanted to. But he recalled an incident when he had to defend this stand to Buck. The Buckaroos had finished a gig in New York City, and Tom needed to get back to Bakersfield for the closing on a house he had just bought. He planned to fly home, but Merle Haggard, who was also on the show, told Tom he had heard that he and Tom were supposed to drive the bus back to Bakersfield. Tom told Buck he had to fly home so he could be there in time for the closing. Buck told him, no, he had to stay and drive the bus. Tom told Buck in the lobby of the hotel, "Buck, I'm going home. Whatever it is, I am going home. Whatever the consequences are—my job, whatever—I don't care. That is the deal we made."

Tom flew home, then Buck called a meeting with him to complain. Tom told Buck that he could make more money driving a bus than what he was earning playing steel for him. He also told Buck, "You ought to think about these boys out here who never missed a date, never been late for a date, in all these years and they would do anything for you," Tom said. "You ought to think about that a little bit, instead of what old Buck is doing for you, because I am tired of hearing of what Buck's doing for me, or hasn't done for me. You know, I have been waiting a long time for you to do for me."

As usual, Tom found that if he stood up to Buck and had the facts to support his argument, Buck would back down.

Though there were sometimes conflicts with Buck, the Buckaroos got along well on the road. For all the traveling they did, they never had any problems or arguments to speak of. Nonetheless, it seemed that whenever the band stopped for gas or to eat, there was always someone who would linger and be left behind. In fact, the only person who was never left behind, or at least threatened with it, was Buck. "It was sort of a hobby to break up the monotony by running off and leaving a member of the band," Doyle said.

Doyle himself got left behind once or twice, but Buck always left him some money so he could get to the next venue. Once, Buck and his Buckaroos were working at a club in Marysville, California, near Sacramento, and they went to a Halloween party after the gig. Doyle met a woman and spent the night at her house. The next morning, she took him back to the motel where the band was staying, but the guys had checked out and gone on to San Francisco, about eighty miles away, without him. Buck had left an envelope at the front office with Doyle's name on it. There was a $20 bill inside, along with a note that said, "Here's $20. If this'll get you to San Francisco, you've still got your job." Doyle gave the woman the $20 and she drove him to San Francisco. When he walked into the hotel, Buck and Don were standing there. "I'm not that easy to get rid of," Doyle said. Buck and Don got a kick out of it.

The drummers—Mel King, Willie, and later Jerry Wiggins—were frequently late. "It must be just a drummer's trait," Doyle said. "We run off and left Jerry Wiggins three or four times. And he never did get the message." Once, Willie got left behind accidentally while dawdling at a truck stop in Wyoming. The bus had gone seventy-five miles down the road when a highway patrolman pulled it over and told the guys they had left one of their band members at their last stop. So they had to turn around and go back for him.

After the band got the bus, Buck started flying more, but there were still times when he rode with the guys—and drove. The last time he drove the bus was near Four Corners, New Mexico, about two or three o'clock in the morning. He had taken a wrong turn off the interstate and ended up on a narrow two-lane highway. When Buck realized his mistake, he proceeded to turn the bus around and got it high-centered, which meant it was straddling the road, front and back wheels on both sides not touching the asphalt, blocking both lanes of traffic. Approaching cars were forced to stop, and when people got out to see what was going on, their headlights illuminated the big "Buck Owens and the Buckaroo's [sic]" sign on either side of the bus. That more or less ended Buck's driving career, which was fine by him.

★ 25 ★

THE GIRL SINGER

The band's new Flex bus was missing one important feature: a lavatory. Until one was added, the guys Okie-rigged a "pisser," which was a funnel attached to a garden hose that emptied through a hole in the door at the front of the bus. That way they could relieve themselves in transit—and leave a stream out on the highway. The only problem was that in wintertime, the hose would freeze, and what was supposed to go outside came inside and there was a mess to clean in the bus. Nevertheless, the pisser helped keep stops to a minimum, which Buck insisted on.

By mid-1966, however, the bus had to make stops for one member of the entourage who couldn't use the funnel: Kay Adams, who was hired as Buck's opening act. Whereas Bonnie Owens had only sung backup, Kay was a featured performer—the group's first real girl singer.

Kay was discovered by Dusty Rhodes when he was scouting new talent. He became mesmerized by her appearances on Dave Stogner's local television variety show, *KLYD's Kountry Korner*. Kay had appeared on only a couple of shows when Dusty showed up at the station and asked if she was interested in getting into music professionally. She said yes, and he took her to see Cliffie Stone, who was a singer, songwriter, bandleader, bass player, disc jockey, booking agent, manager, and record company executive, among other things. He had a knack for discovering and nurturing new talent.

Cliffie took Kay down to the studios of Tower Records, a Capitol Records subsidiary, for an audition. She wore the only dress she owned, and a pair of little brown flats instead of heels because she was recovering from a fluke accident involving a push mower. She just stood there and sang her heart out. Cliffie declared that she was "the most country little thing" he'd ever seen and said he wanted to record her and see what they could do together. Kay was signed to Tower on July 15, 1965.

Her first Tower single, "Honky-Tonk Heartache," went to the top ten in local and regional markets. When she won the most promising female vocalist award from the Academy of Country and Western Music, she almost fainted from the shock. "That was the last thing I would have thought of in my life," she said. "I was too new." (Her counterpart that year as the academy's most promising male vocalist was Buck's chief rival, Merle Haggard.) It was the newly founded organization's first awards show, Kay remembered, and they didn't have trophies made up for the ceremony. They handed her something that looked like a trivet, "a thing you set a hot pot on," she said.

Cliffie was the one who introduced Kay to Buck, who continued his reign as the top artist of the day. On January 3, 1966, he released "Waitin' in Your Welfare Line"/"In the Palm of Your Hand." "Waitin' in Your Welfare Line" climbed to #1. On February 15, he recorded "Think of Me," which was written by a woman named Estrella Olson who had sent some lyrics to Buck. People sent hundreds of lyrics to him all the time, and it was rare for Buck to pay attention to any of them, but he felt these had promise, so he had Don Rich set them to music. "Think of Me" was released May 2—the same day as the *Dust on Mother's Bible* LP—with "Heart of Glass" on the flip side; it marked yet another #1 for Buck. Less than a month after Capitol released *Roll Out the Red Carpet* and *The Buck Owens Song Book* in 1966, both albums had sold more than twenty thousand copies. Since the beginning of the decade, Buck had sold about two million albums in all.

Like Dusty and Cliffie, Buck had an ear and an eye for new talent. He also had a weakness for beautiful brunettes, and at five foot four, 120 pounds, Kay was no exception. Buck decided that the singer, with her stunning looks, country ways, and complementary voice, would be an asset to his road show. "Kay was a wonderful singer," Buck said. "She had a better voice than Susan Raye, but Kay was a hillbilly singer." Kay said, "I didn't sound like anyone else.

I didn't realize that until now, but that is necessary. I was really hilly, just hill-billy to the bone."

Kay was amazed at how quickly her association with Buck materialized. Buck persuaded her to leave Cliffie and signed her to OMAC in spring 1966. Buck told her she would earn $25 per show, all expenses paid, which in addition to the standard $10 per diem meant her own hotel room. Kay was humble enough that she thought she had scored a career coup. After all, she would be touring with the number one country artist in the nation—not bad for a recent transplant from Vernon, Texas, the so-called "Watermelon Capital of the World." Kay did not know to bargain for more money, though. She didn't think to ask about what others on the show were getting paid, even though she had two young sons for whom to provide. She had grown up poor, the fifth child in a family of eight children, and had made do with very little. Still, she didn't possess a mad hunger for money. "We just grew up so happy and with music going on all the time that I never felt poor," she said.

"I think that when the Buck Owens thing came along, she grabbed at it," Cliffie said, "probably because she thought it would help her career. You've got to remember, at the time, Buck was like the major record seller of the damn world. But I think Kay could have gone on to become an individual star herself, and maybe retained a following of her own like Loretta Lynn."

Years later, Kay said she didn't know Cliffie had felt that way, and that if she had, her career might have taken a different turn. She was so new to the business that she was unaware that Buck could spot a future star a light year away, or that he plucked them up so he could control their bookings and chart success, thus ensuring his own place at the top.

Kay was told when to report, and as soon as she climbed on the bus, band-leader Don told her to sit down because the guys needed to talk to her and set down a few rules. "I want it understood that we haven't had a girl on the bus and I want you to know we are not going to wait on you hand and foot," Don said. "I want you to know that no one is going to carry your luggage. You pull your own weight. You carry your own luggage. The other thing is, if we feel like fartin', we're gonna fart."

Kay listened and then said, "I was raised with brothers." But the rules didn't last long. Within six to eight months, she and Don were involved in a love affair, and he was carrying her luggage.

Whenever the Buckaroos went to New Mexico, they came home with an interesting tale. That's where Doyle almost got left behind in the desert, where Mel King was fired, and where Buck blocked a highway with his high-centered bus. It's also where Tom Brumley had a late-night run-in with a horse in the road.

One night in 1966, around 2 A.M., the band had just gassed up in Gallup and had gotten back on the interstate. Tom was driving, and Doyle was his copilot. Tom was just getting up to full speed and reached down for his coffee. When he looked up, three horses appeared out of nowhere, galloping full-speed down the median. He hollered, "Hang on," slammed on the brakes, and cut to the left. Doyle was stunned and said, "Oh, there's a horse."

Kay Adams was asleep in a bottom bunk, and the force of the accident threw her onto the floor of the bus. Don, who was about twice Kay's size, had been in the bunk above hers and was ejected on top of Kay. "It was really frightening," she said. "It knocked everything out of everything that could be knocked out in there and threw us out of the bunks. It damned near killed me"—although she softened the impact for Don.

"It's a miracle that we didn't turn the bus over or slide it over the side into the field," Kay said. "Tom was great. He kept the bus upright and stopped it. It could have been a real disaster. Thank God, it wasn't." After he pulled to a stop, Tom surveyed the damage. The bus was built like a tank, and its front bumper had caught the right front and tail end of the last horse in the trio, an appaloosa-pinto. The horse damaged a bit of sheet metal on the front of the bus and knocked out the headlights before its head slung around and hit the door, bending it inward, and then its body slid down the right side of the bus. The horse was dead and one of its legs had been severed above the knee. "We had horse all over that bus," Kay recalled.

Tom remembered seeing someone in a pickup truck drive through a fenced area with its lights off. Tom was able to drive the bus back to the service station in Gallup so the headlights could be replaced. There was a phone on the bus, and Doyle called the highway patrol and asked them to meet the bus there. The patrolman was Native American, and he told the Buckaroos that the Indians had cut a hole in the fence so their ponies could graze at night on the grass alongside the interstate. He said he was going to have to go shoot the other two horses before they killed somebody.

The only problem the band had on the way back to Bakersfield was wind noise through the bent door.

26

Buck Owens Ranch

At the height of his hit-making powers in 1966, Buck Owens forged a deal with twin brothers Don and Bud Mathis to sponsor his own nationally syndicated show, the *Buck Owens Ranch*. The Mathis brothers owned a furniture store and had a highly rated local television show in Oklahoma City called *Country Social*, which featured Buck as a periodic guest. The brothers approached Buck with a concept for a new half-hour program with him as the star. Buck liked the idea, and the first *Ranch* show was broadcast March 15, 1966.

The show's format was a typical music variety program with an introduction by the emcee, followed by a song by Buck and his Buckaroos, a song by one of the featured guests, a plug for Buck's records and songbooks, a couple more songs by Buck and his guests, and the closing announcement by the emcee. Guests included Bob and Faye Morris, Merle Haggard, Hank Williams Jr., Waylon Jennings, Charley Pride, Conway Twitty, Wanda Jackson, Jimmy Dean, Roy Clark, and Tommy Collins.

When they taped, they did the complete show from start to finish. Buck and the band prerecorded the instrumental tracks in Bakersfield, and then sang live to the tracks while they air-strummed and -drummed to make it look as though they were actually playing on the show. The show's set resembled an outdoor courtyard, with blue and white tile accents, a fountain, and a stucco building with arches. It was designed so viewers would think it was being filmed at Buck's Edison ranch. In reality, it was taped on a soundstage at Oklahoma City's WKY-TV. (That's where Buck first met Tom Brumley's brother Jackson, whom he soon hired to work at OMAC. Jackson drove his parents to watch a *Ranch* show taping; he got to meet Buck and the two hit it off.)

At the end of the first season, Buck bought out the Mathis brothers, but he liked the arrangement with WKY, so he continued to travel four times a year to Oklahoma to shoot thirteen shows over the course of three days.

Initially, Bud Mathis was the show's emcee, but in 1968 Bill Mack, a disc jockey at WBAP-AM radio in Fort Worth, took over. Jack McFadden called Bill and asked if he would be the show's announcer, and Dorothy Owens booked him for the tapings. "Remember that rock 'n' roll song Buck did as Corky Jones on the Pep label?" Bill said. "I used to say, 'Buck, why don't you do "Hot Dog" on the *Ranch* shows?' and he'd look and me and say, 'Well . . .'" Bill was joking with Buck, of course, because they both knew that song would not go over with a country audience.

Bill and Buck had a professional but cordial relationship. Although Bill never got to visit Buck's real ranch, he played golf with Buck sometimes when the star was in the Dallas–Fort Worth area. Tom said they would play golf together all day long and have a great time from sunup till sundown. Bill recalled playing golf one time with Buck, Don, and Doyle in Fort Worth when he noticed dark clouds forming. Buck was coming up out of the sand trap and Bill said, "Buck, have you ever seen a tornado?"

"No," Buck said.

"Turn around."

Buck turned to see a large black funnel cloud behind him.

"You'll do anything to win a golf game!" Buck said, before they ran for cover.

Bill was the *Ranch* show emcee for a year and was all set to go back for the next season, but he hadn't heard from Bakersfield. So he called to see when he should arrive in Oklahoma City, and that is when he found out his services were no longer needed. He was told Mike Owens was going to be the announcer. "I didn't quit or leave," Bill said. "I just didn't hear from Buck anymore." Bill didn't feel too bad about it, though, and joked that it cost him more money to get to the studio than he got paid for doing the show.

Buck made the *Ranch* into a family affair and handed off the job of announcer to his son, who went by the name "Michael Lynn," using his middle name as his last name. Mike eventually became director of the show, and his brother Buddy became a regular guest. "Buddy Alan" used his first name as his last in his musical career.

The Buckaroos neither were paid extra nor received royalties for their work on the show. All they got was their regular weekly pay. Supposedly, Buck had promised the band members 10 percent of the album royalties from *The Buck Owens Songbook* LP to divvy up four ways as payment for their work on the *Ranch*, but that never happened. Doyle maintained that Buck owed him at least $800,000 for his *Ranch* work, which even extended to buying the boss's clothes.

"Go get me some shirts," Buck said.

"What kind you want?"

"You pick 'em out."

Jay Dee Maness, who would replace Tom on steel in 1969, recalled that performing on the *Buck Owens Ranch* was an ordeal in itself, because they would record every day, all day long. "It was OK, because it was a lot of work but it was good experience," he said. "Buck, boy, he had an iron hand with that show."

Buck owned all of 295 of the original shows as well as dozens of repackaged programs with new and previously broadcast performances, which brought the total to 380. Select programs are sold on VHS and DVD formats at his Crystal Palace nightclub in Bakersfield. Buck donated one videotape of *Ranch* snippets to the Country Music Foundation in Nashville.

At its peak, the *Ranch* broadcast in one hundred markets around the country, every week of the year. The reach of the show was enormous, and former Capitol Records producer Earl Poole Ball Jr. recalled overhearing a couple of long-haired hippie rock 'n' rollers at Wallach's Music City in Los Angeles discuss guitar playing:

"You know, I saw a guy on TV the other day, and he plays guitar just exactly how things ought to be played," one long-hair said.

"Well, who is he?"

"It's the guy that plays guitar for Buck Owens. He is just totally amazing, this guy."

Earl said, "They were digging it. Young, hip kids were sitting around digging Don Rich's playing on the *Buck Owens Ranch*." Don was "a guitar player's guitar player," and he never knew how much he would grow to be respected by people in the industry and beyond.

In 1973, *Hee Haw* producers arranged with Buck to end the *Ranch*, because *Hee Haw* was in syndication and the two shows competed against each other in certain markets.

27

CARNEGIE HALL

The first offer for Buck and his Buckaroos to play the legendary Carnegie Hall in New York City had been received by Jack McFadden in fall 1965. Buck was reluctant to take the prestigious booking, however. Even though he had the hottest act in country music at the time, he was insecure enough to worry that New Yorkers might not be interested in country music, and he didn't want to subject himself and his band to the embarrassment of playing to a less-than-sold-out hall.

But when a second offer came in 1966, Buck set aside his insecurities. There is little argument that Friday, March 25, 1966, was the zenith of Buck Owens's career. Not only did he and his band play to two sell-out crowds of twenty-seven hundred in the venerable venue, but also one of his best-selling and most critically acclaimed albums, *Carnegie Hall Concert with Buck Owens and His Buckaroos*, was recorded live that night.

Kay Adams recalled that Carnegie Hall was the second stop on the first tour she went on with the band (the first stop was a dance in an Oklahoma City ballroom, at which she didn't even sing). As a young girl, Princetta Kay Adams would stage performances for pretend audiences down at the salt flats in Knox City, Texas. In the dirt she would draw a big stage, a dressing room, and stairs. In her imagination, she would dress in beautiful gowns, ascend the stairs to the stage, and sing and dance for hours. For her, performing at Carnegie Hall was a childhood dream come true. The house was packed and people were dressed to the hilt with furs and jewels, unlike her. She "wore a little ol' plain blue dress" when she walked onstage, because Buck preferred the plain, homespun look for her. Later, after she had been with the band awhile, she cut her hair, and Buck was very upset. He said, "Let it grow back out. You know we have an image and I'd like you to keep an image like Loretta Lynn with the long hair and the little full skirts and the clean-cut, all-American persona." So she grew out her hair and dressed in gathered skirts to keep the boss happy.

"I went in like a doodlebug," Kay said, meaning she went in backwards, starting with the biggest things first, such as Carnegie Hall. As a result, she had no fear—she didn't know what Carnegie Hall was, let alone what she was doing. Some of the artists on the show were so nervous they could hardly sing, but she had no problem performing. "I just walked right out there and did it out of pure ignorance," she said.

Doyle Holly didn't recall being told the band was going to play Carnegie Hall. In fact, he said he first learned they would be playing there on the building's steps. Buck's mother, Maicie Owens, would create only one itinerary for the whole trip, and if anybody wanted a copy they could get one, but as a rule, there was just one master copy. Doyle, of course, was more concerned about having fun and his next conquest than he was about where the next show was going to be. Still, he was honored to discover they were playing there, because he had heard about Carnegie Hall all his life but always had associated it with either the opera or classical music.

Tom Brumley, who, along with Willie Cantu, was more serious about the music, had a different recollection. He said Jack McFadden had booked the Carnegie Hall appearance quite a bit in advance. "It was a thrill to be a country act playing Carnegie Hall," Tom said. "We weren't the first, but not that many country acts had played there."

The afternoon of the concerts, Buck and the band went to the hall for a photo shoot for the cover of the live album they would be recording that night. For the shoot and their two performances, Buck and the band were dressed in charro-inspired Nathan Turk suits with bolero jackets and a distinctive diamond-shaped embroidery pattern studded with rhinestones. Buck wore mustard yellow with blue embroidery and the Buckaroos wore bright blue with yellow embroidery. Their boots were a dark blue patent leather.

Many accounts have been written about how Buck and his Buckaroos wore suits designed by Nudie Cohn at Carnegie Hall, but they did not. Buck was far too money-conscious to have sprung for five Nudie suits. Usually, the band wore Nathan Turk outfits that weren't so expensive. Nudie suits cost around $700 apiece and the N. Turks were in the $200 range. "Turk was about half as cheap and gave you a lot," Buck said. He favored N. Turk not only because of the lower price tag but also because the tailor would "give you a quick turnaround." They would go into his shop and everybody would be measured within a half-hour. The suits would be ready for a fitting in ten days and ready to pick up two to four days after that. Examples of Buck's N. Turk–designed outfits are on the covers of the "Open Up Your Heart"/"No More Me and You" 45 sleeve, the *I've Got a Tiger by the Tail* LP, and the *Carnegie Hall Concert with Buck Owens and His Buckaroos* LP. The band also bought clothes from Sheplers, a low-priced western wear chain based in Texas.

Buck did own some Nudie-designed suits. He liked glittery, shiny stage clothes, but as a rule, most of the Nudie suits he owned had longer jackets that weren't gussied up with cacti, wagons, and other western motifs a la Porter Wagoner. Buck's Nudie suits were usually understated, impeccably tailored numbers with longer jackets and western accents—with the exception of one gold suit that was so heavily laden with ten thousand rhinestones that he wore it only once in 1964.

When the Buckaroos were done with the photo shoot, they hailed a cab back to their hotel. Upon arrival, Buck turned and told Don Rich: "You tip the guy." So Don handed the cabbie a $5 bill. The incensed cabdriver started ranting, "You clowns! You're obviously somebody and you mean to tell me all you're going to tip me is five bucks?" Don went back to him and apologized. "I'm sorry, give me the $5 back," he said. The cabbie gave back the money and Don put the $5 in his pocket and walked away, leaving the cabdriver empty-handed and fuming.

Anytime Buck did a live album, it was a tense experience. The band tried to make few to no mistakes, because there was no second chance taping a live show. At Carnegie Hall, there were two shows, however, and Capitol Records producer Ken Nelson taped them both and then chose the best version of each song for the album.

The show was a huge extravaganza with Kay Adams, Dick Curless, Freddie Hart, Red Simpson, Wynn Stewart, and Sheb Wooley on the bill. At the time, these artists, all heavyweights in California country music, appeared regularly on Buck's shows. Heavyweights or not, Buck got away with paying the people in his show the least amount possible. For example, Red Simpson only got $100 a show, even though he had had a couple of good records and had written songs for Buck. Red and Jack got into an argument over the money, and after the Carnegie Hall show, Red had to ride the bus back to Bakersfield while Buck flew.

Disc jockey Lee Arnold of New York's WJRZ radio announced all the acts, each of which had either ten or fifteen minutes in the spotlight before Buck's forty-five-minute set. "And now, the moment we've all been waiting for," Arnold said. "Born in Texas, he's an admiral in the Texas Navy, lives in Bakersfield, California, has a great big ranch out there. He's had so many hits, I lost count about twenty years ago. He's won about every conceivable award ever given in the country world, time and time again, year in and year out. Ladies and gentlemen, a warm Carnegie Hall welcome for Buck Owens."

The band immediately took off into the intro of "Act Naturally," Buck's breakthrough hit, as the audience whistled and hooted. Buck then talked to a man in the audience named Ken, probably a disc jockey, to whom he gave a Brownie camera to take a snapshot of the band onstage. (Don had bought the camera in a drugstore, not in Germany as he said onstage; that was one of Don's little jokes on the show.) Then Buck said, "Come on up here, Willie" and Willie Cantu got up from his drum set and pushed everybody out of the way to get up-front when the picture was taken.

"Together Again," with Tom Brumley's trademark steel solo, came next. As the show continued, two main components were comedy and impressions of other country stars, including Ernest Tubb, Tex Ritter, and Johnny Cash. Buck had made sure that the band toned down their usual raunchy routine for the more refined New York audience.

〜✕〜

The Buckaroos usually tried to tailor their stage shows to the audience—for example, if it was a family show, such as a performance at an orphanage, they would not include any risqué jokes. But Buck's shows did lean toward the lewd and the crude at times. Doyle told of how he had seen Del Reeves do a joke in his routine in which he would pump the microphone stand like a toilet plunger. Once, onstage at the Golden Nugget in Las Vegas with Bonnie Owens, Doyle copied Del's act, saying, "I told you a hundred times, Bonnie, you can't put them things in the toilet, they stop it up." Bonnie was genuinely embarrassed and told Doyle afterward that the joke was crude. Buck went along with almost any joke, no matter how off-color it might be, because he liked to see what he could get away with.

The band had talked about toning down the Carnegie Hall shows beforehand. "We're gonna do more serious of a show," Buck said. They left out many jokes, including the "Ex-Lax" routine they usually did at the beginning of every show. But there were still subtle hints about adultery and bestiality, in addition to a few flirtations by Doyle and Buck with select audience members, such as "Edna." In his Johnny Cash impression, Doyle sang, "*I stole your wife and that's a fact. She ain't no good so you can have her back.*" The parody of "Ring of Fire" included Buck's line "*The taste of love is sweet when hearts like ours meet. Love is a burning thing, I know it's love 'cause my thing's aflame,*" but it didn't make the album cut.

Another example from their semi-sanitized Carnegie Hall act was the "Jealous Horse" routine, a parody of Tex Ritter movies and Tex's song "Jealous Heart." The scene was late at night with Tex riding along on his horse, bored, and singing to the animal. That was Doyle's cue to say, "That's not all they did to that horse," which would get a laugh. Then Buck would play the straight man and say, "Doyle, you can't say that!" Doyle would step up and interrupt Buck, saying, "Well, you can't kiss them 'cause their breath stinks." "Oh, their breath stinks, that's what it is?" Then Doyle would say the punchline: "And you gotta walk so damn far to kiss them." It was considered crude at the time, but by today's standards, the suggestion of bestiality might be considered tame. In the 1960s, the bit broke new ground, especially for an allegedly wholesome group such as Buck Owens and his Buckaroos.

Willie recalled that "one of the things Buck needed the most onstage was that he was so intent on being funny. I understand it was entertainment and

Buck used to talk about that, that you have to entertain the people. But I always felt that his music, his songs would have been enough."

The original *Carnegie Hall* LP would be released July 25, 1966, and reissued as *Live at Carnegie Hall* by the Country Music Foundation in December 1988 with previously unreleased material from the concert. The new material included "Fun 'n' Games with Don & Doyle," a comedy routine in which they played homage to Ernest Tubb, and "Twist and Shout," the group's homage to the Beatles. A surprise came at the end of the Beatles skit, Doyle said, when Don fired a muzzleloader onstage. "Ken Nelson didn't know that the gunshot was coming," Doyle recalled. "Ken was in a room by himself; there was no control booth where you could see what was going on," so he was caught off-guard. But Tom Brumley said firing the muzzleloader was a running gag Don did at the end of the Beatles medley in all their shows. He said each night Don would add a little more powder, until "one night that thing went off and just smoke everywhere. He was always puttin' more powder in it until it got so loud and deafening, I was afraid the gun was gonna blow up. I said, 'That's gonna blow up in your face one of these days!' Oh, no. Don never had enough of anything."

Buck told those attending the Carnegie Hall concerts that it was "without a doubt, the warmest audience we've ever performed for." Buck's encore was a medley of hits, followed by a sign-off that was typical Buck: "I think I love ya, and I'd like to kiss all of you, but I don't have time. And one other thing, I have a little saying, and it's for you, that it takes people like you to make people like me. Bye!" Often he would end concerts telling audiences this. It was his small way of acknowledging that he wouldn't be where he was if it were not for his fans.

After the shows, Buck and his entourage returned to their hotel, the name of which no one can recall. "We stayed I think at the Roosevelt or the Americana, I can't remember," Doyle said. No party had been planned in celebration of their milestone performances. "Well, you can party in New York City if you know New York City," Doyle said. "We never did know New York City."

Nevertheless, Buck was like a testosterone-fueled pilot who had greased a DC-10 into a perfect landing and was now in search of a flight attendant to celebrate with. So he homed in on the closest brunette, Kay Adams. Kay and Doyle both recalled how Buck had hit on her earlier that night, saying: "Katie, I just don't understand why you won't go to bed with me. You'd really like it. It's like a loaf of light bread." Kay said, "I guess he meant that big. Well, I didn't pay it any attention because every man will tell you things—usually it's kind of like a fish story." Doyle also remembered Buck saying to Kay, "Why drive a Chevrolet when you can drive a Cadillac?" Meaning that Buck was a Cadillac, and any other man was a lesser ride.

After the show, Jack McFadden got Kay by the arm and whisked her past everybody into a waiting limo; Buck was seated inside. They went on to the hotel and she thought Buck was just being nice to her. She had no inkling that Buck had plans to take her to bed. He said, "I need you and Dick Curless to come to the room and sign papers." He was very charming and nice to her the whole way back to the hotel, talking business and asking questions such as, "How do you think the show went?" Kay was bowled over by the attention and the flattery. When she got to her room, he called her and said, "Please come down to my room and sign these contracts. I have yours here and Dick's here." Dick was leaving the room as Kay was arriving, and she thought everything was cool. But after she signed the papers, Buck leaned over and deep-throated her, then pulled her to the bed and lay down next to her. Her mind was whirling like a Texas tornado, and she thought to herself: "*Oh, my God, how am I going to get out of this? How do I get out of this?*" Then she said, "Oh, I forgot something in my room. I'll be right back." She jumped up and ran from Buck's room to hers. "It just scared the hell out of me," she said.

Kay said something else strange happened that night. About 2 A.M., there was a knock on her door.

"Who is it?" she asked.

"House detectives."

Two men strolled into her room, looked around, and left.

"I never did know what that was about," she said. "I always remembered that. Strange. I don't have any idea why they came in or who they were or if they really were house detectives."

28

RUNNING WITH THE DOGS

Buck's approach to women was much like his approach to money: he loved them both and never got enough of either. He definitely was a numbers runner when it came to the opposite sex, and his superstar status drew groupies in droves. Behind closed doors, he behaved more like a rock star than the wholesome, all-American country singer and family man he purported to be to the public. Playing off Elvis Presley's nickname "Elvis the Pelvis," Buck proclaimed himself "Enos the Penis" and said, "It would be boring to be with the same woman all the time." One thing is certain: Buck was never bored.

By her own admission, Kay Adams was as naive and as green as they came. She was a sweet country girl whose only experience with men before joining Buck Owens's show had been with her husband, with whom she had two young sons. "How I ever survived those days, I don't know," she said, "because sexually maybe Loretta Lynn might have been that dumb, but I just can't think of another woman being as dumb as I was about sex. There's an old saying, 'If you run with the dogs, you'll get fleas,' and I was runnin' with a pack of dogs."

When Kay first started touring with the Buckaroos, Buck directed a lot of sexual innuendo her way. For example, Kay had Native American heritage, and both Buck and Doyle referred to her as "Blanket Ass," supposedly because she had been charmed by many men. But after his failed attempt to bed her in New York City, Buck backed off and became very much a gentleman with her. Of course, it was probably because Don was interested in her.

Kay said Buck disapproved of her and Don's relationship from the start, because it did not look good for a married family man with two children to be involved with a recent divorcée with two children. Of course, Buck never had attacks of morality when it came to the way he, a married man with many children, conducted his personal affairs. Most likely, the only reason he cared was because Kay and Don were both visible members of his road show. If the press found out, it would cast a bad light on his organization—which, in turn, might affect his bottom line.

Kay was caught in an emotional tug-of-war between Don and Buck. She said Buck would call them in and say, "You two have got to stop this!" She would tell Don, "I have two children I have to make a living for. I'm by myself, single. I've got to make a living, you're going to have to go away." Don would get angry and say, "He has no right to tell me this," possibly because he knew Buck was no pillar of purity himself. Then Buck would turn around and tell Kay, "You are going to cause a scandal and it's going to go against the show. You are going to get this big scandal going." Then Don told her, at least twice, "I'm not going to give you up. I'll stop picking for him and start picking for you."

Kay knew that Buck couldn't do without Don but that Buck could easily do without her. Buck began to talk to her about booking her on her own in the hinterlands and not with his road show. This distressed her greatly. She felt backed into a corner, yet Don persisted. The couple had a big argument over it one night, and Kay wouldn't let him into her room. She was trying to get him to leave her alone so she wouldn't lose her job. Don pounded and pounded on her door until somebody called the front office and complained about the racket. Buck then called her room and said, "For God's sake! Open up that door and let him in. This is crazy! The manager's on the phone with me."

Kay also worried that her record company, Tower, would find out and yank her contract, because she was supposed to have a wholesome image. She didn't think her label knew about her affair with Don, though it could have. "They probably prayed every night that I wouldn't cause a bunch of trouble," she said. The fear of being found out created a lot of pressure for her, and the stress was almost unbearable. But "we could no more have stopped that than we could've stopped the heavens being up above," she said. "I swear we were soul mates and there was a magnetism. It was not a sexual thing." Kay insists their attraction went beyond the physical; it was deeper, more cerebral, more spiritual in nature.

⤬⤬⤬

Kay said that Buck Owens and his Buckaroos were some of the most brilliant, intelligent, talented, creative, and good-looking musicians with whom she had ever worked, but she thought they could have been even better if they had put the music first and lost all the distractions—specifically, chasing women and worrying about their next lay. As the singer came to learn, the action that took place after hours was not what one would expect from a wholesome country band. While Willie Cantu and Tom Brumley would repair to their rooms, read a book, listen to music, visit with other musicians, call home, and sleep, Don, Doyle, and Buck took full advantage of their celebrity. Buck exuded warmth and genuine good humor, and whenever he walked either onstage or into a room, the energy would shift and his larger-than-life presence filled the space. As an entertainer, he was known to charm the brassieres off females, who passed their undergarments to their heart-throb onstage.

Buck's promiscuity, in part, stemmed from his insecurity about his looks. Bedding scores of females verified him as a man. "Buck wasn't the prettiest guy in the world, but he always got the prettiest girls," Doyle said. Bipolar disorder may have factored into his behavior, as well; if he truly was manic-depressive, as some of his relatives and associates believe, hypersexuality is one of the symptoms. Kris Black saw his insatiability as a way of dealing with the pressures of fame: "People don't understand what it is like to be a superstar or just a star. Just the grind of being on the road, all the people, all the loneliness. All this has to be factored in when you look at all this behavior because a lot of people hit the bottle, hit drugs, and I think Buck's drug of choice was women."

Buck, Don, and Doyle all were known to share a woman like hippies passing around a bong at a head party. Even though she was Don's steady lover, Kay recalled that "Don had a woman in every port." Buck, on the other hand, often had more than one in every port. There were so many groupies that Buck had sex with women like he passed out autographs. Sometimes he would have relations with as many as eight women in the course of a night. As soon as he was done with one, she'd be sent on her way before the next one was ushered in, and sometimes he demanded more than one at a time.

Doyle recalled that his own sexual experiences on the road were like a cattle call, and that some nights he'd have as many as three or four women in different rooms and he'd be running back and forth all night. When asked why he carried on this way, he answered, "Because Dick needs a hole." He remembered one night when he and Don went to Buck's room after a show and knocked on his door. They knew he had a good-looking woman in there and wanted a piece of the action. Buck came to the door in his bathrobe, arms folded across his chest, with his erection exposed. A big smile spread across Don's face and he said, "Well, would you look at that! It looks just like a little baby's arm holding a tiny red apple." Buck allowed them to enter and the three took turns with the evening's featured attraction.

The groupies sent to Buck's so-called playroom after a show sought bragging rights about how they had been of service to the legendary Buck Owens. Blow jobs were Buck's preferred method of being with a female he didn't know and trust. That way there would be no more unplanned pregnancies or legal hassles.

An unexpected duty foisted upon Kay was that of taking in young women from the playroom after Buck was finished with them. Buck paid for her room, after all, and used that as leverage. "I got acquainted with so damn many women that people wouldn't believe it," Kay said. She always thought Buck hated women, because he never would let any of them sleep in his room. They were always sent to hers. "They'd rattle and talk and most of 'em were kind of naive little things that didn't know not to talk, and they'd all tell me the same thing, that Buck would never make love to a woman. He would only have them do oral sex to him and nothing back to them. I know there is a logical reason for that, so they won't have paternity suits. That it feels good, second. But I thought that he didn't like women because he'd make them bow down on their knees."

Kay was also forced to look after the teenage girls who showed up in the playroom, so they could be returned to their mothers. Kay said some women were huge Buck Owens fans but knew in their heart they were either too old or too heavy to be with him, so they would bring their teen daughters instead and leave the girls there. Countless times Buck would call Kay and say, "Hey, this girl's underage, her mother drove off and left her, and I've got her for the night. I don't want to touch her. It's a lawsuit." So he would send the girl to her room. "I got acquainted with a lot of girls that way," Kay said. "Some of the girls were absolutely beautiful. Just gorgeous and they would be like six-teen to seventeen, some of 'em. I only ran into one that was fourteen and her mother had left her there. I even said to her, 'Can we call your mother and have her come get you?' I finally wound up just letting her sleep in my room. There wasn't anything else I could do."

How many women Buck had relations with is impossible to pinpoint, but it's safe to say they numbered in the thousands. Buck had women at his dis-posal at all times, and he had his favorites in various cities, as well. A few of his regular squeezes included a girl named Judy; a woman named Bettie; a blonde who worked on his fan magazine; and Dolly, a country music groupie who hooked up with other well-known singers whenever they were in Las Vegas, according to those who knew her. Buck knew her well, and saw her often.

Once, Buck and one of his favorite friends, "Luanne," had an argument. She talked to Jack about it, and he tried to reassure her everything would be fine with Buck that evening. When she showed up at dinner that night with Jack, Buck said, "I would like to offer a toast. Here's to Luanne. Yesterday she was mine, tonight she is Jack's, and tomorrow she is the world's." Of course, the poor woman was humiliated, because she and Jack had absolutely noth-ing going on. All they had done was talk about the argument she had had with Buck. Another time, Buck said, he made plans to rendezvous with a lover in Cincinnati, Ohio, only to be surprised by another close bed buddy who had traveled there to see him. He told her he had a previous engagement and apologized that he could not visit with her that trip. According to Buck, the woman got upset and slept with his drummer in retaliation, although he didn't say which drummer.

Buck himself was not above using sex to get revenge on those he thought had wronged him. The year after Kay Adams joined Buck's entourage, Norma Jean Beasler decided to quit *The Porter Wagoner Show* and Porter wanted to hire Kay as her replacement. At the annual disc jockey convention in Nashville in February, Porter called Kay's room and asked if she would dine with him, because he had business to discuss. Don Rich was in her room at the time and overheard the conversation; he was livid, but there was nothing he could do to prevent the meeting. When Porter came to pick her up, Don was hiding behind the door, "dying to come out and let him know he was there," Kay remembered. Porter made his offer, but of course, Buck said, "Absolutely not! You're under contract and I won't let you do it." Later, the guys in the band wouldn't let Kay live it down—they changed her nickname from "Blanket Ass" to "Miss Wagoner."

Because he couldn't get Kay, Porter hired Dolly Parton instead. Buck wasn't one to let bygones be bygones, however. He called Norma Jean and asked her to come visit him. It was his way of getting revenge on his old friend Porter, because everybody knew Porter had a thing for Norma and loved her. When Norma Jean came in, Buck made accommodations for her. She had a seat in the audience and then Buck took her back to his room.

In addition, Buck and some of the guys got their share of professional nooky on the road. Doyle recalled how he, Buck, and Don once picked up some prostitutes and a sexually transmitted disease in Memphis. When they got back to Bakersfield, they rushed off to doctors to get checked. Kris Black said it was funny the way it was handled, because it was as if the men thought they were doing their women a big favor by being honest and telling the truth so no one else would get sick. She said it was a good thing there wasn't AIDS then, otherwise the men would have died an early death.

Buck's later duet partner LaWanda Lindsey, who described herself as a pretty boring person on the road, remembered a trip the entourage took to Alaska. The day after they got back to Bakersfield, her phone started ringing off the hook. It was Buck.

"OK, LaWanda, here's the story: some of the guys came back from Anchorage with a venereal disease. If you are talking to any of the wives and if they ask you if you had to go get a flu shot, you tell them you did."

"Why?"

"Do I have to spell it out?"

"I guess so, because I don't have the flu."

"Well, yes you do. You have to go get a shot because several of the guys have contracted a venereal disease from somebody in Alaska."

It finally dawned on her that is what the guys were doing while she was sitting in her room wondering why she wasn't invited to join them.

Jim Hager recalled that being on tour with Buck in 1972 was "like touring with a rock superstar" and that in Las Vegas, someone had arranged for the guys to get a freebie at the infamous Mustang Ranch brothel. Jim said although he didn't partake of the offerings, his brother Jon did.

Buck still didn't like to be alone, and when females were not at his immediate disposal, he often insisted that Don spend the night in his room. The two would lock themselves away, and the others in Buck's entourage were told not to disturb them. Kay Adams always thought they were working or writing songs, but she said the groupie Dolly told her Buck and Don were making a different kind of music. Doyle was adamant that Don and Buck were not bisexual and that with Dolly, one had to consider the source: Dolly had had a son by Buck, Doyle and Marlane said, but Buck wouldn't marry her. (Kay, on the other hand, didn't seem to think Buck was the father.) "I can tell you this," Doyle said, "Don was not gay. Buck was so horny he'd stick it in anything, and I never saw any indication that Buck was queer."

Everybody who knew Buck and Don said their relationship was heterosexual—they loved each other like brothers. On the road, Buck always stayed in his room and only ventured out to do the shows. He rarely went out to eat and always ordered room service. Usually, Buck and Don and later Jack McFadden conducted business in Buck's room. Tom Brumley recalled that Buck once told him "I want for you to be close to me like Don is," but Tom had no desire to take a more active role in the organization.

Still, there are some people who question Buck's sexuality. Charlie C. Allen, a songwriter, musician, and former WHBQ air personality from Memphis, is one. Charlie recalled meeting Buck one morning in 1975 when Buck was in Nashville taping *Hee Haw*. Charlie and a buddy were having breakfast at the Pancake Pantry in Nashville and saw Buck and Don Harron, who was the KORN Radio announcer on *Hee Haw*. Charlie said Buck and Don Harron started looking at them and they looked back, though they didn't want to make Buck self-conscious. Their thinking was "there's the great Buck Owens, hell, and we're trying to be songwriters so naturally we were interested in that." After Buck finished his meal, he approached Charlie and introduced himself. Charlie and his friend were flattered that Buck had stopped by to say hello. "A couple of young men in that day and time, you dressed differently then," Charlie said. "You slicked up and it was the '70s and it wasn't that peasant look. We thought we looked spiffy, you know, and I think Buck thought that as well. So he came over and introduced himself and we traded compliments. He said, 'You guys might come up. We're staying at the King of the Road, and you might come up and visit with me. Here's my phone number. Give us a call.' I thought that was unusual for a major star to come over to the table of two nobodies and offer the phone number and the opportunity to come up to the motel room. When he left, the other guy said to me, 'Was that what I thought it was?' I said, 'You know, I'm not really sure, but I think it was. I think he just hit on us.'"

★ 29 ★

JAMES, CHARLEY, AND RAY

Between *Buck Owens Ranch* and the Carnegie Hall shows, 1966 was another banner year for Buck. He started billing himself and his show as "all-American" and began strumming a red, white, and blue acoustic guitar built for him by Semie Moseley of Mosrite Guitars (although the design would not be patented and licensed to Gibson until the 1970s). He was showing signs of restlessness, and he decided he wanted to try something new musically as well: he wanted Elvis Presley's guitarist James Burton to play lead guitar on a session. James had done his brand of "chicken pickin'" on a few Merle Haggard songs, and he was friends with Tom Brumley from Tom's days of playing at the Palomino in North Hollywood. Buck asked Tom to call James and arrange a session.

"Buck, you've got Don Rich playin' guitar and you want me to call James Burton!" Tom said.

"Yeah, I want you to call James Burton."

So Tom asked James if he would play and he agreed. James played lead guitar on "Open Up Your Heart," recorded during an afternoon session on April 6, 1966. "He stood up in a chair, Burton did, and just played the greatest solo you ever heard in your life," Tom said. "Buck started laughin' right in the middle of the take because James just knocked him out." James had to start over because Buck had ruined the take, and the subsequent takes never matched the intensity of the first. "I mean, when somebody's playin' like this, leave 'em alone," Tom said. The flip side of "Open Up Your Heart" was "No More Me and You." The single was released August 15 and peaked at #1.

Buck was also a fan of singer Charley Pride, who was brand new to the business in 1966; he had just released Mel Tillis's "The Snakes Crawl at Night." At the time, few people knew Charley was black, because he sounded like a white country crooner. Buck loved Charley's singing, Kay Adams recalled, and when the Buckaroos were in Charley's home state of Mississippi to do a show with Red Foley, Lefty Frizzell, and others, Buck invited Charley to perform.

Charley was thrilled to be invited to share the stage with such legendary performers, especially Lefty Frizzell. "I could tell that night that Lefty had been one of Charley's real idols," Kay said. Everyone was sitting around backstage, so Charley handed his guitar to Lefty and said, "Lefty, I'd be really honored if you could tune my guitar for me. I don't play a lot." Lefty sneered, "I don't tune guitars for niggers." Don Rich reached over and took the guitar from Charley and tuned it without a word. That one small gesture spoke volumes to everybody who witnessed it, and it underscored to them that Don was a big man with an even bigger heart.

The good news of 1966 got even better when Ray Charles recorded his own versions of two Buck Owens tunes, "Together Again" and "Cryin' Time." Ray took "Together Again" to the top ten, making it the biggest commercial hit cover version of Buck's repertoire. "Cryin' Time" was Ray's last entrance into the top forty, and it won him a Grammy Award for best R&B recording. "To have Ray Charles do one of your songs was a financial pleasure," Buck said. "Long before Ray recorded 'Cryin' Time' I was a fan. So to have him make such a huge, monstrous hit out of 'Cryin' Time' in 1966 was a sincere pleasure."

But Buck wasn't eager to share that success with Tom Brumley, according to a story Tom heard from Buck's mother. Like everybody who worked for Buck Owens, Tom held Buck's parents in the highest regard. They were good, honest, salt-of-the-earth folks whom everybody called "Truck Mother" and "Truck Daddy." Tom said that Truck Mother would tell him things Buck didn't want him to know, and that he got really upset with Buck when Truck Mother told him, "You know, Ray Charles called up here and wanted you to do his album with him."

"He did?"

"Yeah, and Buck said no. He wouldn't let you go. He called two or three times. He said, 'That steel player is driving me out of my mind. I want to use him on that album.'"

"Oh man, I jumped old Buck!" Tom remembered. "I told him that he didn't have any right to deny me who I played with. I didn't have an exclusive; I didn't even have a contract with him. And that would've done him some good and me some good. You know, why would you not do that?"

30

IF THE SUIT FITS

During one tour in 1966, Doyle Holly recalled, Buck dressed him down in front of others for not learning "Where Does the Good Times Go." "Looking back, it was all my fault, you know. I should have sat down and did my homework," he said, but at the time he found it especially humiliating. When the band got back home, Doyle called Buck and informed him he wasn't going out of town again—he was giving Buck his two-week notice. Doyle had been doing some recording on the side, including a version of Bob Morris's "Dumb Thing" for Mosrite Records, and he wanted to strike out on his own.

"You're not going to give me a two-week notice," Buck said, "I've got contracts on you."

"You're right. I'm not going to give you a two-week notice," Doyle shot back. "I'm going to give you a *one*-week notice."

Buck then told Doyle that if his recording of "Dumb Thing" hit it big, he'd sue Doyle for breach of contract. He sent Doyle a notice in the mail saying he still had dates to fulfill and that if Doyle missed two recording dates, he would sue him. Doyle didn't make the two recording sessions, but Buck never sued him, because "Dumb Thing" was never a hit.

The band went into the studio on November 8, 1966, without Doyle, for Buck's last session of the year. They recorded the ballad "Your Tender Loving Care" with Bob Morris sitting in on bass. On December 16, just in time for Christmas, Capitol released a single of the song Doyle had struggled to learn, "Where Does the Good Times Go," with "The Way That I Love You" on the flip side.

With Doyle's exit, Buck had to find another permanent bass player. Unlike the typical star, who would choose a replacement himself and personally offer him or her the job, Buck relied on word of mouth, even at the height of his popularity. Although Buck had hired Tom Brumley himself, Tom was an exception; Buck usually asked either his existing or his outgoing personnel to recommend musicians who might fit the position qualifications. Doyle and Willie Cantu joked that the first qualification to becoming a Buckaroo was being "crazy."

All kidding aside, Buck wanted someone with the ability to play the instrument in question, a good personality, and a strong character—and the suit had to fit. Buck would not hire a new musician unless he could wear the stage outfit of the musician he was replacing; he damn well wasn't going to replace a perfectly good costume. "I learned, whenever you leave Buck, the clothes stay," Doyle said. Willie said he had to return everything except his boots, and Doyle had to leave even his size 8½ black patent leather boots behind for his replacement.

At Doyle's suggestion, that replacement was bassist Wayne Wilson. The only problem was that Wayne had size 10 feet. Wayne could wear Doyle's clothes all right, but when it came to the boots he was like one of Cinderella's horsy stepsisters trying to wedge a big foot into a tiny glass slipper. Buck said, "Well, powder 'em!" So Wayne did. When he went onstage, he hobbled because they pinched his feet so bad. At the end of a show, the other guys would have to help him offstage because his feet were in such pain. It was at least six weeks before Wayne got a pair of new size 10 boots, and when they finally arrived, all he could talk about was what pure heaven it was to slip his feet into boots that fit.

Buck Owens and his Buckaroos made their first foray into Asia when they performed at the Koseinenkin Hall in Tokyo in February 1967. The Buckaroo wives went, and Ken Nelson also took his wife, June, who was fascinated by Oriental art and architecture. The Nelsons flew to Japan on February 1 and were met by Warren Birkenhead, who was Capitol's Tokyo representative, and his wife, Mary. Buck, Jack McFadden, and the rest of the entourage arrived two days later. Buck and his Buckaroos were such a big draw in Japan that it took two days to meet with the press and be photographed and interviewed. While in the country, they also visited a geisha house.

"Buck took a very quick trip to Japan in '67," Marlane Ulrich recalled. "It was cold over there then and they wore their parkas, which caused quite a sensation. We really enjoyed that trip." The parkas had been gifts from the Janice Fur Company to the band. Doyle loved his but had to give it back to Buck when he left the group.

The day after the standing-room-only concert, Buck and the band flew back to the states, while the Nelsons took an extended vacation in Asia.

It was a different job requirement than the wardrobe restrictions that brought an end to Wayne's time with the Buckaroos. As Kay Adams noted, an unspoken rule for band members was "you don't take the boss's woman." Wayne made the mistake of getting it on with Dolly, one of Buck's favorite groupies. It didn't seem to bother Buck when he and Don shared a conquest, but he did not appreciate sharing her with Wayne. That's why, in the summer of 1967, Wayne Wilson was fired.

After firing Wayne, Buck rehired Doyle Holly, who had spent six months in Seattle and three months playing around Bakersfield and at the Palomino in North Hollywood. But then Buck fired Doyle; "I am going to have to let you go," Buck told him in the nicest possible way. Doyle didn't remember why he was being canned, but it was most likely because he had threatened to quit again. Buck was kind enough to line up a job for him at Bob's Lucky Spot. Buck told Doyle, "Let me call this guy and get you a job. Let me see if I can remember the number, I haven't called it in three or four years." Buck's photographic memory didn't fail him; he called either the owner or the manager at the club, who said, "Yeah, I want Doyle Holly in here." Doyle put together a band the next day and went to work the day after that.

Ray Salter was hired as Doyle's second replacement. Ray played rhythm guitar for Dave Stogner and his Western Rhythmaires and was a sweet, quiet man with a massive black pompadour and sideburns to match. He was an all-around utility guy; he played both bass and acoustic guitar, and he even helped style the other Buckaroos' hair. Willie recalled that it was obvious that

Ray looked and acted differently from the rest of the band members. At some of the places they worked, people would make veiled references about what Ray's mannerisms meant, but Willie was still a kid and naive about worldly ways, and he had no clue that they were implying Ray was homosexual.

The new bassist often shared a room with either Willie or Tom, more so than with Don. Willie never had any problems with him, except that he was "too neat about everything," and he used to wear strange-smelling cologne that Willie couldn't stand. Willie was rooming with Ray in New York City, where the Buckaroos were to perform on *The Jimmy Dean Show*, when Jack McFadden came to their room to let Ray know his services were no longer needed. Buck had decided that it would look bad for the band if they were to appear on national television with a band member who appeared to be gay. "He stood out too much just by the way he looked," Willie said. "So that was the reason why he got let go."

It seems like a double standard, considering Dorothy Owens was a lesbian and proud of it. The way Buck saw it, Dorothy was kin; he couldn't do anything about her, but Ray he could. And she wasn't onstage for the world to see, either. Ray ended up working with the band for less than a month. He wasn't in the group long enough even to be considered a Buckaroo, although he was there to pose for publicity photos with the band.

Doyle had been at Bob's Lucky Spot only three weeks when Buck called and said, "The Ray Salter thing isn't working out." Doyle had to fly to New York immediately. He passed Ray as he came out of the hotel room in what was a very awkward moment for Doyle, who ended up staying another four and half years with the band. When Ray got back to Bakersfield, he took Doyle's place at Bob's Lucky Spot playing bass for Bobby Durham, who also sported a big black pompadour and sideburns but wasn't gay.

31

THE STUDIO AND THE SNAKE

Also in 1967, singer-songwriter-producer Gary Paxton, who had worked with Buck in Tacoma, Washington, got sick of Los Angeles and relocated to Bakersfield, which had cleaner air and a slower pace. Gary had been doing well in Los Angeles and had several Grammy-nominated songs he had produced, arranged, and engineered, including "Cherish" and "Along Came Mary" by the Association and "Sweet Pea" by Tommy Roe, but he felt he needed to get out of the city.

In Hollywood, Gary's favorite place to mix music had been Capitol Records. Capitol had a huge room about twenty to thirty feet underground with "voice-of-theater" speakers and an echo chamber covered with several coats of epoxy to help buffer outside noise. He wanted to re-create that sort of studio in the Bakersfield area. So he bought an old bank building on North Chester Street in Oildale that had been vacant since 1937 or 1938 and hired Dennis Payne to help him, although Dennis usually didn't get paid. Together they refurbished the upstairs into a music store and turned the vault downstairs into a state-of-the-art echo chamber. When they painted the vault with epoxy, they both got ripped for about a week; nobody had told them they weren't supposed to be inhaling the fumes. Gary also bought the furniture store next door, where he built a twenty-by-forty-foot recording studio with a high ceiling and a grand piano. Then he built a garage between the two buildings to house his Greyhound bus.

Gary and Dennis set to work cutting whatever recordings they could to make money. Gary knew he wasn't going to be drawing much business from the San Joaquin Valley, so he sent out word to all his connections. Before long, they had several country artists, about thirty bands, some from as far away as

Edmonton, Alberta, Canada, and about five other artists who came to his Oildale studio regularly to record. One of their projects was producing 101 Strings budget albums for a man named Al Sherman who lived in Los Angeles.

Gary had known Buck Owens for about eight years, since he played bass for Buck out at Bresemann Park and appeared on Buck's weekly television show, *The Bar-K Jamboree*, in Washington. A bit of bad blood had developed between Buck and Gary, however, over some masters Gary had produced and recorded for Rex and Vern Gosdin. The Gosdin brothers were in Buck's stable of talent, and through Buck Owens Productions they recorded peripherally for Capitol Records. Buck evidently claimed ownership of the masters, and when Gary protested, Buck simply said, "Sue me." Nobody in their right mind went up against the mighty Capitol Records and Buck Owens at that time, though, because no one ever had enough money to fight a major label and the number one country artist of the day. Of course, the Gosdins' recordings never went anywhere; Buck owned them, therefore they languished.

One day, Buck went over to talk to Gary about producing OMAC artists at his studio, but he only wanted to pay Gary a flat weekly salary, the same way he paid the Buckaroos. At least the Buckaroos were able to earn a commission selling concessions, but in Gary's case there was no commission, no percentage, no nothing, and he would have to do all the work. Gary told Buck he didn't want to produce his artists under those terms. Not being one to overlook a slight, Buck tucked it away for future reference, but continued being cordial to Gary and Dennis during his visit. He said he wanted to see their operation; "What are you guys gonna do down there?" he asked about the vault. So they took him downstairs, showed him what they were doing, and told him their plans.

Buck seemed genuinely interested, so Gary let down his guard and told him he also hoped to buy the vacant theater across the street. Buck wanted to see that as well, so they called the real estate agent and went over to do a walk-through. They spent the tour telling Buck exactly where the control room would go, how they wanted to keep the stage intact and film shows there, and so forth. Gary had it all figured out, but he didn't have enough money to buy the theater, and he was hoping Buck would go in on it with him. Buck told him that the plan was too far out, and that he didn't need a studio because he was with Capitol, which had great studios, and he could go there anytime to record. Then he left.

Gary, however, was determined to build his second studio. So he called Al Sherman in L.A. in the hopes of enlisting him as a partner. Al flew to Bakersfield to look at the theater building, but when they called the real estate agent to come show the building again, they were told: "Well, you can't do that because Buck Owens bought this building. He's a genius! He came up with this idea to build a studio over there." Needless to say, Gary, Al, and Dennis were spitting mad. Not only had Buck bought the building, but also he had stolen their idea. So they went back to cutting tracks in the bank studio.

Buck's construction workers came and went, and little by little, the theater studio began to take shape. After a few months had passed, Buck started showing up every couple of days in his expensive Excalibur sports car to monitor the progress. Early one morning, Gary and Dennis saw Buck's fancy car parked outside and exchanged appropriate epithets about the man. Shortly thereafter, they saw Jim Wattenbarger drive up in his truck. Jim was a Bakersfield contractor who built houses and apartments and may have been kin to Buck on his father's side. He was also a songwriter and a buddy of Gary's who had bailed him out of some tight spots a time or two.

"Look at this snake I found!" Jim said. "It's alive!" In the truck bed lay a huge black snake.

Gary and Dennis had been up for three days straight; there were no windows in their studio, so they never knew if it was day or night, let alone what date it was. They were also still fairly drunk from the day before. They began venting to Jim and another guy they knew, Kenny Johnson, about how angry they were at Buck for stealing their idea.

"You know, if anybody really had any balls, they'd put that snake in that car," Jim said.

"I'll do it!" volunteered Dennis, who was all of eighteen or nineteen years old at the time.

"Yeah, do it. Go ahead. Go do it!" the other guys said, egging him on.

So Dennis picked up the writhing reptile. The other three guys hid behind Jim's truck and watched as he carried it over to Buck's Excalibur and dropped it in on the driver's side floorboard, beneath the steering wheel. Dennis wanted the snake to go under the seat so it would come back out when Buck got into the car and scare the living crap out of him. But the snake had no clue as to what Dennis had in mind; it slithered under the dashboard instead. Then the four of them watched and waited for Buck to come out, but he never did. They soon tired of waiting and returned to working and drinking some more.

A month or so later, Merle Haggard came into the Blackboard, where Dennis was playing, and sat in with his band and sang. They were sitting around on a break when Merle said, "You know what I heard? I heard some sick, evil-minded, worthless sonofabitch put a rattlesnake in Buck's car."

"Really?" Dennis said, trying to sound ignorant about the situation.

"What kind of an evil person would do that?" Merle asked.

"God, Merle, I have no idea. Some really sick sonofabitch would do that."

As it happened, Phyllis Owens had driven the car to the grocery store and put her bags in the trunk. When she went to unload them, saw the snake in the spare tire and freaked. Buck never did see the snake, but when he told the story to others, somehow the black snake had morphed into a venomous rattler.

Years later, Gary said Buck had never forgiven him for not working with him. Buck eventually sold the studio and it became Fat Tracks, which closed in 2006.

★ 32 ★

JENNIFER

On the road, Buck was still behaving like the bachelor he was not, keeping an eye out for his next conquest. That is how he noticed twenty-two-year-old Jennifer Joyce Smith at a concert at the Cotillion Ballroom in Wichita, Kansas, in 1967. Jennifer was a long-stemmed beauty with straight dark hair down to her waist; she was so beautiful that she looked as though she had stepped off the pages of a fashion magazine. The young woman was attending the show with a girlfriend and was seated about fifty feet away on the left side of the stage. Buck could not take his eyes off her. He wanted her, and what Buck wanted, he usually got.

When the band took an intermission, Buck asked the manager of the ballroom if he had seen "the cute little girl with her hair down to her waist and the cute little dark girl that was with her." The manager said that he had and Buck told him, "Go find her and tell her I want to meet her." The manager balked, but promoter Mike Oatman told him he had seen her and that they would find her. About ten minutes later, the promoter was back with Jennifer. The older singer and younger woman exchanged pleasantries, and Buck learned that Jennifer had been born in Long Beach, California, but had grown up in Texas and that she was an art major at the University of Oklahoma in Norman. That was a convenient opening for Buck, who told her that he filmed the *Buck Owens Ranch* at WKY-TV and that they were getting ready to tape some shows soon. Ever the gentleman, Buck asked, "Would it be permissible for me to ask you if I could take you to dinner?" Jennifer replied, "Well, yes it would." So he got her phone number and called her in advance of his trip to Oklahoma to make a date.

Doyle recalled that Jennifer initially had eyes for Don, but Buck wanted her so there was no argument as to who would win her. As the Hagers said, Buck always got first pick of the women. "I've never known Buck to take seconds," Jon said. His brother, Jim, agreed. "I don't know anybody who would want seconds after that Empire's been on 'em!"

After their initial meeting and first date, it wasn't long before Buck was jetting Jennifer to concerts whenever her class schedule permitted. "I can vouch for the fact that he always had Jennifer by his side. She was always there," said Jay Dee Maness, who would join the Buckaroos in 1969. "As far as any women he was with any other time, I couldn't tell you, but Jennifer, hands down, she was always around."

Of course, during his courtship with Jennifer, Buck was still married to Phyllis, whom he would not divorce for another five years. Still, Buck moved Jennifer to Bakersfield in 1970 to do artwork for his companies, and he supposedly had her under contract as his housekeeper, too.

33

Forbidden Fruit

As widely as Buck spread his seed, it is no wonder that he fathered more children than he cared to admit. In addition to his acknowledged offspring—Buddy and Mike with Bonnie and Johnny with Phyllis—Buck also sired at least six more children. That total included four daughters—the one from his first marriage, the one with Marjorie from Placerville, the one with his lawyer's wife, and another by a Bakersfield girl whom he impregnated when she was only seventeen—and two more sons, one by the groupie Dolly and another by an unknown woman. Buck treated his unacknowledged children as unpleasant business more than actual flesh and blood. Some of their mothers were paid six- and seven-figure sums to keep their existence quiet, while others got nothing.

Buck usually settled with a pregnant lover quickly and quietly before a matter wound its way to court. There was only one known paternity suit against him, by a woman who accused both him and his bass player Wayne Wilson, who had been fired for sleeping with another of Buck's conquests, of fathering her child.

As he did with business, Buck also sought to perpetuate confusion about his love life. Buck said that there was no way he could have fathered the child over which he was sued, because he had had a vasectomy. Supposedly, he had been snipped on one side either after Johnny was born or when Johnny was about five, and had the other side done later, although usually the vasa deferentia are severed at the same time. Whether Buck really had a vasectomy is anybody's guess, though some women who knew him in the biblical sense said Buck didn't have scars on his scrotum. Buck's later wife Jana Jae recalled that "he wanted me to have children, but he'd had a vasectomy, and he said,

'I'll just get unfixed,'" but she never recalled seeing any scars. And the Hagers were skeptical that a man who prided himself on his virility and the size of his penis would ever submit to such a procedure.

Buck would sometimes make an even more unbelievable claim: that he'd been born with only the vital organs on the left side of his body, and thus he only had one testicle. However, several of his sexual partners confirm that he came with all the standard male operating equipment. Jana Jae said of his lone-testicle tale, "I think that's the bullshit," referring to Doyle's remark about the percentage of truth in whatever Buck said. Doyle said, "He got that from me. I only have one. Well, I got a little one and a bigger one." And Tom Brumley said, "I tell you what, if I just had one I wouldn't be going around telling everybody!"

Despite his ongoing attempts to escape his paternal responsibilities, Buck was a much better father to his sons Buddy and Mike than he was a husband to Bonnie. When Buddy and Mike were young, he hadn't been much of a presence, but as they grew older, he took a firmer hand in their upbringing. Buddy, whom associates say is a great guy and very respectful, got into the music business and toured with Buck and the band. Mike, like his father, became a successful businessman; everything he did for Buck paid off. "They turned out very well, you can't deny that," Tom said. "I don't know about the other kids."

Most friends say Buck failed with the son he had with Phyllis. As a kid, Johnny was big-boned, handsome, and lovable in every way. His mother adored him and spoiled him rotten. Consequently, Johnny began running with a bad crowd and was prone to trouble. A teenage Johnny would develop a crush on LaWanda Lindsey, which worried Buck, although LaWanda would have nothing to do with the boy, because he was three years younger. Kris Black didn't think Buck was a very good father to Johnny; he wasn't there for him and left it up to Phyllis to discipline him. "That is just my theory," Kris said, "but he did try to turn Johnny over to me and asked me to work with Johnny, figuring I was good with people, but with the dynamics of that situation, forget it! Overall, he loved the kids and was very protective of them and he took a lot of time to teach and share and to care. I think he dropped the ball with Johnny, but I don't know the circumstances that he was having to deal with at the time. He was a great father, but he was a rascal."

To one young female relative, however, Buck Owens was worse than a rascal. Buck had always been enamored of teenage girls, and in 1967 or '68 an under-age family member accused him of statutory rape. The scandalous incident was the talk of Bakersfield and lowered Buck in the eyes of many.

Statutory rape charges carry severe legal consequences—unless, of course, the accused happens to be a superstar with money and clout. Buck had plenty of both, and Dennis Payne said Buck was able to work out a settlement with the court and the girl. Doyle Holly said Buck never did time for the incident. Apparently, the arrangement Buck worked out included a large settlement in exchange for the girl's silence, and Buck got all records pertaining to the case.

In April 2000 and July 2002, Buck lent an undetermined amount of non-purchase money to Angels Nest Trust—established for a "minor/ward/client represented by a trustee"—for a 5,830-square-foot stucco Tudor-style single-family residence built in 1940. The house, built on a half-acre lot on prestigious Mulholland Drive in Los Angeles, has six bedrooms, four bathrooms, a swimming pool, and a six-thousand-square-foot basement. In 2007, the house and property were assessed at $2.76 million.

Two properties in Kern County were listed as being jointly owned by the Buck Owens Revocable Trust and the Joni and Oliver Gibson Revocable Trust in 2007. One was a vacant lot, assessed at $20,674, and the other a single-family home, assessed at $148,744, in Bear Valley, California. The trust mailing address is in Tehachapi, California, where Buck also owned a home.

It is not known why Buck funded the trust for the minor child and co-owned these properties with another trust, because nobody is saying. Quite likely, they fall under the category of "Settlement, Lips Sealed."

34

FRIENDS IN HIGH PLACES

Broadcast journalist Lesley Stahl once characterized Ronald Reagan as a "mysterious blend of fakery and authenticity." The same could be said of Buck Owens. In person, he had an undeniable warmth and charm that drew people in. He was jovial, charismatic, and sincere, and people loved him. But then there was a whole other side to him, the selfish, demanding, mean, temperamental side that only close associates saw. Most people were also unaware that Buck had friends in very high places, including Reagan himself.

Although Buck leaned to the right politically, he considered himself an independent but registered as a Republican so he could vote in primaries. Nevertheless, he was no respecter of politicians. He schmoozed Democrats and Republicans alike, because he never knew when he might need a favor from whoever was in office at a given time.

Buck counted presidents, vice presidents, senators, governors, lieutenant governors, state senators, mayors, sheriffs, and other elected officials among his friends. He was able to arrange for a police escort wherever he went and could call upon law enforcement for favors. Future Buckaroo steel player Jay Dee Maness remembered going through good-sized airports with Buck, and he would always have a police escort. "That always somehow bothered me," he said. "It was like, 'This guy's famous and he's rich and all that, but does he really need police leading him around?' I'm just watching all this going, 'Why? He's a country music artist!'" Buck also drew favors from the FBI, and had one agent in particular who investigated people for him. In addition, Buck was able to sway the Kern County sheriff to deputize some of his latter-day Buckaroos. Ronnie Jackson, Doyle Singer, and Jerry Wiggins were sworn in by Captain Al Loustalot (pronounced "Loustalow") so they would be able to pack heat and take care of Buck's needs.

Various press accounts indicate that Ronald Reagan and Buck were acquainted. One photograph shows Reagan in black tie talking with Buck at a dinner held in the then-governor's honor in Bakersfield. The caption reads: "As a close friend and supporter of Reagan, Buck was invited to attend the dinner as a special guest of the Governor." Ken Nelson included the same photograph in his autobiography. Another story tells of Reagan sporting a Buck Owens wristwatch, which Ken also mentions in his book. It's true that Reagan was a country music fan, and he had various country stars perform at functions at his Santa Barbara ranch. According to Ken, it was through Reagan's love of country music that the politician met Buck. They also may have become acquainted through two native sons of Bakersfield, Michael Deaver and Lyn Nofziger, who worked for Reagan when he was governor and president. In Reagan's presidential administration, Deaver served as his chief of staff and Nofziger as press secretary.

"Buck was directly connected to Ronald Reagan," Larry Adamson said, as well as to John F. Kennedy's good friend Jack Warnecke Sr. Doyle Holly said that Buck was also connected to a California senator from the 1960s whose name he could not recall. Vice President Dick Cheney and California lieutenant governor Mike Curb were also friendly with Buck; Mike Curb, as owner of MGM records, would produce Buck's award-winning 1970 album *Big in Vegas*.

Larry recalled attending a fundraiser for Reagan at the St. Francis Hotel in San Francisco during the 1960s "at a time when Buck was hot, hot, hot." At the fundraiser, Larry was invited to join an exclusive men's club, the Bohemian Club. He believed Buck to have been a member at one time, he said, because Buck had approached him about using Larry's ranch, not far from the state capital of Sacramento, for some of the group's activities. In addition, Buck had several friends in politics and the music industry who were members and guests of the group. The club has counted Reagan, Cheney, Democratic senator Robert C. Byrd of West Virginia, rocker Steve Miller, and former Grateful Dead rhythm guitarist Bob Weir among its members, according to a membership list obtained from the son of a late member and articles in the

Wall Street Journal and *Spy* magazine. Buck was a good friend of Byrd, who would appear on *Hee Haw* twice in 1969, and the Dead were big Buck Owens fans. Country crooner Lee Greenwood, who would sing at Jack McFadden's second wedding in 1969, also attended and performed as a guest at the Bohemian Grove, the club's summer bacchanal in Monte Rio, California, near the Russian River. The club gained some notoriety when former president Richard M. Nixon said on one of his infamous White House tapes: "The Bohemian Grove, which I attend from time to time . . . is the most faggy god-damned thing you ever could imagine, with that San Francisco crowd."

The group was founded by about a dozen working newspapermen as a salon of sorts. Before its first election in April 1872, the club had expanded to include other writers, artists, actors, and musicians, "and such others not included in this list as may by reason of knowledge and appreciation of polite literature, science and the fine arts, be deemed worthy of membership," its official hand-book reads. Over the years, the invitation-only membership was opened to include wealthy businessmen and power brokers. Yearly dues top $10,000 and preclude entrance to the average wage earner. According to investigative jour-nalist Philip Weiss, who infiltrated the club for his exhaustively researched first-person account for *Spy* magazine, presidents ever since Teddy Roosevelt, who was a member, have either belonged to the club or have attended club func-tions as guests; U.S. policy is often formulated at its so-called Midsummer Encampments. Members are sworn to secrecy about the club's activities.

The whole idea of being affiliated with the Bohemians spooked Larry. He remembered being taken into a room in which a painting of the devil was hanging over the fireplace. The man recruiting him to join told him: "You, too, can make a deal with the devil." When the man excused himself for a moment, Larry reached into his pocket for his Instamatic camera and snapped a photograph of the painting, because he knew people would never believe him. The whole experience gave him such bad vibes that he couldn't get out of there quickly enough.

Of course, the quickest way to get in bed with a politician is to give him or her money. Buck was said to have contributed money to Reagan's gubernatorial campaign, and there were rumblings in Bakersfield that Buck had funneled money through oil magnate Armand Hammer when Reagan ran for president. Hammer, the late founder of Occidental Petroleum, was convicted of making illegal contributions to President Nixon's re-election campaign in 1972. He was pardoned by President George H. W. Bush in 1989.

Buck, along with his nephew Mel Owens Jr., made campaign contributions over the years to various other politicians, including California state senator Roy Ashburn (R-Bakersfield), who made an ill-fated run for Congress in 2004 and garnered headlines in early 2010 when he came out as gay. The most interesting campaign contributions, however, were made in 2000 by Buck and his brother Mel Owens Sr., to Rick A. Lazio, the New York Republican who unsuccessfully ran for U.S. Senate against Hillary Rodham Clinton. Federal campaign contribution records show that Buck and his brother each contributed $1,000 to Lazio's campaign that year—even though Mel Sr. died in 1971.

Larry Adamson recalled being at his club in Rocklin with his good friend Jack McFadden once trying to figure out a good time to book Wynn Stewart when a call came in for Jack. When Jack got off the telephone, he was pissing mad. Buck had been ordered to play five nights for Reagan on the campaign trail, and they couldn't schedule Wynn for the club because he was part of Buck's show. "Jack was mad," Larry said. "I wish I knew who was on the other end of that phone call." It was a turnabout for Buck, who was used to calling all the shots. In this case, Buck had to jump when they said jump, Larry said.

"Now see, if you've been trying to trace his power line," Dennis Payne said, "you'll find it clear up into the government. It goes beyond business. He enjoys it too much. He preys on people's hopes and dreams. It's really vicious what he does. It really makes me wonder who he answers to. He answers to somebody."

As a rule, only Buck's male associates were privy to his political connections. Women generally had no clue; Buck's later wife Jana Jae never thought of Reagan as being a close friend to Buck, although she had met him once at a performance. Exceptions to this rule probably included Buck's sister

Dorothy, and certainly included Don Rich's wife, Marlane, whose husband knew Reagan, too. Not only did Marlane know that Buck and Reagan were friends, but also she herself was friends with Reagan's sister, whom she had met when he was running for governor. She has an autographed photograph of Reagan on horseback in cowboy garb that says: "To Marlane and the boys, Ronald Reagan."

35

JUMPIN' JERRY WIGGINS

In May 1967, Willie Cantu quit the Buckaroos. It wasn't because he didn't like the music, but he needed a change. There was more to him than being Buck's drummer, more sides to him than playing country music. In all, Willie had spent three and a half years touring with Buck. As Buck gained more fame, the band toured less and played fewer dates. "Everything became a medley, all the tempos got faster and faster, and it just wasn't any fun anymore," Willie said. "I didn't enjoy playing, and I loved to play, and I wanted to play more, which I got from playing in clubs." In his haste to leave, he signed Buck's exit agreement clearing him of receiving any future royalties. "I probably didn't know what I was doing at the end, when I signed all these papers," he said. "I probably lost a lot, but I wanted out, you know."

Since leaving the Buckaroos, Willie Cantu has studied percussion instruments from around the world, including African and Indian drums. By 1981, he was in New York drumming professionally, before settling in Nashville in 1983. His marriage to Geraldine ended in divorce, but he is remarried and lives with his wife, Julie, and their two children in Tennessee. Willie has played sessions as well as in the house band at the Nashville Palace. He continues to indulge his love of musical complexity by leading a Scottish bagpipe corps, the Lovat-Cameron Pipe Band.

Looking back, Doyle said that when Willie was with the Buckaroos, it "was probably the happiest time of the band. I hated to see him go."

Tom Brumley took it upon himself to initiate Willie's replacement, Jerry Wiggins. Tom recalled that when "Jumpin' Jerry," as Buck nicknamed him, started working with them, he said, "Let Jerry stay with me the first night." When they got to their room after the show, Tom sat down on one of the double beds.

"Sit down here, Jerry, I want to talk to you," he said.

Jerry went over and sat on the bed facing Tom.

"Jerry, we have two beds like this," he said as he put his hand on the drummer's knee. "Jerry, man, I'll tell you one thing, it's sure nice to have you in the group." He squeezed Jerry's knee. "No, I mean, it's just really a pleasure to have you for a roommate and everything. I just think you're cuter than the dickens."

Jerry was sober-faced and laughed nervously. He didn't know whether Tom was kidding. Tom kept it up a little while longer, telling Jerry how cute he was and such, then Jerry said, "Just a minute, I'll be right back," and got up and went next door to Don and Doyle's room. Don was in the bathroom brushing his teeth when Jerry came in and said, "Heya, Don. What about Tom, is he . . . is he queer?"

Don looked up and said, "Huh! Well, yeah, we all are, didn't you know that?"

"Old Jerry was so scared he just really got freaked out," Tom remembered.

All kidding aside, though, Tom said he could sleep well when Jerry was rooming with him, because neither one of them went out to prowl. They both went to bed and slept.

On June 8, 1967, Buck recorded "It Takes People Like You (to Make People Like Me)." He said he wrote the song to thank his fans, because he appreciated the phenomenal success they had brought him. The song, backed with "Left Her Lonely Too Long," was released on September 25 and peaked at #2.

Buck was always looking for another "Together Again," which is why, he said, he wrote and sang the ballad "Your Tender Loving Care," which was released as a single on June 26 and hit #1; "What a Liar I Am" was on the flip side. On August 28, one of Buck's idols, Jimmy Bryant, played rhythm guitar on Buck's "How Long Will My Baby Be Gone." Buck's last cut of the year, on December 5, was "Sweet Rosie Jones," the idea of which came from his grandmother. She hummed old melodies about tall, dark strangers, so he included the lines "And then one day, a tall, dark stranger . . . rode into town."

Despite his continuing success, Buck had yet to be recognized by the Nashville-based Country Music Association. He was nominated for two CMA awards in 1967, but he lost to Eddy Arnold for entertainer of the year and to Jack Greene for male vocalist of the year. On the other hand, his Buckaroos had won the CMA award for top instrumental group or band that year.

36

STOLEN GLORY

Gene Price of Shamrock, Texas, was just another young, starry-eyed singer-songwriter when he landed in Bakersfield in 1967. He found full-time work in the oil fields by day and worked as a freelance musician by night. Gene went to Buck's house to talk to him about Buck using some of his songs, but nothing ever came of their meeting. In the meantime, Gene signed an exclusive songwriting contract with Johnny Bond's label, Seashell Music.

Shortly thereafter, Dusty Rhodes started trawling the waters to see if he could hook another unschooled fish for Buck and Blue Book Music. Dusty found a live one in Gene and told the young man that Buck wanted to buy out his contract with Johnny. Gene had wanted to be associated with Buck ever since he moved to town, and in 1968, he finally got his wish. He signed four separate contracts with Buck for "exclusive recording, exclusive writing, exclusive management, and exclusive booking," snagging deals with Blue Book Music, OMAC, and Capitol Records.

By all appearances, Gene was a Capitol recording artist, but the Capitol deal was merely a demo-recording arrangement. Ken Nelson would produce his songs, but Capitol would print just three not-for-sale promotional copies of his music on the Capitol label. Buck would double-bill both the artist and label for studio time. It happened all the time when Buck signed new talent. As Tom Brumley put it, Buck didn't have any real artists working for him, just "meek little people that he controlled" who were in awe of him. Buck took advantage of that awe, and people like Gene would be lured into signing several contracts, without seeking legal advice, just to work with the great Buck Owens. When Gene first signed with Buck, "he was like old 'Buck and Son' and all this" (Mike Owens was working with his dad), and he had Gene completely flummoxed as to what he was signing. "He knew what he was dealing with. I was a young and naive, foolish kid."

Once the contracts were signed, Buck had Gene locked up so he couldn't do anything for anybody else. Buck tried to "control all of the artists he had so they stay down and you stay up. That's what he did to me." Meanwhile, Merle Haggard asked him to sing harmonies for him, which Gene did. So he "was working for Merle and tied to Buck every eight ways from Sunday."

Gene didn't figure out how Buck was using him until after he performed on Merle's *Okie from Muskogee* album, which was recorded live in Muskogee, Oklahoma. Gene was surprised when Merle announced his song "In the Arms of Love," and had him sing the first track he ever cut for Capitol. *Okie from Muskogee* turned out to be a multiplatinum album, and Gene got artist's as well as writer's royalties for the song. He had two songs on that album, as well as cuts on Buck's *Tall Dark Stranger* and *Big in Vegas* albums. In addition, he had songs on Wynn Stewart's albums, and so on.

One day, Gene asked Buck for an advance, which he got only on the condition that Buck got half of the writer's royalties to all of Gene's songs, although Gene contends Buck got "99.9 percent of all of them." Despite all the big hits Gene wrote for Buck, he said he only "got about $10,000 to $11,000 from then till now." All the Form 100s, which register writers' royalties and have to be filed whenever a work or composition is recorded, that Gene filed with BMI as 100 percent writer have conveniently disappeared, he said. The lawyer Buck sent to help Gene figure out his accounting had him turn over all the papers and he never got them back. "So I don't have my copies anymore," Gene said. "Lo and behold! Snake in the grass."

Gene never could get anybody to do an accounting at Capitol, either. "I just wanted to know how many albums were sold of *Okie from Muskogee*, how many were sold on *Easy Lovin'*, how many albums were sold on *Tall Dark Stranger*, how many albums and how many cuts were on each album, and of those cuts, how many were mine, and tally it up," he said. "I'm talking about record sales. That's the Capitol Records company."

Gene said, "I just would never get an attorney that would stay straight with me long enough or a smart enough guy to pursue and follow the numbers.

Never could get anybody interested. When I sued Buck, I found out the attorneys I was using were Buck's attorneys."

In the late 1970s, Gene sued Buck in Los Angeles Superior Court to recoup royalties on the songs he had written for Blue Book Music, including "In the Arms of Love," "Easy Lovin'," "Please Come to Me," and "Across This Town and Gone." Because of the deal Gene made with Buck, Buck's name is the first to be credited on all of these songs. When he went into open court, it was a media circus, Gene said, with photographers and cameras going off and Buck shaking hands with the judge and the jurors. Gene was disgusted by the display: "Buck was so corrupt and so crooked," he said. Even though he lost his case, he felt some satisfaction in knowing that Buck had to spend money on a lawyer and court costs. "I asked him once in the hallway of the courthouse, 'Why? Why?' He just told me he'd ruin me. I had a lot of political enemies during those years because I did fight. Anybody and everybody in the publishing business, in country music." Former Capitol Records producer Earl Poole Ball Jr. said the lawsuit stymied Gene's career. "He wasn't a Buck fan when it was all over somehow."

What Gene couldn't understand is why Buck had talent and could write yet chose to put his name on the work of others. "When fame bit Buck in the fanny, he kinda lost it," he said. "But, like I say, he's still a thief, but he's a thief driving a Rolls Royce convertible."

Tommy Collins recalled that Gene Price was so bitter that he "walked the streets with a pistol in his boot. I mean, walked back and forth in front of Buck's office." But Gene wasn't the only disgruntled singer-songwriter in Buck's camp. Merle Haggard, Red Simpson, Freddie Hart, Ronnie Jackson, and even Buck's compadre Dusty Rhodes had trouble with him, too.

Buck's old friend Oscar Whittington, the fiddle player who lent him a shirt way back when, had a club in the Democrat Hot Springs, a private resort east of Bakersfield where Tommy Collins and Red Simpson used to play. Oscar would give them all they wanted to eat and drink and a motel room to boot.

They performed with the band Oscar had there on weekends. Tommy remembered that he had just finished a show and it was time for Red to perform, but nobody could find him. Finally, Red came onstage, went up to the microphone, and said, "I'm sorry to be so late to my show, but I've been out trying to find somebody that likes Buck Owens. And I can't find anybody."

37

KRIS BLACK

Kris Susan Lynn Black was a seventeen-year-old virgin when she met the man of her dreams. She was to become one of Buck Owens's biggest and best-kept secrets, Buck's private "Priscilla Presley" of sorts.

Kris was born September 19, 1950, in Ladysmith, Wisconsin, but moved to Rapid City, South Dakota, at a young age. Her mother was a big country fan who adored Hank Thompson (Hank, like Buck, was produced by Ken Nelson at Capitol Records), so Kris grew up listening to country music. By the time she was in high school, she had a job at what was then country station KRSD-AM. She came from a home where she was raised to do her father's bidding, even though he barely spoke to her. As a result, she had a recurring dream about an older man who was her best friend and showed her how to become all she could be. While she slept, she had long visits with this tall man with sandy hair. She couldn't wait to fall asleep at night in hopes the man would come talk to her in her dreams.

On April 2, 1968, KRSD sponsored the Buck Owens show at the Rapid City Auditorium, and Kris, a pretty, long-legged redhead, got to be backstage among the activity. She was taking in the scene when a tall man with sandy hair walked in lugging some instruments; she recognized him immediately. "Oh my gosh!" she thought. "God sent me a bus driver to be my husband. This is cool! I'm off and running." By nature, Kris was shy, introverted, and easily embarrassed. But there was no question in her mind that she must talk with the man from her dreams. So she overcame her shyness and approached him. A friend of hers from the station saw them talking and pulled her aside. She asked if she knew who he was.

"Yes, the bus driver," she said.

"No, it is Buck Owens!"

"It is not! Haven't you looked at an album cover lately? This is most certainly not Buck, this is a bus driver."

Then she went back to speak with her bus driver friend, who evidently had overheard the exchange and was smiling at her. Kris was nervous and explained to him, "We've got album covers, and you are not Buck Owens."

The man started laughing. "You're Buck Owens?" He had an ear-to-ear smile by now and nodded in the affirmative. He was dressed in a dark blue suit and a white turtleneck. The band had just started wearing turtlenecks and in the last two weeks, Buck had had his hair restyled so it fell forward on his forehead instead of being slicked back, so he did look different from his album covers.

Kris began to back up and said, "I can't talk to you. You are famous!"

"I don't know what you call me," he answered.

After the show, Buck said to his new friend, "There's a bunch of us that are hungry. Do you know where we can eat?"

"About the only place in town is McDonald's at this hour."

So Buck and Don got in Kris's hot pink Chevrolet and the rest of the guys piled into other vehicles, and they drove to McDonald's—in a blinding snowstorm. Afterward, Buck and the band went back to the Sands where they were staying, and Kris went home to her parents.

By morning, the blizzard had crippled the city, so Kris called Buck at his hotel room. "He was raging a fit from hell, hollering at Jack," she said.

"McFadden, I can go through anything in this business, but I have got to have my breakfast," she heard Buck yell. "You know gawddamn well I've got to have my breakfast! You know I've got to have my breakfast! You booked me at a hotel that doesn't have a restaurant! What is wrong with you?"

Kris told her mother what was going on and she told her daughter, "Take the electric bike, honey, go fix him some breakfast."

"You can't do that," Buck told her. "There is a blizzard."

"Well, I can use the Cadillac and I am used to driving in the weather."

"If you are going to get breakfast, get the bacon one-eighth of an inch thick," he said.

Armed with eggs and an electric skillet, Kris stopped by a butcher shop to make sure she had bacon that was precisely one-eighth of an inch thick. Then she went to Buck's hotel room and cooked him breakfast. Afterward, they were standing outside in the snow talking to Don and Buck put his arm around Kris and he said, "Don, I am going to marry this woman."

Of course, Buck was still married to Phyllis at this time, but Kris didn't know that. "Little details," she said. "That man was never good at details." All the seventeen-year-old girl knew was that a superstar just said he was going to marry her. The way Kris was raised, a man's word was law. So when Buck said he wanted to be her husband, it wasn't hard for Kris to lapse into blind obedience.

As it happened, there was a whiteout at the airport, and all flights had been canceled. Buck and his Buckaroos had a show in Denver that night, but the weather forced them to reschedule for a later date. Because they were stuck in Rapid City, Buck asked Kris to take in a matinee with him, Don, and Kay Adams at the local theater. They were the only people in the theater, and Don had brought along a flask of booze. He told Kris to go get a Coca-Cola and they poured out part of the Coke and mixed it with the contents of Don's flask for them all to share. Don and Kay were in the front of the theater, and Buck and Kris were in the back. Being the joker he was, Don would yell out, "Look out! He is going to kiss her! Turn your head!"

Kris was having the time of her young life. It was the happiest she had ever been. Afterward, Buck told Kris he wanted to meet her family, which seemed to her to be in keeping with what he had told Don that morning: *I'm going to marry this woman.* Kris could not believe how quickly things were moving between her and Buck—they didn't call it Rapid City for nothing. So they went to her home to meet her folks, who sat on a couch with "Oh my God!" looks on their faces, rather like the dour Culhanes on *Hee Haw*. Buck told Kris and her parents that he was going to raise her to be the wife he'd always wanted. Kris was thinking, *This is a formal engagement. He has met my parents and now everything is cool.*

The next time Kris saw Buck was when he went to Denver to do the concert that had been rescheduled. She drove there to meet him and they talked about her plans for the future. Kris told him she wanted to go to school and become an actress someday. He told her about the two radio stations in Phoenix that he had recently acquired, KTUF-AM and KNIX-AM/FM. He encouraged her to think about moving to Arizona, which she eventually did. Kris's parents, like Priscilla Presley's, approved of their daughter being involved with the wealthy superstar, and her mother pushed for marriage.

Once she had settled in Phoenix, Buck continued courting Kris. "He would fly in and we would be together," she said. Even though she wanted to be in California, it was easier for Buck to keep his relationship with her secret if she were a state away. That way Phyllis and Jennifer Smith, as well as any others in his covey of women, would be less likely to find out about her. Buck advised Kris to make it appear as if their relationship was strictly business, and they had an underlying agreement that she was not to go public about their relationship. He also played psychological games with her, telling her that if she kept their agreement quiet, she'd prove to him that she could be a good wife, and people would like her on her own merits. Although many people were unaware of Buck's arrangement with Kris, Don's wife, Marlane, said they were going to be married.

Buck would fly to Phoenix every couple of weeks to visit her, under the guise of checking on his radio stations. He wanted Kris to learn to become a proper lady and enrolled her in the Patricia Stevens finishing school, the same one to which Elvis Presley had sent Priscilla (except that Priscilla attended the Memphis facility).

At one point, Buck asked her if she would like to work at KTUF. They were looking for a pretty girl to serve as station queen and drive around in a Corvette for a car-giveaway promotion. He told her he would have no say in the decision, but that the station manager, Joe Thompson, would decide who would become Miss KTUF. This made her a little nervous and confused, because she thought that Buck ran the world and that if he wanted her to do something, the decision would rest in his hands, not someone else's. That is when she discovered Buck would "strongly influence" people but would leave the final decision up to them.

So she met with Joe, and he did select her as Miss KTUF. Joe proceeded to teach her such things as how to make a quick phone call or drop a note, and how to be more efficient. She did remote broadcasts from various locations, such as a McDonald's where a randy Ronald McDonald kept hitting on her in front of the little kids.

At one point, the promotion staffers were trying to think of a way to link a boat show with country music, and it was Kris who thought of a way to tie it all together: a country cruise. After that, Joe began to think of her as more than just the pretty face of the station. He recommended to Buck that they should channel her talents in a promotional capacity.

Kris dearly loved Buck and always viewed him as her savior, who had rescued her from an unhappy home. "There were many times when Buck would show sensitivity and caring, or insight that was just really amazing," she said. "He, at some level, understood what a nightmare I was in. My parents were not really happy, and I was physically and verbally abused. He was so kind in a lot of ways, so protective in a lot of ways." This, of course, was the polar opposite of how he treated his wife.

★ 38 ★

A Run-In with Rolene

One of the last shows to which Doyle Holly remembered driving the Flex bus was at the Hollywood Bowl. It was a double bill of Buck Owens and his Buckaroos and Merle Haggard and the Strangers. The guys had been back east and had come back to California to do the show before going back out on tour—the last tour they would do on the bus. The Buckaroos had told their wives that they would be staying at a Hollywood hotel, but when they got there, they decided to go home and surprise the women in Bakersfield.

As it turned out, the women had also decided to surprise their husbands—by visiting them in Hollywood. When they arrived at the hotel dolled up in false eyelashes and fake fingernails, they found that only Buck was registered. Rolene Brumley and Marlane Ulrich went up to Buck's room and knocked on the door. When Buck came to the door, his hair was a mess. Unbeknownst to Rolene and Marlane at the time, he'd been rolling around in bed with a female admirer.

"Where are the boys at? Tom and Don?" Rolene asked.

"I don't know and I don't give a gawddamn!" roared Buck, who hated coitus interruptus.

Rolene couldn't stand someone taking the Lord's name in vain; it raised the hair on the back of her neck. "You asshole!" she shot back.

Buck was taken aback and didn't know what to say, so he just closed the door in their faces.

"You can't talk to him like that," a shocked Marlane said. "Oh, you shouldn't have said that!"

"He can't talk to me like that!" Rolene fumed. "And if he goes talkin' like that, that's the way he's gonna be talked to."

By then, Tom was back from Bakersfield and already at the Hollywood Bowl. When Buck arrived, he said, "Tom, I need to talk to you. Come back in the dressing room." When Tom went back, Buck was pacing back and forth, upset. "Tom, I don't know how to . . . I don't know what to say. Well, me and Rolene had a little misunderstanding a while ago. I don't know what to do about it."

"What is it, Buck?"

"Well, I just . . . it's a just a little thing that I don't know what to do about it." Buck hedged but finally told Tom what Rolene had called him and said he wanted an apology.

Tom kind of snickered and said, "Oh, that's a good one! When Rolene gets here, let me talk to her and see what happened, and then I'll tell you what I think."

"OK," Buck said.

Tom left the dressing room and thought that Rolene would be upset because Buck had told her husband what had happened. He knew his wife, though, and knew that she probably had the situation under control. Later, Rolene and Phyllis drove up, laughing and having a big time. In front of Phyllis, he asked Rolene what had happened, and she recounted the incident. Tom went back to Buck and said, "Well, Buck, at that particular moment you were an asshole, so if anybody apologizes to anybody, you need to apologize to Rolene, because she's certainly not going to apologize to you. You instigated it. It's about time she had her rights."

Buck never did apologize to Rolene for his abruptness and crassness, but Rolene and Tom had gotten their rakes in, and that was all that was ever said about the incident.

"He didn't really like women," Rolene said. "He didn't. He didn't like Marlane either. She thinks that he did. He didn't. See, I don't have anything to lose, 'cause I don't really care what he thinks, because he never was nice to me or the kids. He'd say hi to 'em, you know, when we'd all meet out there so they could take off in the lovely camper. He didn't really like me, you know, because of that one incident."

"I don't know if he likes women or not," Tom said. "I am sure he likes women for some reason, but you're asking me if he has any respect for women? Well, I don't know. I can't say that he's any more one way to 'em than he is some men. How would you say this? He's taken advantage of both."

39

FLYING HIGH

By the time Buck Owens retired the Flex bus in 1968, it had 190,000 miles on it. The band members continued to use the bus for personal errands until it was sold to KUZZ, one of Buck's radio stations in Bakersfield. The station crew cut a side out of it and turned it into a remote broadcast unit. In 1971, the bus would be sold to country singer David Houston, who drove it for several years.

After the bus, the band graduated to flying in 747s to and from shows. By this time, Buck owned a travel agency, so he used it to book commercial flights for the band members, who previously had flown only overseas. As always, the band members had as much fun traveling as they did onstage. Marlane Ulrich recalled Don telling her about some of the jokes the guys played on the stewardesses. Don and Jerry Wiggins liked to put Blackjack gum on their teeth so when they smiled for photographs it looked as though they were missing a few teeth. Another favorite trick of theirs was to put dog food inside an airsick bag, pretend they were throwing up, and then hand the smelly bag to the stewardess.

Buck liked to be in control at all times, and he couldn't do that on commercial carriers, because he was at the mercy of airline schedules, baggage handlers, the weather, and more. Even before he got the Flex bus, he began talking about buying his own plane and encouraged both Tom and Doyle to get multiengine flight training so he could have more than one pilot onboard at a given time. Buck paid for Doyle's rating, but Tom paid for his own. "I knew that if Buck paid for it and he didn't get a plane, I might have to pay him back," Tom said. "So I just did it. That way I'm not obligated. It's mine. I had benefits from the Army G.I. Bill of Rights that paid for that."

As time progressed, Buck began to charter private planes. He put Tom in charge of arranging the charters, despite their agreement that all Tom would have to do was play steel guitar. They chartered Learjets from Frank Sinatra, who had an aviation company that catered to celebrities such as Elvis Presley and Paul McCartney, and from Clay Lacy, who not only sold charter flights but piloted them as well. "He also was a United Airlines pilot and he raced a four-engine DC-7 in the Reno Air Races," Tom recalled. "He was a great guy and he could fly, I'll tell ya."

At least one Buckaroo had a fear of flying, and that was new drummer Jerry Wiggins. One practical joke on him wasn't enough for Tom, so once as they were leaving for El Paso, Tom went up to the cockpit and said, "Clay, get me one of those really super-straight-up climb-outs." Clay went down the runway and took off straight up to 24,000 feet in about four minutes. "Vrrroooom!" Tom remembered. "Jerry's going, 'Ohhhhh,' just petrified."

Another time, Clay was flying the band in a super-stretch DC-8 from Los Angeles to Baltimore with a stop in New Orleans. They took off out of New Orleans, and after about thirty minutes or so, one of the engines started shuddering. Tom was sitting next to Don Rich and said, "Well, we just lost an engine, Don."

"Ah, no, no," Don said.

"Yes, we did. We just lost an engine."

"What!" said Jerry, who had turned around and was peeking over the back of his seat at Tom and Don.

"We lost an engine," Tom said matter-of-factly.

"Oh! Oh! Lost an engine!" Jerry was petrified.

Pretty soon, it happened again—the plane shuddered and vibrated.

"We've lost two engines," Tom announced. He knew how to fly and knew the noises planes made, so everyone knew he was dead serious.

Except for Jerry, who didn't want to believe him. The drummer called the stewardess over and said, "What's the matter? What's going on? Tom says we lost two engines."

"No, we haven't lost any engines," she reassured him. "They just started up some kind of engine down in the compartment. It vibrated and we shut it off."

On the approach into Baltimore, they barely missed hitting a Cessna 172. They were so close that they could see the pilot in the Cessna as they zoomed past. When they started to touch down on the runway, fire trucks and emergency vehicles sped alongside the plane on the runway. The DC-8 was rolling full speed, and the landing seemed to go on forever. When they were safely on the ground, Tom asked the stewardess what had happened.

"Yeah, you were right," she said. "We lost two engines."

Clay had done an amazing job flying and landing the crippled plane, Tom said, and the ground crew had to come out and tow the plane.

After that experience, Tom said, every time something went wrong on a flight, "Don and Jerry would ask me what that was. 'What was that noise?' 'What was this?' and 'What was that?'"

Eventually, Buck did buy his own planes so he could get to major airports more easily from Bakersfield. He first bought a twin-engine Beechcraft TC Baron—"the Corvette of airplanes," Doyle said—that flew 250 miles per hour.

Initially, Bob Woods was Buck's promotion director, but Bob knew how to fly and gave flight instruction, so Buck made him his regular pilot. Tom and Doyle both served as copilots. Doyle was in the right seat more than Tom was, but if two planes flew on a trip, Doyle would copilot one and Tom the other. It also fell to Tom to arrange for any chartered planes on which the band flew—yet another example of how Tom's original deal with Buck was ignored.

Tom didn't remember much about Bob Woods but recalled an instance in which he insisted on flying through a big storm against Tom's better judgment. Doyle said that Bob used to do aerobatics in Buck's Baron; "He was crazy. If I'd known then what I know now, I never would have flown with him."

Buck also had his son Mike learn how to fly and eventually replaced Doyle with Mike as copilot, much as he had replaced Bill Mack with Mike as the *Buck Owens Ranch* emcee. "I called Mike 'Aardvark,' because an aardvark can't do nothin' right," Doyle said. "He took my job as Buck's copilot and wrecked Buck's $100,000 airplane. I bought a model of a Beechcraft Baron and messed up the nose of it. Then I painted the word 'Aardvark' on it and gave it to Mike." Evidently, the wrecked Baron didn't faze Buck, because he turned around and bought a Beechcraft Duke in March 1971, which Bob and Mike piloted.

Buck's pilot would later carve out a notorious niche for himself in Bakersfield aviation history. As the story goes, Bob, a married man, met his demise on January 31, 1975, when he and a married lover went for drinks on his thirty-ninth birthday at the airport bar before going up in a Cessna 150 for a mile-high rendezvous. The plane crashed, killing them both.

40

BUCKING TRADITION

The Buckaroos were named top instrumental group or band by the Country Music Association in 1968 for the second straight year. The CMA also honored them with the award for top touring band. Even though CMA recognition still eluded their boss, Buck Owens continued breaking new ground with his music and performing in venues that traditionally did not feature country acts.

In August 1968, Buck traded his freight-train sound for a bluesier approach when he recorded "I've Got You on My Mind Again." Ken Nelson took the tracks Buck laid down and overdubbed them in Nashville with background vocals by the Jordanaires and Anita Kerr. Regarding the style departure, Buck said, "A lot of people ask why I changed my music, you do it out of boredom and you see where radio play is not hardly as good as it was a couple of years ago, the sales are not as good, so you try something different." "I've Got You on My Mind Again" peaked at #5 after its September 30 release.

Among the nontraditional venues Buck and his Buckaroos played that year, the most significant may have been the White House. Buck always said that he and the Buckaroos performed at the White House on the eve of President Lyndon Baines Johnson's announcement on March 31, 1968, that he would not seek re-election. The president himself had told them he was not going to run again, Buck claimed. Of course, this makes for a great tale, but on the back cover of the *Buck Owens Live at the White House* LP it says that Buck played there September 9, 1968, about six months after LBJ made his announcement. (The album itself was not released until 1972.)

LBJ had at least three things in common with Buck: he was a fellow Texan, he loved country music, and he had a nickname for his penis ("Jumbo").

Buck, the band, and Dorothy Owens got the royal treatment, including a special tour of the White House. Buck's son Buddy Alan also joined his father on the trip and sang that night. Buck remembered the audience as being rather uptight until one of LBJ's daughters started "whooping and hollering" when Buck belted out Terry Fell's "Truck Driving Man." After that, "they loosened up a bit and everything was great," he said.

After the White House performance, Don became friends with the pilots of Air Force One. Every now and then, his wife would get a phone call: "Hello, Marlane, this is Air Force One. Just thought I would let you know that Don will be in at 10:45."

The band also played two shows at the Fillmore West, which was primarily a rock venue, on October 11 and 12, 1968. Although the show poster featured photographs of Don Rich, Tom Brumley, Willie Cantu, and Wayne Wilson, both Wayne and Willie were history by then. Doyle Holly played bass and Jerry Wiggins played drums at the Fillmore gigs.

Tom Brumley said the Fillmore was an experience he would never forget. The stage was on the second floor, so they had to lug all their instruments and equipment upstairs. The Fillmore staff wanted to do a light show behind them onstage, so they had to set up on the afternoon of the first show to do a sound check and synchronize the music with the lights. Otherwise, the guys wouldn't have been there until show time.

When Tom walked in, there was not a chair in place. He thought that was rather strange—no seats and everybody with long hippie hair doing a light show. When they returned to do the show that night, concertgoers were sitting on the floor smoking pot, and the building reeked of marijuana. The Buckaroos performed, but Tom could tell that Buck was nervous about all the pot smoking. Then somebody walked up to Buck and handed him something. He was talking to someone else, not paying much attention. He thought it was a request rolled up in a piece of paper, so he took it. When he looked at the rolled-up request, he said, "Don! What is it?"

"Geez, Chief, that's a joint!"

"Well, take it!" Buck said.

"I don't want it!"

"Let me have it!" Doyle said. "I'll take it! I'll take it!"

They had a good laugh over it. Later, Buck asked the cops on security detail upstairs what they did about the pot smoking and they said, "As long as they stay in here smoking, we don't do anything; they step outside, they get nabbed."

By 1968, Kay Adams could no longer take the pressure of being caught between her lover Don and a disapproving Buck. She knew Don couldn't leave Buck's show, so she did. Buck needed a new duet partner, and on Kay's recommendation, he chose Susan Raye, who had been touring with Buck since either 1964 or 1965, depending on the account. Doyle had a thing for Susan, who stood at the microphone next to his on *Buck Owens Ranch*. He confessed that he was always looking down on the shiny part of the stand so he could see up her dress. Kay, meanwhile, continued her relationship with Don.

When 1969 rolled around, Buck was still committed to shaking things up musically. On January 8, he again used the Jordanaires as dubbed-in backup singers, this time on "Tall Dark Stranger." The track, with "Sing That Kind of Song" on the flip side, was released as a single on July 21 and hit #1. The *Tall Dark Stranger* LP was released on September 29. On "Who's Gonna Mow Your Grass," he had Don Rich play a fuzztone guitar and again caught flak for not singing country music. "Who's Gonna Mow Your Grass"/"There's Gotta Be Some Changes Made" was released as a single on January 13, 1969. It, too, hit #1. In February, Buck and his Buckaroos played at the Houston Astrodome to 112,000 people over the course of three days.

After two years of construction, Buck Owens Studios in Oildale opened for business in March 1969, and Buck started recording all his songs there instead of in Hollywood at the Capitol studio. Buck and Jack also set up a new agency called Performers Management, where they put their new young talent such as Buddy Alan, Tony Booth, the Hagers, and Susan Raye. In the fall, Don Rich received a Country Music Association nomination for instrumentalist of the year but lost to a Nashville guitar legend, Chet Atkins.

Around this same time, Don and his wife, Marlane, made a big change of their own. In 1968 they bought a lot in Park Stockdale, an upper-middle-class subdivision of Bakersfield, and they moved into the house they built there the following year. Don and Marlane were close friends with many of their neighbors, including Marvin and Jeanne Mason and Jack and Diane Immel. Buckaroos Tom Brumley, Doyle Holly, and soon-to-be-added bassist Doyle Singer lived in the area as well. Marvin said that Don's was one of the better homes in the area, and that he had done some custom work, installing a soundproof room where he could play and record his music.

The Ulriches lived at the corner of Angell Street, and the Masons lived in the middle of the block. (The Masons still live in that house today, and Marlane still owns hers but rents it out.) Marvin was friends with Don for about five years. He remembered him as a devoted father who loved being involved in his sons' activities. Marvin described their subdivision as a fun, family-oriented place with a swim team, Little League baseball, and a game a week with all the dads.

Don made sure his sons, Vance and Vic, were involved in all the sports, because his parents had denied him that experience as a boy. Don himself was a complete klutz, totally lacking in coordination. He was ambidextrous, however; he did most everything with his right hand but batted and played golf with his left. "He wasn't very athletic," Marvin recalled. "He was a hell of a musician, but, hell, he was left-handed! He tried to play golf a couple of times and he got the golf cart on the wrong side and he shagged the ball right through our golf cart one time." Still, Don wanted to be involved. He loved to volunteer as a Little League umpire, even though he didn't know a lick about baseball. He'd call something behind the plate, and then ask the catcher, Marvin's son, Marc, "Was that good or bad?" He wanted Marc to signal him with a nod so he would know what to call.

Marc and his sister, Janet, were the same ages as the Ulrich boys, and Marlane and Jeanne were both Scout leaders. The families got together often, and whenever Don was home, he and Marvin would have a beer after work. In February 1973, Marvin poured some concrete around the flower beds at his house and Don came over to help; he scrawled "Big D" in the wet cement, and it is there to this day.

Don was an avid photographer who enjoyed documenting the neighborhood parties with his Nikon. Marlane said he also took his camera on every trip and would have to take it to the photography shop when he got home, because the vibrations from traveling in the airplanes caused the small screws to loosen. Don was always the life of the party and would purposely mispronounce such words as "champagne," which would become "cham-pag-nee."

Whenever the band traveled through Washington, they would stop and visit Don's folks. Don would bring back seafood from those trips. Being the jokester he was, he always made sure to get a couple of geoducks, pronounced "gooey-ducks," a sea animal that looks like a male organ, and put them on display at neighborhood get-togethers. "Don was just a fun, a fun-hearted guy," Marvin said. "He always had a smile on his face, and was game for anything."

The Owenses, too, moved into a new home in the late 1960s. In 1968, Buck and Phyllis sold their Edison ranch and bought a ranch-style showplace home at 309 Panorama Drive, overlooking the Panorama Bluffs. It was Phyllis's dream house.

But Phyllis was the type of person who would smile on the outside while hurting deeply on the inside. Her husband's statutory rape scandal still weighed on her; she had started looking old and weary. The stress and humiliation became too much to endure, and the couple separated and eventually divorced. The *Bakersfield Californian* has reported at various times that Buck and Phyllis divorced the second time in 1968, 1971, and 1972. In fact, the divorce was not finalized until May 1972, although there is also an earlier filing in Kern County dated February 1972. Doyle said Phyllis got $7 million in the divorce settlement.

The newspaper also reported that Buck lived in the Panorama Drive house until 1974, but after he and Phyllis went their separate ways he moved to a ranch he bought from oil magnate J. Paul Getty for $500,000 on Zerker Road in Bakersfield. Buck nicknamed it "Tortilla Flat," a nod to author John Steinbeck's book of the same name.

When Phyllis was dying of emphysema years later, she was also suffering from a cognitive disorder. "She kind of lost her mind, and she didn't know anybody right at the last," Rolene recalled. "Phyllis was always good to me," Jo said. "I remember Phyllis coming to my house and not knowing where she was and I took her to the hospital. Sad." According to Kris, Johnny got power of attorney over his mother. Phyllis's maternal aunt, Ona Stevens, took care of her in her final days, Rolene said. She died in a convalescent home on February 2, 1996.

41

THE SHOW MUST GO ON

Buck Owens was the consummate performer—any applause he received was always earned, never requested with a hand motion. "Buck knew how to run a crowd," Doyle Holly said. "If you have ever been to the *Grand Ole Opry*, you'll see whenever the people start to applaud there's somebody over on the side holding up an applause sign. Buck never did that one time. If you didn't deserve applause you wasn't gonna get it, but he would sit there and milk you for applause. He would never interrupt the audience while they were applauding."

He also was the prototypical performer in that he believed the old adage "The show must go on." Sure, he may have cut a show short a couple of times, but he still put on a show.

It often fell to Jim Pierce, who played piano for Buck's opening act, Wynn Stewart and the Tourists, to keep the show going through a number of obstacles, including his share of the Buckaroo's pranks. Doyle Holly was often the culprit. During sound check before the show, Jim would have less to do than the other musicians. While the rest of the Tourists tuned up and adjusted the balance, he would go eat a steak. Doyle would take this opportunity to sabotage his piano.

Jim started every show with a piano boogie as the curtain opened. One night he was on an upright piano, trying to play the opener, but the keys sagged and no sound came out of the amp. The curtain was open, fifteen thousand people were in the audience, and he was just going through the motions. He rose from the bench and opened the top of the piano to see what the problem was. Doyle had stuffed the piano full of newspapers, preventing the hammers from striking the strings. So Jim reached in and pulled out the papers. Meanwhile, the audience was in stitches—they thought it was part of the act.

Because that trick had been so effective, Doyle began pulling more. Jim thought he would be safe when the venue had a grand piano instead of an upright; he played with the lid up and would be able to see if something was amiss. Of course, he was wrong. During one concert, he was on a grand piano, and he could see that there were no newspapers between the hammers and the strings. But as the curtains opened, the keys were sagging again. Doyle had Scotch-taped all the keys together. So as the band played, Jim had to pull off the tape. In between fills and such, he would push down a key, raise another, and so forth, just trying to get his fingers in between to hold the tape and pull it out. It was a fiasco.

After that, Jim tried to get even with Doyle. On one show, before Buck came on, Jim lifted the fuse out of Doyle's amplifier. Doyle played through the opening song, but no bass could be heard. Buck was extremely upset. Jim was sitting alongside the stage, tossing the fuse up in the air and catching it in his hand. Doyle looked over at him and saw the fuse, so Jim went over and plugged it back in.

From that experience, Doyle learned to check his fuses before Buck came onstage. So another time, Jim turned down all of the keys on Doyle's bass so it was nowhere in tune. On the opening number, Doyle's playing sounded like "*kerplomp, kerplomp, buzz, buzz*," and he had to tune up as quickly as possible because Buck was giving him dirty looks.

"It's funny," Jim said. "When a show goes with no problems, it kind of becomes obscure in your memory. It's these little stupid or unusual things that happen that bring certain shows back into mind."

To Buck, not even a car accident and a head injury were valid reasons not to perform as planned.

During the winter of early 1969, his entourage was doing a series of package shows in Iowa. As usual, Wynn Stewart and the Tourists opened the show, followed by several other acts before Buck and his Buckaroos closed out the bill. They had played in one town and the next was about 150 miles south, so they decided to base in the first town and travel to the second show. Wynn was traveling with the Buckaroos, and the Tourists were in Wynn's station

Buck Owens meets the Japanese press in 1967.

Courtesy of Marlane Ulrich-Dunivent

Buck Owens's parents, Alvis Owens Sr. and Maicie Owens.

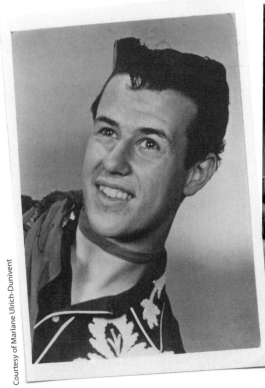

Don Rich in his midteens, around the time he met Buck Owens.

An early publicity shot of Don, wearing a suit borrowed from Buck.

Buck Owens, Kenny Pierce, Don Rich, Mel King, and Jay McDonald in front of Don's parents' house in Tumwater, Washington, in July 1963.

Marlane Ulrich, Voni Morrison, Phyllis Owens, and Jacky Owens with a float promoting the Big Fresno Barn dance hall, circa 1961. Voni got a cowriting credit on Johnny Russell's "Act Naturally," which would become Buck Owens's breakthrough #1 in 1963.

Don Rich, Buck Owens, and his ex-wife Bonnie Owens onstage in 1963. Buck is wearing the watermelon-colored Nudie suit that was stolen not long after this photo was taken.

Doyle Holly, Buck Owens, Willie Cantu, Tom Brumley, and Don Rich with the band's Winnebago, the Green Goose.

Merle Haggard and Buck Owens, 1965.

Buck examines a supersized brassiere that a fan handed to him onstage, 1965.

Buck Owens, Wanda Jackson, an unidentified fan, promoter Smokey Smith, and George Jones in Des Moines, Iowa, 1964.

Glen Campbell, Buck Owens, and unknown fans.

...uck with his old friend Loretta Lynn.

Maicie Owens, Buck Owens, Phyllis Owens, and Jack McFadden.

...om left, Ken Nelson, Buck Owens, and ...ck McFadden in the Capitol studio.

Clockwise from foreground, Tom Brumley, Doyle Holly, Bob Morris, and Buck Owens in the Capitol studio.

The publicity shot and cover photograph for the *Roll Out the Red Carpet* album, 1966.

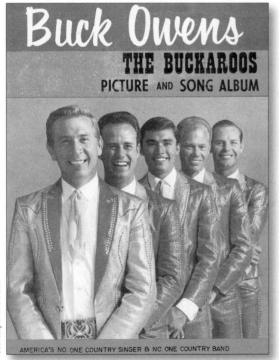

Doyle Holly, Don Rich, Tom Brumley, and Buck Owens on *KLYD's Kountry Korner*, which Dave Stogner hosted.

The cover of the band's picture and song album, a book from the mid-1960s.

Don Rich (top), Doyle Holly (center), and Tom Brumley (bottom), in Ray-Bans that were given to the band.

On the tour of Japan, 1967. In the second row, from left, Buck Owens and Don Rich; behind them, Jack McFadden and Wayne Wilson. Tom Brumley is at far right in the window seat.

Wayne Wilson, Don Rich, Buck Owens, Willie Cantu, and Tom Brumley meet the Japanese press in 1967.

Lady Bird Johnson, Billy Deaton, Dorothy Owens, Don Rich, President Lyndon Baines Johnson, and Tom Brumley in 1968.

From left, Jerry Wiggins, Tom Brumley, Don Rich, Doyle Holly, Jack McFadden, and Buck Owens get a tour of the White House from LBJ's secretary.

Courtesy of Marlene Ulrich-Dunivent

Buck Owens playfully points a shotgun at Don Rich.

Author's collection

From left, Doyle Holly, Don Rich, Buck Owens, Willie Cantu, and Tom Brumley at a show sponsored by Buck's Phoenix radio station KTUF.

Don Rich snapped this photo of Bob Woods (left) and Doyle Holly in the cockpit of Buck's private plane. Buck Owens is seated at right in the foreground.

On the *Hee Haw* set, Jim Shaw, Doyle Singer, Buck Owens, Don Rich, Ronnie Jackson, and Jerry Brightman. The instrumental tracks for the show were prerecorded, so the band is "air-strumming."

Marlane Ulrich, left, and Jennifer Smith, on tour with Buck and his Buckaroos.

Hi!! I'm Kris Black and I'll be your All-American Oriental tour guide —

BUCK OWENS
MADE IN JAPAN

Kris Black in the promotional photo for "Made in Japan," 1972.

Don Rich does his best *Easy Rider* pose as he takes his wife Marlane for a spin on his 1971 Harley-Davidson Sportster.

THREE POSSIBLE ROUTES FOR DON RICH'S LAST JOURNEY

Possible routes

San Simeon
Cambria ❹
Cholame ❸
⑤ McFarland ㉕
CALIFORNIA
❺
㊻
Morro Bay ❻ ㊽
San Luis Obispo
❷
❶
San Francisco
DETAIL
㉝
Bakersfield
⑨⑨ ㊽
Los Angeles
①
⑯⑥ Taft
Maricopa
Pacific
Ocean

❶ Buck Owens's recording studio.

❷ Buck Owens's ranch.

❸ The most direct route to Cambria.

❹ Don Rich's destination.

❺ Site of motorcycle accident.

❻ Don Rich pronounced dead at Sierra Vista Hospital, San Luis Obispo.

Pallbearers carry Don Rich's casket to its final resting spot in 1974.

Buck Owens'
CRYSTAL PALACE
MUSEUM AND THEATER

Artist's rendering of the honky-tonk that Buck built, the Crystal Palace.

wagon. Jim Pierce was driving when the car developed mechanical problems; he was able to get the car to limp into a dealership. Because the Tourists were the opening act, Jim left the car to be repaired and rented another so they could make the date on time.

After the show, they headed back to their hotel in the first town. It was about two or three in the morning when it started to snow. Larry Wellborn, Wynn's guitarist, was driving the rental car. He had never seen snow, let alone driven in it. Jim had fallen asleep in the front passenger side and in the back seat were bass player Hap Arnold and a couple of other musicians. Larry was driving down a small hill as a semi truck was coming up the other side. He panicked and slammed on the brakes. The car went into a skid and hit the truck head-on.

Just before the accident, Larry hollered, "Look out!" Jim opened his eyes in time for the collision. The truck driver had seen the car coming, so he braked and was able to slow down a bit, but "we hit that sucker and it was a weird experience," Jim said. "It was like everything was going in circles and like being in a very strong, scary earthquake." Back then, cars weren't equipped with seat belts, and the guys in the back seat slammed against the front seat and were bruised. Larry wasn't hurt, but Jim hit the rearview mirror and the windshield. "I was able to open the passenger-side door and I sat there for a minute dazed," he said. "I'm thinking, 'Boy, it's been quite an accident. I am getting snow all over me,' and I go to wipe my hand and there's blood all over my shirt. I knew I didn't feel it, but I knew that I was bloody. Then I was afraid to put my hand up; I didn't know what I was going to reach. I started getting a little woozy."

A family in a farmhouse several hundred feet off the road heard the collision and came to their aid. The couple's daughter, who was a registered nurse, happened to be staying there that night. They saw what bad shape Jim was in and got him into the farmhouse, laid him on the floor, and gave him cold compresses until an ambulance came and took him to the University of Iowa Hospital for surgery. Jim forgets how long he was in surgery, but he had more than twenty stitches along his hairline. Basically, he had been scalped, which was why he was bleeding so profusely. After the surgery, he was moved to the recovery room; when he came to, he had no idea where he was. His head was bandaged, and he was in bad shape. His right leg had been hurt in the wreck, too. (The hospital went after him for all the medical costs, which he wasn't fully aware of until they sent him a bill later. Larry was uninsured, so Jim had nobody to sue.)

About twelve hours later, an Iowa state trooper showed up at the hospital to check Jim out and take him back to the hotel. "It shows what impact Buck Owens had when he was playing in places," Jim said. "Who could say to a state trooper, 'I want you to pick up a musician?'" Back at the hotel, Jim felt awful. He had taken pain pills but his head was still throbbing. He was in no shape for anything. Word came through Jack McFadden that Buck said he had to perform another show that night. Jim sent word back: "I'm in no shape to play." Word came back from Buck: "You're going to play anyway."

Smokey Smith, the promoter of that particular show, went onstage and announced, "You've heard about how the show must go on? We're going to show you the loyalty of the people that work with Buck Owens. Jim insisted, regardless of the unfortunate accident that he had early this morning, that he had to go onstage and play piano for you folks."

The curtains opened and Jim was sitting at the piano bandaged and dazed, trying to play. He barely remembered the show and didn't think he played well because mentally he was souped on pain pills, and physically he hurt. Buck and the promoter had made such an issue about how the show must go on because of Jim's loyalty, but "it was a bunch of bull!" he later insisted. "That was not the case. I have never forgotten that, and I still think that was sort of an unreasonable request."

That winter tour turned out to be so grueling that Wynn's band members split up and the Tourists had to re-form with almost all new personnel. Jim stayed a while longer, but left in May 1969.

★ 42 ★

JAY DEE

By early 1969, Tom Brumley sensed that Buck Owens's star had peaked, that his career was starting to slow—and that money had become his be-all and end-all. "I told Buck he needed help," the steel player said. "That if money was causing problems for him to get rid of it. I was sick of it all." So Tom left the Buckaroos. "I got off the boat when I saw the first leak. Some boats sink faster than others and you don't know how fast it's gonna go. I overstayed anyway."

Tom said Buck tried to get him to sign an exit contract when he left, but he refused. Once he was gone, however, Buck kept calling him wanting to talk about the contract.

"I'll sue you for $50,000," Buck told him.

"What for?"

"For ruining my sound."

"Buck, the first thing is, you wouldn't admit that I had anything to do with your sound in public," Tom said. "I mean, you know I did, but you wouldn't admit that, so that don't scare me. Besides that, if you sued me for $50,000, I'd sue you for $250,000. And there's gonna be a lot of people hurt if you do this and a lot of stuff's gonna come out."

At the time, Tom had some heavy-hitting managers behind him who were prepared to battle Buck in court. Tom was right; it could have gotten very ugly for Buck if he had opted to sue. Instead, Buck backed off. Tom never signed an exit contract and Buck never sued him.

"He could have kept us together so easy, by keeping us happy, which would have been so easy to do," Tom said. "He screwed us all."

Buck hired Jay Dee Maness to replace Tom on steel guitar. Jay Dee was twenty-four years old, just a "green kid." He doesn't recall whether he had to sign a contract, but he does remember Buck telling him, "If you're going to record with the Buckaroos, you've got to be a member of BMI. So we have to get you signed up." That was to Jay Dee's benefit, of course, but also Buck's, because "he wound up with all the publishing on anything anybody wrote," Jay Dee said. He was paid $125 a week and never knew what the other guys made. "Buck had a way of only letting you earn as much money as he wanted you to earn," he recalled.

After years of being stiffed by ne'er-do-well club owners and promoters, Buck had learned to insist on being paid part of his fee upfront in cash and the rest when the job was finished. Cash also gave him an advantage come tax time because "he had plenty of ways to hide it," Jay Dee said. "He figured that out early."

Sometimes Buck would figure ways to get more money for less, which meant sometimes the fans got burned. Jay Dee recalled one show they played after a race on a small dirt track in the Midwest. It was really cold that evening, the wind was blowing, and not many people were there. Buck had gotten his upfront money, and before they'd even finished their performance, he sent Jack to get the remainder. "When you get the money," he told Jack, "you nod to me, we're outta here." The band hadn't played a half-hour when Jack nodded and Buck ended the show. "It's too cold, too uncomfortable, we're outta here," Buck said.

Jay Dee also recalled that Jack McFadden came up to him once in an airport and said, "Hey, I want you to carry this bag through for us. We've got so much stuff, take this bag and carry it on through. Everybody's gotta take a turn at this, 'cause we've gotta carry this bag."

"Ah, well, OK," Jay Dee said.

It was a good-sized duffel bag with a broken handle, so it had to be carried under an arm and on a hip. As it happened, the duffel was filled with cash; when Buck would get to the next big town, he would bank the money. "That was real normal," Jay Dee said, though he doesn't recall seeing anybody else carry the duffel, because he never paid attention to it until he had to lug it.

Jay Dee also used to warehouse all the Buckaroos' Telecasters for free after the band got in off a tour. He'd pack them in his Firebird Pontiac at Los Angeles International Airport and take them home, where he would keep them until the band left on the next tour. There wasn't room for the instruments on the smaller plane that flew back to Bakersfield. Jay Dee figured it was just another part of his job description.

Late in 1969, Jay Dee experienced the wrath of Buck. They were at a baggage carousel in an airport somewhere in the Midwest waiting on their bags. Buck walked up to Jay Dee with fire in his eyes and his lip aquiver. "Let me tell you something, you tell your wife to stay off of the fucking phone!" he yelled. "I hired you, I didn't hire her!"

Jay Dee was taken aback. The reason Buck was dressing him down in public was because Jay Dee's wife had called Dorothy Owens to get her husband's paycheck, which was always late. "Dorothy, we're starving to death out here. Can we get the money?" his wife pleaded. They were living in a rental house in Van Nuys, California, and had an infant son. As it was, they were living hand-to-mouth and $125 didn't stretch too far. They needed the money when it was due, not later. A couple of times his wife even had to drive from Van Nuys to Bakersfield to get the check just so they could pay their bills on time.

"I just thought it was another way for him to control me," Jay Dee said. He never suspected that either Dorothy or Buck might be holding onto the money longer than necessary to extract all the interest they could from it. In any case, "I knew when that happened that my time was limited—either by him or by me."

A couple of years after leaving Buck, Tom Brumley joined the Stone Canyon Band with Rick Nelson, who, unlike Buck, was a generous and considerate boss. Tom stayed with Rick for ten years. Tom also went on to manufacture steel guitars and play with many other performers, including the Desert Rose Band, Merle Haggard, Chris Isaak, Waylon Jennings, Rose Maddox, Rod

Stewart, and Dwight Yoakam. For many years, he had his own show in Branson, Missouri, before buying into a UPS Store there. Later, he moved back to Texas. In addition, he was inducted into in the Texas Steel Guitar Hall of Fame and the International Steel Guitar Hall of Fame.

Despite everything, Tom was glad he had hung in as a Buckaroo and had been part of the band during its heyday. "I just have some really good memories of Buck being really super-nice in a lot of ways," he said. "I hear people say what he did to them and everything, but I could say he never did it to me."

43

HEE HAW

Both the big and the small screens beckoned Buck Owens in 1969. He starred in his second film, an eighty-seven-minute musical with a thin plotline about a husband and wife who are given tickets to the *Grand Ole Opry* by singer Marty Robbins. *From Nashville with Music* featured an unlikely all-star Bakersfield cast, including Buddy Alan and Eddie Fukano, onstage at the *Opry*. Only Hollywood would have thought to depict West Coast artists onstage in Music City. Also that year, producers of *Hee Haw*, an hourlong country comedy-variety television program, asked Buck to become one of the homespun cohosts of the new show.

The weekly national television exposure of *Hee Haw* would forever change the public's perception of Buck Owens. To the television viewers of the era, and those of later generations, Buck would no longer be known as the number one country artist of the 1960s; he would be seen instead as a silly bumpkin in backward overalls. Many people feel the show eroded Buck's standing as a stellar musician and pioneering artist and contributed to the demise of his music career. "People were oblivious to country music and how it was done and why it was done and so on and so forth, and my contention always was if left alone, country music is a rather prestigious product and will stand on its own," said Buck's contemporary, Jimmy Dean. "You don't have to gussy it up, you don't have to corn it down, just let it be what it will be." However, the "corning down" of country music is exactly what happened with the advent of *Hee Haw*.

Hee Haw got its start with another CBS comedy show of the 1960s, *The Jonathan Winters Show*. Sam Lovullo, who would go on to produce *Hee Haw*, was an associate producer, and two Canadians, John Aylesworth and Frank Peppiatt, were writers. Although Winters was funny, his humor was quirky and did not appeal to folks in the South, where ratings were abysmal. By its third season, the network sought to widen the show's appeal by booking six country acts as guests: Roy Clark, Jimmy Dean, Dale Evans, Buck Owens, Minnie Pearl, and Roy Rogers. The producers found that each time a country act was booked, the ratings spiked. It wasn't enough to save the flagging show, though, and by season's end it was canceled. Still, CBS was having some success with *The Glen Campbell Goodtime Hour*, a 1968 summer replacement for *The Smothers Brothers Comedy Hour*.

The Smothers Brothers Comedy Hour experienced ratings trouble when Tommy Smothers voiced his political opinions on air, and after several warnings to Tommy to stay off his bully pulpit, CBS killed the show in 1969. As its summer replacement, the network produced a one-hour special called *Hee Haw*, based on a concept John and Frank had devised for a country version of *Laugh-In*, the popular NBC comedy show that featured one-liners, running gags, and skits throughout. Like the show's creators, Gordie Tapp was Canadian. Gordie and Archie Campbell wrote the first *Hee Haw* show, along with George Yanok and Jack Burns. They got the green light to tape the special the first week of May 1969, and the show was scheduled to air in the middle of June. That meant they had a little more than a month to put together the show.

Hee Haw was created with a Southern audience in mind, with a passel of rural characters. It would be a fast-paced show that mixed corny jokes and country music with a shot of country wisdom. The producers approached Buck to host, and shortly thereafter they offered Roy Clark the job of cohost. Roy was hired for his comedic abilities and Buck for his musical abilities, even though both were excellent musicians and both were funny. Buck, with his engaging personality and exaggerated facial expressions, fit well on the small screen.

The first episode aired on June 15, 1969. It featured Roy on the banjo and Buck on his red, white, and blue acoustic guitar picking out a musical intro as they introduced themselves: "I'm Buck and I'm Roy, let's go, right now!" One-liners such as "There's more corn around here than in the whole state of Kansas" were plentiful. Gordie Tapp and Archie Campbell, dressed as farmers, sang "Pfft You Was Gone," the verses of which were interspersed throughout the show. The Culhanes, a small-town country family who sat on a sofa like birds on a wire, also had running spots throughout the show, discussing such things as astrology and a "Playcow of the Month" calendar that Hugh Heifer had sent Grandpa Jones. Don Harron, as the KORN Radio announcer, gave farm and weather reports and told of a chicken that had laid the same egg five times while being blown backward by a big wind. A Mark Twain character dispensed such wisdoms as "You can lead a horse to water, but nothing smells worse than a wet horse."

Buck and his Buckaroos, dressed in cheesy yellow ochre and brown plaid coats, sang "Johnny B. Goode" and "Who's Gonna Mow Your Grass." The latter was accompanied by a video of various overall-clad farmers, including a midget, running around frantically with push mowers. Loretta Lynn was on the first show singing "Your Squaw Is on the Warpath." Another friend of Buck's, Charley Pride, sang "I Can't Help It (If I'm Still in Love With You)" and "Kaw-Liga." Roy Clark grimaced and sang "Sally Was a Good Old Girl" while a chorus line of scantily clad animated sows danced in front of him a la the Rockettes. Minnie Pearl, the show's special guest star, held court on a front porch delivering a monologue to the enraptured cast.

Sometime after the pilot was produced, Buck hired Doyle Curtsinger to play bass, on Doyle Holly's recommendation, while the latter switched to playing electric rhythm guitar. For stage purposes, Buck shortened the name of his new bassist to "Doyle Singer."

Hee Haw was added to the permanent CBS lineup on December 17, 1969, and fifty-one episodes were produced through February 23, 1971. When CBS canceled the show in 1971, it moved into syndication, where it thrived. Five hundred thirty-four episodes were produced between September 8, 1971, and May 30, 1992. Doyle Holly said, "The day *Hee Haw* went into syndication it went into 112 or 122 markets better than when it was with the network." It is said to be the longest-running show in television and is now in reruns on the RFD-TV network. In all, 585 shows were taped in Nashville, first at the CBS affiliate studios at what was then WLAC-TV and later at the Opryland Complex–Studio A.

Buck admittedly did the show for the money: $400,000 a season, or $20,000 a day for the twenty days he worked on the show each year. His cohost was paid the same. In other words, Buck and Roy made in one day what the Buckaroos would have grossed had they played all fifty-one episodes of the show at union scale, which at the time was a little more than $400 per episode. Even Sam Lovullo, the show's producer, made only $500 a week, or $26,000 a year.

"These armchair critics that say that Buck Owens sold out when he went on *Hee Haw*—fuck them," Jon Hager said. "They're just jealous they weren't on *Hee Haw*. Buck was the perfect match. Roy Clark was the perfect match. And with those two, and that talent, it was wonderful." Jim said, "Buck didn't need the money. He already had $37 million." Jon said Buck deserved whatever money he got for doing the show because "Buck never showed up late, never showed up fucked up, on the set of *Hee Haw*."

Initially, Don Rich was the show's music director, and he and the Buckaroos were the house band. While in Nashville for the two weeks it took for them to tape the show, the band stayed at various hotels, including the old King of the Road, a Ramada Inn, a Holiday Inn, the Millennium Maxwell House Nashville, and a Howard Johnson's. The cast got price breaks on rooms at most of the hotels and free rooms at Maxwell House and Howard Johnson's; the show had trade agreements with the latter two hotels and mentioned them in the credits. Jay Dee Maness recalled that when they were staying at the Holiday Inn, where they only got a price break, Buck deducted the cost from their weekly paychecks. In the early 1980s, after Gaylord Entertainment Company took over the syndication of the show, Sam Lovullo said, Buck would be the only one on the cast who got to stay at the opulent Gaylord Opryland Resort & Convention Center, which the company also owned.

On the Saturday and Sunday between the two weeks of production, Buck and his Buckaroos played gigs. Although they were making union scale for their *Hee Haw* appearances, the Buckaroos didn't make any money for the weekend bookings. "That was Buck's way," Jay Dee said. "He had all kinds of ways of just controlling everything you did as long as you worked for him. He didn't allow us to do any other outside sessions for any other artists. Demos or not. He said, 'You're mine. You work for me and when you record, it's gonna be for me or my artists.' So that was another sore spot with me and Buck. You know, it just kind of went on from there."

"Buck was crucial to *Hee Haw*'s original chemistry," producer Sam Lovullo wrote in his book *Life in the Kornfield: My 25 Years with Hee Haw*, "so much so that we even brought aboard his personal manager Jack McFadden as talent coordinator." Sam had first met Jack on the set of *The Jonathan Winters Show*, on which Buck had appeared as a guest. The producer said that Buck and Jack brought in just the right people to appear on the show but was quick to point out that he had final say on all the acts booked: "No one, let me repeat that, no one—neither Buck nor Roy—no one had control over Sam Lovullo." In fact, Sam felt that both Buck's and Roy's agencies directly benefited from their association with him and the show, because it helped them to attract better artists to their respective folds.

Still, with Jack in charge of lining up talent, Buck was able to pocket even more money, because many of the guests were artists signed to his management and booking agencies, including the Hagers, Lulu Roman, and Sheb Wooley. Sheb not only played Ben Colder, the resident drunk, but also created the show's theme song, which turned out to be a lucrative deal—and Buck quite likely got 50 percent of that take as well.

Sam, who majored in business administration at UCLA and worked in business affairs at CBS before moving over to programming, gave Buck high marks for being "one of the shrewdest, smartest businessmen in the world."

Hee Haw's guests were a Who's Who of country music, and over the course of the show, every major country artist appeared on the show. Buck's old friend from Washington State, Loretta Lynn, appeared fifty-one times. The show's eclectic cast changed over the years, but viewer favorites included Sheb Wooley, Lulu Roman, and the Hagers, as well as Grandpa Jones, Minnie Pearl, Junior Samples, Archie Campbell, Gordie Tapp, George "Goober" Lindsey, Stringbean, Kingfish, the Wonder Dog, and of course, the Hee Haw Honeys.

Among the Honeys were such starlets as Gunilla Hutton, Jeanine Riley, Lisa Todd, Barbi Benton, Victoria Hallman, Elvis Presley's former flame Linda Thompson, and Misty Rowe. Sam singled out Misty as "brilliant" and a "very smart, shrewd negotiator." He also recalled that at one time or another Buck wanted to cast both Susan Raye and Jana Jae as Hee Haw Honeys, but Sam balked because he felt the Honeys needed to exude a sexier persona; like banjo picker Roni Stoneman, Susan and Jana projected a more wholesome image to him. Of course, Buck had a thing for both women, which is why he pictured them as Honeys. In addition, Buck was romantically linked to at least three of the regular Honeys, although he never allowed his playboy side to surface on the set. When he was at work, it was all work; the playing came after the work was done.

Aside from lining up guests for the show, Buck's second-biggest contribution was when he put his overalls on backward. It was a form of protest against having to wear them. He said he had never in his life worn overalls (though that doesn't exactly fit with his claim that he had to work the fields as a boy), and he had an aversion to the dirt-farmer image that overalls portrayed. His small act of defiance backfired, though, and ever after, he had to wear backward overalls on the show.

Silly jokes and one-liners were peppered throughout the show and were told in every possible setting: the Kornfield, a barbershop, a barnyard, a classroom, a general store, a front porch, and so on. When a joke was told standing next to the fence, a board would pop out and slap the joker on the fanny. A typical gag is this exchange between Grandpa Jones and Junior Samples:

GRANDPA JONES: "How come I seen you eating with a knife at supper?"
JUNIOR SAMPLES: "My fork leaked."

And this one in which Minnie Pearl plays a teacher and Roy Clark plays a student licking a giant lollipop:

MINNIE: "Who makes the sun shine?"
ROY: "The good Lord does."

MINNIE: "Who makes the moon shine?"
ROY: "My daddy does."

In between joke and song segments, producers broadcast animated spots of donkeys and cows telling one-liners and short videos, including one with Superman bursting out of an outhouse. All said, the show was a mindless romp, the kind of escapism that viewers loved.

Behind the scenes, however, things were not so carefree. Buck and Roy came across on television as buddies, but there was friction on the set. Sam Lovullo may be in line for sainthood for juggling egos and seamlessly producing the show. The first and biggest hurdle Sam had to deal with was which cohost would get top billing. Roy had it in his contract that he was entitled to the top spot, whereas Jack and Buck had failed to address that issue in Buck's contract. Still, Buck threatened to pull out of the show if his name wasn't mentioned first. Sam resolved the issue by giving Buck top billing the first season then rotating the billing in each subsequent season. Two openings had to be shot and alternated in the post-production phase. It was costly and a "technical pain in the ass," Sam said, but it had to be done to keep the peace. Eventually, the issue was resolved for good when Roy went to Sam and told him he thought it sounded better as "Buck Owens and Roy Clark."

Both Buck and Roy wanted assurance that neither one was earning more than the other. Buck was also determined that Roy not get more time onscreen; he actually had Jack watch the shows with a stopwatch to make sure. And Buck got jealous because Roy delivered all the punch lines while he was stuck playing the straight man. He told Sam, "If I can't be part of the joke, why don't you use someone else?"

To keep tension on the set to a minimum, Sam kept the two men as far away from each other as possible. Buck was scheduled to come in early in the production cycle, when he'd perform enough songs for all thirteen shows. Roy would join Buck later to tape the "Pickin' and Grinnin'" segments and the closing numbers. Buck was then free to either return to Bakersfield or go out on tour while Roy wrapped up the comedy segments.

Of the friction that remained, most of it stemmed from Buck's high and mighty attitude. Once, Buck lit into Jay Dee Maness about something he didn't like in front of other people. Jay Dee was new to the band and didn't know what to make of it, but he was embarrassed as all get-out. One well-known Nashville steel player, who later became one of Jay Dee's idols, came through the door and saw Buck berating the twenty-four-year-old. About five minutes later, the older steel player passed Jay Dee a note that said: "You tell that sonofabitch to go fuck himself." Jay Dee still has the note.

Another time, according to Roy, "Buck was onstage and got all over Sam Lovullo, an absolute sweetheart of a guy." They were finishing taping, and Buck had reservations for a flight back to Bakersfield. The producers discovered they were missing a camera shot, so the cast was forced to wait until it was done. Buck called Sam out of the control room and yelled, "How dare you keep me waiting here!" Roy had become friendly with Sam at this point and wanted to throttle Buck and shake some sense into him, but he restrained himself.

Once, according to a story Jack McFadden told latter-day Buckaroo Ronnie Jackson, the conflict between the two hosts nearly led Roy to quit the show. Buck wanted to bring banjoist Buck Trent onto the show, but Sam was complaining that he already had too many banjo players: Ronnie Jackson, Roni Stoneman, Bobby Thompson—and Roy Clark. Roy threatened to leave if Buck added another banjoist to the lineup. (Perhaps confirming what Jack was saying, Ronnie had noticed that Roy wouldn't speak to him in the dressing room anymore.) Roy finally got fed up and tendered his resignation. Jack had his assistant, Lee Ann Enns, call around and poll station managers on whether they would buy the show if Roy left. Not a single one said they would. It was clear to everyone involved in the production of the show that Roy was more popular with the stations than his cohost. Buck knew then he didn't have that much pull.

Despite the on-set conflicts, Buck's former cohost never forgot Buck's contribution to music. "His music came natural to him," Roy said. "He was a session guitar player. A lot of people don't remember that he played guitar on a lot of records. He could come up with different sounding little things that were good. He must have been creative. I wasn't there, so I would just imagine that it would be Buck that just came up with these things and he just had a very unique voice. I remember when he was the hottest thing going."

Roy stopped short of saying he was friends with Buck. In his autobiography *My Life—In Spite of Myself*, he wrote, "He wasn't a laid-back country boy I felt comfortable being around. He was, and still is, very opinionated, very set in his way, very dollar-conscious. If he doesn't have the first dollar he ever made, he knows where it's at. What can I say? Buck is just a strange guy." However, Buck was known to visit Roy on his boat in Fort Lauderdale, Florida. It was docked next to the houseboat on which a girl named Sandy Fox lived. Sandy was an aspiring artist, and at seventeen she hung out on Roy's deck pickin' and grinnin' with him, while Buck was down below with a woman rockin' and rollin'.

44

DRUGS OF CHOICE

Hee Haw costar Roni Stoneman wrote in her autobiography, "Buck always seemed to me like a businessman. He was 100 percent professional. I never saw him drunk, or pilled or cocained up. He wasn't that kind of guy."

Jay Dee Maness agreed. "I know Buck didn't do drugs and I only saw him drink one time," he said. It was March 9, 1969, and they were in London on the way to the Palladium to do the *Buck Owens in London* live album. Buck and his Buckaroos were riding in a limousine to the venue and were drinking. Buck and Don were sitting next to each other and Buck looked at Jay Dee and said, "Gimme that bottle!" Jay Dee handed him the bottle of whiskey, which Buck chugalugged. "*Glug-glug-glug-glug-glug-glug-glug*. That much," Jay Dee said. Buck handed back the bottle. The steel player figured Buck was just nervous about doing the show. "I never, ever saw him drink any other time," he said.

"We all liked to drink," Jay Dee said, "but it was never out of hand, it was purely recreational." Don even taught him how to drink boilermakers—that's beer and whiskey—in the morning.

"Here, try this!" Don said.

Who was Jay Dee to say no?

The *Buck Owens in London* LP was released June 2. A month earlier, on May 5, Capitol had released a song from the London performance, Chuck Berry's "Johnny B. Goode," as a single, with "Maybe If I Close My Eyes (It'll Go Away)" on the flip side. "Johnny B. Goode" shot to #1, though some fans criticized him, saying it was far from a country song. "If 'Johnny B. Goode' ain't a country rock song, what is it?" Buck asked.

Though Buck generally abstained from drugs, the same couldn't be said for some of the *Hee Haw* cast. Jim and Jon Hager, who joined Buck's show in 1969, said that Buck was lenient enough to allow them to smoke pot, and wasn't so naive as to think Don Rich didn't either.

The Hagers were high-energy young men who were always yammering and bickering with one another. It was a constant back and forth. They recalled Buck summoning them to his room one time to talk about the continual friction. "You guys can go ahead and smoke that grass, or whatever you call it," Buck told them. "I don't know. Maybe you need to smoke more of it, or something. You know, so you can be more lethargic."

Doyle Holly recalled that once, after they got settled in their rooms after a show, Buck was looking for Don. Buck called Doyle, and said, "Hey, Doyle, have you seen Don?"

"No, I haven't, Chief."

"Check the Hagers' room."

They all had a big laugh over that, because they knew Buck wasn't blind to what was going on behind his back. Buck, of course, didn't need pot to calm him. Women were his panacea.

Jim told of how one time in Las Vegas, they went knocking on the door to Buck's room when he had a woman inside because they wanted a salary advance to buy pot. An annoyed Buck answered the door and told them, "If this is what you want, I'll buy it!" Jim said he never did, though. He just told them that so they would leave him alone.

Jon Hager recalled yet another incident in July 1969, when they were doing the live album *Big in Vegas*. (Buck recorded the *single* "Big in Vegas" on August 19, 1969, at his recording studio in Oildale. It was released October 20, with "White Satin Bed" on the flip side, and peaked at #5.) Buck was in his dressing room at the Bonanza in Las Vegas, which had speakers so artists could be aware of what was happening onstage and hear their stage calls, but Buck was oblivious because he was busy entertaining yet another female— or "having his knob polished," as the Hagers put it.

The twins ran down to Buck's dressing room, which was next door to theirs, to tell him it was almost curtain time. They knocked on the door and said,

"Hey, Geese, this is the last song, get ready." Buck opened the door, and there he was in all his glory, or as Jon said, "There was the whole Owens Empire."

"The Owens Empire," Jim echoed.

"And Buck had the biggest grin on his face, you know," Jim said. "It was like, 'Yes, boys, that's what you get for being Buck Owens.'"

The Hagers recalled that at times Buck gave them prescription drugs for their own recreational use. In addition, a Nashville physician named Dr. Landon B. Snapp II prescribed medications on demand to Buck's entourage. Whenever they were in town to do *Hee Haw*, they would visit Dr. Snapp and get "speckled birds," the prescription diet pill phentermine. Jim Hager, who weighed all of 158 pounds, said Dr. Snapp would prescribe him the drug for weight loss. Don used the same excuse: "I need to lose weight." Jon Hager remembered that he and Don would go visit Dr. Snapp together, and "Don always got his prescription filled."

Buck wasn't always tolerant of his musicians' drug use, though. In 1971, *Hee Haw* regular Lulu Roman was busted for having dangerous drugs, the first of two such busts. One of the sponsors wanted her off the show, so Buck practiced tough love with her and said to the producers, "Get her off! Get her off!" So she was fired. It forced her to clean up her act, and she was eased back into the show the following year.

45

JO MCFADDEN

Soon after Jack McFadden began working as talent coordinator for the yet-unaired *Hee Haw*, he met his second wife, Virginia Jo Williams. (Jack and his first wife Peggy, whom some called a "spitfire," had divorced in 1967.) The petite brunette was a single mother who had recently moved from Tabor City, North Carolina, to Tennessee. She was working at WLAC-TV in Nashville when she bumped into Jack in the hall. As she was leaving the studio, he was heading in, talking to someone, looking the other way. Someone said something to Jo and she turned, then Jack and Jo crashed into each other. They both had their arms loaded with paperwork, which scattered everywhere. Of course, Jack had noticed the pretty young woman before, but until then she hadn't really noticed him. She figured he was attracted to her because she didn't look twice at him and only said "hello" now and then. "I wasn't out trying to get attention," she said. "I wasn't aware that he was watching me or anything, but I have been told over the years, time after time again, that I was probably the only woman in the world that he ever trusted."

Jack and Jo got married at the Bonanza in Las Vegas on July 20, 1969, while Buck Owens and his Buckaroos were in town recording *Big in Vegas*. Jo said they planned their nuptials so they would coincide with the taping of the album and fall after the premiere of *Hee Haw*. A Baptist minister officiated, Lee Greenwood played the organ, and Freddie Hart sang. Buck was Jack's best man. Among those in attendance were the couple's four children (Jack's three with Peggy and Jo's daughter, Ginger), longtime friend Larry Adamson, Phyllis Owens, Doyle Holly, Don Rich, Jerry Wiggins, Susan Raye, Jim and Jon Hager, and Charley and Rosine Pride. Other guests included people from Capitol, the amusement business, Nashville, and Washington. It was overwhelming to Jo, because she was a quiet person, while Jack was the more-the-merrier type.

They were so unlike each other in many ways. Jo was not a fan of Buck and Dorothy Owens, while Jack would never say a negative word about them. Shortly after they wed, Jack said to her, "Is there anything in your past that I need to know about?"

"Like what?" Jo asked. "Anything you want to know, I'll tell you. I don't have any deep, dark secrets, any great big confessions to make. I haven't done anything that's really terrible or anything like that."

"Well, it's not so much me, but if there's anything that is a secret in your life, Dorothy will find out about it and she'll use it against you," Jack said.

That was exactly what Jo did not need to hear. Whereas Jack might roll over and play dead about something like this, it set Jo afire. She had a short fuse back then, especially when it came to the Owenses nosing around in her personal life. Oh, she was mad.

"Jack, my life is mine!" she said. "I've not done anything that I wished I hadn't done. I don't think that I've done anything that I couldn't hold my head up about. No."

"Well, if there is, Dorothy will find out about it and she will use it."

"Jack, if Dorothy ever comes to you with any story, I'll know about it," Jo said, because she knew her husband would not have been able to keep it a secret from her. "If she starts asking you, 'Did you know this or did you know that,' you tell her to make an appointment with me and anything she wants to know, I'll tell her, but she can stay out of my damn private life! I don't have anything to do with that office, and she has nothing to do with my private life. If I find out she has found anything in my life that she wants to try to hold over your head, I'll certainly have a problem with that and I'll go tell her about it."

Dorothy was always very nice to Jo, though, because that was still how she operated—she'd smile at someone's face then stab him or her in the back. Fortunately, Jo and Dorothy had little contact; Jo made sure to keep a distance so she would not be open either to criticism or to investigation. As Jo said, "That office was like a hotbed of disease and I wanted no part of it!"

"Jack, I'm going to stay out of your business and out of your life as far as the office goes," she told her husband. "I am going to be a little house frau. I am going to do my own thing, you do your own thing, and whenever we're at the home, we're doing our thing together. This way, it won't be 'Jo said this' or 'Jo did that.'" Jo never visited Jack's office five times during the whole time she lived in Bakersfield, she said. And when Jo had to attend various functions with Jack, she stayed by his side and did not wander off and socialize. "I guess maybe some of them might have thought I was kind of antisocial, but I had already heard enough to know I didn't want to get in the middle of that mad stream."

Jo said that she personally never really had any problems with Buck, she just didn't like him from day one—nor did she like the way he mistreated her husband. "I think Jack is probably one of the most loyal people that Buck would ever have on his side," she said. "Jack ate and breathed his job. He ate and breathed loyalty to Buck. Buck did not know a loyal friend when he saw one." She felt Buck's screaming and yelling at him in front of other people was uncalled for. "That's just strictly my opinion, not Jack's," she said. "He didn't really talk about it. I saw it and heard it. I didn't like that. I thought it was very demeaning, but that was Jack's gig, it was not my gig. I probably would have been very angry had it been me, or I would have let it be known."

Jack's wife agreed that her husband had been responsible for much of his boss's success. "If they told Jack it couldn't be done, he would prove them wrong," Jo said. "Jack was not passive about doing it; he was very aggressive. I think maybe some of the things, the big things would not have happened without Jack. Course, Buck's a pretty smart man and the two of them together made a lot of things happen that seemed totally impossible."

Indeed, Jack was the reason Buck had made record profits in concert fees and the like. As Tom Brumley recalled, promoters were used to paying country acts just so much money and that's all they'd pay. "They was sellin' out," he said. "They'd sell out those big concerts, and . . . they were there to see them, not there to see the promoter," and yet they'd only pay the bands maybe $2,500. "Jack just broke that barrier all the devil to fuck. Just shattered it completely." For example, he had gotten the minimum going rate for a package show in 1969 with Tommy Collins, Rose Maddox, Sheb Wooley, and Buck and his Buckaroos up to $7,500 a night.

"He made Buck a lot of money," Tom said. "A lot of money."

Though Buck often failed to appreciate Jack's efforts, one incident from around 1974 stood out in Jo's mind as particularly strange. Jack had been on the road with Buck for a few weeks, and when he came home, the Buckaroos were taking a weekend off, so the McFaddens decided to take it off, too. They drove up to Lake Shasta in Northern California, where they docked their boat. No sooner had they arrived and put their boat in the water when the dock master came out and told them there had been several telephone calls for Jack and he had taken a number for him. Jo was rather frightened, because not many people knew they were going out of town; she feared there was a crisis of some sort. Jack took the number and returned the call. It was Buck. When he came back to the boat, he looked beaten down, disappointed.

"What's wrong?" Jo asked.

Jack stood there in a daze.

"Well, what is it?" Jo pressed. "What in the hell is wrong!"

"When I called Buck, he started yelling into the phone, 'You're fired! What do you mean going off on a weekend like this?' I guess when I get home I won't have a job."

"So? What's the big deal?" Jo asked. Of course, Jack didn't take kindly to her remark, and Jo had already resigned herself to the idea that they'd have to go back home so Jack could save his job.

"Are we going back down?" she asked.

"No," Jack said. "No use to go back now."

He never said another word about the incident, and Jo didn't bring it up either. In fact, she never knew what the deal was. But when Jack got back to Bakersfield, he still had his job.

In the mid-1970s, Jack bought a radio station in Manteca, California, which he and Jo rebuilt from the ground up. "I didn't know anything about radio but the knob to turn it on," Jo said, but her attitude was, if that was what Jack wanted to do, they would figure out how to go about it. They changed the station's format to country music and operated it for several years, until a man came in with an offer to buy and Jack sold it to him outright.

"We were successful in building a radio station. We built, bought, and paid for this business," Jo said of their later endeavor, a Nashville management agency. "Jack got his Mercedes and he got his boat, and you know, it didn't come through any Owens money. We were not hangers-on, and so I'm kind of proud of that."

46

BUCK CHANGES HIS TUNES

At the turn of the decade, change was in the air. On November 5, 1969, Doyle Holly married Virginia Mae Driskill—or Ginny, as she was known—the petite blonde he had first glimpsed through the window of the band's tour bus in 1966. They had met in Los Angeles in the late 1960s, where Ginny was dating comedian Gary Mule Deer, teaching school, and doing a little modeling on the side. Ginny was good friends with Betty Hager, Jim's wife. Doyle had been driving all night and crashed at Jim's place. When he awoke, Ginny was there and sparks flew.

Ginny was a descendant of the famous cattle baron Jesse Driskill, who established the historic Driskill Hotel in Austin, Texas, but later became destitute. Although Doyle had chemistry with Ginny, he still loved his regular squeeze, the pretty brunette, too, so he dated both the blonde and brunette, who were probably unaware of each other.

Like Jack and Jo McFadden, Doyle and Ginny got married in Las Vegas, with Marty Robbins as best man. Shortly thereafter, however, his previous wife Letha informed him that their Mexican divorce was illegal. He had to untie the knot with Letha before he could make Ginny his fourth and last wife again in Las Vegas on August 27, 1970, this time with Don Rich as best man. Ginny bore Doyle two children, Jess Austin and Heather Ramona, who called him "Uncle Daddy" because he was gone so much of the time. In true country song fashion, his brunette girlfriend was pregnant with twins, but she didn't tell Doyle because he had married Ginny.

Buck Owens continued to make artistic changes, as well—and not always for the better. In early 1970, he dropped one of the instruments from his band.

Although the steel guitar had been a crucial component of his unique sound, he decided he no longer needed one. So after being a Buckaroo for only eleven months, Jay Dee Maness and his wife were in bed one Sunday morning when the phone rang. It was Buck. He said, "Son, I'm sending Mike down to pick up all the boots, all the clothes you have, and all the guitars. I've decided to not have a steel in my band at all, so he's coming down to pick up that stuff." Click. He hung up.

Being let go was probably the best thing Buck could have done for the young steel player, because it forced him to stand on his own. He became a session musician and got back to working the clubs, which he couldn't do while employed by Buck. "That whole Buck Owens thing has done me more good, if you will, more mileage than anything I've ever done," Jay Dee said. "People remember, just that short time I was with him. People still say, 'Oh, I saw you and so-and-so, you played with Buck.' In that way, it was really good for me and I appreciate that."

A week after he was fired, Jay Dee heard that Buck raised everybody's pay, "or raised what I thought everybody was getting," to $150. In June 1970, Buck added keyboard player Jim Shaw to the Buckaroo lineup.

Buck stooped to a new low at a concert in Lynchburg, Virginia, around 1970. He was performing at E. C. Glass High School when a sandy-haired ten-year-old musical prodigy went backstage to meet him and the Buckaroos—in particular, his idol, Don Rich. The boy told Don that he, too, was a guitarist. Don asked him to play something and handed his silver sparkle Telecaster to the boy, who launched into "Buckaroo." Buck leaned over to Don and whispered, loud enough for the boy to overhear: "He won't amount to a hill of shit." The words stung the boy and stuck with him all his life, although Don's reply to Buck stuck more: "You wait and see!"

No doubt, Don, as the father of two young sons, knew the damage Buck's words would inflict upon the child and sought to smooth things over. The boy went on to win state championships and play lead guitar for such artists as Big Al Downing and Dottie West. He even played on *Hee Haw* twice. What Buck felt he could gain by belittling a child is anybody's guess, but that was the kind of man he had become.

By September 1, Buck had sold almost ten million records. In a ceremony at the Capitol Tower in Hollywood, Capitol Records named him "Capitol's Country Artist of the Decade." More than a thousand people attended, and Capitol president Sal Iannucci lauded Buck for "a record unmatched by any other artist."

Shortly thereafter, however, Buck's musical star began to dim. Although he was still a popular concert draw, his chart hits were falling off, mostly because of the direction his music was taking. He was in what he called his "experimental phase."

Buck was tired of churning out similar-sounding tunes, and one of the ways he branched out was to record duets, both with Susan Raye and with his son Buddy Alan. On February 2, 1970, Buck and Susan's single "We're Gonna Get Together"/"Everybody Needs Somebody" was released. "We're Gonna Get Together" was more in keeping with Buck's freight-train sound than their subsequent duets; it peaked at #13. Their *We're Gonna Get Together* LP was released April 6, the same day as "Togetherness"/"Fallin' for You" was released as a single. On July 3, he and Susan recorded "The Great White Horse," utilizing a Moog synthesizer and echo chambers. "The Great White Horse"/"Your Tender Loving Care" duets were released as a single on July 27. "The Great White Horse" was Buck's biggest hit with Susan; it went to #8. The LP of the same name was released on September 8.

Then Buck started writing songs about different geographical places, including "The Kansas City Song," which he cowrote with Red Simpson. Doyle Holly felt the song was slamming the city; he told Buck, "I hope you never get pissed off at Oklahoma," his home state. At the next recording session, Buck sang a song for Doyle: "*Oh, the wind blows every day in Oklahoma . . .*" "The Kansas City Song"/"I'd Love to Be Your Man" was released as a single on May 18, 1970, and peaked at #2. *The Kansas City Song* LP was released a couple of months later, on July 6.

But perhaps the most famous song Buck wrote about a place was "I Wouldn't Live in New York City (If You Gave Me the Whole Dang Town)." It wasn't that Buck didn't like New York, because he appreciated his fans there, and he eventually bought a place off Central Park West. The vocals were recorded live on Forty-Sixth Street in New York City on August 14, 1970, and the siren on the track is from an actual police car. Buck regretted one thing about the song, though, and that was changing the word "damn" to "dang" on the advice of label executives. Somehow, it didn't have the same ring to it. "I Wouldn't Live in New York City"/"No Milk and Honey in Baltimore" was released as single on October 5 and peaked at #9. The album *I Wouldn't Live in New York City* was released November 2.

"I Wouldn't Live in New York City" was one of four songs—along with "Tall Dark Stranger," "Sweet Rosie Jones," and "Big in Vegas"— for which Buck and the Buckaroos shot film shorts on 35mm film. It was a ground-breaking venture, and through it Buck has been credited with creating the world's first country music videos.

Buck continued his experiments in December 1970 by covering such songs as Simon and Garfunkel's "Bridge over Troubled Water." Producer Ken Nelson got perturbed; he didn't think the song fit Buck's sound, and he accused the star of trying to be "hep." Buck also courted controversy with this cut because both teachers and religious leaders thought the song was about drugs. Still, after "Bridge over Troubled Water"/"(I'm Goin') Home" was released as single on January 11, 1971, it climbed to #9.

The *Bridge over Troubled Water* LP was released February 15. Doyle recalled spending 102 hours in the studio on the *Bridge over Troubled Water* album and only getting paid for six hours.

Around this time, motorcycle mania struck the Buckaroos, and all the guys had to have one. Buck got so worried he started posting news clippings about motorcycle accidents on the bulletin board at the studio. Gene Price recalled going with Don when he picked up his blue Harley-Davidson Sportster. Don had had risers put on it to lift the front end and extend the front wheel like the chopper in *Easy Rider*, starring Peter Fonda. Aficionados believe a raked cycle improves performance; the downside is the front end is heavier and less responsive on turns and curves. Gene said it "looked like a Tijuana special." Doyle Holly had a Honda motorcycle and, according to Don's neighbor Marvin Mason, Don also had two other bikes, both Hondas.

In November, Doyle Holly left the Buckaroos for good. As he had with Tom Brumley, Buck asked him to sign an exit agreement to void all his contracts. Buck wanted him to sign over all songwriting royalties, which he did, and any monies that he were due to him through OMAC or Buck's other companies, which he didn't. By this time, Buck had instituted a profit-sharing plan, which was a good deal, but it had only been in effect for about eight months when Doyle left, so it only earned him around $400 or $500.

Doyle formed the band Vanishing Breed and was signed to Barnaby Records, a label singer Andy Williams started. "Nobody at that time realized the success that Buck was going to have or that we were going to have," he said. "You can't foresee success and I didn't foresee success until after I quit the band." Doyle was named bass player of the year by the Academy of Country Music the following year. He had minor success as a solo artist with one top twenty single, "Lila," and one top thirty single, Shel Silverstein's "Queen of the Silver Dollar." He also kept busy working gigs in clubs and making guest appearances on *Hee Haw*.

In early 2001, Doyle discovered he was the father of his old brunette girlfriend's identical twin daughters when the girls tracked him down via the Internet. He left Ginny and went to live with the twins' mother in her mobile home in California. He was with her for about a year and a half, until he called her "trailer trash" and she booted him out. Then he went back to Tennessee and Ginny.

"They say that hindsight is 20/20," Doyle said. "Looking back, I know that Buck was responsible for getting me away from the oil fields of Bakersfield and putting me onstage full time. And back in the '60s, money was not my concern. It was just eight years of a long party. Because if it was about money, I would've quit the first month I worked for him."

For Buck, of course, it was about money. And in 1971, he made one of the most brilliant financial moves of his career when he signed a new four-year contract with Capitol Records that eventually gave him unprecedented control over his master recordings. According to the agreement, the record company would retain control of Buck's masters only as long as he remained under contract.

47

RUBY AND THE MASTER OF SPIN

In 1971, Buck added five-string banjoist Ronnie Jackson to the Buckaroos and launched into his bluegrass phase—although Ronnie, who had lived and breathed bluegrass in Kentucky, felt the tempos were far too "draggy" to be called real bluegrass. The outspoken musician would often clash with Buck; "I don't know who was fired most," he recalled. "Doyle Holly or me!"

Shortly after he joined the group, around the time *Hee Haw* went into syndication, Ronnie began to feel as though he was being shoved to the back burner of the television program. None of the Buckaroos' songs on *Hee Haw* featured banjo tracks, and he would purposely be left off camera. The guys started ribbing him about Buck phasing out the banjo. Ronnie got upset and went to Buck to ask him what was going on. Buck told him, "Son, if you don't like working, you just pick up your paycheck when we get on home." Ronnie shot back, "Well, I just may do that!" Jack McFadden ended up taking Ronnie for a ride to calm him down, and things settled down after that.

Buck recorded the country-bluegrass song "Ruby (Are You Mad)" on March 23, and released it as a single with "Heartbreak Mountain" on the flip side on April 12. It peaked at #3 on *Billboard* and #1 on *Cashbox*. The *Ruby* LP was released June 21.

The red-haired beauty on the album cover was Buck's employee and secret lover in Phoenix, Kris Black. She was paid $100 for her modeling fee. Capitol Records and Buck flew her around the country as Ruby to promote the album to various radio stations. "I'd do promo things, 'Hi, I am Buck Owens's

Ruby. I am mad all right, just mad about KFWB radio here in Amarillo,' and that sort of thing."

Beyond "Ruby," Buck stayed busy in the studio throughout 1971. He cut "I'll Still Be Waiting for You," which was not released as a single until January 17, 1972. The song peaked at #8, with "Full Time Daddy" on the flip side. He continued to focus on bluegrass-flavored songs that featured the banjo, such as "Rollin' in My Sweet Baby's Arms," which he recorded on May 4, 1971. The single was released August 16 with "Corn Liquor" on the flip side. It peaked at #2 on *Billboard* but made it to #1 on *Cashbox*. On October 4, Capitol released another "best of" LP, *The Best of Buck Owens, Vol. 4.* Two duets followed: "Too Old to Cut the Mustard"/"Wham Bam" with Buddy Alan was released November 8, and "Santa's Gonna Come in a Stagecoach"/"One of Everything You Got" with Susan Raye was released November 22.

Things went so well with the *Ruby* promotion, Kris Black said, that Buck and Wade Pepper from Capitol decided that she should be Buck's national promotion director at his headquarters in Bakersfield. Buck went to Kris and asked her, "Careerwise, what are your aspirations?"

"I am putting everything together to be an actress," she said.

He told her that Bakersfield was a lot closer to Hollywood than Phoenix was. He offered her the job of promotion director, and told her she would have a secretary, so if she needed to take off and do a movie, the secretary could run things. Kris was floored. When Buck moved her to Bakersfield in 1972, she felt like they were stepping into their future together. As Buck did for nearly everyone on his payroll, he had a contract drawn up for Kris to sign. The most telling parts of hers read:

> Black acknowledges that this employment may require being on call at all hours, and that said engagement is not based on the hours of the normal working days, that she may be required to work odd hours and weekends, which Black hereby agrees to do. . . . Black acknowledges that the services to be rendered by her hereunder are of a special nature and a unique character which gives them a peculiar value, the loss of which

cannot be reasonably or adequately compensated for in damages in an action at law, and that a breach by Black of the provisions of the agreement will cause Owens great and irreparable injury and damage.

Around the same time, LaWanda Lindsey also moved to town to work for Buck. LaWanda, who had just turned nineteen, was hired as a replacement for Buck's duet partner Susan Raye. Somewhere along the way, Susan and drummer Jerry Wiggins had fallen in love. On October 3, 1971, they got married in Bakersfield, with their boss as best man. By early 1972, they were expecting a baby, and Susan knew it would be easier for her to tell Buck she was pregnant and didn't want to travel as much if she could say, "Here's another girl singer." She suggested to Buck that he hire LaWanda Lindsey, whom she had met a year earlier at the annual disc jockey convention in Nashville. LaWanda agreed to take her place on the road show, though Susan still recorded with Buck. LaWanda stayed a month at Susan and Jerry's before getting a small apartment by herself.

Kris, too, was living alone in Bakersfield. Buck, meanwhile, was living at the Zerker Road ranch while pretending to live at his folks' old house. (His parents were in Paso Robles, running one of Buck's cattle ranches.) Kris would go to his parents' old place to visit him and make him margaritas and his favorite recipes. "Everything had to be his mama's recipe, his mama's banana pudding, his mama's biscuits," she said. (Of course, eating such fattening food caused Buck to struggle with his weight, and he went on and off the Atkins diet.) Kris would stay and watch TV with him, but it would drive her crazy because he always had the remote control in his hand and just when a show was getting to the good part, he would switch the channel on purpose. After Kris went back to her apartment, Buck often went off to consort with Jennifer Smith.

Kris recalled that she and Buck were dining in the restaurant at the Bakersfield Airport when he asked her to move out to his ranch with him. She told him she would rather wait until they were married, and he told her, "You won't embarrass my mother." Still, Kris wanted to wait, because she thought they were very close to marriage at that point.

Shortly thereafter, Kris told Buck that her parents were coming to California for a visit—and he fired her. After her folks returned to South Dakota a week later, Buck called her into his office and rehired her. Kris was baffled, and then realized Buck had fired her only to avoid having to be around her parents.

Then Buck suggested that she and LaWanda live together. "I think LaWanda's getting a little homesick and is not real happy," he said. "I think that you and LaWanda should become roommates. It will give LaWanda a little more stability here." So the two young women upgraded their digs, moving into a larger apartment together.

Even though Kris was a little more than two years older, LaWanda said her roommate was very innocent, naive almost. Kris was "the kind of person you could knock down and she'd stay down and let you hit her again," LaWanda said. Jo McFadden agreed. "Kris is so overwhelmingly good to people. She overdoes it, and she does it with all good intentions. She is so generous, so thoughtful, so good." LaWanda felt that Buck used Kris for a long time, that he simply liked the idea of having girl singers and other young women on his payroll.

At the time, LaWanda had no idea that Kris was involved with Buck. LaWanda thought their relationship seemed friendly—but, then, Buck was friendly with most of the people with whom he did business. "It didn't seem like a boyfriend and a girlfriend or somebody that had had a relationship, you know?" she said. "But then maybe he told her not to act that way when other people were around"—which, of course, was exactly what Buck had done.

Then Buck quit inviting Kris out to his parents' old house. "I thought he was punishing me for saying that I wouldn't live with him, and I figured, 'Well, if I do just what I am supposed to do everything will be all right,'" she said. "Talk about a complete idiot, but I was just trying to make the best of a bad situation."

When Kris started work at her new job, she was so unfamiliar with the business that she was still asking, "What is a promotion director? Somebody please tell me." But within her first year, she was formulating many of the most highly visible promotions of Buck's career, campaigns that brought him to the attention of both disc jockeys and the public.

For instance, she came up with the campaign to plug Buck's song "Made in Japan," which was recorded March 7, 1972. Don Rich played three violin parts that were dubbed over one another to sound like a whole string section. The single was released April 3, with "Black Texas Dirt" on the flip side. Kris decided to produce a series of promotional photos that would be sent to various radio stations and newspapers to encourage them to play and write about the song. Since she had been raised somewhat like a Midwestern geisha, it was no wonder that the photos drew upon that theme; Kris herself dressed as a geisha for the shoot. "Made in Japan" became Buck's last #1 as a solo artist, and Buck said the song was among his most requested.

By this time, Buck had decided he needed a steel player again. He hired an eighteen-year-old Ohioan named Jerry Brightman. On April 26, 1972, Buck recorded "Ain't It Amazing, Gracie," written by Glen Garrison. As Buck often did with other writers' compositions, he changed some things and gave himself top billing. The single was not released until March 5, 1973, with his first version of "The Good Old Days (Are Here Again)" (recorded November 6, 1972) on the flip side. The song only went to #14. The *Ain't It Amazing, Gracie* LP was released May 14, 1973.

Capitol released another duet with Buck and Susan Raye on June 19, 1972, "Looking Back to See," which peaked at #13. A duet of "Cryin' Time" was on the flip side. The next day, June 20, Buck recorded "You Ain't Gonna Have Ol' Buck to Kick Around No More," which he wrote after hearing Richard Nixon say "you won't have Dick Nixon to kick around anymore" when he lost the 1962 gubernatorial race to Edmund G. "Pat" Brown. The song was released on August 28 and peaked at #13 on *Billboard* and at #2 on *Cashbox*. "I Love You So Much It Hurts" was on the flip side.

On December 4, 1972, Capitol released the single "In the Palm of Your Hand"/"Get Out of Town Before Sundown." "In the Palm of Your Hand" had also been on the flip side of Buck's "Waitin' in Your Welfare Line" single back in 1966, and it was one of the songs he performed at Carnegie Hall that year. The *In the Palm of Your Hand* LP was released January 8, 1973. Buck rerecorded

"The Good Old Days (Are Here Again)" as a duet with Susan Raye in February. It was released May 21, with "When You Get to Heaven (I'll Be There)" on the flip side. Another single, "Arms Full of Empty"/"Songwriter's Lament," was released on July 30.

On October 8, 1973, Buck recorded "Big Game Hunter," which also benefited from a high-profile campaign by Kris Black. She released posters that depicted a sexy woman with a male trophy underfoot, though this time she was not the model. The single was released November 5 and peaked at #8.

Also in 1973, Buck sent his gorgeous emissary on a cross-country tour in a hot pink Firebird convertible to meet face-to-face with male program directors at key country radio stations and thank them for playing his records. Buck told Kris to buy the car for the trip and that the company would pay for it. She did, but then Buck reneged on his promise and Kris got stuck with the monthly payments.

Buck himself was a brilliant master of promotion, the original spinmeister who instinctively knew how to get his name out there and believed the axiom that there is no such thing as bad publicity. What's more, as Kris Black said, "He was a master manipulator; he knew exactly when to be nice to people to make them stay with him."

Wade Pepper remembered one year when they went to New York to promote Buck to national singles sales managers. They got one of the big rock stations in New York to play "I've Got a Tiger by the Tail" and contacted Macy's to set up a promotion. Buck brought in "the whole crew, Tony Booth, Susan Raye, Wynn Stewart," and they all played, which was a first for Macy's. "Buck was a very creative man," Wade said.

One publicity stunt Buck wanted to make happen in 1973 was to pose nude for *Playgirl* magazine. He told Kris to go out and buy a copy of the magazine for him so he could study the way the guys posed. She did, but she told him "no way" should he pose for the skin magazine, because it would ruin his wholesome image. "Well, it's either that or the wife contest," he told her. She never knew if he had really wanted to pose for *Playgirl*, or if he had made up the story so she would let him do a "wife contest" instead.

The following June, the wife contest seed was planted during an interview with a magazine reporter who spoke with Buck at his ranch. The star played up how lonely he had been since his divorce from Phyllis two years earlier and told how he wanted to find a wife—he said he would even consider a mail-order bride. The reporter then put out the call for all wife prospects to write to the singer. It wasn't really a contest per se—there wasn't even a prize. It was just another publicity stunt Buck set in motion to draw attention to himself. As his DJ friend Larry Scott of KLAC-AM in Los Angeles said at the time, "He's quite a promoter. If I know Buck, he'll probably get four or five hit records out of all those letters and he'll probably find a wonderful woman." Neither of these things happened. By August 1974, Buck said, he had been inundated with at least twenty thousand letters, some from skeptics, some from lovelorn women, and one from a married man with two children, who wrote, "We're gonna have to dispense with this sexual discrimination. I can make you just as happy as any woman."

The next year, Buck formed the Buck Owens International Lonely Hearts Club, which coincided with the release of his single "Weekend Daddy"/"41st Street Lonely Hearts' Club" on March 10, 1975. Of course, Buck was anything but lonely; he was busy juggling Kris and Jennifer.

In 1974, Buck cut a novelty song that was a take-off on Shel Silverstein's "On the Cover of the Rolling Stone," which Dr. Hook & the Medicine Show had taken to the top ten on the rock chart early the previous year. Buck contacted Shel to see if he could do a country version of it; he found out that Shel had already written a hillbilly version. When Buck heard his version, he decided to rewrite it, with the songwriter's approval. Once again he snagged a piece of the writing action and top billing, though not only Shel but also Buck's keyboardist Jim Shaw got a writing credit. On February 6, 1974, Buck recorded the parody, "On the Cover of the Music City News," which referred to the Nashville-based magazine founded by singer Faron Young. The song was released as a single on February 25 and peaked at #9, with "Stony Mountain West Virginia" on the flip side.

That year also marked the release of "(It's a) Monster's Holiday," a song Kris called "the promoter's nightmare." It had been recorded the day before

Halloween in 1973, but it was not released until June 24, 1974—when radio stations were not looking for Halloween fare. Station program directors were telling Kris, "We can't play that stupid song. If we do, the kids will cover us up with their dumb little phone calls." So she decided to target children specifically. She contacted General Mills and got cases of Franken Berry and Boo Berry cereal, which she mailed to the stations for listener call-in giveaways, and she made a crossword puzzle just for kids. "The kids got it up to #6 with a bullet," she said. The *(It's a) Monster's Holiday* LP was released closer to the holiday, in September 1974.

What would ultimately strike Kris, however, was that Buck decided to come out with a song about monsters roughly three weeks before Don Rich died. "Really and truly, 'Monster's Holiday' in June by a man who is brilliant about promotion? I mean, it really doesn't fit. Why would he come up with that song then?" she asked. "I think in a very deep and subconscious level he was just thinking of some kind of horrible thing.

"That is just the way I look at things," she said. "I look at things different, sometimes."

★ 48 ★

DEATH OF A BUCKAROO

Buck Owens and his Buckaroos took their longest road trip ever in 1974 when they did a thirty-one-concert, thirty-three-thousand-mile tour of the Pacific Rim. During the seven-week tour, they produced three live albums in Japan, Australia, and New Zealand. Ronnie Jackson said the grueling trip seemed even more difficult because they were separated from their wives for so long.

In Hong Kong about halfway through the tour, Don hurt his back lugging equipment and had to see a doctor. Medical costs were high there, however, so they waited to get him to a doctor in New Zealand, which had socialized medicine. Buck called Don's wife, Marlane, and asked her to fly over so she could attend to her husband. Marlane went with her friends Jeanne Mason and Diane Immel to get a visa at an embassy in Los Angeles before flying into Dunedin International Airport, where Don picked her up. She then traveled with him the rest of the tour—two weeks in New Zealand and two weeks in Australia. Despite Don's injury, they had a wonderful time.

In October 1999, Buck would tell historian Kathryn Burke a different story. It was a horrible trip, he claimed, and everybody was in hate with everybody else by the time they returned to the States. He also said he had discovered on the tour that Don was an alcoholic, when he botched the lyrics to "Diggy Liggy Lo." Buck said that he wanted to bring Marlane over to effect an intervention of sorts to help Don confront his drinking, but that Marlane's passport had expired. He said he was able to get Kern County congressman Bill Thomas to step in and get Marlane to New Zealand immediately. Upon hearing this tale, Marlane was incensed. "Bull! God!" she exclaimed. Ronnie Jackson concurred with Marlane: "I never heard anything of that story," he said. "There was never a problem with Don and he played his butt off. I never saw Don drunk and he sure didn't screw up any shows. The live records proved we cooked."

"Buck must have been delusional in his later years," Marlane said. "Sure, we all had cocktails [in New Zealand], but not excessively." Marlane also said that Buck knew Don enjoyed his scotch, and that she would get mad when Buck would send Don a case of Chivas Regal "too often." Jerry Wiggins, who roomed with Don on the road, recalled that the bandleader would sleep with a fifth of scotch by his bedside and drink throughout the night. In addition, a lover of Don's at the time of his death said Don favored Johnnie Walker Red and would suck cloves to sweeten his breath. But other bandmates and Marlane insisted that in spite of his drinking, Don "never got drunk."

Kay Adams recalled that Don Rich said to her in early 1974, "I want to taste everything there is to taste. I want to go ninety miles per hour until I run into a brick wall."

The fact is, Don was growing frustrated. According to Kay, he had talked about divorcing his wife so that the two of them could be together. However, a photo of Don and Marlane fishing on a boat with Buck's son Buddy off the waters near Sydney, Australia, shows a happy couple. The truth is, if Don was thinking about leaving anyone, it wasn't Marlane—it was Buck. In addition to quitting the band, Don was planning to launch a solo career and write a tell-all book. Even Tom Brumley had warned Buck when he left that if Buck sued him "a lot of stuff's gonna come out."

If Don had gone solo, he would have been formidable competition for Buck if he'd signed with the man he'd talked to about becoming his future manager—Larry Adamson. Capitol's Wade Pepper said, "Some people used to comment that if Don was out on his own, he would be his own star, but we will never know that." Nevertheless, many people, including singer Jimmy Dean and former Capitol Nashville president Jim Foglesong, admitted that they were bigger Don Rich fans than Buck Owens fans.

In spite of Don's jovial facade, he was tired of the road, and quite likely tired of Buck's badgering and deceit. Don may have been so tired that he didn't much care about himself or keeping up an impossible image. Even though Don loved

Buck, working half his life for such a demanding boss had taken a physical and mental toll. He began to vocalize his feelings, something he had never done before. "I can't deal with this shit anymore," he told Dennis Payne after accompanying Buck to make an $800,000 cash payoff to someone in the dark of night. Don told his wife that he had to go with Buck whenever he bought a "business"—and that Buck always paid for it in cash.

There was one problem: Buck didn't want Don to leave—just as he hadn't wanted Tom to leave—because he knew it would ruin his sound. Don may have told Buck he was going to sign with Larry, because when asked about managing Don, Larry said: "Well, that was a long time ago. They paid me a bunch of money and I am out of it. It's one of those things, it is over with, you know. You count your chips, and you either cash in or cash out. I decided to get out of it, and they said, 'OK. That's fine; we're done right there.' So, for your information, Jack [McFadden] wrote me a check."

If his prospective manager was out of the picture, it could explain, in part, why Don began to behave contrary to the image Buck wanted his band members to project. He moved from uppers to appetite-stimulating marijuana, which might explain why he was packing anywhere from 220 to 250 pounds on his six-foot frame. He grew his hair longer, and with it, he grew a little more reckless.

Around the end of June 1974, Tom Brumley, who was then playing steel guitar in Rick Nelson's Stone Canyon Band, saw his former bandmate after a session at Buck's recording studio in Oildale. Don was on his raked Harley-Davidson Sportster and Tom told him, "The last guy in the world that ought to be on a motorcycle, especially raked like that, is you. You know, because you don't pay attention to anything." He replied, "Nah, man, if I died tomorrow I would have lived more than most people have in a whole lifetime. I love that motorcycle so I'm going to keep on riding it."

Buck always lectured Don on the dangers of motorcycle riding. Tom didn't recall hearing him do so, "but I know he did. We all did."

In the summer of 1974, Buck and his Buckaroos were in Redding, California, to perform a couple of shows. There was a talented fiddle player who lived in Redding at the time, and some of the faculty at Redding College urged her to go to the concert and meet Buck Owens backstage.

Jana Jae was a musical prodigy who was born in Great Falls, Montana, and grew up in Weiser, Idaho. Her Juilliard-schooled parents taught her to play violin when she was two and a half years old. She studied classical violin on scholarships at the famed Interlochen Music Camp in Michigan and the Vienna Academy of Music in Austria. She went to the college that gave her the best scholarship, Colorado Women's College. By 1974, she had won numerous awards and was teaching fiddle and playing in a bluegrass band in Redding while raising two young children, Matt and Katy.

From what she had heard about Buck, she was intrigued. So she took her fiddle and a single she had recorded and went to meet him between shows. They were talking about music and Buck asked her, "Do you have your fiddle with you?" She said, "Well, yes, it's in the car," and he said, "Go get it. I want to hear you play." So she got it and she played a little for him backstage. "Do you do 'Orange Blossom Special'?" he asked. She told him she did and played a bit of it for him. He liked what he heard and said that for the next show, he would bring her onstage. "You'll be playing with Don Rich. You'll love it," he said. "Just come on out when I call you, and it will be kind of a surprise for the audience." So that is what happened. Don and Jana really got into it onstage and knocked the audience dead. Don was thrilled to be playing with someone of his caliber and had a huge smile on his face the entire time.

After Buck and the band left Redding, Jana kept in touch with Jack McFadden, because she thought he could help book the bluegrass band in which she played. Jack was always her contact, not Buck, and she called Jack every couple of weeks to see about bookings.

Back in Bakersfield, Don was preparing for a deep sea fishing holiday with his family in San Simeon, California. Marlane had gone deep sea fishing several times before with their sons and their neighbors Jack and Diane Immel and the Masons, but Don had never been able to go because he was always working. Now he was going to have some time off, so they made plans for the whole family to go on Wednesday, July 17, 1974.

The vacation, in part, was to renew Don and Marlane's bond as husband and wife after a recent reconciliation. God knows the couple had traveled a rocky road during their thirteen-year marriage, but they had survived in spite of Don's various infidelities and lengthy absences working as Buck Owens's main man. They had been separated briefly because of Don's most recent dalliance, a blonde New Yorker he'd met in Nashville who hung out with Kenny Rogers and the First Edition. Because Don was music director of *Hee Haw*, he spent more time in Nashville than the other Buckaroos. The affair supposedly had been going on for three years before Don finally told his wife about it. Don described trysts he'd had with the woman in excruciating detail, and told Marlane he planned to marry her. Whenever the blonde showed up, he would tell Marlane about it and say, "Well, I thought you should know." Marlane had even called the blonde at one point and told her to say hello to her young sons since she was going to be their stepmother. Of course, Don got mad at Marlane and told her, "You shouldn't have done that."

Marlane was heartbroken, but she hung tough, because she loved Don and he was a good father to their sons. Don genuinely loved Marlane, too, but working with Buck, the absences were long and the temptations many. Not to mention, he didn't have the best role model in Buck when it came to being a faithful husband. As Kris Black put it, "Madonna stayed at home with the kids, and the whores were out on the road to play with. That is just exactly where their little minds were."

Then there were Kay Adams and a former OMAC employee, both brunettes, who also loved Don. From the beginning, Buck had discouraged their affairs, yet he had never protested about Don and the blonde. The former OMAC employee Don was seeing said the blonde had prompted their only argument. "I think he was using her as an excuse to leave Bakersfield and to leave Buck because he was really unhappy there at the end," she said.

The Ulriches' vacation plans changed when Buck set a recording session for the night of July 17 and Don was told he had to stay and overdub tracks. Night sessions were not the norm for Buck, though. He had gotten into the habit of doing only day sessions with Capitol Records producer Ken Nelson, who liked to be out of the studio by four in the afternoon and home before peak rush hour. Besides, Buck was a morning person, up at five-thirty or six o'clock every morning to play tennis or golf before eating a big breakfast and going to work. When Tom Brumley was with the band, he said, "We never ever did night sessions. We always did it during the day. We'd start anywhere from ten to one o'clock. We'd do no more than two sessions a day."

Marlane wanted Don to stick to their original plan and leave with the family the morning of the seventeenth, but Don, ever the peacemaker, opted to appease the Chief. He told Marlane there was a chance Buck would cancel the night session, and that he might be able to go fishing on the eighteenth after all. The family could leave as scheduled, and Don would drive over as soon as he finished with Buck.

On the night of July 16, Don told his wife he wanted to ride the Harley to the coast, because it was something he had wanted to do for some time. She protested, though, because she did not feel comfortable about him riding the chopper at night. "No, I really want to take the Harley over," Don said. "I am going to take a gun with me in case somebody harasses me and I'll take a sleeping bag and if I get too tired, I will pull over and rest. Please don't worry, I really want to take the motorcycle." Marlane prevailed, however, and Don agreed to drive his 1961 Austin-Healey sports car instead.

Before Don left for the studio the morning of July 17, his wife gave him a sheet of paper with detailed instructions on where to find her at the coast. Don tucked it in his shirt pocket and then left in the Austin-Healey, but he returned a few minutes later. The vintage ragtop had developed mechanical problems, which was unusual, because it was Don's baby and he kept it in top condition. "The Healey is really making a funny noise," he told his wife. So he parked it by the side of the house and rode the Harley-Davidson Sportster to the studio instead.

But Marlane knew that Don still had a safer, albeit not-so-pretty, ride he could take to the coast: their new station wagon. She wouldn't need it, because she and the boys would be traveling with their friends Jack and Diane Immel and their son, John, in the Immels' Ford LTD. Around 11 A.M. the two families headed to the small coastal town of Cambria, California, roughly halfway between Morro Bay and San Simeon. It was a long ride to the coast back then; Marlane said it took a good three or four hours.

After Marlane and the Immels checked into the Cambria Pines Lodge, they went out to play a round of golf. They had chosen to stay there because it had a golf course and even though Don wasn't any good at the game, he had clubs and enjoyed going out with the guys, having fun and drinking a beer or two. This trip was going to be some much-needed down time for him.

At the studio, the band was backed up on sessions for various artists and was scrambling to catch up—which, in part, was why Buck wanted Don there for three sessions that day. Nobody remembers what the first session entailed, but it was either to overdub *Hee Haw* tracks or to back up Susan Raye; it started at either 10 or 11 A.M. and tension was high. Don had done either a modulation or a run that Buck didn't like, and Buck told him not to do it again. When they did another run-through, Don did it again. This went on a few times until Buck got pissing mad, stopped the session, and threw Don out of the studio. Don took off on his motorcycle to blow off steam.

Kris Black said she saw Don that day and got a strange feeling when she saw him on the chopper. "Don, why are you riding that?" she asked.

"Oh, I just got it out because my brakes are out, so I need to drive this."

"Please be careful. That is so dangerous. That chopper has an extended wheel, and you don't have any center balance."

"Oh, Krissy, a coward will die a thousand times and a brave man only once."

When the band broke for lunch, the Buckaroos' banjoist, Ronnie Jackson, went over to the Foster Freeze for a burger. When he returned to the studio, Don rode up on his chopper and said, "C'mon, Ronnie, c'mon. Let's go for a ride." Ronnie had never ridden before and didn't want to because motorcycles scared him, but Don finally persuaded him to hop on for a quick spin. Neither wore a helmet. When they were walking back into the building, Ronnie told Don he could see why he loved riding because he, too, had enjoyed his first ride on the open road with the fresh air snapping against his face. Their conversation then turned to the dangers of riding, and Don said, "Yeah, you know, Ronnie, if anything ever happened to my hands where I couldn't play music, I wouldn't want to live."

Don and Ronnie went back into the studio for the afternoon session, and the earlier storm between Buck and Don seemed to have blown over. As they were ending the session, Ronnie was playing guitar and still had a part to play, but Don offered to finish it. So Ronnie left his D-28 Martin behind for Don to play and went on home. Steel player Jerry Brightman also stayed behind, to work with Don on overdubs for Buck's son Buddy Alan. After Jerry and Don finished the session around either two or three in the afternoon, they talked for twenty or thirty minutes, which was not the norm. It wasn't as though they never talked, they just never talked at length. Jerry remembered Don being on his bike, wearing cutoff jeans; he was talking about going to the coast to meet his family and some friends. It was the last time he saw Don alive.

Don, however, returned to the studio for session with Tony Booth. Tony recalled doing a session that day, though his memory is fuzzy. He couldn't remember the last song he played with Don, let alone the time. He thought it was sometime in the late afternoon, because he was not a morning person. Tony said that he thought Don, Doyle Singer, Jim Shaw, and Jerry Wiggins played on the session. He recalled talking to Don during daylight hours—it was midsummer, when the days were longer—about a session set for the following Monday. He knew Don liked playing other music besides country, and told him he would get to play guitar on a cover of Jim Croce's "Workin' at the Car Wash Blues."

Afterward, Don called his Bakersfield lover, who had been fired at OMAC because Buck disapproved of her relationship with Don, and told her he didn't want to go to the coast and wanted to stay with her that night. She told him it wasn't a good idea because she had just started a new job and needed to be fresh for it. He then called Cambria Pines Lodge and left a message for Marlane saying the night session had been canceled and he would soon be on his way. The sun set at 8:19 P.M. in Cambria and it was dusk before Marlane got his note. She expected he would arrive after ten that night, so she put a note and some streamers on the Immels' car antenna so he would know where to find them if the front office was closed.

Kris remembered that "Tony and Larry Booth both told me that as Don was leaving, Buck was pleading with Don not to go to the coast, to please not go that night. He seemed to have a bad feeling, and Buck almost got down on his knees. He talked to Don for almost an hour saying: 'Please, don't go.'" All Tony remembered was Buck asking Don not to ride the motorcycle to the coast.

After he finished the Tony Booth session, Don returned to the Park Stockdale subdivision, where he lived. He evidently stopped by Doyle Singer's house to borrow a fully loaded five-shot revolver, a Model 36 .38 caliber Chief Special Smith & Wesson. Don loved collecting firearms and had a mini-arsenal of his own at home, from muzzleloaders to revolvers. Why, friends wonder, did Don borrow a gun from Doyle Singer when he lived in the same neighborhood and could have taken one of his own?

It was a cool, moonless night as Marlane paced outside her quarters at the Cambria Pines Lodge. Inside, her two young sons, eleven-year-old Vance and nine-year-old Vic, lay sleeping. The note she had attached to the antenna of their friends' car fluttered in the ocean breeze. As minutes became hours, Marlane became annoyed. Why was Don so late? Where was he? "Damn it!" Eventually, she gave up her vigil and retired. Sometime during the night, she heard sirens and she knew something was wrong, very wrong. "I probably heard the sirens because he was killed in Morro Bay," she said. "Maybe I did. I don't know."

Looking back, Marlane was certain Don had taken Highway 46 through Paso Robles, not only because it was the most direct route but also because it was a good bike road with all its twists and turns. The highway, a treacherous two-lane stretch of asphalt in 1974, gained notoriety after actor James Dean died on a side road in a head-on collision in 1955 near Cholame in San Luis Obispo County. But it appears Don made a fatal change in plans that night and did not take the shortest path to his destination. Most likely, he traveled north on Highway 1 through Morro Bay on his way to Cambria. Highway 1 was also a dangerous car ride along the coast, especially on a chopper such as Don's. Upon realizing that Don would have had to travel south on Highway 1 to get to Morro Bay and then double back to Cambria, Marlane said she had never really thought about which way he had gone because the outcome had been so "crappy."

The moon was two days shy of being new that night, so it was dark on that stretch of Highway 1 two miles south of the Morro Bay city limits, near the intersection of Yerba Buena Road. At 10:05 P.M., something caused Don to slam his chest against the handlebars, rupturing his pulmonary artery and cracking his ribs. He then hit the median and lost control of the motorcycle, which turned over; his body was ejected about 150 feet off to the right of the road.

Because the accident occurred outside the city limits and on a main highway, the California Highway Patrol and the San Luis Obispo Sheriff's Office had jurisdiction. According to the sheriff's report, the CHP was notified of an injury accident "by an unknown Morro Bay Police Department officer." Highway patrolman R. Whittington arrived at the scene and called a private ambulance to the scene, because only Cambria had a public ambulance service at that time. Doyle Holly said Buck had told him there were no witnesses to the accident, but the San Luis Obispo Sheriff's Office incident report noted otherwise: Whittington told reporting officer D. Okel of the sheriff's department that Peter Charles Martinez, 39, of Brentwood, California, had seen Don traveling northbound on Highway 1 when the accident occurred. The sheriff's report did not note any adverse weather conditions, such as fog, or any road construction that might have contributed to the wreck.

The Smith & Wesson that Don had borrowed from Doyle Singer was found at the scene, with extensive damage. There were four live .38 Special Smith & Wesson brand hollow-point bullets, the kind that expand on impact, found in the chamber. The bullet by the hammer was missing, but Doyle Holly said it was Don's usual practice to remove it when carrying a loaded weapon. After the accident, Doyle Singer gave the gun to Ronnie Jackson, who, like Doyle Singer and Jerry Wiggins, was one of Buck's deputized, gun-carrying Buckaroos. Ronnie said the snub-nosed revolver was damaged and that the CHP said it had been fired twice. He speculated that Don had probably stopped somewhere and fired off a couple of shots. The CHP only keeps records on file five years and said the files for Don's accident no longer exist.

Also recovered at the scene was "one blue motorcycle helmet (damaged)," which raised questions among friends. Jerry Brightman said, "Don never wore a helmet," while Marvin Mason said Don always wore one. As a rule, Don did not wear one in California, which did not have a helmet law at the time. He did own two blue helmets, which he and whoever happened to ride with him wore only when riding in Nevada, which had a helmet law.

While Don's Sportster was being hauled to Tex's Towing in Morro Bay, the ambulance sped him to what was then Sierra Vista Hospital in San Luis Obispo. Fifty minutes after the accident occurred, Donald Eugene Ulrich was pronounced dead on arrival by Dr. Clifford Wright. Emergency room nurse Janette Jones, who was twenty-nine at the time, had the unpleasant task of preparing Don's body for the funeral home and packaging his personal effects so they could be turned over to the sheriff's office. When asked whether she had seen anything out of the ordinary that night, she said yes but would not discuss it on the record.

About midnight on the morning of Thursday, July 18, the Bakersfield Police Department was contacted by Lieutenant A. Wood of the San Luis Obispo Sheriff's Office, and a request was made to notify Don's wife. When Bakersfield police found no one home at their house on Angell Street, they contacted Jack McFadden, who called Don's neighbor Marvin.

What wasn't noted in the sheriff's incident report, however, was that an unidentified California Highway Patrol officer notified Kern County sheriff's captain Al Loustalot, who, in turn, called Buck and broke the news to him that Don had been killed in a motorcycle accident. Ronnie Jackson said Buck called his private pilot Bob Woods and told him to get the plane ready immediately. Then, he said, Buck and his son Mike, the copilot, flew to San Luis Obispo to identify Don's body.

Around 6 A.M. in Bakersfield, KUZZ news director Hal Lafoon broadcast the report of Donald Eugene Ulrich's death on the radio station Buck owned and his son Mike managed. Soon thereafter, Lafoon was fired, supposedly for being insensitive and announcing Don's death on the air before the next-of-kin had been notified (though, as it happened, Marlane and her children would not have been able to pick up the station's signal in Cambria). Doyle Holly said that the broadcaster hadn't made the connection when he reported the name: "Hal knew who Don Rich was, but he didn't know who Donald Eugene Ulrich was." Kris Black, however, recalled hearing a report about "Don Rich, leader of the Buckaroos" and thinking, "'Oh, what did Don do now?' because he was such a clown."

Marlane awoke early Thursday morning and Don still wasn't there. She, of course, was very worried. She called the Immels and told them Don had never arrived. Jack Immel said, "Maybe he went to where the boats are taking off?" So they got into the Immels' car and drove to San Simeon, just below Hearst Castle, which was a smaller place than Morro Bay. He wasn't there. Then they thought that perhaps Don had lost the name of the motel, so they drove around to every motel in the area looking for the chopper. They didn't see it anywhere. Then they went back to where the boats were and Jack said, "Something isn't right. I am going to call Bakersfield." So Jack called Marvin Mason, their friend down the street, and Marvin told him that the police had been there looking for Marlane, and that Don had been killed.

Jack didn't tell Marlane, though. He said, "Just a minute," and when he got off the phone with Marvin, he called the San Luis Obispo Sheriff's Office. When he hung up, he said, "OK, Mar, there is a police escort coming to meet us. We ought to leave right away, because we have to go and identify stuff." Marlane was numb. From that moment on, everything was a blur to her. As Jack Immel sped past the accident scene on Highway 1, she recalled seeing police cars and trying to keep her two sons, who were crying uncontrollably in the back seat, from looking out the window and seeing where their daddy had died.

At 6:15 A.M., two sheriff's deputies were dispatched to the Cambria Pines Lodge to inform Marlane of her husband's death. When they arrived, the deputies were notified by a dispatcher that she had already been told about the accident and was southbound on Highway 1. The deputies were told to overtake their car and request that Marlane pick up her husband's belongings at the sheriff's office.

"Right outside of Morro Bay, all of a sudden it was cops all around us," Marlane said, "and here we were going from Morro Bay at 60 miles an hour. They were getting us past where he was killed, just as fast as they could."

According to a supplementary report by the sheriff's office, Marlane picked up her husband's belongings at the sheriff's office on July 18. The report read:

Mrs. Ulrich signed for the following property:
1. $40.25 in U.S. currency.
2. One Masterchange credit card.

3. One Shell Oil credit card.

4. One Texaco credit card.

5. One Union Oil credit card.

6. Miscellaneous papers.

7. One Buck Owens wristwatch.

8. One Smith and Wesson, model 36, .38 Chief Special, serial number 211838.

9. One blue helmet.

The initial incident report, however, listed several other items: a Chapstick, a blue pocket comb, dark glasses, a yellow metal ring with a white stone, a yellow metal neckchain, Don's California driver's license, and an American Express card. Marlane said she had gotten back the ring, which supposedly was on Don's body when it was turned over to the mortuary, and which she remembered as being onyx with a diamond in the center. She could not remember what had become of Don's driver's license, but thought that it might still be in his wallet, which one of her sons now has. (A copy of the driver's license was attached to the death certificate.) Marlane also did not know whether someone may have kept the smaller items as souvenirs. The "yellow metal neckchain" was a gift from Buck to Don, with a gold coin pendant attached. Marlane was unaware that the pendant had been recovered along with Don's body, because she was not privy to the accident reports. But she knew how much Don had cherished that gift from Buck; he had worn it all the time. Jack Immel and Marvin Mason had even returned to the scene of the accident on July 18 to search for it, along with the instructions on how to find Marlane in Cambria, but they found neither. As for the American Express card, when asked whether it had been returned, she said, "We didn't have an American Express card." Buck did, though, and he had given Don a corporate card to carry in his wallet. Given Buck's attitude about money, it seems possible that when he identified Don's body, he asked for—and got—both the gold coin pendant and the American Express card.

After retrieving Don's effects, Marlane returned to Bakersfield with her sons, in a state of shock over her husband's sudden death. Friends and loved ones gathered at her home to offer condolences and support.

When Don Rich's death was announced, the people at Buck Owens Enterprises and OMAC sprang into action. The office staff answered calls and letters from people expressing shock and offering condolences. Kris Black wrote a press release and a tribute to send to the media.

Don didn't have a will, but he had an accidental death provision in his home insurance policy that if something happened to him, his widow could collect double the amount. Marlane notified the insurance agent, a musician friend. Then Dorothy Owens oversaw the filing of union insurance claims and the funeral arrangements. Marlane was asked to sign a contract, because Don had produced some records and was entitled to royalties. "Buck really helped me out a lot on that, and he lined everything up for me," she said. "And then when I got the money, he introduced me to his banker."

Buck was the go-to man and a demon for details. He wanted to take care of the burial and Don's affairs so that his distraught widow would not have to deal with them. "Buck was so good to me," Marlane recalled. "He and Dorothy took care of everything." Buck arranged for the quick disposal of the wrecked Harley-Davidson Sportster, as well as Don's Austin-Healey. He paid one of Don's honorary pallbearers to move the motorcycle from Morro Bay to a Bakersfield salvage yard. Bob McClain, who also had a Sportster, noticed some of the front spokes had been knocked out, which probably caused Don to lose control and hit the median. The sports car was sold to Jack McFadden, who, in turn, sold it to Lefty Frizzell's brother, David Frizzell. Jackson Brumley remembers driving the ragtop, which seemed to be having trouble with the overdrive, to a man in Porterville, who was to deliver it to David.

Buck went so far as to advise Kay Adams not to show up for Don's funeral—out of deference for Marlane's feelings, he said. The blonde Don had met in Nashville, on the other hand, was not discouraged from attending, which made no sense to Kay. Wouldn't the blonde's presence at the funeral be as hurtful to Marlane as Kay's?

More puzzling still, Buck never told the full truth about how he learned of Don's death. Buck's Rhino Records CD booklet and his Web site tell his version of the story, while propagating an error that has been repeated time and again in the press: that he had heard about Don's death the *morning* of July 17, and that Don had died the evening of July 16. The account read:

At 6:30 on the morning of July 17, 1974, Buck's home phone rang. It was his son Michael, who managed KUZZ. He informed him that Don Rich had been killed earlier that evening when his motorcycle struck a highway divider. "He said, 'Dad, I have to tell you something.' And then he told me about Don. It's something that I always wanted to forget and never to remember . . . and I had to call his wife and tell her—she was in Morro Bay."

As usual, Buck embellished the story. In reality, he was not the one who told Marlane about Don's death. But why would he claim to have played *less* of a role than he did, by concealing the fact that he learned of the accident six or seven hours earlier from Captain Loustalot, then flew in and identified Don's body?

Buck seemed to go to great lengths to confuse people about the events surrounding Don's accident. "I'm sure he was depressed during that time and I think Don's death itself, you know, he said, 'Well, I told him not to go,' " Jana Jae said. "But there was something that happened, I think, in the studio or something that Don was upset about. I never did ask, I don't know. But, for some reason I think Buck probably felt personally responsible for that death."

Most die-hard Buckaroo fans and people who work in the country music industry can remember where they were and what they were doing the moment they heard about Don Rich's death. Earl Poole Ball Jr. and Doyle Holly were in Nashville. Tom Brumley and his brother Jackson were in Hawaii on tour with Rick Nelson.

Jerry Brightman was in Bakersfield when Buckaroo drummer Jerry Wiggins called him early on July 18 to ask if he remembered what vehicle Don had been driving the day before.

"The bike," the steel player said. "What's going on?"

"The bike? OK, well, I gotta call you back."

After about an hour, Wiggins called back to tell him that the San Luis Obispo sheriff's department had issued a bulletin "about a thirty-year-old male that was killed on a bike." Wiggins also called Ronnie Jackson about 5 A.M. that morning to tell him Don had been killed.

Bill Mack was working as an overnight disc jockey at WBAP-AM in Fort Worth. "I called Buck when I heard about Rich having his motorcycle accident," Bill said. "My first reaction was that Buck was taking it rather well. He told me, 'Well, life must go on.' It was business as usual. But I found out later he wasn't, because he sank into a deep depression. Maybe he was just in shock."

Jerry Brightman said, "He kept a stiff upper lip—life's going on."

Larry Adamson, however, took a dimmer view: "Nobody in that whole organization was torn up about Don's death."

LaWanda Lindsey saw a different side of Buck shortly after the accident. She had arrived in Missoula, Montana, the morning of the eighteenth for the next show in a string of OMAC gigs, and had found a message waiting for her: "Jack McFadden needs you to call him." Because she was tired, she decided to rest and call him later. When she returned the call, Jack told her Don had been killed.

"His death really crushed me," LaWanda said. "I had not, to that point, had any member of my family pass away. That was the closest I had. That death devastated me."

LaWanda caught the next flight back to Bakersfield. When she arrived at Marlane's, the front door was open and Buck was standing in the entryway. "I'll never forget the look on Buck's face," she said. "He was as white as your shirt. I had never seen him look that way and I stopped and hugged him and told him how sorry I was."

She went inside, and someone told her that Marlane would want to go into detail about Don's death but advised her not to go there because Marlane would lose control. After saying hello to everybody, LaWanda found Marlane and sat down on the couch next to her. Marlane hugged her and said, "Did you hear how it happened?" LaWanda told her, "Yes, I did. Yes, I did, Marlane." It didn't matter, though; Marlane wanted to tell her friend the story. The Savannah, Georgia–born singer didn't have a problem with that. "I remember thinking people in the South would go ahead and let you tell that story over again," she recalled. "Folks in the South were sensitive to the needs of others and would listen with an open heart." Then she said Marlane said, "Did you hear how the handlebar went right through Don's helmet and into his head?"

Years later, Don's widow remembered the helmet as being damaged in the back, and that it had "cracked like he hit his head." Don's Bakersfield lover recalled she had cracked one of the helmets on its side while on a trip to Reno when a dragonfly buzzed under it and she tossed it to the ground.

At 1 P.M. the day after the accident, Dr. Karl E. Kirschner, the same controversial medical examiner in the death of Church of Scientology founder L. Ron Hubbard, conducted an autopsy on Don's embalmed body at what was then Sutcliffe Mortuary in San Luis Obispo, before two witnesses. According to the autopsy report, the external examination revealed a tall, obese, Caucasian male with an estimated height of six feet, with short, wavy, brownish hair and puffy facial features. There were extensive abrasions on his right and left shoulders, back, and chest, and to a lesser degree, his right chin. His skull was intact and no fluid was coming out of the ears. Still, Kirschner didn't follow protocol and Don's brain tissue was not examined, even though blood welled in both nostrils, nor was the vitreous humor in his eyes checked for blood alcohol.

According to Don's death certificate, the immediate cause of death was "hemorrhagic shock due to or as a consequence of rupture, right pulmonary artery, due to or as a consequence of motorcycle accident." The certificate also noted that "deceased lost control of motorcycle when it struck divider strip." The autopsy report noted that Don broke several ribs and his chest cavity had filled with blood. He also had "bruises and excoriations [on] skin of back, shoulders and face."

Buck said the coroner called him the next day to tell him that Don had a high alcoholic content, but Don's blood alcohol report was not issued until two weeks later, on July 30, 1974. Back in the 1970s, blood alcohol tests were not done on a regular basis as they are today, but ER nurse Janette Jones said such a test could have been completed at the hospital in a matter of hours if necessary. It wasn't in Don's case, though, because he was already dead. Since the hospital didn't collect a blood sample, the nurse said, it had to have been drawn either by law enforcement at the scene or later at the mortuary. Whatever the source, the Central Pathology Labs report said Don's blood alcohol level was a whopping 0.42 percent. Later, this additional remark was added to Don's autopsy report: "The blood alcohol of this deceased was at a near comatose level and was without doubt contributory to his demise."

Blood alcohol tests are fallible, however, and their accuracy may vary from individual to individual depending on tolerance level, when the blood was drawn, whether it was venous or arterial blood, and whether it was taken from an embalmed body. For example, if a body is embalmed prior to a sample being taken, results will be corrupted because of the alcohol in the embalming fluid. In addition, law enforcement officers say it is possible, although rare, for someone with an extremely high blood-alcohol level to remain coherent. "I have arrested two people in nineteen years with blood alcohol higher than 0.40," said a former military police officer from nearby Fort Ord who requested anonymity. "Both walked and talked better than some with 0.08. Tolerance by your body is a hard one. They say 0.40 is the death limit, but it's not." Many of Don's associates and even Marlane said they had seen Don drink many times without alcohol having any effect on him. Tom Brumley and Ronnie Jackson are two who doubted Don was drunk at the time of the accident.

Buck, however, told historian Burke that he pleaded with the coroner not to release Don's blood alcohol level to the media but the coroner told him, "It's the law." Somehow, though, Buck was able to keep the coroner from releasing that information and earned him Buck's "eternal gratitude," Burke claimed. Although if Buck wanted to protect Don's memory, it is odd that he made a big deal of telling people, including Doyle Holly and Tom Brumley, that Don had gone on a binge that night, hitting every bar up and down the coast.

Other oddities complicate matters further. First, although a coroner's inquest is often conducted when a high-profile person is killed, in Don's case there was only a standard investigation. Second, no photographs exist of the autopsy, even though they were a recommended practice in death investigations in California in 1974. And finally, key records are missing from Don's file at the mortuary where the autopsy was performed. Sandra Smith of what is now Wheeler-Smith Mortuary in San Luis Obispo said, "It's the strangest thing: nothing was in the file except the death certificate"—which was incomplete. "Normally, everything is in there. All the papers, autopsy reports, etc. As you can see, besides the three handwritten notes and copy of the certificate of death, there is very little information."

The three notes to which Smith referred were handwritten on the letter-head of a Champion Company insurance representative in Fresno named Gene R. Bowen. Two notes detail the particulars of the accident. The third is a memo to "Chet" to arrange for "Don Olrick" to be taken by Robert Shaffer in a car to Greenlawn Memorial Park. There the body was to be prepared for the funeral, which was set for 11 A.M. Monday, July 22, 1974, at Hillcrest Memorial Chapel, with interment to follow at Hillcrest Memorial Park.

Don's funeral was a small affair by celebrity standards and was by invitation only. Buck was accompanied by Jennifer and kept Kris busy by putting her in charge of making sure that only invited people were admitted. About 250 people showed up to pay their respects. The small chapel was packed.

On the day of the funeral, Bonnie Owens's mother, Davis McKinney Campbell, died, so Bonnie and then-husband Merle Haggard did not attend. Nevertheless, *Country Town News* writer Dick Davis said the service "was like looking in to the pages of the West Coast edition to the Country Music Who's Who." In attendance were Ken Nelson, Rolene Brumley, LaWanda Lindsey, Susan Raye, the Hager twins, and local country singers Tommy Hays, Jimmy Phillips, and Gene Moles. The pallbearers were Buddy Alan, Jerry Brightman, Ronnie Jackson, Jim Shaw, Doyle Singer, and Jerry Wiggins, and honorary pallbearers were Tony Booth, Don Hall, Jack Immel, John Kelly, Gene Luttrell, Bob McClain, Jack McFadden, Larry Martin, Marvin Mason, Tex Mitchell, Woody Morrison, Mayf Nutter, Buck Owens, Mike Owens, Charley Pride, Lloyd Pudiwitr, Jack Shipman, Wayne "Moose" Stone, and Jim Torrance.

The Rev. Richard C. Lewis officiated and W. L. Hargis sang. Don's wife was numb with grief and sedated, and she remembers little about the service. It was an open-casket funeral and LaWanda said Don looked like himself, although his head was swollen. He was dressed in a nice suit, a white one like the Buckaroos wore at the time. He also wore white gloves. Ronnie Jackson said he could hear the last words Don had spoken to him echoing in his head: *"If anything ever happened to my hands where I couldn't play music, I wouldn't want to live."*

After the service, mourners filed past the body. Jon Hager reached inside the casket and put both hands on Don "to get the juju from his suit." Jim Hager put a guitar pick on Don's chest, and said, "You're gonna need this."

Also in attendance was Don's alleged lover. Marlane had sent her friend Diane Immel to retrieve the blonde at the airport and take her to the funeral. At the graveside ceremony, which immediately followed the service, the blonde reached out to try to touch Marlane. LaWanda recalled somebody saying, "Did you see . . . !" She remembered a woman trying to reach out for Marlane. LaWanda said, "Who? Who was that? Who was that!" She remembered others saying in disgust, "Ugh. I can't believe she came!" Kris Black said she was profoundly moved by the way Marlane handled the situation. "She was nothing but compassionate to this woman," Kris said. "I just thought, 'How incredibly loving can a human being be?' And she really was. She loved her man, and if that was where he was at, what was going on with him, she just loved him." Marlane was crying and said, "We both loved him very much and there is nothing to fight about now because he is dead."

Diane took the blonde back to the airport immediately after the funeral. As requested, Kay Adams did not attend, but she said she would have loved to put her arms around Marlane, "because I know what it did to me," she said. "I know it was devastating to her. It was devastating to me, and I regret that I caused her pain. I really do."

At age thirty-two, Don Rich had lived more, seen more, and done more than others twice his age, Buck Owens excepted. After almost sixteen years with Don at his side, Buck knew all of his bandleader's strengths and weaknesses. Don worked hard and partied hard, and had always been there for Buck. As Jon Hager said, "He was the son. He was the brother. He was the confidant of Buck. He knew Buck better than Buck did. Again, and that's why it hit Buck so hard when Don passed on."

After Don's death, Buck was lost. "First you can't talk," Buck told A&E in 2000. "This is a brother. It's a son. It's a soul thing. And I never got over it and I never will. Maybe in the next world."

Kris Black recalled that Don had told her in Nashville once, "If two men could love each other, I loved Buck Owens enough." After Don's death, she was in Buck's office with him, and he was crying. He told her, "If two men could love each other, I love Don Rich." She comforted him and told him that "Don told me that he loved you so much." Yet they had never said those words to each other.

Don's final resting place is not what one would expect for a major star of his day. He is buried in the Owenses' plot at Hillcrest. Buck's brother, Mel, and Buck's parents are buried nearby. As always, Buck spared expenses when he purchased Don's modest gravestone. It is a cheap recessed concrete marker with a pine bough in each of the bottom corners. It reads:

HUSBAND, DADDY & SON
DONALD EUGENE ULRICH
"DON RICH"
1941   1974
ALWAYS SMILING

★ 49 ★

LIFE AFTER DON

Buck Owens auditioned several guitarists to replace Don Rich, but none seemed to fit. He finally settled on Don Lee, who had a rhythmic style of playing as opposed to Don Rich's hard-driving style. The band rehearsed as it never had before trying to get back to where it needed to be. As Jerry Brightman said, "We were trying to replace the rock that didn't exist."

About a month after Don's death, Buck was back on the road. His entourage at that time included Susan Raye and *Grand Ole Opry* star George Morgan, whose daughter Lorrie Morgan would be represented years later by Jack McFadden. Jerry said their first show without Don Rich was at the Red Rocks Amphitheater in Denver, but he couldn't recall the date. They then headed to Buck's old stomping grounds in the Pacific Northwest. They played two shows at the Civic Auditorium in Portland, Oregon, on Sunday, August 18, 1974, and two shows two nights later at the Opera House in Spokane, Washington. The *Spokane Daily Chronicle* wrote an advance story promoting the Tuesday night concerts; the newspaper must have based the story off an old press release, because it listed Don Rich as one of the featured performers. The next day, the *Chronicle*'s review of the two-hour concerts said, "There is no doubt Buck and his band missed the multiple talents of fiddle player supreme Don Rich, killed in a recent accident. But duets on a single guitar and banjo by Buck and members of the backup group were still appreciated. . . . The guitar work of newcomer Don Lee, in his second show with Owens, was superb." Later in that same review, it mentioned that the music of Seattle balladeer Pat Roberts and his Evergreen Drifters "was a pleasing contrast to the bombastic Owens."

The week after his Northwest shows, Buck headed south to perform in Jackson, Mississippi, then northeast to perform with Susan Raye at the Lorain County Fair in Elyria, Ohio, where he played to a crowd of about seven thousand people on August 24, 1974. "When I get a crowd like that, it turns me on to do my best," Buck told a reporter. "I am raring to go for my second show." He was still milking his "wife contest" scheme, before talk turned to Don's death. He said he was still in shock, but "I am going to take time off during October, November, and December and just try to work things out. I don't know how I am going to replace Don." From Ohio, he went on to play a show in Kansas.

Buck then hired fiddle player Mark Moseley, who was kin to guitar maker Semie Moseley. Mark played on a few sessions and one December 1974 show, Toys for Tots, before he was let go.

Without Don next to him onstage, Buck was nothing. Everybody knew that, including Buck. "I never quite got over that," he told the *Nashville Banner* in 1992. "I went through the motions for another six years, but there are certain things that you can't take a particular ingredient out of and have it remain the same."

Tom Brumley said he found it strange that Buck talked about how great Don was after he died. "Buck calls me up saying how much he misses Don," he said. "Well, let me tell you, if Don was still here, Buck wouldn't be giving him any credit."

Kris Black recalled that after Don's death, Buck sunk into a terrible depression, and things were rough at Buck Owens Enterprises as a result. She transferred over to the KUZZ radio division to work under Buck's son Mike for a while. Mike had always been very nice to her when they worked together in Phoenix, and she thought he was one of the greatest people in the world. "But from the day that I set my foot in that Bakersfield office," she said, "all hell broke loose."

Buck believed in fostering creative tension, so he would pit people against one another. Kris didn't find out about this until years later, but Mike had told Buck the promotion job could not be done from the KUZZ offices. So as soon as she was brought in, they were at odds. Kris also believed that Mike felt threatened by her. "It was very clear. I think he was pretty much aware that I was in line to be, or supposed to be, Buck's wife, and also to have part ownership of the company. So Mike was just really in a constant state of downright controlling me, and I always felt like I was the Road Runner—'Beep beep'—and he was really trying to come up with his next scheme."

While working at the station, Kris also had to deal with death threats. "One guy was always telling me he was going to kill Buck after Don Rich died," she remembered. "There was a lot of that sort of thing." The police took the threats seriously, she said, and they suggested that she start taking her dog to work to make herself feel safer. Of course, Mike got mad at her when the dog messed on the carpet.

In fall 1974, the Country Music Association posthumously bestowed its instrumentalist of the year award on Don Rich. Winning instrumentalist of the year was a huge deal for a West Coast artist and it validated Don's talent, especially since Buck Owens had been ignored by Nashville over the years. Earl Poole Ball Jr. recalled being incensed that no one from Bakersfield went to accept the CMA award on Don's behalf. Kris Black did go to Nashville to accept a *Music City News* award for Don, though, and also tried to accept the CMA award, but the CMA told her she couldn't.

"Great Expectations," which had been released on the flip side of "(It's a) Monster's Holiday," was rereleased as a single on November 4, 1974, with "Let the Fun Begin" on the flip side.

The time had come for Buck to renew his contract with Capitol Records, but Buck was holding out for a better deal. His sales had dropped and he hadn't had a #1 hit since 1972's "Made in Japan," so the record company chose not to re-sign him. Under the terms of Buck's 1971 agreement, Capitol would have five years to sell Buck's records after the end of the contract, so he wouldn't assume ownership of his masters until 1980. For now, it was a crippling blow not only to Buck but also to the other artists whose Capitol deals were tied to Buck's contract, including Buddy Alan, Tony Booth, LaWanda Lindsey, Mayf Nutter, and Susan Raye.

When the other artists lost their deals, Buck placed all the blame on Capitol, but that was the agreement Buck had made with the label: they were all part of Buck Owens Productions, and if Buck went, they went, too. Mayf said that he had seen a document on a desk at Capitol in Hollywood that indicated only sixty copies of his upcoming record were to be pressed. Sixty records wouldn't give him much chance for national distribution, but it would allow Capitol's lawyers to argue that the company had released Mayf's record, so it blocked any legal recourse Mayf may have had. Mayf complained to Buck for about three years that Capitol wasn't getting his records into areas where he was getting airplay. Buck's stock answer was, "Son, they're not gonna help ya. You didn't do nothin' wrong, but they're not gonna help ya, and there's nothin' you or me can do about it." Buck told Mayf that he was in legal talks with Capitol, and if he discussed any details about what either side was doing during the negotiation process, he'd risk losing his battle with the label. As always, Buck's interests took priority, and it didn't matter that even his own son Buddy Alan was losing his recording deal.

Buck fared better than the other dropped artists, and in 1975 he signed a deal with Warner Brothers Records, recording for the first time in Nashville. "He landed himself a recording contract with Warner Brothers and never really did anything with the rest of us," LaWanda said. "I didn't feel too bad because he didn't get his son either. I would certainly think he would be more devoted to him."

Jerry Brightman left the Buckaroos, and on April 1, 1975, Buck hired his last steel guitarist, Terry Christofferson, to whom Jim Shaw had introduced him in January of that year. But Buck's chart success continued to dwindle. He worked fewer dates as well, limiting his appearances mostly to performances on *Hee Haw*. He shifted his focus to his business concerns in Bakersfield.

By 1976, Marlane had moved away from Bakersfield, and Buck, she said, went off on a drinking binge and kind of lost it. Later, she heard he'd had a breakdown. Buck himself later said he was indeed diagnosed with an extended nervous breakdown. He'd been depressed for almost eighteen months, he said, and wasn't able to either sing or write. "It took me a while to realize a problem did exist," he recalled. "I guess the Lord needs Don more than we needed him here."

Buckaroo Jim Shaw, who worked closely with the singer in later years, told A&E in 2000 that Buck basically "had gone a little crazy" and didn't know how to handle it. So Buck quit working for a while and only did what absolutely had to be done. Jo McFadden said of his work, "His heart wasn't in it." Buckaroo Ronnie Jackson noticed another change in Buck, too: "Buck was never the same after Don Rich got killed. Buck could care less about anybody after that."

★ 50 ★

JANA JAE

About six months after Don Rich died, fiddle player Jana Jae called Jack McFadden to check in, and to her surprise, he asked her to come for an audition. She told him her bluegrass band had a busy schedule and she was an integral part of the group, so she didn't know whether she could break away. He advised her that it would be in her best interest to come to Bakersfield, and he would not take no for an answer. He told her what day she needed to be there and asked her to get a room near the airport.

At that point, Jana was struggling to meet expenses and raise her two children, and the thought of leaving her $50-a-night gig and her band in a lurch worried her. Still, she went to Bakersfield and holed up in a hotel room, where she practiced to a tape she had made of all the fiddle parts of Buck Owens's songs on a big reel-to-reel recorder while she awaited word. Jack had ordered her not to leave her room for any reason until he called, because Buck was mourning Don and refusing to see anyone. He had to catch Buck at just the right moment.

After about three days, Jack finally called and told her to get to the studio immediately. "Can I just take the fiddle and come back?" she asked, but Jack told her to bring everything with her. Jana threw her clothes in her suitcase, grabbed her fiddle and reel-to-reel, and went to audition for Buck and Jack. She did an extensive audition and had every fiddle part down, because she had been practicing nonstop for three straight days. They took a long break during which Jack and Buck conferred, and then Jack called her in and said, "Well, we're going to Las Vegas."

Buck later told her it took three people to replace Don Rich: Don Lee on lead guitar, Doyle Singer on high harmony, and Jana on fiddle. Buck thought she might do well because fans would be less likely to compare a woman with Don. Jana was blown away by the speed of everything. Prior to this, she had only played at local and state venues; this was the big time and she felt it from the very first show. Jana felt as though she and Buck connected musically from the start. She knew music and was good for the show, and she loved it.

Before they went to Las Vegas, though, they performed three shows at the Warehouse at the University of Colorado in Denver. Although Jana didn't play at the gigs, she was backstage taking in the scene. Both Jerry Brightman and Ronnie Jackson saw her and wondered who she was and what she was doing there. Jana, on the other hand, noticed a young girl named Judy who had been brought in to see Buck. At first, Jana thought Judy was just a young fan, but then she found out Judy and Buck were involved. When Jana saw the two of them together, she remembered thinking that this really young girl made Buck look terribly old. Later, she learned that Buck wanted Judy to meet Jennifer. Jana felt that Buck was no different from most men, especially men in the music business, who are fascinated by both youth and threesomes.

Next, the band went to Vegas to play for a couple of weeks. While they were there, Jack presented her with a contract, and she realized she would not be making much money as the group's first Buckarette—only $700 a month. It was far less than what she had earned teaching fiddle. She was in tears.

"I can't make this and take care of my kids."

"This is what everybody gets. Period," Jack said.

Of course, that was not true. Pay hinged on whatever deal someone was able to finagle with Buck and on how valuable he felt that person was to him. Jack assured her that Buck had never let anybody starve and that he would take care of her, which she said he did—"in a very minimal way." More importantly, despite his stinginess, he demonstrated a commitment to quality that Jana admired. "He did have the best sound equipment. He did have a good recording studio. He was a quality showman and I think he had quality around him. I probably never would have gone on the road for seven hundred dollars a month if I hadn't felt this quality."

Upon returning to Bakersfield, Jana had no place to stay, so Buck arranged for her to bunk at Kris Black and LaWanda Lindsey's apartment in between tour dates. Dorothy Owens also offered to put Jana up at her place, but Jana declined, because she was comfortable at the apartment. Even though Jana had only a professional relationship with Buck at that point, Kris's female antennae went up immediately. Jana, on the other hand, did not recall feeling any bad vibes from either LaWanda or Kris. Jana knew LaWanda from the shows, and Kris was in the head office. "I think I was told that Kris was seeing Buck, sort of," Jana said. "So, you know, it was fine with me, I didn't think anything about it. I was only focused on music. Any of the relationship-type things really were not where my head was." Of course, Kris was only following orders by keeping her relationship with Buck silent, so Jana had no way of knowing they were involved. Besides, Jana had seen the way Buck behaved on the road. She figured he was living the life of a bachelor.

The romance between Buck and Jana did not begin until fall 1975, after Jana had been with the show for about nine months. "He was a single man, so I didn't have a problem with that," she said. "He did court me for quite a while. He'd take me to dinner after the shows and he was always fun. He wanted to be fun, just real fun and funny, charming, and definitely good to me. There was nothing kinky, nothing weird. Just really a wonderful relationship."

Buck was obviously infatuated with Jana, if not in love. According to Roni Stoneman, who appeared on *Hee Haw* with Buck and Jana, people were talking about how Buck followed Jana around the country, "staring up at her when she did a show." *People* magazine also commented on how Buck would sit "cow-eyed" in the front row watching her perform. His attraction for her was not a figment of her imagination.

Even so, Buck involved her in his cats-in-a-gunnysack approach with women. Joe McFadden, Jack's son, noted that she and Kris were "two ladies who were at ground zero for all the perversion." Buck took sport in throwing his lovers into close proximity with one another to see how they would interact with him as well as with each other. He had still been married to Phyllis when he moved Jennifer to Bakersfield, and he was with Jennifer when he brought Kris to town. Then along came Jana, whom Buck had stay with Kris while he cohabited with Jennifer. His love life resembled a Mormon polygamist's, except without the religion. Eventually, Jana got her own house and moved her children down from Northern California, and Buck courted her there and on the road. Buck courted her children, too, she said, and he was always at her house in Bakersfield. He had even gone to visit her second home in Idaho. During their courtship, Buck continued wooing Kris and Jennifer on the sly. "I was part of a fucking harem," Kris said. "I think he was a sheik in a former life."

As far as the show was concerned, Jana felt from the get-go that there was a lot of jealousy surrounding her, and she thought that it was up to the guy in charge either to squelch it or allow it to happen. Of course, Buck didn't do anything. It was more fun watching how people interacted and let them duke it out.

Whenever anybody new started with the show, Buck would give him or her a lot of attention onstage. It was no different with Jana, who got standing ovations doing songs such as "Orange Blossom Special." Jana said the music was the best part about her time with Buck. She was very comfortable with the show and Buck was good to her and understood and respected her musicianship, and that came long before anything personal transpired between them. "Every single show, we got a huge standing ovation for me and an encore, and maybe two encores," Jana said. "But I think it was good for his show, and good for his spirit. He really enjoyed it, and we really sparked on the stage."

Ronnie Jackson, too, had gotten a lot of attention when he started playing banjo for Buck a few years earlier; Buck would do songs such as "Dueling Banjos" that featured his skills. So Ronnie knew how it was when Jana came onboard. Still, it seemed to him that Buck was trying to make Jana the star of the show, that she was just another publicity stunt to keep his name out there at a time when his career was flagging. And Ronnie felt as though Jana treated the guys in the band like her flunkies, making them lug her amplifiers around and such while she told them what to do. He said the other guys felt the same as he did, but they didn't say anything. Although the musicians respected her talent as a fiddle player, he said, they felt she was not carrying her own weight. "She was the queen. Of course, she was sleeping with Buck. We had to bow to her like she was the Queen of Sheba or something." In addition, he said, Jana had her sights set on landing Buck as a husband and was very open about it.

Ronnie and Buck had many run-ins as a result of his outspokenness about Jana. One night in Las Vegas, Ronnie told him, "Jana is a good musician. The thing is, the Buckaroos are getting really uptight over everything that's going on with her."

"You're not telling me who to marry or who I can go to bed with," Buck shot back.

Kris did not like Jana at all. She felt she was homing in on Buck after Don's death. "She was trying to psych Buck out by coming over and asking me questions," Kris said. "She was very, very dominating. When she came down, she had a taped-up fiddle case—violin case I should say—as she had studied violin in Vienna. She was very motivated. She was bullying people when she first got there, and everybody was upset about it, because Don Rich had died. Buck was so vulnerable emotionally to that particular instrument. It was a very strange situation. Jennifer really loved Buck, but Jana was capitalizing on Don's death." Kris remembered Buck being depressed and locking himself away and being very quiet, and when she would go to his room to see him, his face would be covered with stubble.

Jana, on the other hand, said that Buck had his ups and downs, highs and lows, like many in the music business. He might have gotten down and quiet, and he might have led a rather confined existence, she said, "but I never thought of him as a depressed person."

In spring 1976, Jana took a history class at Bakersfield College and wrote a paper titled "Nashville West: The Musical Heritage of Bakersfield." This upset Buck, who seemed not to want her talking to local musicians for fear of what she might learn about him. He didn't get furious about it; he just told her in a playful way, "Why would you do that? You're opening a can of worms."

It reminded her of the defensive reaction he'd had one night when they went to a jam at a local nightclub. Some of their musician friends were there, and they got Jana up to play and they had a great time. "Why would you do something like that?" Buck said. "You know, you're working for us."

Jana went ahead and wrote the paper, interviewing local musicians and "somebody's wife." She said she didn't pay much mind to the gossip she heard, because most of it was unfounded, "but there were one or two people who said, 'You leave. You get out of this situation. This is not a good situation. This is not a good man.' And I didn't see that."

★ 51 ★

THE NO-RECORD DEAL

There is a common misconception that Buck Owens had little to no influence in Nashville. Perhaps he couldn't change the way the Nashville establishment produced music, but because of his money and his position in music history, he wielded much power behind the scenes. Singer-songwriter Dennis Payne told the story of how Buck used that power against him. The rest of this chapter is based on Dennis's account, which may at first glance seem implausible, but Dennis was a believable, reliable source whose information on other subjects always checked out. People such as Jo McFadden and Doyle Holly swore by the man, and Doyle himself insisted that Dennis go on the record with his story.

For some reason, Dennis said, Buck set out on a personal mission to blackball him and went to great lengths to make sure he never had a music career. It could be that Buck was jealous of Dennis's looks and talent, or it may have gone back to that incident when Dennis was a teenager just starting out—when he told Dorothy he would rather be an artist than a star and Buck seemed to turn on him. Whatever the cause, Buck's strange behavior escalated when he summoned Dennis to the studio early one morning.

Buck was sitting at his "throne desk" when Dennis arrived. "How do you like the sound of this?" Buck asked. Dennis thought he was going to play him a song to get his input, but he just spoke a name: "Armand Hammer."

"What about it?" Dennis asked.

"That's your name, son. We're changing your name to Armand Hammer. That's going to do it for you. You have that Armand Hammer look, that Greek kind of look. That *thing*."

"I don't think so, Buck."

Buck was insistent. He told Dennis changing his name to that would make him a household name. Household name is right, Dennis thought; he didn't want to be named after a brand of baking soda.

"I don't think so, Buck," he said. "I don't want to be known as Arm and Hammer." Dennis thought Buck was really losing it. He had never heard of Armand Hammer, founder of Occidental Petroleum, to whom Buck was referring. But he would later connect Buck's idea with his own father, Charles Payne, whom Dennis did not meet until he was about twenty years old. Charles had worked in the petroleum industry before his untimely death.

Dennis told several people about his strange conversation with Buck, and everybody had a big laugh about it—except Jim Shaw, who couldn't understand why Dennis wouldn't go along with Buck's idea. "Well, Buck will really do it for you if you let him do this," Jim said.

In 1976, Dennis decided to leave Buck's organization. The songwriter was having marital problems and decided he needed to focus on his marriage, so he went to Buck's office and told him he wanted to get out of his contracts, his songwriting, everything. Buck never let anybody leave without a fight. Nobody. Much to Dennis's surprise, Buck said, "OK." Dennis was suspicious: "I don't know if you understand, but I want out of everything." Buck replied, "No problem," then got Dorothy on the phone and said, "Got Dennis over here and he wants to get out of everything. Draw up all the paperwork." So they sat in his office the rest of the afternoon talking like the old friends they weren't. A few hours later, Dorothy called and said the papers were ready. Buck went over and signed the papers and that was it. Dennis was free to go. He couldn't believe it.

A couple months later, Dennis received a check from music licensing organization BMI. Most of his royalty checks were in the $100–$400 range. He was shocked, because this one was for $21,025. He suspected right away that something was wrong, but the check had his name and address on it. Sometimes when a songwriter leaves a publisher, a large royalty payment will be made, but Dennis didn't think that was the issue in this case. He called Buck to ask about what he thought was a gross overpayment, but Buck wouldn't take his call. Then he called Dorothy, and she wouldn't take his call. Next, he called Jack McFadden, and he wouldn't take his call either. No one would take his calls. Dennis didn't know what to do, so he called his father-in-law, who was a businessman, and he came over and looked at the check. "Hell, son! It's got your address on it, your name. Go cash it." So Dennis took the check to the bank where he had his accounts, where he was told, "No, we can't cash this check. You might not be this person." He asked them what he was supposed to do and the clerk told him, "We'll give you a receipt and run a check, and if it's really yours, then we will cash it."

About a week later, the bank called and said, "Mr. Payne, you can come and get your money." So Dennis and his brother-in-law went down to pick up his money. He took a briefcase with him to put the money in. He had a gut feeling something wasn't right, that something was going to happen, and he didn't even know why he felt that way. The bank teller told him the money had been deposited in his account, so Dennis wrote out a check for the full amount. "They took me into the vault and put me in this nice big red chair with a high back and went and got me Coca-Colas and whatever I wanted," he remembered. "Two little pretty girls got down on their hands and knees and counted out $20,000 in cash all over the floor." Dennis stashed the bills neatly in his briefcase and walked out to the counter. He expected something to happen—maybe for the FBI to show up—but nothing did. He then walked outside the bank and waited. Again, nothing happened. So he got in the car where his brother-in-law had been waiting.

"What in the hell have you been doing in there?" his brother-in-law asked.

"I'm not really sure," Dennis said, opening the briefcase to show him the money.

"Hell, you robbed the bank, didn't you!"

"I'm not sure. I might have. I don't know."

Meantime, a guy named Bob Jones, whom Dennis had known when he worked for Buck, had left Bakersfield and taken a job with ATV Music in Nashville. Bob was working with record producer George Richey, who was married to Tammy Wynette, and had shared some of Dennis's music with

George. The producer called Dennis in Bakersfield and told him he should come to Nashville; he wanted to produce Dennis and thought he could get him a record deal. So Dennis took about $5,000, stashed the rest of his money in his father-in-law's safe, and flew to Tennessee. He stayed with Bob and met George, who was very optimistic about working with Dennis. Everything seemed bright.

About a week later, Dennis was at Bob's when he got a phone call from the district attorney in Bakersfield. He told Dennis he had issued a warrant for his arrest. "You need to surrender yourself to the Davidson County Sheriff's Department, because you're going to jail," the DA said.

"What did I do?"

"We've got you on forgery."

"Are you sure of that?"

"Oh, yeah, I have the check right here."

"Would you read me the name that is on the check?"

"Dennis Bruce Payne."

"Well, buddy, that's my name," Dennis said. "When you guys get together and figure out how I forged my own name, call me back."

When Dennis signed the BMI check, he signed it "Dennis B. Payne," which was the only name he had ever known or used. He wondered if Buck had somehow set him up for forgery, and thought back to another strange incident a few years earlier. Dennis had been arrested by federal marshals for being underage in a bar, and he was grilled about people with foreign-sounding names. The feds called him "Martin," and when Dennis insisted he wasn't Martin, they looked at each other and laughed. One of the marshals who had been shoving him around said to the others, "This guy doesn't even know who he is!"

Had someone in the Bakersfield music business found out that there were questions about his identity?

After the DA's call, Dennis figured it was time to leave Bakersfield for good. He flew back, packed everything he owned, and moved to Nashville. He told George Richey about what was going on, and George was tickled. He had produced Freddie Hart's *Easy Lovin'* album for Buck and had never gotten paid. Needless to say, George wasn't too happy about that, but he was happy to think that Buck was out a substantial chunk of money. The producer hired Dennis an attorney, who got the issue cleared up so Dennis could keep the money. George encouraged him to do so, but Dennis knew it wasn't his and was having trouble sleeping at night. He decided that "being the way I was raised, it just wasn't right."

So he took all the money to the office of a BMI executive in Nashville and dumped $20,000 on his desk.

"No, no, no! I don't want that," the executive said. "You're going to go to prison."

"Why would I go to prison?"

"You're a criminal."

"No, I'm not, and here's the money. You can have it back."

The executive refused to take cash, so Dennis gathered it up. The two men went to a bank, where Dennis counted all the money and had a cashier's check made out to BMI. He gave the executive the check and told him he could shove it, that he didn't want the money. The songwriter felt he had done the right thing and finally felt at peace inside, because he had suspected all along that the money wasn't his.

When he told George what he'd done, George was upset. In fact, just about everybody Dennis knew was mad at him for returning the money.

"That was the start of the no-record deal," Dennis said.

Dennis remained in Nashville for the next thirty years and beyond. He had deals arranged with every major label—Capitol Records, Columbia, Poly-gram—but when the day came to sign the contract, someone always said, "Well, we just had a call from somebody, and we can't tell you who, but we're not gonna sign you."

At one point, Dennis was being managed by Johnny Cash's drummer, W. S. Holland. Dennis was set to do a showcase, and he called his manager to check in. W.S. said, "Hey, I've got a good buddy here sitting across the desk from me. He told me to tell you that he's got his eye on you, he's still watch-ing you."

"Buck Owens, right?" Dennis said.

"Yeah, how did you know?"

"There's no record deal."

When he went to do the showcase, nobody showed up to listen.

Another time, Dennis had a millionaire in Kentucky set to invest in him, but even he couldn't buy Dennis a deal. Jimmy Bowen, then-president of Capitol Nashville, told the investor, "Dennis Payne never gets a record deal ever, never in the history of music. Never. He never gets anything. That's the way it is." When Dennis's manager took the late Lynn Shults, the A&R man at Capitol Nashville who signed Garth Brooks to his first record deal, a demo tape, Lynn loved it and wanted to know who was singing. As soon as he was told it was Dennis Payne, Lynn threw Dennis's tape out the window and said, "Don't ever bring this guy's stuff in here again. We can't do anything with him."

"That's the way it has been for all these years," Dennis said. "Every time I almost get a cut, something happens."

Although Dennis still plays music, "it's tough," he said. "If I knew how to do anything else, I'd go do it, because it's been a struggle just to exist. Sometimes I feel like I've bought this American dream thing, that if you had a talent and you worked really hard at it and you did the best you can do and you didn't screw nobody you'll be rewarded and good things will come to you. Well, it ain't how it is. I'm tired. Wore out. Fried."

Dennis loved Buck Owens's music—but added that "a lot of that music wasn't all his. Buck robbed a lot of people and claimed it was his. He uses everybody. He uses up people's talent. He's kind of like a vampire. He sucks the life out of them, drains off all their life for his own purpose. He takes pleasure in it. That's the real sad part about it."

Two Goodbyes

In 1976, Kris Black was beginning to see the darker side of her boss and lover Buck Owens. As she aged, she noticed a distinct change in the way he treated her. Kris agreed with Jana Jae that Buck preferred younger women; "When I hit 25, I was starting to turn into the old hag."

In addition, she said, "Buck wouldn't let me sing." Kris had always wanted to, and she had the voice for it. Her roommate LaWanda Lindsey was surprised to discover that Kris had a nice voice, though she thought it was more pop than country. But Buck told Kris she had no business being in the limelight, because she was very important to him and would someday be part owner of the company. Kris did cut a record in 1976, but Buck blackballed it for airplay at radio stations across the country, she said. It was a tactic he often used when keeping other artists in their place.

Kris's record did not trigger the split between her and Buck, but it happened around the same time, when Kris found out that Buck was living with Jennifer Smith. LaWanda still didn't know that Kris and Buck were involved, so once when she got back from the road, she let something slip about how Jennifer had gone with them. Kris wanted to know who Jennifer was, and LaWanda replied, "That model that lives with Buck out at the ranch." Then Kris told LaWanda about her relationship with Buck.

After that, Kris started to rebuff Buck's advances, though he kept coming on to her. She wanted out, and not just as Buck's lover. She wanted out of Buck Owens Enterprises altogether. She refused to continue there with Mike Owens constantly on her case and Jennifer living with the man she loved. She decided she would quit on April 20, 1976, the day her annual profit-sharing matured. Mike fired her the day before that was to happen, though. On April

19, he informed Kris in a terse, two-sentence letter that she was being relieved of her duties. When she was packing up her office, Buck begged her not to go, but she could take no more. Buck and Kris had been together exactly nine years, from April 1968 to April 1976.

A month later, on May 13, Kris's roommate, LaWanda Lindsey, married Billy Smith and set up housekeeping in Albuquerque. By the following year, LaWanda's singing career had rebounded, and she signed a recording contract with Mercury Records.

While working for Buck, Kris had attended Bakersfield College, and she graduated with honors with an associate of arts degree in broadcast journalism in 1976. She began pursuing endeavors unrelated to her former boss, such as getting one of her mother's favorite country artists, Hank Thompson, inducted into the Country Music Hall of Fame.

Four months after she left Buck, she sat at his dying father's bedside at Bakersfield Memorial Hospital, holding his hand and listening to his stories. Buck was mad at his father and wouldn't visit him. The way Kris saw it, Buck's softer side was the result of his strong ties with his mother, and he associated her with goodness. Conversely, he associated his father with badness. As much as Buck loved and cared for Maicie, he could be very cruel to Alvis Sr., in an underhanded, passive-aggressive way. Although he had put his father in charge of overseeing a couple of his ranches, he used that responsibility against him.

Alvis Sr. told Kris about how Buck had once made him use a half-inch pipe for irrigation instead of one-inch pipe, because it was cheaper. The half-inch pipe kept breaking and his father had to keep replacing it, back-breaking work under the hot California sun. Alvis Sr. could not understand why his son, who had more money than he could ever hope to spend, would not go with the better pipe that would hold up. "Son, why do you do that?" he asked.

Buck's father, who had leukemia, died of acute pulmonary edema at age sixty-seven on August 26, 1976. After Alvis Sr.'s funeral, Maicie wrote Kris the following letter:

Dear Kris:

Thank you very much for the pink carnations in a straw basket. They were beautiful. Kris, thank you also for always being so nice and good to Dad. Dad liked you a lot.

Kris, I miss him so much. I don't know how I can go on without him. We all loved him so much, our loss seems more than I can bear.

Thank you again for all the nice things you have done—

All our love,
Mother Owens & family

Kris did offer Buck comfort after the death of his father, but he took the opportunity to let her know that he was very displeased with her efforts on behalf of Hank Thompson. Buck was insanely jealous of Hank, whom Ken Nelson also produced at Capitol Records. ("Buck hated his dad, but he loved Ken Nelson," Kris said. "Buck loved him like he loved Don Rich. Ken Nelson was the father he wished he'd had.")

Even after all the trauma she endured while working for Buck, Kris still loves the man. "You know, when I look back, some of my friends say, 'You should be so bitter, you should hate him,'" she said, "but I am so grateful for the opportunity to find out what I was made of, to know the people in the country music business, the people that made things happen in that time and era. I really learned a lot that I am glad for now. As far as being OK financially and stuff, there's great resentment that I was misled."

Jo McFadden said she told Kris she should "thank God every day that you're alive that you didn't get a hold of him and marry him, 'cause she would have been a miserable sonofabitch. Kris does not know how lucky she is not to have that man. 'Cause he would have made her life hell.'"

After Kris left him, Buck went forward with his aborted plan to pose nude for *Playgirl.* The photos were shot in 1977 at his ranch on Zerker Road. He never intended for Enos the Penis to see print, because he made sure he had photo approval prior to publication, which he never provided. Still, the pre-publication hype got his name bandied about at a time when his career was on the skids, and he reveled in cavorting "Buck nekkid" for the magazine's female photographers.

And yet, it was not the most shocking thing Buck did in 1977. Because that was the year when, as Kris put it, "he went and married Jana."

★ 53 ★

THE "THREE-DAY" MARRIAGE

The marriage between Buck Owens and Jana Jae would become one of the most talked-about in country music history, and contrary to popular belief, it was no snap decision. Buck told Jana he loved her for a long time and talked about marrying her—just as he had talked to Kris about marrying her. "I was in love," Jana said. "I was really in love and I knew he was also. We sparked onstage, personally, everything—we had fun every single night. We'd go out after the shows, and it was just fun."

Their relationship began to shift, however, after Jana started recording a fiddle album for Buck and he presented her with a contract that sought to tie up any albums she recorded for the next twelve years. They were in the studio at the time, and she told him she wanted to look over the thick document first. When she wouldn't sign it on the spot, he flipped out. It was the first time she had ever seen him truly angry. In an attempt to calm him down, she said, "I would check out any contract I signed even if it was with a dishwasher repairman."

Buck told her the contract was nonnegotiable. He was not about to forget what he saw as an act of defiance, and during the time the two wrangled over the terms, Buck did to Jana what he had done with other Buckaroos such as Doyle Holly and Ronnie Jackson—he fired her repeatedly. All told, he hired and fired her three times during the period she worked with him. "Maybe if I had signed that recording contract blindly, it may have been the most wonderful thing in the world," she said. "The fact that I didn't was what made him furious, and that's what changed the relationship. He wanted this precise and total control: *He had been good to me. Why did I question him? Or not trust him?* So that was sort of the beginning of a roller-coaster traumatic." Eventually she signed the contract, but only after she had a lawyer review it, and ultimately she recorded the fiddle album.

Still, the damage had been done. After the ordeal, Jana remembered times on the road when Buck would disappear to a room down the hall. "It was like he was trying to make me jealous," she said. "I would be left in the room while he would go meet with so-and-so and so-and-so. I remember one time in Nashville at Spence Manor he was meeting with Linda Ronstadt and Emmylou Harris and I said, 'Oh, I would love to talk to them.' When it came right down to it, he said, 'Stay here and I'll be back,'" she recalled with a nervous laugh. "He would disappear sometimes and I would begin to wonder where in the heck he was, and I knew there had to be something going on the whole time. I remember lots of ups and downs."

Then he threatened to hire a girl fiddle player from Weiser, Idaho, Jana's hometown. He would do things such as touch another woman's leg or breast on purpose in front of her to make her jealous. "He had no shame," Jana said. "He would do something like that to get a rise out of not only me but everybody. We were so close that it was obviously hurtful to me."

Then one day, Buck called her with an order: "I need you to come to the office and I really need to talk to you and I want you to come right now!"

When Jana got to his office, he told her, "This is ridiculous what we've been going through. I've got a private plane out there. The engines are running and we are going to go get married."

"But, Buck, are you sure?" In Jana's mind, their relationship had soured and things weren't as cohesive as they had been. She did not want to make a mistake, particularly when she had two small children who were part of the package.

Buck proceeded to persuade her for an hour and a half to two hours, using every reasonable argument he could present. "Haven't I always been good to you? Couldn't I be good for Matt and Katy? What else do you want? Here you've got your children taken care of, you've got your music, we're good onstage. We're happy together."

Jana felt herself being reeled in again.

"I've got the plane ready. You have to say yes."

Then he gave her a ring, a beautiful diamond ring with either nine or eleven diamonds. "Rows of diamonds, big diamonds," she remembered. That is when she let herself go over the edge. She thought to herself that every-thing he said made perfect sense, and it probably would end their emotional roller-coaster ride. She heard herself say, "OK."

"Well, go pack your bags real quick and come right back and we'll go to the airport."

Buck and Jana married May 2, 1977, at the Little Church of the West wed-ding chapel in Las Vegas. They stayed two nights at the Landmark in the hon-eymoon suite and were supposed to go to Phoenix next, but Buck changed the plan and said they were going back to Bakersfield to get some things before going on to Phoenix.

When word got out about their marriage, most people were incredulous. Ronnie Jackson couldn't believe Buck was leaving Jennifer, because she'd been with him a long time and he couldn't imagine them ever splitting up. Neither could Jo McFadden, who really liked Jennifer. The consensus among many in Buck's camp was that Buck wasn't thinking clearly. He was still reeling from Don's death, they thought, and didn't know what to do with his life or career. They felt he associated the fiddle with Don and because Jana played the fid-dle, he convinced himself he was in love. As for Jana, they didn't believe she really loved Buck; they saw her as a gold-digger.

Others disagreed. LaWanda Lindsey, who genuinely liked Jana, wasn't sur-prised by the union, and she felt Jana actually cared for Buck more than he cared for her. Jana herself denied that she had married Buck for financial gain, but agreed that money played a big part in the ugliness that followed. "I think when someone is earning the money, and the family members are helping with it—you know, they are not really earning their own money but are using his or her career, his or her money—they become very paranoid about any-body coming into the scene who might throw a curve. I understand that."

The newlyweds landed in Bakersfield, where they were met with an ice-cold reception from Dorothy and Mike. Buck's relatives were worried, Jana later concluded, that there had been no prenuptial agreement, not even a dis-cussion of one. "They wanted a contract. I think they had been so used to contracts with everything else for everybody else, and Buck hadn't even mentioned it. I am sure after that recording-contract deal, he knew I probably would not have agreed."

Buck was then whisked away. When she called looking for him, no Buck. He had told her, "I'll pick you up at four o'clock." So she sat and waited and waited and waited. Her children were there, but not Buck. She called Jack and Dorothy and left messages. Someone finally returned her call and told her Buck had been taken to the hospital and could not be reached. The hospital story didn't make any sense to her; she knew something was very wrong.

After a day or so, Buck's lawyer paid her a visit and told her: "There's no more Buck. We have filed an annulment." Jana sensed that this new development hadn't originated with Buck; she suspected that Mike and Dorothy, or maybe just Dorothy, had had something to do with it. "I just couldn't believe it. I was so shocked. I said, 'I need to talk to Buck.' I said, 'What have you done with Buck? Where is Buck?' They wanted the simplest thing, to just annul it, but it was a consummated marriage. So they whisked him away and hospitalized him, which just, to me, was outlandish!"

"Look I have this ring!" Jana told the lawyer. "Don't you know that we have been in love and that this marriage is what he wants? Look at this ring!"

"Oh, yeah, well, he probably does love you, but he's just confused."

Buck's appearances in four cities were postponed or canceled, and the official story was that Buck had been hospitalized after a riding accident. The Associated Press, quoting Jack McFadden, reported that Buck had injured his left hip in a fall from a horse. Supposedly, he was hospitalized for bruises and to make sure blood clots didn't form, though he told Nashville music journalist Stacy Harris that he'd torn some leg ligaments. "His story was that he had fallen off a horse in distraction when Jana left him," Roni Stoneman wrote in her autobiography, and Tom Brumley said, "The story I heard was he got married on Monday, fell off his horse on Tuesday, got annulled on Wednesday."

What really happened may never be clear, because some of the parties involved aren't talking. Some believe that Dorothy and Mike were behind the hospitalization, perhaps because Dorothy was trying to have Buck psychologically evaluated in addition to pressuring him to annul the marriage on grounds that Jana was insane. Others claim that Jennifer played a role. According to the version of the story Kris Black heard, when Buck took off to Las Vegas to marry Jana, he called Dorothy and told her to let Jennifer know she had to move back to Texas, because he had just married Jana in Las Vegas. "If that had been me," Kris said, "I would have been boo-hooing hysterically."

Jennifer, of course, knew that the best way to stir Buck's emotions was to hit him below the belt—in his wallet. Even though California would not have recognized Buck and Jennifer's relationship as a common-law marriage, Kris said, "Well, Jennifer is nobody's fool, so she just promptly said, 'You tell him that he is going to owe me half of everything he owns and he doesn't have time to hide his assets.' She stood her ground, so when Buck got back, he told Jana, to my understanding, to go to the house with her children and wait for Daddy to call when the coast was clear and then they could all move in and live happily ever after. He gets on the phone with the lawyers in Los Angeles to get this thing figured out. He needed to get out of the mess because Jennifer had him, big time." Jana herself told *People* magazine: "There are other girls in his life."

In any event, during the time he was feuding with his new wife, Buck moved Jennifer into the ranch on Poso Creek Lane where Dorothy lived with her companion. Dorothy's ranch was adjacent to his own, and he wanted Jennifer around in case it didn't work out with Jana.

When Jana received the annulment papers from Buck's camp, filed May 3, 1977, in Bakersfield, she saw the grounds were that she was insane. However, Buck's camp told the wire services the grounds were "irreconcilable differences." Jana and her Los Angeles attorney Marvin Mitchelson fought back, filing for annulment on grounds of fraud.

By mid-May, Buck had retracted his initial petition for annulment. "I love that pretty fiddle player and I won't stop until I get her back," he told the *Herald-Examiner* in Los Angeles. "I just got cold feet. Gee whiz, I thought, here I play golf or tennis every day and I might have to give all that up. Then I thought that for the first time in my life, I am really in love. Why did I serve those annulment papers? I spent two years talking her into marrying me and now I did this? I'm just a poor country boy from Texas and I hadn't been married in a long time."

He started a full-scale blitz to win Jana back, including a contrite appearance on the *Tonight* show, which Steve Allen hosted that night, begging Jana to come home. There were also radio spots, full-page ads in the *San Francisco Chronicle* and the *Los Angeles Times*, and billboard ads, which Jana thought were tacky, that said: "Jana Jae Owens, I need you, Matt and Katy. Buck," "Jana Jae Owens, I love you. Buck," and "Come back." Then-WBAP disc jockey Bill Mack said, "I remember going on the air and saying, 'Buck wants you back,' and I didn't even charge him for it."

The *Los Angeles Times* reported that on July 21, Jana agreed to reconcile with Buck and moved out to his ranch with her two children, Matt, nine, and Katy, seven, and her grand piano in tow. Within twenty-four hours, he disappeared without explanation until July 30. Again he begged her to stay, only to disappear again four days later.

Buck filed for divorce in Kern County on August 17, in spite of Jana's annulment petition that was filed in Los Angeles. She filed a motion on August 18, to change her grounds to "mental incompetence" and asked that the court order a psychiatric evaluation for Buck.

Jana and her children left Bakersfield and moved in with her father in Playa Del Rey. She then filed a restraining order against Buck, but the court order did not deter him. He hounded her "almost every day," she told the Associated Press. He sent presents to her father's house: "He sent like three dozen flowers every day and a diamond watch, and gifts for the kids. There were truckloads of things coming constantly. I was so traumatized that I just hid out. I couldn't stand it."

Buck told the *Nashville Banner*, "After five weeks, I'm still apologizing. This ain't no publicity thing. What the hell do I need with publicity, especially this kind? I've always been a guy who could walk away from a girl, but I can't this time. Jana's not the kind of girl to walk away from. She's the kind to get next to." He told *People* magazine, "There has never been another girl like Jana."

Jana agreed that the ads he bought were not a publicity stunt, but "knowing Buck, he was going to use it. I mean, he wanted me back. He wanted truly to get me back, OK. He was not going to just be mincing about it. He's just gonna get me back! You know, for the world! And make a big splash and he probably subconsciously thought it's gonna be a lot of publicity, too."

What did go unpublicized, however, is that Jana finally agreed to reconcile again and she and her kids moved back out to the ranch, where she lived about a year and a half as Buck's wife. After she returned, he never talked business with her again; instead, he kept everything at a personal level. "He was always very aware that I was totally concentrated on my children. I mean, that was my whole thing. Children and music."

The emotional roller coaster continued, however, and she kept journals to keep her sanity. She was presented at some point with a marriage contract, which she never signed. She just said, "If I am not supposed to be here, I don't want to be here." If he had presented her with the contract in the beginning and said, "This is a prenuptial I think that will do right by both of us. Have your lawyer look at it and we will talk about it," she would have had no problem with that. But now it was being presented in such a way that she didn't feel like it was coming from Buck. She felt people were thinking: "Oh, he just doesn't know what he is doing"—the same reason, she suspected, that they wanted to hospitalize him after their marriage. "He had known what he was doing for the past several years," Jana insisted.

Then there was the matter of Jennifer. Jana recalled being on a trip with her husband when Dorothy called and said, "Jennifer's in the hospital." They cut their trip short and went back to Bakersfield. Jana didn't know exactly what happened. "I think it was something pretty dramatic. I think Dorothy insisted that he come take care of her," she said. "So there was always that pull. Later on, he would sing about Jennifer and that relationship, 'It ain't love, but it ain't bad.' In retrospect, I think he truly was torn by what was already there: contracted family"—i.e., family members on Buck's payroll. "The family was very comfortable with that relationship, because there was nothing that could hurt them whatsoever. For me to come in with no marriage contract, and blissfully in love, I mean, that was a real threat to them. There was definitely a connection between us, and it was more of a love connection than an arrangement that was comfortable for everybody else."

Also in 1977, Buck wanted to leave *Hee Haw* because he was really burnt out, but the producers talked him into staying. And banjoist Ronnie Jackson had had enough and left the Buckaroos.

Then in 1978, after a seventeen-month ride on the "roller-coaster traumatic," Jana wanted off. She realized that she wasn't being fair either to herself or to her children, and that if she didn't leave, nothing would change. So she called talent manager Jim Halsey and told him she might be moving and was in need of management. After leaving Buck, Jana moved to Burbank and then to Tulsa, which had a thriving country music scene. "The only thing I wanted out of the divorce settlement was just to pay the bills," she said. "I just wanted to go on with things, and as long as I got enough to pay the legal fees and my moving expenses, I was gone."

In total, there were four divorce filings for Jana and Buck. The first two were entered in Los Angeles in May and August 1977 and the last two were entered in Bakersfield on August 17, 1977, and August 30, 1978. The last one finally took and was entered into the official record on August 31. Mitchelson, who went on to become a famed palimony lawyer, won Jana a settlement of at least $1 million, though she would not say how much she got.

Jana also had to end her working relationship with Buck, which meant she had to sign exit papers for her Buckarette contract. Any future payments she received for her previous work, such as reruns of *Hee Haw*, fell under that agreement, she said—which meant she had to keep signing over all those checks to him. With *Hee Haw* reruns continuing to this day, over time it turned out to be a huge amount of money Jana lost. "The hardest part of the actual split," Jana said, "I mean aside from the emotional part, the only real on-paper part that was difficult was getting the release from my album." She ended up paying Buck $5,000 to gain ownership of the album. In spite of all the hassles, Jana maintained that working with Buck had been a boost to her career.

After their divorce, Jana said she felt Buck did not want producer Sam Lovullo to put her in any of the *Hee Haw* reruns, because Buck wanted to pretend that her appearances had never happened. "Of course, it happened. It happened big time and in a big way and it was a very important section there, but that would be hurtful to me and that would be the last word so to speak." Sam said there was no way Buck could have prevented Jana from being featured in reruns, however, because it was a union show that had to abide by the Screen Actors Guild and American Federation of Television and Radio Artist rules.

Jana said a friend in Nashville had read her a portion of Sam's book and it gave the impression that she wanted to stay on the show and hounded Sam at his office, even hiding in the closet until he came back so that he could not avoid seeing her, "which is total bull. They wanted me to be on the show. Sam was very helpful, very appreciative of my talents. He is the one who recommended Jim Halsey to me, which I think probably infuriated Buck." However, she said she was never asked to continue on *Hee Haw* and no one even called to let her know she wouldn't be appearing anymore, much the same way Bill Mack had never been told that he would not be continuing in his role as emcee of the *Buck Owens Ranch*. It didn't much matter to her, though, because it was not a financial gain for her to do *Hee Haw*—Buck got all her money for that anyway. Besides, she was busy developing her new stage show.

Some time after Jana and Buck's divorce, Kris Black remembered, she was being interviewed by various radio people, including Billy Parker at KBRO in Tulsa. "He was interviewing me in just a general sense, and we had about fifteen guys sitting in the back of the control room, because there in Tulsa, Oklahoma, they would let people in to sit in and hear the show and see what was going on," Kris said. "Well, Billy says to me, 'Kris, why do you think Buck married Jana Jae? Do you have any idea on that?' And I said, 'Well, I guess he just liked the way she fiddled.' Everybody in the control room laughed."

In 1978, not long after Jana's exit, Buck's in-studio partnership with Susan Raye ended as well. By this point, Buck's behavior had become increasingly erratic.

Bradley Hartman, the engineer who recorded "Play Together Again Again" on March 21, 1979, recalled that when Buck, Jack McFadden, and producer Norro Wilson showed up to cut the song at the Enactron truck outside Emmylou Harris's house in the Coldwater Canyon section of Beverly Hills, Buck was antsy and didn't want to do it because he wanted to go to Las Vegas. "He was kind of bossing him around a little bit," Bradley said of Buck's treatment of Jack. "They could have just stayed and finished up, but it was like they had to go party." When the three men returned after being gone a few days, Brad recalled, "they came back pretty wasted."

With Kris and Jana both out of the picture, Buck Owens married Jennifer on June 21, 1979. This time he made sure to have his bride-to-be sign a prenuptial agreement before she signed the marriage license. Buck told *Country Weekly*, "I figured I wasn't ever going to find anybody that would put up with me the way she did and I liked her style, so one morning I said, 'Let's go get married.'"

It's true that Jennifer stuck with Buck through a lot of crap. She was still there for him even after he broke her heart by marrying Jana Jae. Friends say she genuinely loved him and was not after his money. She was content to stay on the ranch, following her childhood dream of riding and owning thoroughbred horses. Although she and Buck never had any children together, they ran a rescue operation of sorts for dogs and cats on their ranch, complete with kennels. Whenever strays wandered onto their land, they got them veterinary care and had them either spayed or neutered, then found homes for the critters. Their union would end up being the longest of all Buck's marriages.

Jo McFadden said she could not imagine that Buck's marriage to Jana would have worked, because Jana was very career-oriented, whereas Jennifer was content to stay home. Jo always felt Buck was very lucky to have a woman such as Jennifer.

Jana, on the other hand, lamented that she had lost the attention not only of the fans but also of every record company in the world. Buck had black-balled her in the business, she said. He also didn't want her to use his last name, which is why she uses "Jana Jae" professionally, even though "Jana Jae Owens" is her legal name. It amazed her to find that Buck dealt with their marriage by pretending it never existed; he just "swept everything under the rug," she said. "Professionally, he knows that's what would hurt me."

54

THE '80S

Finally, it seemed, Buck Owens was able to slow down and enjoy life. In the evenings, he and Jennifer would sit in the yard to watch the sun set and the coyotes play. In January 1980, he told the Buckaroos he was not going to be doing many dates anymore and disbanded the group. He offered them jobs in his organization doing other things besides playing music. Keyboardist Jim Shaw became his right-hand man (or "yes" man, as some associates put it) and steel player Terry Christofferson worked in the research department. Bassist Doyle Singer stayed on to play occasional gigs, while drummer Jerry Wiggins left that year and was replaced by Rick Taylor on the few gigs they played. No one seems to remember what lead guitarist Don Lee did or when he bowed out, but Terry doubled on lead and steel after Don's exit.

After his Warner Brothers contract expired later in 1980, Buck Owens announced his retirement from recording and touring altogether. His heart wasn't in the music anymore. So he focused on his business concerns in Bakersfield, continued to cohost *Hee Haw*, and acted in a made-for-television movie. Buck's third and last movie was a 1980 spoof of crime dramas titled *Murder Can Hurt You*. It had an all-star cast, including Hee Haw Honey Gunilla Hutton. Buck played the role of Sheriff Tim MacSkye, a cornpone version of Dennis Weaver's TV character Dennis McCloud.

As Buck withdrew from the performing life, Jack McFadden found he had little to do as Buck's manager, and he focused his time and attention on other OMAC artists instead. Then in 1983, International Creative Management called. ICM was looking for someone to run its Nashville office, and Jackson

Brumley, who was working in Nashville at the time, recommended his former boss. Jack did not want to live in Nashville, but he flew to New York and talked to the ICM executives anyway. They offered him an attractive deal, which he accepted. Then he and his wife, Jo, went to Nashville and bought a house. "I can't believe I am moving to Nashville," Jack told Jo. "You know, I never would have thought that I would have moved to Nashville." As far as Jo knew, Buck had very little say about Jack leaving Bakersfield. Even though Jack was working a new job in a different city, he would continue to represent Buck until Jack's death in 1998.

Jack was not very happy at ICM and after seeking legal advice broke his contract in the first half of 1984. Then in August, he and his wife broke ground on a building on Eighteenth Avenue South in Nashville and opened their own office together. They set up a booking agency, McFadden & Associates Inc., which longtime agent Paul Bryant headed up, and a management company, McFadden Artists Corporation, which Jack and Jo ran. They managed such country stars as Billy Ray Cyrus, Freddie Hart, David Frizzell, Sonny James, Lorrie Morgan, Gene Watson, Shelly West, and Keith Whitley, among others.

Buck went to Nashville not long after the McFaddens opened their agencies, and Jo recalled that Buck seemed envious of the modest building and businesses that she and Jack had built together, even though they paled in comparison with the business behemoth Buck had built. Most likely, Buck envied the fact that he himself hadn't had a hand in it, and that Jack had a supportive mate in Jo, who had helped him become a success in his own right. Buck had never had that in a woman, beyond his sister Dorothy.

Larry Adamson also went to visit his old friend in Nashville, and while he was in Jack's office, the phone rang. "Here, I've got somebody for you to talk to," Jack said, handing Larry the telephone. It was Buck, of course. "Jack always wanted me to patch it up with Buck," Larry said. "I didn't want to patch it up."

In 1991, Jack was named man of the year by the Nashville Association of Talent Directors. In addition, he served on the board of governors for the Nashville chapter of the National Academy of Recording Arts and Sciences and on the board of directors for the Country Music Association. Jack was credited with getting Billy Ray Cyrus his first contract in 1992 for his smash album *Achy Breaky Heart*.

Back in Bakersfield, life took a downward slide for Buck in 1986. First, after seventeen years on *Hee Haw*, he was relieved of his cohosting duties. He told the press he'd made the decision to leave, because the producers told him they were going to change the show's image. "They said, 'Next year we're going to wear tuxedos,' I said, 'You are, but I ain't,'" Buck told *Country Weekly* magazine. He told the Associated Press, "As I get older, I wanted to get away from having my time orchestrated: 'Buck be here at 1, do that at 2.' I'm rebelling against that more and more, and I was really starting to consider the show an infringement on my time." He said he wanted to "redirect his energies" to his own business interests, such as his broadcasting and newspaper holdings.

However, the truth is that Buck was asked to leave. Nobody has said why, only that it was a well-thought-out decision. *Hee Haw* spokesman Tom Adkinson told the Associated Press in March 1986 that Buck was leaving the show and that Buck "and the show's producer had spoken about this, so it's not a sudden thing." Jack McFadden agreed that the leave-taking was not an overnight decision and that there was "no animosity on either side. This parting is very sad, like Buck is right now. When you work with someone for 17 years, you don't just walk away and say, 'I'll see you.'" Roni Stoneman said she and Buck were fired the same day. "I was stunned," she wrote in her autobiography. "Buck Owens was one of the stars. Sam's face was blood red when he told me the head office had ordered the move."

Then, to borrow from one of the running-gag songs on the show, "pfft he was gone."

A few months after he was fired from *Hee Haw*, Buck's beloved mother passed away. Maicie Owens died at age seventy-seven on May 27, 1986, in Bakersfield. Pastor Roger C. Spradlin of the Valley Baptist Church in Fruitvale, where Maicie had been a Sunday school teacher for more than forty years, officiated at the funeral.

Kris Black tried to get to the funeral, she recalled, but arrived too late, although she made it to where the mourners gathered afterward. Buck was with Jennifer when he saw Kris, and he got away long enough to tell her, "Meet me at my office," which she did. "His heart was truly broken" over the loss of his mother, said Kris, who had set up her own marketing company in Dallas, Texas, in 1982 and had become a Reiki master and certified massage therapist instructor. "He sobbed in my arms like a child. I held him for over half an hour, doing Reiki and transferring energy to his heart chakra, and rocked him like a mother would rock a child."

"Oh my gosh," he said. "I want to take you to dinner!"

Kris told him he didn't have to, that he had Jennifer, and to go home and be with his wife, but he insisted. They agreed to meet at a Chinese restaurant. Kris got there around five o'clock and waited, but Buck being Buck, never showed up.

In the mid-1980s, Buck sold Blue Book Music and its catalog for $1.6 million to Buddy Killen at what was then Tree Publishing in Nashville. Killen felt that it was a wise investment and that the catalog would earn back the money spent on it many times over. Songs in the catalog included many Merle Haggard standards such as "Mama Tried," "Okie from Muskogee," and "Today I Started Loving You Again" as well as Gene Price's "Easy Lovin'." Of course, when a publishing company sells a song catalog, the songwriters do not reap any profits from the sale.

Buck also focused on mentoring up-and-coming country artists, most notably Dwight Yoakam. Before they met, Dwight had recorded two albums, *Guitars, Cadillacs, Etc., Etc.* in 1984 and *Hillbilly Deluxe* in 1987. Dwight, one of the so-called neotraditionalists in country music, was a big fan of Buck Owens and a proponent of the Bakersfield Sound. He had patterned much of his work on that Telecaster-infused style. He even dedicated *Hillbilly Deluxe* to Buck and wrote the song "Little Ways" as a tribute to Buck's musical influence. The admiration and respect was mutual.

The story of how Buck and Dwight met is almost legend in itself. In 1987, Dwight called his musical hero and arranged to meet at Buck's office. Dwight was performing at a fair that night and asked Buck to join him onstage. Buck decided, why not? That performance led to a duet of Homer Joy's "Streets of

Bakersfield," which was recorded April 4, 1988, with Pete Anderson as the producer. It was released June 17 and became Buck's first #1 in sixteen years, and Dwight's very first.

Buck first recorded "Streets of Bakersfield" on November 6, 1972. Homer Joy had written the song about Buck, because when he first blew into town, Buck refused to talk to him. Homer was persistent, however, and eventually gained an audience with him. Buck liked the song and offered him $50 for it, but Homer stood his ground and got his fair share. The 1972 recording was not released as a single; it was an album cut on Buck's 1973 album *Ain't It Amazing, Gracie*.

Not since Don Rich had Buck felt such a kinship with a young musician, and he and Dwight became fast friends. Buck told A&E *Biography*, "Dwight should've been one of my sons." Buck even toured occasionally with Dwight. Although both artists championed the honky-tonk sound, their approach to music was different. As author Colin Escott noted, "Yoakam saw his music as an art form; Buck just saw it as something he did."

Before setting out on the road with Dwight in 1988, Buck called Marlane Ulrich and told her someone had stolen his blue guitar. He asked her to return Don Rich's silver sparkle Telecaster, so she sent it back to him. He kept it, playing it on his gigs with Dwight as a talisman of sorts. Years later, he sent it to Marty Stuart as a gift.

In July 1988, James P. McCarty, better known as Jim, took over the drums for the not-quite-disbanded Buckaroos. He also began working as a computer wizard for Buck. Jim said, "Outside of having the opportunity of working with Ringo Starr in 1989, for the most part, [it was] not a pleasurable experience."

Jim Foglesong, then president of Capitol Nashville, persuaded Buck to sign another recording contract with Capitol. Buck resurrected his old rockabilly number "Hot Dog," rerecording it at Capitol Records in Hollywood on August 3, 1988, with Jim Shaw producing. "Hot Dog" was released as a single on September 28, but it only peaked at #46 on the *Billboard* country chart. The *Hot Dog!* LP was released November 16.

Also in 1988, the Country Music Foundation released the compact disc version of the Buckaroos' *Live at Carnegie Hall*. In a rare act of benevolence, Buck lent the masters, which he now owned, to be digitally remastered. The proceeds went to the foundation.

❧

In March 1989, Buck was invited to the Bay Area Music Awards, sponsored by San Francisco–based rock magazine BAM (Bay Area Music). Buck was photographed at the event, better known as the Bammy Awards, with rockers Neil Young, Sammy Hagar, Chris Isaak and John Fogerty, all self-confessed Buck Owens fans. Fogerty even mentioned Buck in a 1970 Credence Clearwater Revival song "Lookin' Out My Back Door." The producers of the Bammies suggested that Buck and Ringo Starr sing a duet of "Act Naturally," which they each had performed separately. Ringo declined, but Buck got the idea to rerecord the song with the former Beatle. He got his old friend British country music promoter Mervyn Conn to arrange a recording session with Ringo at the Abbey Road Studios in London on March 27, 1989. Jerry Crutchfield and Jim Shaw produced the session. Buck and Ringo also shot a video for the song. Buck and Ringo's "Act Naturally" duet was released as a single on June 21, 1989, and it peaked at #27. The song was nominated for a Grammy Award.

The *Act Naturally* LP was released October 4, 1989. Guitarist Richard Bennett, who worked with Buck on the album in Nashville, remembered him as "a serious professional." Richard recalled that "Buck was very involved with how things were going; he wasn't passive, nor was he dictatorial. He was there on time and knew all the tunes. I was kind of wishing it was a little less Nashville and a little more of him," he said of the session. Buck let his comedic side come out during the Nashville sessions; he had a running gag where he would pull up his sleeve and there would be three or four watches on his wrist. "It was like a *Three Stooges* routine," Richard said. "We'd say, 'Hey, Buck, what time is it?' He was the nicest man."

On April 10, 1989, the Academy of Country Music gave Buck its Pioneer Award. It was the West Coast equivalent to being named to the Country Music Hall of Fame, which Buck would not be inducted into for another seven years. On the other hand, Kris Black, his former lover and promotion director, was victorious in getting Buck's rival Hank Thompson inducted into the Hall of Fame in the fall of 1989.

55

THE '90S

In August 1992, guitarist Casper Rawls planned a party at the Continental Club in Austin, Texas, to celebrate the birthday of his hero Buck Owens. It turned into a yearly event known as the Buck Owens Birthday Bash, and spawned similar tributes at various honk-tonks across the country.

As more birthdays passed, Buck began to experience health problems, but at least he had the financial means to deal with them. Being a hypochondriac also served Buck well; in 1993, he worried that a nagging sore throat might be cancer, and doctors did discover a small tumor on the back of his tongue. Surgeons at Stanford Medical Center cut into a crease in his neck and excised the tumor and a good portion of his tongue. Buck rebounded well and remained fairly healthy until acquiring pneumonia in 1997. He bounced back again, despite the arthritis in his knees. He would suffer a minor stroke in 2004 and would not perform much in the last year of his life, when, Doyle Holly said, Buck reportedly was diagnosed with spinal cancer.

Buck outlived his remaining siblings. His older sister, Mary Ethel McKinney, who also had cancer, died January 3, 1990, of complications due to hardening of the arteries (arteriosclerosis), according to her autopsy report. His younger sister, Dorothy, succumbed to multiple myeloma on November 20, 1995. After she died, Jennifer Owens bought Dorothy's Poso Creek Lane ranch, which neighbored her husband's. Buck, in turn, bought it from Jennifer in 1998.

Bakersfield College bestowed an honorary associate of arts degree on Buck in 1994, and in April 1996, Kris Black, Buck's cousin Mary Lou Cushman, and then-mayor Harry Reynolds teamed up and led a successful drive to get the main street in Buck's hometown of Sherman, Texas, renamed Buck Owens Highway. Buck and his sons Buddy and Mike attended the ceremony.

Later that year, Buck finally got some respect from Nashville, when he was named not only to the Nashville Songwriters Hall of Fame but also to the Country Music Hall of Fame. For years, people had tried to get him to buy a house in Nashville to improve his chances of being admitted to the Country Music Hall of Fame, but he refused to "sell his soul." Recognition had been a long time coming, and Jack McFadden had worked relentlessly to make it happen, but it was well deserved. Over his career, he had his name on 450 songs as the writer and recorded at least 93 singles, 47 of which had made the top ten and 21 of which hit #1. At this writing, more than 60 Buck Owens albums have been released on various labels.

At the Country Music Hall of Fame induction, Dwight Yoakam had the honor of introducing his mentor as the latest member of the Hall of Fame. They sang a truncated duet of "Act Naturally." When Buck accepted the award, his wife Jennifer and sons Buddy and Mike watched from the front row. Buck's speech was somewhat slurred and he appeared to be drunk. Everybody was buzzing about what in the heck was wrong with Buck. "A lot of people thought he was ripped," Jon Hager recalled. "And he was, boy, he was really sedate."

Jay Dee Maness attributed his slurred speech to the surgery on his tongue a few years before. "You'd be surprised at the people who thought he was either on drugs or drunk after he had his little cancer," Jay Dee said. "I actually went to bat for him when people would say that; I'd go, 'No, you're wrong. It's not true.'" Jon Hager thought that Buck was "on OxyContin or something like that, something that they give for a painkiller," but he agreed that the guest of honor had not shown up intoxicated out of disrespect. "People say when he went to accept the Country Music Hall of Fame award, you know, that was no big deal to him. No, he could give a flying shit what they do out here in Nashville. He showed up anyway."

After years of working in juke joints and honky-tonks, Buck had a dream of taking country music clubs to a higher level. His would be a classy joint with nothing but the best of everything. He soaked at least $6.7 million in the initial construction of the Crystal Palace, the star in Buck's Bakersfield business crown, which opened in 1996. Jim Shaw told CMT.com in 2007 that he watched it grow into a $7.4 million investment, mostly because of his boss's frequent design changes.

The club houses his collection of country music memorabilia in a mini-museum, which was established as a nonprofit venture called the Buck Owens American Music Foundation and was incorporated with the California secretary of state as the Buck Owens American Music Corporation for the "public benefit" on January 26, 1998. Buck's nephew Mel Owens Jr. was listed as the registered agent and Buck was president at the time. Assets and income were listed as zero in 1998. An IRS Form 990 for the Buck Owens American Music Foundation lists May 1998 as the date the foundation was officially recognized as tax exempt for a "museum" and "museum activities." Dwight Yoakam announced in October 2007 that a portion of the proceeds from his *Dwight Sings Buck* tribute CD would be donated to the foundation.

Prior to the grand opening of the Palace, Buck contacted Don Rich's widow and asked her to send all Don's suits and instruments to him so he could put them on display in the museum. Marlane and her sons went to the trouble of gathering everything and shipping the items off to Buck, but he never invited them to the event.

One of the more interesting items on display in Buck's collection is the first Nudie suit he owned. How the museum came by the suit is a story in itself. Russ Varnell, a die-hard Buck Owens follower from North Carolina, who fronts a group called the Too Country Band, performs every year at the North Carolina State Fair. In the 1990s, the fair featured a wax exhibit with a Buck Owens likeness in it. The wax "Buck" wore a watermelon-colored suit, and he played a red, white, and blue guitar that Russ coveted. He offered to buy the guitar from the curator of the exhibit, but the man refused to sell. One year, Russ didn't see "Buck" in the exhibit and asked the owner why. He told Russ he had sold the statue but still had the guitar if Russ was interested in buying it. They struck a deal by which Russ would buy the guitar—but only if he got the suit, too. When Russ received the package, he saw that the suit was in bad shape. It had holes in the lining, was ripped, and smelled bad. Russ thought it looked similar to the one Buck was wearing on the *Together Again* and *On the Bandstand* album covers. Then he noticed a tag inside the suit with Buck's name and a Nudie of Hollywood label. He called Jim Shaw at Buck's office and told him about it. A few weeks later, Jim called back and told him that it was indeed Buck's very first Nudie suit, one of two that had been stolen from Buck backstage at a show in either 1963 or 1964. In 1998, after Russ took some photos of himself wearing the suit, he returned it to Buck, and Buck put it on display in the Crystal Palace with a sign that tells the story of its return.

The Crystal Palace itself is unlike such legendary honky-tonks as James White's Broken Spoke in Austin, Texas, which has duct tape patching the linoleum floor and a leaky ceiling. At the Palace, everything is shiny and in top condition. Jay Dee Maness said Jim Shaw told him Buck had put $1 million into the lighting system alone. A 1973 Pontiac Grand Ville, which Nudie Cohn embellished for Elvis Presley, is mounted on the wall like a trophy behind the bar. Buck bought the silver-dollar-bedecked vehicle after Elvis's people wouldn't let the designer deliver it in person, so Nudie kept it and ended up selling it to Buck.

The club also has a state-of-the-art surveillance system with a control room. There were rumors that Buck used it for more than security purposes. "I heard that at his club, the Palace, he goes upstairs and he's got all the tables bugged and he has cameras and he can zoom in on people's conversations and he videotapes them and listens to what's going on," Dennis Payne said. "I don't have any proof of this, but I envision him having this big file cabinet full of files on all these people he's had dealings with or is having things done to or tracked."

High-tech accoutrements aside, Buck was clearly proud of his venture. He wanted it to be his lasting legacy to the city of Bakersfield, which he had grown to love. Building the nightclub, especially the museum, put a spark in his life again. In a personal letter dated "July ?? [sic], 1996," his excitement is evident: "About the 1st of Oct 96 I expect to open the Buck Owens Museum & Theatre. . . . Full restaurant. 2000 ft Dance floor. Some of merchandise is

Elvis car on wall behind the bar—also Bar upstairs—seat approx 550. Dwight Yoakam motorcycle. Prototype of red white blue guitar. 34ft-x-12ft mural in entrance lobby."

In May 2005, Buck unveiled a collection of nine-foot-tall statues in the entrance of the Palace called Legends in Bronze, which pay tribute to ten country music superstars, most notably himself, Merle Haggard, and Garth Brooks. At the unveiling, Garth asked his former backup singer Trisha Yearwood to marry him.

Another thing that Buck wanted at the Palace was good food at reasonable prices that regular folks could appreciate and afford. The servings are large, and the club is known for its chicken fried steak, french fries, and Dwight Yoakam's Bakersfield Biscuits.

The Crystal Palace features live music nightly. Until his death, Buck took the stage, sharing lead guitar duties with steel player Terry Christofferson, on Friday and Saturday nights. At this writing, Buddy Owens replaces Buck on vocals and plays guitar twice a month along with the Buckaroos. The rest of the time, Kim McAbee, who resembles first Buckarette Jana Jae in her younger years and is billed as "the world's only Buckarette," sings while Doyle Singer still plays bass, Terry Christofferson still doubles up on lead and steel guitar, Jim Shaw still plays piano, and David Wulfekuehler plays drums. David came onboard in 2003 after Jim McCarty's exit in December 2002.

In the spring of 1998, years of working a stressful job took a toll on Buck's longtime manager, Jack McFadden, and he died of cirrhosis of the liver. Jack passed away peacefully at his Nashville home on June 16, the day after his former client Billy Ray Cyrus won five trophies at the TNN Music City News Country Awards. His beloved and trusted wife, Jo McFadden, was by his side until the end. "I called hospice first, 'cause that's one of the first things you have to do is notify them," Jo said. She said she didn't call Buck's office until that evening, when she asked to speak to Jim Shaw. She knew he was close to Buck and "would be able to go in and tell Buck. Emotionally, I did not feel like I could talk to Buck and I figured that Jim was capable of just walking in his office and telling him. So I put the burden on Jim Shaw. The office and Buck sent beautiful flower arrangements."

The next day, Stan Barnett of McFadden & Associates placed a call to Alf Wigen in Norway. Wigen (pronounced "Veegen") was an office manager moonlighting as a concert organizer, and he was helping plan two concerts for a Down on the Farm Festival in Norway and Sweden set for July 1998. The festival promoter wanted to bring in Buck Owens as the main act and had put Wigen in charge of negotiations, which had begun in May with Jim Shaw at Buck Owens Enterprises. Stan called to inform Wigen that Buck's longtime manager had died and therefore Buck was canceling all his shows, because he was too distraught and he had to attend the funeral, even though the concerts were a month away.

Evidently, Buck was so devastated that he couldn't even attend Jack's funeral. Buck called Jo to offer his condolences, but only said, "I can't talk now. I'll talk to you later." Jack's widow said she never got an explanation as to why Buck didn't attend Jack's funeral. Jo confessed that she didn't feel that loyal to Buck, "only through Jack's memory." She added, "I know how I feel." After her husband's death, Jo ran their management and booking firms until they were dissolved in 2007.

Meantime, Wigen was left trying to recover the $20,000 advance the concert company had paid Buck. The star had been very difficult in his demands, and Wigen had tried his best to accommodate his requests. Buck had wanted airfare and accommodations for twelve people, which included the musicians' wives. He also wanted a jet to fly them between the towns in Norway and Sweden where the concerts were to be held. Wigen explained that would be impossible because of the mountainous terrain, so they would have to fly by turbo-prop. According to the contract, if Buck canceled, he was to repay the advance, but Buck refused. He also refused to provide proof that he could not make the concert dates, which Wigen needed to cash in on the event's insurance policy. No matter how hard Wigen tried to get the money back from Buck to repay investors, Buck ignored his requests. Eventually, Wigen went to court to sue Buck for breach of contract but was told it would cost $25,000 just to file a lawsuit. Buck then threatened to sue the beleaguered concert company. Wigen said Buck's action caused the company to go bankrupt and ruined his reputation. The promoter who asked Wigen to book Buck for the concerts ended up having a nervous breakdown and was hospitalized for six weeks.

Also in 1998, Bakersfield renamed Pierce Road, the road that ran in front of the Crystal Palace, Buck Owens Boulevard. Buck appeared at the ceremony with his wife, Jennifer, who was sporting a chin-length bob. Buck then led a drive in 1999 to resurrect a version of the famous Bakersfield gateway sign, which now arches near the road that bears his name.

In June 1999, Buck appeared live at the Kern County Fair with Dwight Yoakam and Merle Haggard. Two months later, he turned seventy. "I am still having a hell of a time," he said. Buck borrowed an idea from his old friend Casper Rawls at the Continental Club, and threw himself a money-making birthday bash at the Crystal Palace. He arranged for Tom Brumley, Willie Cantu, and Doyle Holly to join him and paid their expenses, though they did not get paid any performance fees. Buck told Doyle, "I expect to live to be ninety."

The event was held on August 15, 1999; it was front-page news for the *Bakersfield Californian*. Tickets sold for $50 each, and other performers included Gary Allan, John Berry, Chris Hillman, Jim Lauderdale, Danni Leigh, Bonnie Owens, Brad Paisley, Lee Roy Parnell, Herb Pedersen, Susan Raye, Red Simpson, and Rick Trevino.

Jay Dee Maness was also there, though he had not been invited. "I invited myself. I called Jim Shaw and I said, 'Buck's having the birthday party and he's bringing all the guys in. I want to come,' because I didn't think I would get an invitation on my own. He said, 'Well . . . OK.' I said, 'I'm going to be there early and I'm going to set up my guitar and I'm going to play.' And he said, 'Well, then, come on.'" Jay Dee noted that Jerry Wiggins was there as well but wasn't asked to perform. "I thought it was pretty damn bad, you know, that they didn't even ask him to play, and he was a Buckaroo for years."

Dennis Payne also showed up uninvited. He wasn't about to pay the fifty bucks to get in the door, though, and talked them down to $6. When Buck caught sight of him, Dennis said, "Buck screwed up, almost dropped his guitar." He said that KNIX program director Larry Daniels was real nice to him and that Bonnie Owens tried to get him up to sing, but he told her it wasn't a good idea. "I even enjoyed the show," he said.

Buck was not one to forget a kindness, so he paid for plane tickets so that Russ Varnell, the man who had found his suit, could attend the birthday bash. Then, to Russ's surprise, Buck called him onstage to perform a couple of songs with him and the Buckaroos. From then on, Russ traveled to Bakersfield periodically to visit Buck when his schedule allowed. Each time, Buck would call him onstage to sing with him, and always told the audience the story of how Russ had returned his first Nudie suit.

But there was someone Buck seemed to have forgotten. His birthday bash took place on what would have been Don Rich's fifty-eighth birthday. Once again, his widow, Marlane, was not invited.

In the end, Buck effectively turned his back on Don Rich's family. Not only did he snub Marlane by not inviting her to the birthday party on her dead husband's birthday, but also on another occasion he stood up her two grown sons when they arranged a meeting with Buck to talk to him about their father. "He had told Don he would make him vice president and take care of him," Jo McFadden said, "then nothing." It was just another part of his life on which Buck had slammed the door, just as he had with Jo after Jack died. Jo said, "I don't think he said two words to me after that."

★ 56 ★

TOGETHER AGAIN

Buck closed out the 1990s by performing with his saddle pal, Dwight Yoakam, in a concert at the Crystal Palace. On June 28, 2001, he received another career accolade, the Country Radio Broadcasters' Career Achievement Award. Brad Paisley and Billy Yates were among the artists who performed some of Buck's hits at the Nashville ceremony.

In 2001, everybody was shocked when Buck filed for divorce from Jennifer. They'd been married for more than twenty years and together for more than thirty. Doyle Holly, Jay Dee Maness, and Jim Shaw were all of the belief that Jennifer was the one who wanted out; Doyle had heard that "it hadn't been a marriage for the last twelve years" because Jennifer was gone most of the time doing horse shows. But Jennifer's friend Jo McFadden said that was not true. "Jennifer loved Buck. He got rid of his wife and was gonna marry this other girl. No, she didn't leave him. It was a battle."

Even at age seventy-two, Buck was simply not the type of man who could be happy with one long-term love in his life. In May 2000, he had begun securing control of his sizable holdings by moving everything, including the ranch where he and Jennifer lived, into a revocable trust of which he was the conservator/trustee. This way, his wife would be unable to liquidate any of his assets, and he could keep his affairs out of the public eye.

His lawyers advised him to keep a low profile, so unlike during his attempted annulment with Jana, there wasn't much in the press. But he told the *San Diego Union-Tribune* it was "the nastiest divorce you've ever seen." Friends said their prenuptial agreement gave Jennifer $10,000 a month in support until the divorce was final.

During all this, Buck shamelessly pursued a young, dark-haired woman he had met briefly at a *Family Feud* taping with the Dixie Chicks earlier that year. The personal ad that the aging horn dog placed in several publications read, in part, "Buck has lost contact and would like you to call. Please call. . . . Extremely Important." Spokesman Jim Shaw said nothing ever came of this stunt. Buck then took up with a woman twenty-five years his junior whom he met at the Crystal Palace that year. The woman, Karen Rotan, tooled around in a black 1998 Jaguar Buck had given her.

Buck's divorce from Jennifer was finalized in 2002. The terms of the settlement are not known, but Buck gained control over the thoroughbred horse operation, which had been Jennifer's. Jennifer still owns some horses, however, because in 2003 her horse Just Plain Star was a finalist in the National Reined Cow Horse Association's Greatest Horseman competition, sponsored by *Western Horseman* magazine.

In his final years, Buck lived at his ranch with his new lover, Karen. She told the *Bakersfield Californian*, "It was kind of like being with Elvis. I'd heard stories about Linda Thompson. Buck was kinda like, 'That's you.' I always teased him that we were in love with the same person: him." In 2006 he gave her a $68,000, nine-carat diamond promise ring. He didn't get a chance to keep or break that promise, though, because just two days later, he passed away.

Buck spent the last day of his life, March 24, 2006, driving around, inspecting the ranch he loved, before having his son Johnny drive him to the Crystal Palace around 4 P.M. Buck noodled on his guitar in preparation for his show that night and ordered french fries and a chicken fried steak. After dinner, Buck wasn't feeling so well; he told the band he was going home. On his way out the door, "fans on their way in told him they'd come from Bend, Oregon, and how much they were looking forward to hearing him sing," Jim Shaw told the *Los Angeles Times*. So Buck went back inside and did the show. He mentioned onstage, "If somebody's come all that way, I'm gonna do the show and give it my best shot," Jim said.

Buck's last song that night was "Big in Vegas," which he usually closed his show with. Then he went home and fell asleep forever. On March 25, 2006, forty years to the day after Buck Owens and his Buckaroos played Carnegie Hall, Buck was gone.

Karen told Doyle Holly that Buck died about 3:30 A.M., and that she called 911 and tried to resuscitate him. She told Doyle no one showed up until 8 A.M. to take his body to Bakersfield Memorial Hospital, where he was pronounced dead. Heart failure was cited as the cause of death. After Buck was gone, she said, she "cried all day, and has been crying ever since." She said the next day Buddy and Mike ordered her off the ranch, but Owens family friend Cheryl Albers, who was at the ranch the night Buck died, said Karen was given several weels to move. Karen said she left with only her clothes, the Jaguar, and the promise ring Buck had just given her. In comparison, Doyle Holly said, Buck's nephew Mel Jr. got several million dollars, while Johnny inherited the ranch. Property records from 2007, however, list the Alvis E. Owens (Life Estate) Buck Owens American Music Corporation as the owner.

At the Academy of Country Music Awards show in Las Vegas that spring, the ACM paid tribute to Buck; Buddy and Dwight Yoakam performed a reprise of "Streets of Bakersfield." Karen had complimentary tickets to the show, but she told Doyle that Buddy and Mike took the tickets and told her she couldn't go. She bought her own and went in spite of Buck's offspring, who have ignored her ever since.

Karen told Doyle she had no money and he advised her to sell the ring, but she told him she couldn't because it had sentimental value. Karen has since moved back to her home state of Oregon.

When Buck's obituary appeared in the *Bakersfield Californian*, it included a special request from his family. In lieu of flowers, the obit said, Buck had asked that well-wishers send donations to the Bakersfield SPCA, where he and his former wife had given money to help build the Jennifer and Buck Owens Puppy Room to house puppies for adoption.

After Buck's death was announced, his illegitimate daughter by the unnamed Bakersfield girl left a message about Buck's death in a post at Bakosphere.com. Lisa Aguilar—who was born January 21, 1960, and put up for adoption—wrote:

This is to the Owens boys, it's sad to know that you grow up in a town knowing who your father is—and all you ever wanted was to get to know the man and let him know that he has a daughter and you guys have a half sister, he now knows, and is smiling from heaven.

At least Lisa had gotten to meet her famous father, at the Crystal Palace in 2001. He talked to her much as he would a fan but asked her all sorts of questions, such as what year she was born and whether she had lived in Bakersfield all her life. It is possible Lisa caught his eye because she is the spitting image of his sister Dorothy.

"The entire city of Bakersfield mourned Buck with signs, banners, and memories in every hotel, restaurant and club I visited the night before his funeral," neotraditionalist country singer Jann Browne remembered. On Saturday, April 1, 2006, as early as 1 A.M., people began to line up at the Crystal Palace to pay their last respects to their honky-tonk hero. More than sixty-two hundred mourners showed up for the all-day public viewing. They filed past his open casket, which was decorated with red roses and set in the center of the two-thousand-square-foot dance floor. He was dressed in a black Nudie suit and a red shirt, a black cowboy hat resting on his stomach. It was a fitting goodbye for someone who had scraped his way to the top singing in honky-tonks.

Kris Black attended the viewing, where she encountered Buck's former wife Jana Jae. Jana acted as though she didn't know who she was, Kris said, so Kris talked in a twang and said, "Well, I'm Josephine Simpson." Then, Kris said, Jana told her, "Oh, now I know who you are. You're Kris Black. I recognize you by your mouth, and it's a good thing, because you don't look anything like you used to." Kris said Jana told her she had reconciled with Buck within the last two years and they had been seeing each other again, which, of course, did not sit well with Kris. She found it hard to believe, seeing as how Buck had just given Karen a ring—although she was forgetting that juggling women was nothing new to him.

Someone suggested they all go to dinner, and Kris found herself at the same table with Jana, *Hee Haw* producer Sam Lovullo and his wife, and *Hee Haw's* Lulu Roman. Lulu said she sensed some friction between Kris and Jana that evening, though "nothing really was spoken out loud, but I know that several people made mention of 'who is she and why is she here,'" referring to Kris. Lulu did not know who Kris was or why she was there, either. "I may have met her earlier in life, but I didn't remember it," Lulu said. "Kris, she's a talker. I remember she just talked everybody's heads off. Jana was very polite. Perhaps I heard her growl under her breath once or twice. Because Jana's really a nice person. She really is. She's very much a lady and there's always two sides to every story."

Kris, on the other hand, said she had kept quiet during dinner because "Jana was saying the most unbelievable things." Sam mentioned to Kris later that he couldn't believe how quiet she was, Kris said, and she told him, "Contrary to popular belief, I do have an edit button. It's just that Jana was saying such unbelievable things, I had to keep my mouth shut."

Buck Owens's memorial service was held at Valley Baptist Church, where, like his mother, Buck had been a member for many years. The service was held at 2 P.M. on April 2, 2006, a sunny day with popcorn clouds and a clear blue sky after rain the week before. Any trace of smog had been cleared from the air, and the Sierra Mountains were visible to the east and the Tehachapi Mountains to the south.

"It was a beautiful, spectacular, and very emotional send-off for my much-loved friend and mentor," Mayf Nutter said of the service, which was simulcast on three Bakersfield radio stations and three local TV stations, as well as online at www.buckowens.com.

As the mourners gathered, Kris Black noted that Buddy and Mike seemed to be snubbing their adopted stepbrother Jacky Owens. She also asked Don Rich's widow, Marlane, to introduce her to Jennifer, but Marlane begged off, saying, "I don't want to get in the middle of anything." So Kris asked her to point Jennifer out, which she did. Kris then went over and introduced herself, gave Jennifer her business card, and told her how much she had admired her for standing up to Jana.

Herb Pedersen and Chris Hillman opened the service, singing "Turn, Turn, Turn," accompanying themselves on mandolin and acoustic guitar. Then Pastor Roger Spradlin gave the opening prayer, which was followed by the eulogy by Larry Daniels. Buck's recording of "Dust on Mother's Bible" was then played. Buck's nephew Mel Owens Jr., who had been a key part of Buck's management team for many years, shared some memories about his uncle, and John Berry sang "Blessed Assurance." Buck's son Johnny took the podium next and almost broke down a few times as he told how his father had spent the last day of life. Trace Adkins sang "Wayfaring Stranger" and recalled Buck telling him, "Always throw in that low note. That's about all you've got going for ya," which brought laughter from the crowd. Buck's sons Mike and Buddy were next, giving touching remembrances of their father. They spoke of his wisdom and firm guidance and their love for him.

Dwight Yoakam, who was also like a son to Buck, then walked onstage from the front pew, hat in hand, carrying his guitar. He apologized to his mother, who, he said, would not have approved of his singing with a musical instrument in church, and asked that the crowd forgive him for wearing his hat while he sang. He said Buck once told him, "You look good in that hat, Dwight. You oughta keep it on more." With that said, Dwight donned his classic Stetson with the bull-rider brim and rodeo crown and sang "In the Garden."

Brad Paisley made a surprise visit, having flown in from Memphis. He gave a heartfelt testimony to Buck's influence and friendship before singing "When I Get Where I'm Goin'." Pastor Spradlin then talked about how Buck had been born again, and told how Buck often would call him at home late at night and ask questions about passages he had read in the Bible. Few knew that about Buck, he said.

Lulu Roman, now an ordained minister, then shared her story of how Buck had taken her from a grungy nightclub in Texas and put her in front of the world on television's most popular show. She told of her love for him. "I sang at his funeral," Lulu later recalled. "I was the only female that sang. He had it all planned out—'Amazing Grace,' 'cause it was his mama's favorite and it was his, too."

After the service, people stood around and shared memories of Buck. Kris said one young woman was telling her tidbits Kris had never known about Buck and pointed a mourner out to her. "See that woman over there? She's married to the FBI guy that Buck used to investigate people," she blabbed.

Mike Owens told Mayf Nutter, "It's like I'm dreaming, Mayf. I keep hoping any minute now I'll wake up and find out it's not really happening."

Lulu echoed Mike's statement. "Buck's funeral was surreal. It was like, it's not really happening. The grief factor was just huge, almost to the same degree for those who didn't know him."

Jann Browne didn't hang around long after that. "I was sad and ready to go home," she said.

Then came the hugs. "Mike dissolved in my arms at Buck's funeral," Kris said. Lots of hugs were shared, Mayf said, "but no one gave a hug like Buck Owens."

The Owens family held a private burial service at Greenlawn Southwest Mortuary & Cemetery in Bakersfield, where Buck was interred in a white marble mausoleum called Buck's Place. They provided security and limousines to drive Buck's friends to a private celebration of Buck's life at the Crystal Palace. The farewell dinner had free all-you-can-eat food for the guests.

According to Mayf, "the Buckaroos, Buddy Alan, Brad Paisley, Dwight Yoakam and I sang and spoke about Buck. Also, Lulu Roman and Susan Raye sang for us." Even Russ Varnell from North Carolina got to sing. Mayf called it one of the most difficult experiences of his life: "There were lots of laughs and great music and lots of hugs and exchanging of current phone numbers, but the air of frivolity still had a strange feeling about it that I cannot find the words to describe or explain."

Almost a month to the day after Buck passed away, his second wife, Bonnie Owens, died at 4:28 P.M. on April 24, 2006, of complications from Alzheimer's disease. At the time of her death, Bonnie was married to one of her early lovers, Fred McMillen. She had been living in Missouri, but moved back to Bakersfield after being diagnosed. She died in hospice care there and was cremated. A memorial service was held April 27, 2006, and her sons, Buddy and Mike, made sure her remains were interred in Buck's mausoleum at Greenlawn.

Buck Owens had lived hard, worked hard, played hard, and loved hard. Even though he left behind a lucrative business empire and an everlasting musical legacy, it seemed something was missing from his life. Jay Dee

Maness recalled that at Buck's funeral somebody said they had talked to him in his office not long before his death. Buck was having a quiet moment and said, "You know, I've got everything I've ever wanted and I'm still unhappy."

"That is an absolute shame," Jay Dee said. "He touted all this about growing up and being poor and picking cotton, 'and when I get out of here, I'm never gonna be hungry again!' Well, he hurt a lot of people doing that. I don't know if it ever really bothered him or not. We will never know, but to die feeling as lonely and alone is an absolute tragedy."

EPILOGUE

Though Buck remained haunted by his dark, selfish urges to the end, he did seem to have mellowed as he aged. Instead of being jealous of young, talented artists, he had become a friend, mentor, and trusted father figure to many young musicians. Over the years, in addition to Dwight Yoakam, Russ Varnell, Jann Browne, and Brad Paisley, Buck forged friendships with many younger people in the business, including GAC-TV host Storme Warren and artists such as Trace Adkins, Dierks Bentley, Garth Brooks, Monty Byrom, the Derailers, John Fogerty, Emmylou Harris, Chris Hillman, Herb Pedersen, Marty Stuart, and George Ducas. Buck encouraged those he felt best supported and carried on the honky-tonk tradition, and the really special ones got his trademark red, white, and blue Telecasters and acoustic guitars as gifts.

Browne holds a special memory of Buck from when she was nominated for Top New Female Vocalist by the Academy of Country Music in 1989. During the rehearsal before the awards ceremony, Buck read the names of the nominees and then opened the card and said, "And the winner is . . . Jann Browne." She didn't win, though; Mary Chapin Carpenter took the honor that evening. After the show, Buck was walking out just ahead of her and she got his attention. He turned and said, "Hey there, young lady!" and put his arm around her. As they walked to the after party a few blocks away, Browne was trying to wrap her brain around the fact that she was walking down the street with Buck Owens, who had his arm around her. "Not only did he know my name," she said, "he knew a lot of my music and was talking about songs like 'Louisville' and 'Mexican Wind' and was complimenting my voice and writing. 'You had my vote,' he told me. He felt like an old shoe, comfortable." Before they got to the party, he reached into the pocket of his pony coat and pulled out the "rehearsal card" that had Browne's name on it. "Here, you keep this," he said. "Next year you'll be giving your thank-you speech." Browne said the only thing that could have been better than walking with Buck would have been walking between Buck Owens and Don Rich.

George Ducas also has fond memories of Buck. After the young singer got sucked into the backdraft of Garth Brooks amid label upheaval at Liberty/Capitol Nashville, his second album *Where I Stand* languished on the charts and in sales, which sent Ducas into a very dark period. Buck, who was no stranger to depression, was there to offer George encouragement and told him to keep making country music his way, because it was the real thing. Ducas said that Buck "was a very intelligent man. He was so intuitive—so many people in our business are not. They are so ingrained in whatever it is they're trying to accomplish and it's part of the creative dilemma. If you're talking to them, they hear you, but they're not really listening. Buck was the opposite. You didn't even need to say anything and he kind of knew where you were with things."

By the end of his life, Buck had also become a pop cultural icon to a new generation of fans. They posted videos of old *Buck Owens Ranch* performances on YouTube and blogged about the influence his music had on their lives. Die-hard fan Russ Varnell said, "I know everyone has bad sides, some more than most, but I always felt that Buck mellowed into a kind soul for the most part in his final years, and he did so much for Bakersfield and country music and people in general."

And former Buckaroo Jay Dee Maness recalled that working for Buck "was a horribly bad experience, but on the other hand I gained so much out of it and in the end—not the very end, but later on—Buck and I got along really good. I mean, he mellowed out and I guess so did I. I don't hold any grudges. I look at it as a learning experience all the way down the line."

Although Buck is gone, his memory is kept alive in many ways. The Buck Owens Birthday Bashes continue. Younger artists honor his music by performing their own versions of his hits. Jann Browne was the first to release a tribute album, *Buckin' Around: A Tribute to the Legendary Buck Owens*, in

2007. The Derailers and Dwight Yoakam followed later that year with *Under the Influence of Buck* and *Dwight Sings Buck*, respectively. All three CDs feature Buck's biggest career hit, "Love's Gonna Live Here." On Brad Paisley's mostly instrumental 2008 album *Play*, the guitarist and singer included a duet with Buck, a song Buck wrote and demoed shortly before he died, titled "Come On In." (In 2009, Paisley joined his mentor to become one of eight country artists in *Billboard* history to chart ten consecutive #1 hits. Other artists who share that distinction are Alabama, Earl Thomas Conley, Sonny James, Ronnie Milsap, George Strait, and Conway Twitty.) Tanya Tucker's *My Turn*, released in June 2009, included a duet of "Love's Gonna Live Here" with alt-country singer-songwriter Jim Lauderdale, who sounds eerily like Buck. John Fogerty did a cover of "I Don't Care (Just As Long As You Love Me)" on his album *The Blue Ridge Rangers Ride Again* in September 2009.

Other artists paid tribute by writing original songs about Buck. In 2006, Mayf Nutter's "You Got It Now (The Buck Owens Song)," incorporated twanging Telecasters and painted a romanticized portrait of a man giving advice about putting family and Jesus over fame. In the 2007 song "Out in Bakersfield," Nashville singer-songwriters Bruce-jon Brigham, Julie Grower, and Lynne Manderson recalled the man behind the music with a decidedly Nashville sound and construction.

On August 16, 2008, Buck was inducted posthumously into the Texas Country Music Hall of Fame in Carthage, Texas. In May of the following year, Rhino Records released a compendium of the legendary singer's #1 songs in *Buck Owens 21 #1 Hits: The Ultimate Collection*. Also in 2009, Kris Black, Mary Lou Cushman, and former Sherman, Texas, mayor Harry Reynolds teamed up again, this time to commission a bronze statue of Sherman's native son to be erected on the town square at a future date.

Buck's musical legacy and business concerns are carried on by his family and close associates in Bakersfield. His sons Buddy and Johnny, whose mannerisms and voices are eerily like their father's, have taken up the musical mantle. Buddy performs with the Buckaroos at the Crystal Palace, while Johnny fronted a country band called BuckShot for a while. Buddy, Mike, and Buck's nephew Mel Jr. are at the helm of Buck Owens Enterprises, along with Buck's longtime and trusted associates Larry Daniels and Jim Shaw, while Terry Christofferson is general manager of the Crystal Palace.

Over the years, many key players in Buck Owens's life have died. In addition to those whose passing was mentioned in previous chapters, the deceased include Kris Black, Tommy Collins, Dick Curless, Dolly the groupie, Vern Gosdin, Diane Immel, Loretta Johnson, Grandpa Jones, Mel King, Karl E. Kirschner, Don Lee, Rose Maddox, Peter C. Martinez, Roy Nichols, Alan Pierce, Kenny Pierce, Johnny Russell, Lynn Shults, Wynn Stewart, Porter Wagoner, Wayne Wilson, and Bill Woods.

Doyle Holly had been diagnosed with prostate cancer around 2002 and opted for alternative treatment before beginning chemotherapy. His plight had even moved Buck to open his wallet a little; in 2006 he wrote Doyle a $10,000 check to help defray his medical expenses (although it was nothing compared with the money Doyle said was owed him over the years). Doyle died of prostate cancer in a Hendersonville, Tennessee, hospice at 2:30 A.M. on January 13, 2007. In his later years, he'd become a born-again Christian. No services were held; his widow, Ginny, had his body cremated and said she planned to scatter his ashes near her family home in the Black Hills.

Before his death, Doyle had expressed concern that the contributions of latter-day Buckaroos were being ignored. "Doyle Singer and Jim Shaw are good friends of mine, and I'm kinda sorry that they're not getting the recognition that they're due as members of Buck Owens's band. They've been there for twenty years. You know, it's funny that, well, Willie and I were with him a short time compared to the Buckaroos now. We're getting more recognition now as the Buckaroos than we did back in the '60s."

Tom Brumley was getting ready to open a classic country music show in San Antonio when he suffered a fatal heart attack and died February 4, 2009. Memorial services were held in Texas, Nashville, and Missouri, where he was laid to rest. His widow, Rolene, has since moved back to Branson to be near their children and grandchildren.

Jim and Jon Hager died in true twin fashion—less than a year apart, on May 1, 2008, and January 9, 2009, respectively. They were sixty-seven. The brothers had talked of writing their own book, which would have paid homage to the man who gave them their break in show business. The working title was *Hee Haw? My Ass.*

"We could end it on the Owens Empire," Jon said. "Oh, what a chapter, what a chapter!"

"The Owens Empire," Jim said.

"The Owens Empire," Jon echoed. "On the Road with the Owens Empire."

CHAPTER NOTES

Sources of information for each chapter are listed alphabetically by category. Interviews were conducted by the author in person, by telephone, and via e-mail. Publication dates have been noted whenever possible, but some clips culled from Country Music Foundation archives and scrapbooks fail to note publication dates and/or page numbers. In addition, because Internet sites frequently change domains, cease operations, and/or delete entries, some links to online sources may no longer be functional.

Epigraph

Audiovisual
Buck Owens Ranch. TV series, WKY-TV, Oklahoma City, OK, n.d.

Preface

Interviews
Gene Price.

1. Son of a Tenant Farmer

Articles
Bakersfield Californian. Obituary of Maicie A. Owens. May 1986.
Black, Kris. Bio of Kris Black. Press release, Sunflower Marketing (Dallas, TX), November 1995.
Buck Booster fan club newsletter, vol. 6 (December 1978).
Freeman, Donald. "Buck Owens . . . He Hee Haws All the Way to the Bank." *San Diego Union TV Week*, June 21–27, 1970.
Price, Robert. "Buck Had the World by the Tail." *Bakersfield Californian*, April 2, 2006.

Audiovisual
"Acting Naturally." *Biography*. TV series, A&E, 2000.
The Life and Times of Buck Owens. TV special, TNN, 1997.

Books
Burke, Kathryn. *The Dust Bowl, Bakersfield Sound, and Buck*. North Charleston, SC: BookSurge Publishers, 2007.
Dawidoff, Nicholas. "Honky-Tonk Man." In *In the Country of Country*. New York: Pantheon Books, 1997.
Hively, Kay, and Albert E. Brumley Jr. *I'll Fly Away*. Branson, MO: Mountaineer Books, 1990.
Kienzle, Rich. *The Buck Owens Collection 1959–1990*. Santa Monica, CA: Rhino Records, 1992.
La Chapelle, Peter. *Proud to Be an Okie*. Berkeley, CA: University of California Press, 2007.

Documents
National Climatic Data Center statistics for Sherman, TX; Social Security applications, Alvis E. Owens Sr., Maicie Azel Ellington Owens, Dorothy Juanita Owens, Melvin Leo Owens; Social Security Death Index listings, Alvis E. Owens Sr., Alvis E. Owens Jr., Maicie

Azel Ellington Owens, Dorothy Owens, Mel Owens Sr.; U.S. Census records, 1880, 1910, 1920, 1930.

Interviews
Mary Agee, Kris Black, Mary Lou Cushman, Doyle Holly, Loudilla Johnson, Steve LaNore, Buck Owens.

Web Sites
Ancestry.com, Answers.com, Garland Landmark Society (www.garlandhistorical.org), Geneaology.com (no longer available), Handbook of Texas Online (www.tshaonline.org/handbook/online/), Oklahoma State University Library Electronic Publishing Center (http://digital.library.okstate.edu), Weather Notebook (www.weathernotebook.org).

2. The Exodus

Articles
Forte, Dan, and Rick Rawls. "The Return of the Bakersfield Sound: An Exclusive Interview with Buck Owens." *Guitar Player*, February 1989.
Freeman, Donald. "Buck Owens . . . He Hee Haws All the Way to the Bank." *San Diego Union TV Week*, June 21–27, 1970.
Goldsmith, Thomas. "Buck Owens: Sound of Success Is Twang." *Tennessean*, December 16, 1989.
Price, Robert. "Buck Had the World by the Tail." *Bakersfield Californian*, April 2, 2006.

Audiovisual
"Acting Naturally." *Biography*. TV series, A&E, 2000.
The Life and Times of Buck Owens. TV special, TNN, 1997.

Books
Burke, Kathryn. *The Dust Bowl, Bakersfield Sound, and Buck*. North Charleston, SC: BookSurge Publishers, 2007.
Dawidoff, Nicholas. "Honky-Tonk Man." In *In the Country of Country*. New York: Pantheon Books, 1997.
Hively, Kay, and Albert E. Brumley Jr. *I'll Fly Away*. Branson, MO: Mountaineer Books, 1990.
Kienzle, Rich. *The Buck Owens Collection 1959–1990*. Santa Monica, CA: Rhino Records, 1992.
La Chapelle, Peter. *Proud to Be an Okie*. Berkeley, CA: University of California Press, 2007.

Documents
Social Security applications, Alvis E. Owens Sr., Maicie Azel Ellington Owens, Dorothy Juanita Owens, Melvin Leo Owens; U.S. Census records, 1880, 1910, 1920, 1930.

Interviews
Mary Agee, Kris Black, Mary Lou Cushman, Doyle Holly, Loudilla Johnson, Buck Owens.

Letters
Owens, Maicie. Maicie Owens to Thurston Moore, January 26, 1966. Country Music Hall of Fame and Museum Archives, Nashville, TN.
Thurston Moore to Maicie Owens (incomplete copy), January 27, 1966, Country Music Hall of Fame and Museum Archives, Nashville, TN.

Web Sites
Ancestry.com, Answers.com, Garland Landmark Society (www.garlandhistorical.org), Geneaology.com (no longer available), Handbook of Texas Online (www.tshaonline.org/handbook/online/), RootsWeb.com.

3. Bonnie

Articles
Grissim, John Jr. "California White Man's Shit Kickin' Blues." *Rolling Stone*, June 28, 1969.
Harris, Stacy. "Buck Owens: Sometimes It Just Ain't Easy." *Country Song Roundup*, August 1978.

Price, Robert. "Bakersfield Sound: The Blackboard." *Bakersfield Californian*, n.d.
———. "Bakersfield Sound: Two Kings, One Queen." *Bakersfield Californian*, n.d.
———. "Buck Had the World by the Tail." *Bakersfield Californian*, April 2, 2006.

Audiovisual
"Acting Naturally." *Biography*. TV series, A&E, 2000.
The Life and Times of Buck Owens. TV special, TNN, 1997.

Books
Burke, Kathryn. *The Dust Bowl, Bakersfield Sound, and Buck*. North Charleston, SC: BookSurge Publishers, 2007.
Haggard, Merle, with Peggy Russell. *Sing Me Back Home*. New York: Times Books, 1981.
Kienzle, Rich. *The Buck Owens Collection 1959–1990*. Santa Monica, CA: Rhino Records, 1992.

Documents
Bonnie Owens, affidavit for order to show cause, November 12, 1952; Bonnie Owens, complaint for divorce, November 12, 1952.

Interviews
Larry Adamson, Mary Agee, Kris Black, Tom Brumley, Doyle Holly, Dennis Payne, Tex Whitson.

Web Sites
Ancestry.com.

4. The Promised Land

Articles
Freeman, Donald. "Buck Owens . . . He Hee Haws All the Way to the Bank." *San Diego Union TV Week*, June 21–27, 1970.
Fulmer, Douglas. "Buck Owens: From Cotton Fields to Jets, He's Charted His Own Course." *Country Weekly*, August 21–September 17, 1999.
Lawrence County Record. Obituaries. April 1, 2009.
Price, Robert. "Bakersfield Sound: Two Kings, One Queen." *Bakersfield Californian*, n.d.
———. "Bakersfield Sound: The Blackboard." *Bakersfield Californian*, n.d.
———. "Buck Had the World by the Tail." *Bakersfield Californian*, April 2, 2006.
Shaw, Arnold. "Bakersfield—City with a Flair for Country Music." *Los Angeles Times*, July 24, 1969.

Audiovisual
"Acting Naturally." *Biography*. TV series, A&E, 2000.
The Life and Times of Buck Owens. TV special, TNN, 1997.

Books
Burke, Kathryn. *The Dust Bowl, Bakersfield Sound, and Buck*. North Charleston, SC: BookSurge Publishers, 2007.
Country Music Foundation, ed. *Encyclopedia of Country Music*. New York: Oxford University Press, 1998.
Dawidoff, Nicholas. "Honky-Tonk Man." In *In the Country of Country*. New York: Pantheon Books, 1997.
Escott, Colin. *Tattooed on Their Tongues*. New York: Schirmer Books, 1996.
Golomb, Elan. *Trapped in the Mirror: Adult Children of Narcissists in Their Struggle for Self*. New York: William Morrow and Co., 1992.
Kienzle, Rich. *The Buck Owens Collection 1959–1990*. Santa Monica, CA: Rhino Records, 1992.
La Chapelle, Peter. *Proud to Be an Okie*. Berkeley, CA: University of California Press, 2007.
Nelson, Ken. *My First 90 Years Plus 3*. Pittsburgh, PA: Dorrance Publishing Co., 2007.
Reed Elsevier, Inc. *The Complete Who's Who Biographies*. New Providence, NJ: Reed Elsevier, 2000.
Reed Elsevier, Inc. *Who's Who in Entertainment*. 1st and 2nd eds. New Providence, NJ: Reed Elsevier, 1991 and 1997.

Interviews
Larry Adamson, Keith Bilbrey, Kris Black, Tom Brumley, Doyle Holly, Kay Johnson, Loretta Johnson, Loudilla Johnson, Eugene Moles, Buck Owens, Dennis Payne, Wade Pepper, Jim Pierce, Gus Snijdewind, Daryl Stogner, Porter Wagoner.

Web Sites
Ancestry.com, City of Bakersfield (www.bakersfieldcity.us), Corralitos California History (www.corralitoshistory.com), Geneaology.com (no longer available), Kern County Museum (www.kcmuseum.org), Rockabilly Hall of Fame (www.rockabillyhall.com).

5. Capitol

Articles
Price, Robert. "A Buck Owens Bonfire." *Bakersfield Californian*, n.d.

Audiovisual
Farmer Boys. *Flash, Crash, and Thunder*. Bear Family, 1991. Compact disc.

Books
Burke, Kathryn. *The Dust Bowl, Bakersfield Sound, and Buck*. North Charleston, SC: BookSurge Publishers, 2007.
George-Warren, Holly, and Michelle Freedman. *How the West Was Worn*. New York: Harry N. Abrams, 2001.
Kienzle, Rich. *The Buck Owens Collection 1959–1990*. Santa Monica, CA: Rhino Records, 1992.
Nelson, Ken. *My First 90 Years Plus 3*. Pittsburgh, PA: Dorrance Publishing Co., 2007.

Documents
California marriage records, Phyllis Buford and Alvis E. Owens; Social Security applications, Phyllis Irene Buford; SSDI listing, Phyllis Irene Buford; U.S. Census records, 1930.

Interviews
Kay Adams, Richard Bennett, Keith Bilbrey, Rolene Brumley, Tom Brumley, Willie Cantu, Tommy Collins, Doyle Holly, Dennis Payne, Jim Pierce, Billy Sipes, Porter Wagoner.

Web Sites
Ancestry.com, *Bakersfield Californian* (www.bakersfield.com), Ray Stevens's official Web site (www.raystevens.com).

6. Washington

Articles
Bessman, Jim. "Owens Cohort Rich Gets Due on Anthology Project from Sundazed." *Billboard*, November 4, 2000.
Blecha, Peter. "Country Music in the Pacific Northwest." HistoryLink.org, August 18, 2005, www.historylink.org/index.cfm?DisplayPage=output.cfm&file_id=7441.
Bristol, Marc. "Buck Owens & Don Rich Together Again." *Blue Suede News*, Summer 2006.
Erlewein, Stephen Thomas. "Buck Owens: Biography." Allmusic.com, www.allmusic.com/cg/amg.dll?p=amg&sql=11:jiftxql5ldde~T1.
Forte, Dan, and Rick Rawls. "The Return of the Bakersfield Sound: An Exclusive Interview with Buck Owens." *Guitar Player*, February 1989.

Audiovisual
"Acting Naturally." *Biography*. TV series, A&E, 2000.
The Life and Times of Buck Owens. TV special, TNN, 1997.

Books
Burke, Kathryn. *The Dust Bowl, Bakersfield Sound, and Buck*. North Charleston, SC: BookSurge Publishers, 2007.
Fredson, Michael. *Hood Canal*. Mount Pleasant, SC: Arcadia Publishing, 2007

Kienzle, Rich. *The Buck Owens Collection 1959–1990*. Santa Monica, CA: Rhino Records, 1992.
Stambler, Irwin, and Grelun Landon. *The Encyclopedia of Folk, Country & Western Music*. New York: St. Martin's Press, 1984.

Documents
Buck Owens, *Who's Who* application, Heather Publications, Denver, CO.

Interviews
Rolene Brumley, Tom Brumley, Ralph Emery, Jim Pierce, Marlane Ulrich-Dunivent.

Web Sites
HistoryLink.org Online Encyclopedia of Washington State History (www.historylink.org), *Olympian* (www.theolympian.com), Rockabilly Hall of Fame (www.rockabillyhall.com).

7. Dangerous Don

Articles
Bessman, Jim. "Owens Cohort Rich Gets Due on Anthology Project from Sundazed." *Billboard*, November 4, 2000.
Black, Kris. "The Man We Knew." *Country Town News* (Bakersfield, CA), July 1974.
Blecha, Peter. "Country Music in the Pacific Northwest." HistoryLink.org, August 18, 2005, www.historylink.org/index.cfm?DisplayPage=output.cfm&file_id=7441.
Bristol, Marc. "Buck Owens & Don Rich Together Again." *Blue Suede News*, Summer 2006.
Contra Costa Times. "Don Rich." November 11, 1966.
Erlewein, Stephen Thomas. "Buck Owens: Biography." Allmusic.com, www.allmusic.com/cg/amg.dll?p=amg&sql=11:jiftxql5ldde~T1.
Forte, Dan, and Rick Rawls. "The Return of the Bakersfield Sound: An Exclusive Interview with Buck Owens." *Guitar Player*, February 1989.
Fox, Darrin. "Heroes: Don Rich." *Guitar Player*, April 2002.
Kienzle, Rich. "Buck Owens and the Buckaroos." *Vintage Guitar Magazine*, December 15, 2009, www.vguitar.com/features/artists/details.asp?AID=3117.
Price, Robert. "Buck Had the World by the Tail." *Bakersfield Californian*, April 2, 2006.
Stern, Mark. "Biography: Don Rich." Press release, Capitol Records, May 12, 1971.

Audiovisual
"Acting Naturally." *Biography*. TV series, A&E, 2000.
The Life and Times of Buck Owens. TV special, TNN, 1997.
Owens, Buck. Interview by Chris Comer and Rob Ervin. *The Chris & Rob Late Night Talk Show*, WAIF-FM, Cincinnati, OH, July 16, 1997, www.chriscomerradio.com/buck_owens/buck_owens7-16-97.htm.

Books
Burke, Kathryn. *The Dust Bowl, Bakersfield Sound, and Buck*. North Charleston, SC: BookSurge Publishers, 2007.
Fenster, Mark. "Don Rich." In *Encyclopedia of Country Music*, edited by Country Music Foundation. New York: Oxford University Press, 1998.
Kienzle, Rich. *The Buck Owens Collection 1959–1990*. Santa Monica, CA: Rhino Records, 1992.
Stambler, Irwin, and Grelun Landon. *The Encyclopedia of Folk, Country & Western Music*. New York: St. Martin's Press, 1984.

Documents
Buck Owens, *Who's Who* application, Heather Publications, Denver, CO.

Interviews
Kay Adams, Earl Poole Ball Jr., Kris Black, Rolene Brumley, Tom Brumley, Roy Clark, Jimmy Dean, Frank Delaney, Dave Gant, Jim Hager, Jon Hager, Doyle Holly, Ronnie Jackson, Kay Johnson, Loretta Johnson, Loudilla Johnson, LaWanda Lindsey Smith, Sam Lovullo,

Marvin Mason, Jo McFadden, Dennis Payne, Gary Paxton, Wade Pepper, Johnny Russell, Daryl Stogner, Viola Stogner, Marlane Ulrich-Dunivent.

Web Sites
Olympian (www.theolympian.com), Rockabilly Hall of Fame (www.rockabillyhall.com).

8. Bakersfield Redux

Articles
Price, Robert. "Buck Had the World by the Tail." *Bakersfield Californian*, April 2, 2006.

Books
Burke, Kathryn. *The Dust Bowl, Bakersfield Sound, and Buck.* North Charleston, SC: BookSurge Publishers, 2007.
Haggard, Merle, with Peggy Russell. *Sing Me Back Home.* New York: Times Books, 1981.
Kienzle, Rich. *The Buck Owens Collection 1959–1990.* Santa Monica, CA: Rhino Records, 1992.

Documents
Bonnie Owens, complaint for support, February 25, 1959; Nevada Marriage Index, 1956–2005.

Interviews
Rolene Brumley, Tommy Collins, Doyle Holly, Jo McFadden, Johnny Russell, Daryl Stogner, Viola Stogner, Marlane Ulrich-Dunivent.

Letters
Rich, Don. Don Rich to Vance Ulrich, n.d.

Web Sites
Corralitos California History (www.corralitoshistory.com), Kern County Museum (www.kcmuseum.org).

9. General Jack

Articles
Associated Press. "Country Music Manager Jack McFadden, 71." *Chicago Tribune*, June 21, 1998.
Battle, Bob. "Country Music Manager Jack McFadden Helps Stars Shine." *Nashville Banner*, [exact date not noted], 1985.
———. "Music Exec Sees Boom in Entertainment Here." *Nashville Banner*, August 30, 1984.
Grissim, John Jr. "California White Man's Shit Kickin' Blues." *Rolling Stone*, June 28, 1969.
Variety. "Jack McFadden." Monday, June 22, 1998.

Books
Burke, Kathryn. *The Dust Bowl, Bakersfield Sound, and Buck.* North Charleston, SC: BookSurge Publishers, 2007.
Country Music Foundation. *Encyclopedia of Country Music.* New York: Oxford University Press, 1998.
Haggard, Merle, with Tom Carter. *My House of Memories: For the Record.* New York: HarperCollins, 1999.
Kienzle, Rich. *The Buck Owens Collection 1959–1990.* Santa Monica, CA: Rhino Records, 1992.
McCloud, Barry. *Definitive Country.* New York: Perigee Books, 1995.
Stambler, Irwin, and Grelun Landon. *The Encyclopedia of Folk, Country & Western Music.* New York: St. Martin's Press, 1984.
Reed Elsevier, Inc. *Who's Who in Entertainment.* 1st and 2nd eds. New Providence, NJ: Reed Elsevier, 1991 and 1997.

Documents
OMAC Artist Corporation report, Dun & Bradstreet, February 1, 2000.

Interviews
Kay Adams, Larry Adamson, Kris Black, Jackson Brumley, Tom Brumley, Willie Cantu, Jimmy Dean, Jon Hager, Doyle Holly, Sam Lovullo, Jo McFadden, Joe McFadden, Bill Mack, Jay Dee Maness, Jana Jae, Dennis Payne, Wade Pepper, Jim Pierce, LaWanda Lindsey Smith.

Web Sites
Buckowensfan.com, Crystal Palace official Web site (www.buckowens.com), Texas State Historical Association Online (www.tshaonline.org).

10. Uncle Dorothy

Books
Burke, Kathryn. *The Dust Bowl, Bakersfield Sound, and Buck.* North Charleston, SC: BookSurge Publishers, 2007.
Kienzle, Rich. *The Buck Owens Collection 1959–1990.* Santa Monica, CA: Rhino Records, 1992.

Interviews
Kay Adams, Kris Black, Jim Hager, Jon Hager, Doyle Holly, Jo McFadden, Dennis Payne, Marlane Ulrich-Dunivent.

11. "Act Naturally"

Articles
Freeman, Donald. "Buck Owens . . . He Hee Haws All the Way to the Bank." *San Diego Union TV Week*, June 21–27, 1970.
Keel, Pinckney. "Buck Owens Picks, Sings, Pulls in Millions." Pt. 1. *Nashville Banner*, November 21, 1969.

Books
Burke, Kathryn. *The Dust Bowl, Bakersfield Sound, and Buck.* North Charleston, SC: BookSurge Publishers, 2007.
Collins, Ace. *The Stories Behind Country Music's All-Time Greatest 100 Songs.* New York: Boulevard Books, 1996.
Kienzle, Rich. *The Buck Owens Collection 1959–1990.* Santa Monica, CA: Rhino Records, 1992.

Interviews
Tom Brumley, Doyle Holly, Ronnie Jackson, Loudilla Johnson, Mayf Nutter, Dennis Payne, Jim Pierce, Johnny Russell, Daryl Stogner.

12. Merle and the Moose Medicine

Books
Haggard, Merle, with Tom Carter. *My House of Memories: For the Record.* New York: HarperCollins, 1999.
Haggard, Merle, with Peggy Russell. *Sing Me Back Home.* New York: Times Books, 1981.
Kienzle, Rich. *The Buck Owens Collection 1959–1990.* Santa Monica, CA: Rhino Records, 1992.

Interviews
Kay Adams, Larry Adamson, Kris Black, Tom Brumley, Willie Cantu, Jim Hager, Jon Hager, Doyle Holly, Jim Pierce, Marlane Ulrich-Dunivent.

Web Sites
Allmusic.com, Billboard.com, Rockabilly Hall of Fame (www.rockabillyhall.com).

13. Dashing Doyle

Articles
Cashbox. "Country Artist of the Week: Doyle Holly." December 1, 1973.

Christie, Bob. "Buckaroos Reunite for Buck Owens Birthday Extravaganza." *Bakersfield Californian*, August 15, 1999.
Jarvis, Elena. "Doyle Holly Plays Hard Country Pure and Simple." *Colorado Springs Gazette Telegraph*, March 6, 1981.
Rhodes, Don. "Doyle Holly Had His Share of Bad Breaks." *Augusta Chronicle*, May 31, 1981.
Johnson, Jon. "Doyle Holly and the Buckaroos Are Together Again." *Country Standard Time*, June 2003.
Johnson, Loudilla. "Doyle Holly: From Sideman to Headman." *Country Song Roundup*, September 1974.
Stuhr, Evelyn, and Jeanne Stuhr. Press release for Doyle Holly International Fan Club, n.d.

Books
Reed Elsevier, Inc. *Who's Who in Entertainment*. 1st and 3rd eds. New Providence, NJ: Reed Elsevier, 1997.

Documents
Buckaroos service mark registration, U.S. Patent and Trademark Office, January 28, 1969; Doyle Holly Music report, Dun & Bradstreet, 1982; Nevada Marriage Index, 1956–2005, Doyle Floyd Hendricks.

Interviews
Rolene Brumley, Tom Brumley, Willie Cantu, Jim Hager, Jon Hager, Doyle Holly, Marlane Ulrich-Dunivent.

Web Sites
Internet Movie Database (www.imdb.com).

14. Timid Tom

Articles
Christie, Bob. "Buckaroos Reunite for Buck Owens Birthday Extravaganza." *Bakersfield Californian*, August 15, 1999.
Forte, Dan, and Rick Rawls. "The Return of the Bakersfield Sound: An Exclusive Interview with Buck Owens." *Guitar Player*, February 1989.

Audiovisual
Owens, Buck. *Buck Owens & the Buckaroos Live at Carnegie Hall*. Country Music Foundation, 1988. Compact disc.

Books
Hively, Kay, and Albert E. Brumley Jr. *I'll Fly Away*. Branson, MO: Mountaineer Books, 1990.
McCloud, Barry. *Definitive Country*. New York: Perigee Books, 1995.

Interviews
Kay Adams, Rolene Brumley, Tom Brumley, Willie Cantu, Doyle Holly.

15. The Peacemakers

Articles
Associated Press. "Buck Owens Needs Mental Exam: Wife." *Tennessean*, August 19, 1977.
Harris, Stacy. "Buck Owens: Sometimes It Just Ain't Easy." *Country Song Roundup*, August 1978.

Books
Burke, Kathryn. *The Dust Bowl, Bakersfield Sound, and Buck*. North Charleston, SC: BookSurge Publishers, 2007.
Golomb, Elan. *Trapped in the Mirror: Adult Children of Narcissists in Their Struggle for Self*. New York: William Morrow and Co., 1992.
Kienzle, Rich. *The Buck Owens Collection 1959–1990*. Santa Monica, CA: Rhino Records, 1992.

Interviews
Kay Adams, Kris Black, Jerry Brightman, Rolene Brumley, Tom Brumley, Willie Cantu, Mary Lou Cushman, Jim Hager, Jon Hager, Stacy Harris, Ronnie Jackson, Jana Jae, Doyle Holly, Sam Lovullo, Jo McFadden, Dennis Payne, Wade Pepper, Russ Varnell.

Web Sites
Ancestry.com.

16. Dennis Payne

Interviews
Doyle Holly, Dennis Payne, Daryl Stogner.

Documents
Social Security application, Charles Bruce Payne.

Web Sites
Rockabilly Hall of Fame (www.rockabillyhall.com).

17. The Firing of Mel King

Audiovisual
Nelson, Willie. Interview by Bill Mack. *The Bill Mack Show*, Sirius XM Radio, February 2010.

Interviews
Tom Brumley, Willie Cantu, Doyle Holly.

Web Sites
Bakersfield Californian (www.bakersfield.com).

18. Willing Willie

Articles
Christie, Bob. "Buckaroos Reunite for Buck Owens Birthday Extravaganza." *Bakersfield Californian*, August 15, 1999.

Audiovisual
Owens, Buck. *Buck Owens & the Buckaroos Live at Carnegie Hall*. Country Music Foundation, 1988. Compact disc.

Books
Kienzle, Rich. *The Buck Owens Collection 1959–1990*. Santa Monica, CA: Rhino Records, 1992.

Interviews
Kay Adams, Tom Brumley, Willie Cantu, Doyle Holly.

19. Road Stories

Articles
Hollywood Reporter. "Owens Hit in Garden." January 28, 1974.
Rhodes, Don. "Doyle Holly Had His Share of Bad Breaks." *Augusta Chronicle*, May 31, 1981.

Books
Kienzle, Rich. *The Buck Owens Collection 1959–1990*. Santa Monica, CA: Rhino Records, 1992.

Interviews
Kay Adams, Larry Adamson, Tom Brumley, Willie Cantu, Jimmy Dean, Ralph Emery, Doyle Holly, Jim Pierce.

Web Sites
Internet Movie Database (www.imdb.com), Rockabilly Hall of Fame (www.rockabillyhall.com), Songfacts.com.

20. Buck's Pledge

Articles
Forte, Dan, and Rick Rawls. "The Return of the Bakersfield Sound: An Exclusive Interview with Buck Owens." *Guitar Player*, February 1989.
Price, Robert. "A Buck Owens Bonfire." *Bakersfield Californian*, n.d.
———. "Buck: Raw, Real—Not Nashville." *Bakersfield Californian*, April 2, 2006.

Audiovisual
Owens, Buck. Interview by Chris Comer and Rob Ervin. *The Chris & Rob Late Night Talk Show*, WAIF-FM, Cincinnati, OH, July 16, 1997, www.chriscomerradio.com/buck_owens/buck_owens7-16-97.htm.

Books
Burke, Kathryn. *The Dust Bowl, Bakersfield Sound, and Buck*. North Charleston, SC: BookSurge Publishers, 2007.
Kienzle, Rich. *The Buck Owens Collection 1959–1990*. Santa Monica, CA: Rhino Records, 1992.
Nelson, Ken. *My First 90 Years Plus 3*. Pittsburgh, PA: Dorrance Publishing Co., 2007.
Stambler, Irwin, and Grelun Landon. *The Encyclopedia of Folk, Country & Western Music*. New York: St. Martin's Press, 1984.

Interviews
Keith Bilbrey, Tom Brumley, Dan Rogers, Marlane Ulrich-Dunivent.

Web Sites
Grand Ole Opry official Web site (www.opry.com).

21. The Baron of Buckersfield

Articles
Dougherty, John. "Award-Winning KNIX Began as Tax Write-Off for Singer Buck Owens." *Tempe Daily News Tribune*, November 1, 1988.
Forte, Dan, and Rick Rawls. "The Return of the Bakersfield Sound: An Exclusive Interview with Buck Owens." *Guitar Player*, February 1989.
Freeman, Donald. "Buck Owens . . . He Hee Haws All the Way to the Bank." *San Diego Union TV Week*, June 21–27, 1970.
Fulmer, Douglas. "Buck Owens: From Cotton Fields to Jets, He's Charted His Own Course." *Country Weekly*, August 21–September 17, 1999.
Grissim, John Jr. "California White Man's Shit Kickin' Blues." *Rolling Stone*, June 28, 1969.
Harris, Stacy. "Buck Owens: Sometimes It Just Ain't Easy." *Country Song Roundup*, August 1978.
Hollywood Reporter. "Owens Hit in Garden." January 28, 1974.
Keel, Pinckney. "Buck Owens Picks, Sings, Pulls in Millions." Pt. 1. *Nashville Banner*, November 21, 1969.
———. "Buck Owens: Dropout Worth Millions." Pt. 2. *Nashville Banner*, November 28, 1970.
Lewis, Randy. "Buck Owens: Gone but Not Forgotten." *Los Angeles Times*, October 14, 2007.
Price, Robert. "Buck Had the World by the Tail." *Bakersfield Californian*, April 2, 2006.
Scott, John L. "Pop Sales Spur Cowboy Singer." *Los Angeles Times*, March [exact date not noted], 1966.

Books
Burke, Kathryn. *The Dust Bowl, Bakersfield Sound, and Buck*. North Charleston, SC: BookSurge Publishers, 2007.

Dawidoff, Nicholas. "Honky-Tonk Man." In *In the Country of Country*. New York: Pantheon Books, 1997.

Kienzle, Rich. *The Buck Owens Collection 1959–1990*. Santa Monica, CA: Rhino Records, 1992.

Stambler, Irwin, and Grelun Landon. *The Encyclopedia of Folk, Country & Western Music*. New York: St. Martin's Press, 1984.

Reed Elsevier, Inc. *The Complete Who's Who Biographies*. New Providence, NJ: Reed Elsevier, 2000.

Documents
California Secretary of State filings, various years; Dun & Bradstreet, Inc., reports, various years.

Interviews
Larry Adamson, Kris Black, Jackson Brumley, Rolene Brumley, Tom Brumley, Jimmy Dean, Jim Hager, Jon Hager, Stacy Harris, Doyle Holly, Ronnie Jackson, Jana Jae, Bill Mack, Jay Dee Maness, Jo McFadden, Joe McFadden, Mayf Nutter, Dennis Payne, Wade Pepper, Jim Pierce, Gene Price, Lulu Roman, LaWanda Lindsey Smith, Marlane Ulrich-Dunivent.

Web sites
Federal Communications Commission (www.fcc.gov), KUZZ-AM/FM (www.kuzzradio.com), Rockabilly Hall of Fame (www.rockabillyhall.com).

22. Phyllis

Articles
Price, Robert. "Buck Had a Lot of Ladies in His Life." *Bakersfield Californian*, April 2, 2006.

Books
Burke, Kathryn. *The Dust Bowl, Bakersfield Sound, and Buck*. North Charleston, SC: BookSurge Publishers, 2007.

Haggard, Merle, with Tom Carter. *My House of Memories: For the Record*. New York: HarperCollins, 1999.

Documents
California Death Index, various years; California Divorce Index, 1966–1977; Social Security Death Index listings, Phyllis Irene Buford, Melvin Leo Owens.

Interviews
Kay Adams, Rolene Brumley, Tom Brumley, Willie Cantu, Doyle Holly, Sam Lovullo, Jo McFadden, Dennis Payne, Wade Pepper, LaWanda Lindsey Smith, Marlane Ulrich-Dunivent.

Web Sites
Ancestry.com.

23. Professional Jealousy

Articles
Lewis, Randy. "Buck Owens: Gone but Not Forgotten." *Los Angeles Times*, October 14, 2007.

Books
Collins, Ace. *The Stories Behind Country Music's All-Time Greatest 100 Songs*. New York: Boulevard Books, 1996.

Cooper, Daniel. *Merle Haggard: Down Every Road*. Nashville: Capitol Nashville, 1996.

Emery, Ralph, with Patsi Bale Cox. *The View from Nashville: On the Record with Country Music's Greatest Stars*. New York: Quill, 1998.

Golomb, Elan. *Trapped in the Mirror: Adult Children of Narcissists in Their Struggle for Self*. New York: William Morrow and Co., 1992.

Haggard, Merle, with Tom Carter. *My House of Memories: For the Record*. New York: HarperCollins, 1999.
Jones, George, with Tom Carter. *I Lived to Tell It All*. New York: Villard, 1996.
Kienzle, Rich. *The Buck Owens Collection 1959–1990*. Santa Monica, CA: Rhino Records, 1992.
Nelson, Ken. *My First 90 Years Plus 3*. Pittsburgh, PA: Dorrance Publishing Co., 2007.
Oermann, Robert K. *America's Music*. Atlanta: Turner Publishing, 1996.

Interviews
Tom Brumley, Doyle Holly, Dennis Payne.

24. The Flex Bus

Interviews
Kay Adams, Tom Brumley, Willie Cantu, Doyle Holly, Loudilla Johnson.

25. The Girl Singer

Articles
Journal of Country Music. "Gear-Swappin' Mama Kay Adams from Bakersfield." N.d.

Books
Kienzle, Rich. *The Buck Owens Collection 1959–1990*. Santa Monica, CA: Rhino Records, 1992.

Interviews
Kay Adams, Tom Brumley, Willie Cantu, Jim Hager, Jon Hager, Doyle Holly.

26. *Buck Owens Ranch*

Articles
Price, Robert. "Buck Had the World by the Tail." *Bakersfield Californian*, April 2, 2006.
Weldon, Michael J. "Hillbilly Hollywood." WFMU-FM official Web site, www.wfmu.org/LCD/24/hollybilly.html.

Audiovisual
Buck Owens Ranch. TV series, WKY-TV, Oklahoma City, OK, 1966–1973.
The Life and Times of Buck Owens. TV special, TNN, 1997.

Books
Burke, Kathryn. *The Dust Bowl, Bakersfield Sound, and Buck*. North Charleston, SC: BookSurge Publishers, 2007.
Kienzle, Rich. *The Buck Owens Collection 1959–1990*. Santa Monica, CA: Rhino Records, 1992.

Interviews
Kay Adams, Earl Poole Ball Jr., Jackson Brumley, Tom Brumley, Doyle Holly, Ronnie Jackson, Bill Mack, Jay Dee Maness, Jo McFadden, Wade Pepper, LaWanda Lindsey Smith, Lee Allan Smith, Russ Varnell.

Web Sites
Mathis Brothers Furniture (www.mathisbrothers.com), Songfacts.com.

27. Carnegie Hall

Articles
Price, Robert. "Buck Had the World by the Tail." *Bakersfield Californian*, April 2, 2006.

Audiovisual
Owens, Buck. *Buck Owens & the Buckaroos Live at Carnegie Hall*. Country Music Foundation, 1988. Compact disc.

———. *Carnegie Hall Concert with Buck Owens and His Buckaroos*, Capitol Records. Hollywood, California. July 25, 1966. LP.

Books

Burke, Kathryn. *The Dust Bowl, Bakersfield Sound, and Buck*. North Charleston, SC: BookSurge Publishers, 2007.

Englehardt, Kristofer. *Beatles Undercover*. Burlington, Ontario: Collector's Guide Publishing, 1998.

George-Warren, Holly, and Michelle Freedman. *How the West Was Worn*. New York: Harry N. Abrams, 2001.

Kienzle, Rich. *The Buck Owens Collection 1959–1990*. Santa Monica, CA: Rhino Records, 1992.

Wiener, Allen J. *The Beatles: The Ultimate Recording Guide*. Holbrook, MA: Bob Adams, 1994.

Interviews

Kay Adams, Tom Brumley, Willie Cantu, Doyle Holly, Bill Mack.

28. Running with the Dogs

Books

Woodstra, Chris, Stephen Thomas Erlewine, Vladimir Bogdanov, and Michael Erlewine, eds. *All Music Guide to Country: The Experts' Guide to the Best Country Recordings*. San Francisco: Backbeat Books, 1997.

Interviews

Kay Adams, Charlie C. Allen, Kris Black, Maxine Brown, Tom Brumley, Willie Cantu, Roy Clark, Jim Hager, Jon Hager, Doyle Holly, Jana Jae, "Luanne," Buck Owens, LaWanda Lindsey Smith.

29. James, Charley, and Ray

Books

Kienzle, Rich. *The Buck Owens Collection 1959–1990*. Santa Monica, CA: Rhino Records, 1992.

Interviews

Kay Adams, Rolene Brumley, Tom Brumley.

Web Sites

Ed Roman Guitars (www.edroman.com), Songfacts.com.

30. If the Suit Fits

Books

Kienzle, Rich. *The Buck Owens Collection 1959–1990*. Santa Monica, CA: Rhino Records, 1992.

Nelson, Ken. *My First 90 Years Plus 3*. Pittsburgh, PA: Dorrance Publishing Co., 2007.

Interviews

Kay Adams, Tom Brumley, Willie Cantu, Doyle Holly, Marlane Ulrich-Dunivent.

31. The Studio and the Snake

Books

Burke, Kathryn. *The Dust Bowl, Bakersfield Sound, and Buck*. North Charleston, SC: BookSurge Publishers, 2007.

Interviews

Doyle Holly, Dennis Payne, Gary Paxton, Pete Pittman.

Web Sites
Bakersfield Californian (www.bakersfield.com), KGET-TV (www.kget.com).

32. Jennifer

Articles
Fulmer, Douglas. "Buck Owens: From Cotton Fields to Jets, He's Charted His Own Course."
   Country Weekly, August 21–September 17, 1999.
Price, Robert. "Buck Had a Lot of Ladies in His Life." *Bakersfield Californian*, April 2, 2006.

Books
Burke, Kathryn. *The Dust Bowl, Bakersfield Sound, and Buck*. North Charleston, SC:
   BookSurge Publishers, 2007.
Kienzle, Rich. *The Buck Owens Collection 1959–1990*. Santa Monica, CA: Rhino Records, 1992.

Interviews
Kris Black, Jim Hager, Jon Hager, Doyle Holly, Jana Jae, Jay Dee Maness, Jo McFadden.

33. Forbidden Fruit

Articles
Lawrence County Record. Obituaries. April 1, 2009.

Books
Carnes, Patrick, Ph.D. *Contrary to Love*. Center City, MN: Hazelden, 1989.

Documents
California Birth Index, 1905–1995; California criminal case filings, John D. Owens; Kern
   County Property Records, 2007; Los Angeles County mortgage records, 2000, 2002; Social
   Security Death Index.

Interviews
Kay Adams, Larry Adamson, Kris Black, Rolene Brumley, Tom Brumley, Doyle Holly, Jana
   Jae, Buck Owens, Dennis Payne, LaWanda Lindsey Smith, Marlane Ulrich-Dunivent.

Web Sites
Ancestry.com, Tributes.com.

34. Friends in High Places

Articles
Anders, George. "Bohemian Rhapsody: One Thing in Flux at the Grove Is Music." *Wall Street
   Journal*, July 15, 2004.
Bakersfield Californian. "The Buckster Sure Got Around." April 2, 2006.
Schenectady Gazette. "Buck Hosts Birch Bayh." March 2, 1974.
Schultz, Valerie. "Sympathy for Ashburn Turns to Outrage." *Bakersfield Californian*, March 17,
   2010.
Trueheart, Charles. "Pagans and Peerless Leaders." *Washington Post*, October 24, 1989.
Weiss, Philip. "Masters of the Universe Go to Camp: Inside Bohemian Grove." *Spy*, November
   1989.

Audiovisual
"Acting Naturally." *Biography*. TV series, A&E, 2000.
"Buck Owens Honored." Stand-alone photo of Buck Owens and Governor Ronald Reagan, n.d.

Books
Bohemian Club. *Bohemian Club*. San Francisco: Bohemian Club, 1965.
Burke, Kathryn. *The Dust Bowl, Bakersfield Sound, and Buck*. North Charleston, SC:
   BookSurge Publishers, 2007.

Epstein, Edward Jay. *Dossier: The Secret History of Armand Hammer*. New York: Random House, 1996.
Nelson, Ken. *My First 90 Years Plus 3*. Pittsburgh, PA: Dorrance Publishing Co., 2007.
O'Brien, Cathy, with Mark Phillips. *Tranceformation of America*. Las Vegas: Reality Marketing, 1995.
Stahl, Lesley. *Reporting Live*. New York: Simon & Schuster, 1999.

Interviews

Kay Adams, Larry Adamson, Kris Black, Tom Brumley, Doyle Holly, Ronnie Jackson, Jana Jae, Cathy O'Brien, Jo McFadden, Jay Dee Maness, Dennis Payne, Mark Phillips, Gene Price, LaWanda Lindsey Smith, Marlane Ulrich-Dunivent.

Web Sites

OpenSecrets.org, RootsWeb.com.

35. Jumpin' Jerry Wiggins

Books

Burke, Kathryn. *The Dust Bowl, Bakersfield Sound, and Buck*. North Charleston, SC: BookSurge Publishers, 2007.
Kienzle, Rich. *The Buck Owens Collection 1959–1990*. Santa Monica, CA: Rhino Records, 1992.
Nelson, Ken. *My First 90 Years Plus 3*. Pittsburgh, PA: Dorrance Publishing Co., 2007.
Stambler, Irwin, and Grelun Landon. *The Encyclopedia of Folk, Country & Western Music*. New York: St. Martin's Press, 1984.

Interviews

Tom Brumley, Willie Cantu, Marlane Ulrich-Dunivent.

36. Stolen Glory

Books

Burke, Kathryn. *The Dust Bowl, Bakersfield Sound, and Buck*. North Charleston, SC: BookSurge Publishers, 2007.

Documents

California civil case filings, Willard E. Price/Gene Price, June 12, 1970, and February 10, 1981, and Fred Winston Segrest/Freddie Hart, May 1, 1974.

Interviews

Earl Poole Ball Jr., Tommy Collins, Doyle Holly, Dennis Payne, Gene Price, LaWanda Lindsey Smith.

Web Sites

Democrat Hot Springs (www.democrathotsprings.com).

37. Kris Black

Articles

Martin, Bryce. "Owens Uses Pretty Promoter." *Bakersfield Californian*, n.d.

Books

Burke, Kathryn. *The Dust Bowl, Bakersfield Sound, and Buck*. North Charleston, SC: BookSurge Publishers, 2007.
Finstad, Suzanne. *Child Bride*. New York: Harmony Books, 1997.
Kienzle, Rich. *The Buck Owens Collection 1959–1990*. Santa Monica, CA: Rhino Records, 1992.

Documents

Employment contract, Kris Black; Kern County property records.

Interviews

Kris Black, Doyle Holly, Ronnie Jackson, LaWanda Lindsey Smith, Marlane Ulrich-Dunivent.

38. A Run-In With Rolene

Interviews
Rolene Brumley, Tom Brumley, Doyle Holly, Marlane Ulrich-Dunivent.

39. Flying High

Books
Burke, Kathryn. *The Dust Bowl, Bakersfield Sound, and Buck.* North Charleston, SC:
BookSurge Publishers, 2007.
Kienzle, Rich. *The Buck Owens Collection 1959–1990.* Santa Monica, CA: Rhino Records,
1992.

Documents
Death certificate, Bob Woods, January 31, 1975.

Interviews
Tom Brumley, Willie Cantu, Doyle Holly, Jay Dee Maness, Marlane Ulrich-Dunivent.

Web Sites
Billboard.com, Sun Lakes Aero Club (www.sunlakesaeroclub.org).

40. Bucking Tradition

Articles
Price, Robert. "His History Will Live On at These Places." *Bakersfield Californian,* April 2,
2006.

Audiovisual
Owens, Buck. *Buck Owens Live at the White House.* Capitol Records, September 5, 1972. LP.

Books
Burke, Kathryn. *The Dust Bowl, Bakersfield Sound, and Buck.* North Charleston, SC:
BookSurge Publishers, 2007.
Kienzle, Rich. *The Buck Owens Collection 1959–1990.* Santa Monica, CA: Rhino Records,
1992.

Interviews
Kay Adams, Rolene Brumley, Tom Brumley, Doyle Holly, Marvin Mason, Jo McFadden, Dennis Payne, Marlane Ulrich-Dunivent, Russ Varnell.

Web Sites
Bakersfield Californian (www.bakersfield.com).

41. The Show Must Go On

Interviews
Doyle Holly, Jim Pierce.

Web Sites
Rockabilly Hall of Fame (www.rockabillyhall.com).

42. Jay Dee

Articles
Forte, Dan, and Rick Rawls. "The Return of the Bakersfield Sound: An Exclusive Interview
with Buck Owens." *Guitar Player,* February 1989.

Interviews
Tom Brumley, Mary Ellen Duerr, Ronnie Jackson, Jay Dee Maness.

43. *Hee Haw*

Articles
Price, Robert. "A Buck Owens Bonfire." *Bakersfield Californian*, n.d.
———. "Buck Had the World by the Tail." *Bakersfield Californian*, April 2, 2006.

Audiovisual
Clark, Roy. Interview on Country Music Television, 2006.
The Hee Haw Collection. Time Life, 1996. DVD.
Owens, Buck. Interview by Chris Comer and Rob Ervin. *The Chris & Rob Late Night Talk Show*, WAIF-FM, Cincinnati, OH, July 16, 1997, www.chriscomerradio.com/buck_owens/buck_owens7-16-97.htm.

Books
Burke, Kathryn. *The Dust Bowl, Bakersfield Sound, and Buck*. North Charleston, SC: BookSurge Publishers, 2007.
Campbell, Glen, with Tom Carter. *Rhinestone Cowboy*. New York: Villard Books, 1994.
Clark, Roy, with Marc Eliot. *My Life in Spite of Myself!* New York: Simon & Schuster, 1994.
Kienzle, Rich. *The Buck Owens Collection 1959–1990*. Santa Monica, CA: Rhino Records, 1992.
Lovullo, Sam, and Marc Eliot. *Life in the Kornfield*. New York: Boulevard Books, 1996.
Stoneman, Roni, as told to Ellen Wright. *Pressing On*. Urbana, IL: University of Illinois Press, 2007.

Interviews
Richard Bennett, Kris Black, Rolene Brumley, Tom Brumley, Roy Clark, Jimmy Dean, Sandy Fox, Jim Hager, Jon Hager, Doyle Holly, Ronnie Jackson, Kay Johnson, Loretta Johnson, Loudilla Johnson, Sandy Liles, Sam Lovullo, Jay Dee Maness, Jo McFadden, Dennis Payne, Lulu Roman, Russ Varnell.

Web Sites
Hee Haw official Web site (www.heehaw.com), Internet Movie Database (www.imdb.com).

44. Drugs of Choice

Books
Burke, Kathryn. *The Dust Bowl, Bakersfield Sound, and Buck*. North Charleston, SC: BookSurge Publishers, 2007.
Kienzle, Rich. *The Buck Owens Collection 1959–1990*. Santa Monica, CA: Rhino Records, 1992.
Stoneman, Roni, as told to Ellen Wright. *Pressing On*. Urbana, IL: University of Illinois Press, 2007.

Interviews
Tom Brumley, Jim Hager, Jon Hager, Doyle Holly, Jay Dee Maness, Jo McFadden, Lulu Roman.

Web Sites
Phentermine.com.

45. Jo McFadden

Interviews
Tom Brumley, Jo McFadden.

46. Buck Changes His Tunes

Audiovisual
Owens, Buck. Interview by Chris Comer and Rob Ervin. *The Chris & Rob Late Night Talk Show*, WAIF-FM, Cincinnati, OH, July 16, 1997, www.chriscomerradio.com/buck_owens/buck_owens7-16-97.htm.

Books

Burke, Kathryn. *The Dust Bowl, Bakersfield Sound, and Buck.* North Charleston, SC: BookSurge Publishers, 2007.

Kienzle, Rich. *The Buck Owens Collection 1959–1990.* Santa Monica, CA: Rhino Records, 1992.

Nelson, Ken. *My First 90 Years Plus 3.* Pittsburgh, PA: Dorrance Publishing Co., 2007.

Interviews

Jerry Brightman, Jim Hager, Jon Hager, Wes Holcomb, Doyle Holly, Jay Dee Maness, Marvin Mason, Gene Price, Marlane Ulrich-Dunivent.

Web Sites

Traditional Country Hall of Fame (www.talentondisplay.com).

47. Ruby and the Master of Spin

Articles

Clark, Eddie. "'Lover-ly Ad' Campaign Ruled Off-Key." *Los Angeles Herald-Examiner*, May 31, 1977.

Dahlbeck, Emily. "Buck Owens' Search for a Mail-Order Bride: How You Can Become Buck's Wife." [Publication not noted], June 1974.

Eder, Shirley. "'Pore' Buck Still Seeking a Wife." *Detroit Free Press*, August 22, 1974.

Galesburg (IL) Register Mail. "Buck in the Buff and Playgirl's Got the Evidence." September 2, 1977.

Jones, Norma. "Singer Will Stay a Bachelor." *Chronicle-Telegram* (Elyria, OH), August 25, 1974.

Martin, Bryce. "Owens Uses Pretty Promoter." *Bakersfield Californian*, n.d.

Peterson, John. "Buck Owens' Mail Order Bride Stampede." *National Observer*, n.d. Reprinted in *Charleston Daily Mail*, June 20, 1974.

———. "C-W Singer Owes Target of Lovelorn Letters, Calls." *National Observer*, n.d. Reprinted in *Charleston Daily Mail*, July 5, 1974.

Books

Burke, Kathryn. *The Dust Bowl, Bakersfield Sound, and Buck.* North Charleston, SC: BookSurge Publishers, 2007.

Kienzle, Rich. *The Buck Owens Collection 1959–1990.* Santa Monica, CA: Rhino Records, 1992.

Documents

Employment contract, Kris Black.

Interviews

Kris Black, Jerry Brightman, Ronnie Jackson, Jo McFadden, Wade Pepper, LaWanda Lindsey Smith.

48. Death of a Buckaroo

Articles

Bessman, Jim. "Owens Cohort Rich Gets Due on Anthology Project from Sundazed." *Billboard*, November 4, 2000.

Black, Kris. "The Man We Knew." *Country Town News* (Bakersfield, CA), July 1974.

Christie, Bob. "Buckaroos Reunite for Buck Owens Birthday Extravaganza." *Bakersfield Californian*, August 15, 1999.

Davis, Dick. "Mrs. Davis Campbell, Mother and Grandmother of Country Music Artists." *Country Town News* (Bakersfield, CA), July 1974.

———. "Superstar Sideman." *Country Town News* (Bakersfield, CA), July 1974.

Eder, Shirley. "'Pore' Buck Still Seeking a Wife." *Detroit Free Press*, August 22, 1974.

Fox, Darrin. "Heroes: Don Rich." *Guitar Player*, April 2002.

Hance, Bill. "Buck Owens Back and 'Enemy' Is Gone." *Nashville Banner*, June 11, 1976.

Nashville Banner. "Don Rich, Guitarist for Owens, Killed." July 18, 1974.
Oregonian. "Buck Owens Headlines Show." August 13, 1974.
Paxman, Bob. "Flashback: Buck's 'Right Arm' Gone." *Country Weekly,* July 2004.
Spokane Daily Chronicle. "Buck Owens Due Tomorrow." August 19, 1974.
Tennessean. "Buck Owens' Lead Guitar Player Killed." July 19, 1974.
Yakley, Carrie. "Country Music Stars Highlight Lorain County Fair." *Journal* (Lorain, OH). August 18, 1974.

Audiovisual
"Acting Naturally." *Biography.* TV series, A&E, 2000.

Books
Burke, Kathryn. *The Dust Bowl, Bakersfield Sound, and Buck.* North Charleston, SC: BookSurge Publishers, 2007.
Cochran, Johnnie L., Jr. with Tim Rutten. *Journey to Justice.* New York: Ballantine Books, 1996.
Fenster, Mark. "Don Rich." In *Encyclopedia of Country Music,* edited by Country Music Foundation. New York: Oxford University Press, 1998.
Kienzle, Rich. *The Buck Owens Collection 1959–1990.* Santa Monica, CA: Rhino Records, 1992.
Saferstein, Richard, Ph.D. "Forensic Toxicology." In *Criminalistics.* Englewood Cliffs, NJ: Prentice Hall, 1995.
Spitz, Werner U., M.D. and Russell S. Fisher, M.D., eds. *Medicolegal Investigation of Death.* Springfield, IL: Charles C. Thomas, 1973.

Documents
California State Code; Central Pathology Laboratory, blood alcohol report; certificate of death; San Luis Obispo Office of Coroner report, July 21, 1974; San Luis Obispo Sheriff-Coroner autopsy report; San Luis Obispo Sheriff-Coroner synopsis of microscopic examination; San Luis Obispo Sheriff's Office incident report, July 17, 1974; San Luis Obispo Sheriff's Office supplemental report, July 18, 1974; Sutcliffe Mortuary funeral arrangement folder, San Luis Obispo Sheriff Coroner report on post-mortem examination, January 25, 1986.

Interviews
Kay Adams, Larry Adamson, Earl Poole Ball Jr., Kris Black, Tony Booth, Jerry Brightman, Jackson Brumley, Tom Brumley, Jimmy Dean, Jim Foglesong, former MPO at Fort Ord and the Presidio, former OMAC employee, Jim Hager, Jon Hager, Wes Holcomb, Doyle Holly, Ronnie Jackson, Jana Jae, Janette Jones, Sam Lovullo, Bill Mack, Marvin Mason, Mayf Nutter, Dennis Payne, Wade Pepper, Gene Price, Lulu Roman, LaWanda Lindsey Smith, Daryl Stogner, Marlane Ulrich-Dunivent, Jim White, Jerry Wiggins.

Web Sites
Cambria Pines Lodge (www.cambriapineslodge.com), Crystal Palace official Web site (www.buckowens.com), Fender Musical Instruments Corporation (www.fender.com), Old Farmer's Almanac (www.almanac.com), WWW Tide and Current Predictor (http://tbone .biol.sc.edu/tide/).

49. Life After Don

Articles
Brown, Bruce. "Buck Owens Wows Fans." *Spokane Daily Chronicle,* August 21, 1974.
Jones, Norma. "Singer Will Stay a Bachelor." *Chronicle-Telegram* (Elyria, OH), August 25, 1974.
Orr, Jay. "Owens Remembers Old Friend: Singer's Memories of Don Rich Vivid." *Nashville Banner,* September 4, 1992.

Audiovisual
"Acting Naturally." *Biography.* TV series, A&E, 2000.

Books
Burke, Kathryn. *The Dust Bowl, Bakersfield Sound, and Buck.* North Charleston, SC: BookSurge Publishers, 2007.
Kienzle, Rich. *The Buck Owens Collection 1959–1990.* Santa Monica, CA: Rhino Records, 1992.
Nelson, Ken. *My First 90 Years Plus 3.* Pittsburgh, PA: Dorrance Publishing Co., 2007.

Interviews
Earl Poole Ball Jr., Kris Black, Jerry Brightman, Tom Brumley, Jana Jae, Ronnie Jackson, Jo McFadden, Mayf Nutter, LaWanda Lindsey Smith, Marlane Ulrich-Dunivent.

Web Sites
Sound Control Productions (www.soundcontrolstudio.com).

50. Jana Jae

Articles
Associated Press. "Buck Owens Files to End 5-Day-Old Marriage." *Nashville Banner,* May 7, 1977.
———. "Buck Owens Needs Mental Exam: Wife." *Tennessean,* August 19, 1977.
———. "Buck Owens Takes Out Marriage License." *Nashville Banner,* May 4, 1977.
———. "Buck Owens Wants to End Annulment." *Nashville Banner,* August 19, 1977.
———. "Horse Has Last Hee Haw." *Tennessean,* May 7, 1977.
———. "Owens Has Short Honeymoon—Hospitalized." *Nashville Banner,* May 6, 1977.
Bacon, James. "Buck Owens Wants Wife Back." *Los Angeles Herald-Examiner,* May 17, 1977.
Bristol, Marc. "Buck Owens & Don Rich Together Again." *Blue Suede News,* Summer 2006.
Clark, Eddie. "'Lover-ly Ad' Campaign Ruled Off-Key." *Los Angeles Herald-Examiner,* May 31, 1977.
Demaret, Kent. "Buck Owens Roamed While His Fiddler Burned, but Now He's Back on Bended Knee." *People,* July 18, 1977.
Greif, Jana Jae. "Nashville West: The Musical Heritage of Bakersfield." Research paper, 1976.
Hance, Bill. "Buck Owens Says He's Sorry; Wants Jana Jae Back." *Nashville Banner,* June 10, 1977.
Harris, Stacy. "Buck Owens: Sometimes It Just Ain't Easy." *Country Song Roundup,* August 1978.
Hurst, Jack. "Bad Publicity May Result in Happy Ending." *Valley News* (Van Nuys, CA), November 4, 1977.
———. "Fiddler Jana Jae Won't Bow to Personal Unhappiness." *Chicago Tribune,* [exact date not noted], 1977.
———. "Owens: Shining in the Shadow of Other Country Stars." *Chicago Tribune,* November 29, 1981.
Keel, Pinckney. "Buck Owens Picks, Sings, Pulls in Millions." Pt. 1. *Nashville Banner,* November 21, 1969.
Luther, Claudia. "Singer Buck Owens Mentally Incompetent, His Wife Claims." *Los Angeles Times,* August 19, 1977.
Masullo, Bob. "Owens: It Was a Mistake; I Love Her." [Publication not noted], n.d.
United Press International. "Buck Owens Told to Quit Running Ads." *Tennessean,* May 24, 1977.
———. "Owens Ordered to Stop Ads to Wife." *Nashville Banner.* May 21, 1977.
White, John. "Hey Diddle-Diddle, Who's That Playin' The Fiddle?! . . . It's Jana Jae." *Country Music,* January–February 1979.

Books
Stoneman, Roni, as told to Ellen Wright. *Pressing On.* Urbana, IL: University of Illinois Press, 2007.

Documents
California Divorce Index, 1966–1977; Nevada Marriage Index, 1975.

Interviews
Kris Black, Doyle Holly, Ronnie Jackson, Jana Jae, Sam Lovullo, Bill Mack, Jo McFadden, Joe McFadden, LaWanda Lindsey Smith.

Web Sites
Crystal Palace official Web site (www.buckowens.com), Jana Jae's official Web site (www.janajae.com).

51. The No-Record Deal

Books
Epstein, Edward Jay. *Dossier: The Secret History of Armand Hammer.* New York: Random House, 1996.

Documents
Social Security application, Charles Bruce Payne.

Interviews
Larry Adamson, Dennis Payne, Gene Price, Lynn Schults.

Web Sites
Rockabilly Hall of Fame (www.rockabillyhall.com).

52. Two Goodbyes

Documents
Social Security Death Index listing, Alvis E. Owens.

Interviews
Kris Black, LaWanda Lindsey Smith.

Letters
Owens, Maicie. Maicie Owens to Kris Black, n.d.
Owens, Mike. Mike Owens to Kris Black, April 19, 1976

53. The "Three-Day" Marriage

Articles
Associated Press. "Buck Owens Files to End 5-Day-Old Marriage." *Nashville Banner,* May 7, 1977.
———. "Buck Owens Needs Mental Exam: Wife." *Tennessean,* August 19, 1977.
———. "Buck Owens Takes Out Marriage License." *Nashville Banner,* May 4, 1977.
———. "Buck Owens Wants to End Annulment." *Nashville Banner,* August 19, 1977.
———. "Horse Has Last Hee Haw." *Tennessean,* May 7, 1977.
———. "Owens Has Short Honeymoon—Hospitalized." *Nashville Banner,* May 6, 1977.
Bacon, James. "Buck Owens Wants Wife Back." *Los Angeles Herald-Examiner,* May 17, 1977.
Bristol, Marc. "Buck Owens & Don Rich Together Again." *Blue Suede News,* Summer 2006.
Clark, Eddie. "'Lover-ly Ad' Campaign Ruled Off-Key." *Los Angeles Herald-Examiner,* May 31, 1977.
Demaret, Kent. "Buck Owens Roamed While His Fiddler Burned, but Now He's Back on Bended Knee." *People,* July 18, 1977.
Hance, Bill. "Buck Owens Says He's Sorry; Wants Jana Jae Back." *Nashville Banner,* June 10, 1977.
Harris, Stacy. "Buck Owens: Sometimes It Just Ain't Easy." *Country Song Roundup,* August 1978.
Hurst, Jack. "Bad Publicity May Result in Happy Ending." *Valley News* (Van Nuys, CA), November 4, 1977.

———. "Fiddler Jana Jae Won't Bow to Personal Unhappiness." *Chicago Tribune*, [exact date not noted], 1977.

———. "Owens: Shining in the Shadow of Other Country Stars." *Chicago Tribune*, November 29, 1981.

Keel, Pinckney. "Buck Owens Picks, Sings, Pulls in Millions." Pt. 1. *Nashville Banner*, November 21, 1969.

Luther, Claudia. "Singer Buck Owens Mentally Incompetent, His Wife Claims." *Los Angeles Times*, August 19, 1977.

Masullo, Bob. "Owens: It Was a Mistake; I Love Her." [Publication not noted], n.d.

Price, Robert. "Buck Had the World by the Tail." *Bakersfield Californian*, April 2, 2006.

United Press International. "Owens Ordered to Stop Ads to Wife." *Nashville Banner*. May 21, 1977.

———. "Buck Owens Told to Quit Running Ads." *Tennessean*, May 24, 1977.

White, John. "Hey Diddle-Diddle, Who's That Playin' The Fiddle?! . . . It's Jana Jae." *Country Music*, January–February 1979.

Books

Stoneman, Roni, as told to Ellen Wright. *Pressing On*. Urbana, IL: University of Illinois Press, 2007.

Documents

California Divorce Index, 1966–1977; Nevada Marriage Index, 1975.

Interviews

Kris Black, Stacy Harris, Doyle Holly, Ronnie Jackson, Jana Jae, Sam Lovullo, Bill Mack, Jo McFadden, LaWanda Lindsey Smith.

Web Sites

Crystal Palace official Web site (www.buckowens.com), Jana Jae's official Web site (www.janajae.com).

54. The '80s

Articles

Fulmer, Douglas. "Buck Owens: From Cotton Fields to Jets, He's Charted His Own Course." *Country Weekly*, August 21–September 17, 1999.

Oermann, Robert K. "Tree Attains Buck Owens Song List." *Tennessean*, October 9, 1984.

Price, Robert. "Bakersfield City Anthem Has a Twang." *Bakersfield Californian*, April 2, 2006.

———. "Buck Had the World by the Tail." *Bakersfield Californian*, April 2, 2006.

———. "Much More Than a Hit Musical Duo." *Bakersfield Californian*, April 2, 2006.

Audiovisual

"Acting Naturally." *Biography*. TV series, A&E, 2000.

Owens, Buck. Interview by Chris Comer and Rob Ervin. *The Chris & Rob Late Night Talk Show*, WAIF-FM, Cincinnati, OH, July 16, 1997, www.chriscomerradio.com/buck_owens/buck_owens7-16-97.htm.

Books

Burke, Kathryn. *The Dust Bowl, Bakersfield Sound, and Buck*. North Charleston, SC: BookSurge Publishers, 2007.

Kienzle, Rich. *The Buck Owens Collection 1959–1990*. Santa Monica, CA: Rhino Records, 1992.

Killen, Buddy, with Tom Carter. *By the Seat of My Pants*. New York: Simon & Schuster, 1993.

Stoneman, Roni, as told to Ellen Wright. *Pressing On*. Urbana, IL: University of Illinois Press, 2007.

Documents

California Secretary of State LTP/LLC record, Buck Owens Horse Ranch, LLC; Kern County property records, October 2000; Kern County property transfer records, 1994, October

1998, and May 2000; San Luis Obispo County property transfer records, May 2000; Social Security Death Index listing, Maicie Owens.

Interviews
Larry Adamson, Richard Bennett, Kris Black, Jackson Brumley, Liz Cavanaugh, Jim Foglesong, Doyle Holly, Jay Dee Maness, Jo McFadden, Buck Owens.

Web Sites
Crystal Palace official Web site (www.buckowens.com), Internet Movie Database (www.imdb.com).

55. The '90s

Articles
Associated Press. "Buck Owens: Country Singer Has Surgery for Throat Cancer." *Tennessean*, August 20, 1993.
Bakersfield Californian. "Original Buckaroos Back for Birthday." July 15, 1999.
Connell, Sally Ann. "Bakersfield Rallies to Save Piece of Its Past." *Los Angeles Times*, July 19, 1999.
Ehlert, Bob. "Welcome to Bakersfield CA." *Country America*, January 1998.
Fulmer, Douglas. "Buck Owens: From Cotton Fields to Jets, He's Charted His Own Course." *Country Weekly*, August 21–September 17, 1999.
Garcia, Victor. "Buck Owens' Legacy Lives On," *Visalia Times-Delta*, May 19, 2008.
Price, Robert. "Buck and Bakersfield: Two of a Kind." *Bakersfield Californian*, April 2, 2006.
———. "Buck Had the World by the Tail." *Bakersfield Californian*, April 2, 2006.
———. "A Buck Owens Bonfire." *Bakersfield Californian*, n.d.
Roland, Tom. "Buck Owens' Legacy Continues at Crystal Palace." CMT.com, September 14, 2007.
Tennessean. "Owens Plans No More Concerts." September 19, 1991.
Variety. "Jack McFadden." Monday, June 22, 1998.

Audiovisual
Owens, Buck. Interview by Chris Comer and Rob Ervin. *The Chris & Rob Late Night Talk Show*, WAIF-FM, Cincinnati, OH, July 16, 1997, www.chriscomerradio.com/buck_owens/buck_owens7-16-97.htm.

Books
Burke, Kathryn. *The Dust Bowl, Bakersfield Sound, and Buck*. North Charleston, SC: BookSurge Publishers, 2007.
Kienzle, Rich. *The Buck Owens Collection 1959–1990*. Santa Monica, CA: Rhino Records, 1992.
Sisk, Eileen. *Honky-Tonks*. San Francisco: HarperCollins West, 1995.

Documents
California Secretary of State filings, Buck Owens American Music Corporation; IRS Form 990, Buck Owens American Music Corporation, September 2002; Social Security Death Index listings, Mary Ethel McKinney, Dorothy Owens.

Interviews
Kris Black, Jim Hager, Jon Hager, Jay Dee Maness, Jo McFadden, Buck Owens, Dennis Payne, Jim Pierce, Marlane Ulrich-Dunivent, Russ Varnell, Alf Wigen.

Letters
Owens, Buck. Buck Owens to Eileen Sisk, July 1996.

Web Sites
Casper Rawls's official Web site (www.planetcasper.com), Country Music Television (www.cmt.com), Crystal Palace official Web site (www.buckowens.com), Kim McAbee's official Web site (www.kimmcabee.com), TaxExemptWorld.com.

56. Together Again

Articles

Lewis, Randy. "Bakersfield Sadly Says So Long." *Los Angeles Times*, April 2, 2006.
———. "Country Music Innovator Buck Owens, 76, Dies." *Los Angeles Times*, March 26, 2006.
Munoz, Olivia. "Family, Friends and Fans Pay Last Respects to Singer Buck Owens." Associated Press, April, 2, 2006.
Nudd, Tim, ed. "Buck Got the Lovesick Blues." *Adweek*, October 22, 2001.
Page, Chris. "Buck Searches for Mystery Lady." *Bakersfield Californian*, October 16, 2001.
Price, Robert. "Buck Had a Lot of Ladies in His Life." *Bakersfield Californian*, April 2, 2006.
———. "Buck Had the World by the Tail." *Bakersfield Californian*, April 2, 2006.
———. "Buck Week Can't Corral the Legend." *Bakersfield Californian*, April, 2, 2006.
———. "Legend Laid to Rest." *Bakersfield Californian*, April, 2, 2006.
Reed, Christopher. "Obituaries: Bobbie Nudie; Seamstress to Such Stars as Elvis, Roy Rogers and John Lennon." *Guardian*, May 6, 2006.
Ruby, Sarah. "Chauffeur Recalls Years Driving Famous Passenger." *Bakersfield Californian*, April, 2, 2006.
———. "Thousands Descend on Palace." *Bakersfield Californian*, April, 2, 2006.

Audiovisual

"Acting Naturally." *Biography*. TV series, A&E, 2000.
Funeral of Buck Owens. April 2, 2006. Privately recorded DVD.

Books

Burke, Kathryn. *The Dust Bowl, Bakersfield Sound, and Buck*. North Charleston, SC: BookSurge Publishers, 2007.
Kienzle, Rich. *The Buck Owens Collection 1959–1990*. Santa Monica, CA: Rhino Records, 1992.

Documents

Various court filings, Buck Owens Revocable Trust, May 2000.

Interviews

Cheryl Albers, Kris Black, Jann Browne, Doyle Holly, Jay Dee Maness, Jo McFadden, Mayf Nutter, Buck Owens, Dennis Payne, Wade Pepper, Lulu Roman, Russ Varnell.

Web Sites

Adweek.com, Bakosphere.com, Buckowensfan.com, Horsedaily.com.

Epilogue

Articles

King, Caitlin. "Brad Paisley Goes No. 1 for the 10th Time in a Row." Associated Press, May 29, 2009.
Lewis, Randy. "Buck Owens: Gone but Not Forgotten." *Los Angeles Times*, October 14, 2007.
Mclean, Thomas J. "ASIFA Screenings Promote Pop Cultural Literacy." *Animation Magazine*, June 28, 2009, www.animationmagazine.net/article/10238.

Audiovisual

Brigham, Bruce-jon, Julie Grower, and Lynne Manderson. "Out in Bakersfield." Be Ready Music, ASCAP, 2007. Demo on compact disc.
Browne, Jann. *Buckin' Around*. Plan B records!, 2007. Compact disc.
Derailers. *Under the Influence of Buck*. Palo Duro Records, 2007. Compact disc.
Fogerty, John. *John Fogerty the Blue Ridge Rangers Ride Again*. Verve Forecast, 2009. Compact disc.
Nutter, Mayf. "You Got It Now (The Buck Owens Song)." Mayf Nutter Music, BMI, 2006. Demo on compact disc.

Paisley, Brad. *Play*. RCA, 2008. Compact disc.
Tucker, Tanya. *My Turn*. Saguaro Road Records, 2009. Compact disc.
Yoakam, Dwight. *Dwight Sings Buck*. New West Records, 2007. Compact disc.

Books
Burke, Kathryn. *The Dust Bowl, Bakersfield Sound, and Buck*. North Charleston, SC:
  BookSurge Publishers, 2007.
Escott, Colin. *Tattooed on Their Tongues*. New York: Schirmer Books, 1996.
Kienzle, Rich. *The Buck Owens Collection 1959–1990*. Santa Monica, CA: Rhino Records, 1992.

Documents
Social Security Death Index, Doyle F. Hendricks.

Interviews
Cheryl Albers, Kris Black, Jann Browne, George Ducas, Doyle Holly, Jim Hager, Jon Hager, Jay
  Dee Maness, Mayf Nutter, Thomas Rockwell, Russ Varnell, Storme Warren.

Web Sites
ASIFA Hollywood: The International Animated Film Society (www.asifa-hollywood.org),
  Bakosphere.com, Casper Rawls's official Web site (www.planetcasper.com), Country
  Music Television (www.cmt.com), Crystal Palace official Web site (www.buckowens.com),
  George Ducas's official Web site (www.georgeducas.com), Jann Browne's official Web
  site www.jannbrowne.com), Kim McAbee's official Web site (www.kimmcabee.com),
  Napster.com, TwangtownUSA.com, YouTube.com.

SELECTED SESSIONOGRAPHY
AND DISCOGRAPHY

Sessions

Below is a partial listing of Buck Owens's official and unofficial recording sessions. Buck's recorded output has been subject to countless reissues over time; not all custom and reissued works are listed. Information on session dates, times, and personnel are detailed where available. According to some sources, sessions from January 1967 through March 1969 were recorded in Bakersfield, although the Buck Owens Studios in Oildale did not open until March 1969. Track numbers prefaced by "B" indicate tracks by the Buckaroos. Catalog numbers in *italics* represent samplers, compilations, reissues, and releases by the Buckaroos that are not included in the discography. Most recordings are listed by stereo version rather than mono version.

c. 1953, Hollywood, CA: Buck Owens (Billy Mize [steel], Cliff Crawford [trumpet], more unknown musicians)

001 "Blue Love"   unissued / AUD-CD-8124

c. August 1955, Capitol Recording Studio, 5515 Melrose Ave., Hollywood, CA: Buck Owens (Lewis Talley [rhythm guitar], Fuzzy Owen [steel], Glen Ayers [bass], Jelly Sanders [fiddle], Jack Trent [piano]; producers: Terry Fell & Buck Owens)

002 "Down on the Corner of Love"   Pep 105 588 7010 / L/LS-8017 AUD-CD-8124
                                         BCD-16850; [alt.] AUD-CD-8124 BCD-16850
003 "It Don't Show on Me"   Pep 105 45-571 / SLP-172 L/LS-8017 AUD-
                                         CD-8124 BCD-16850; [alt.] AUD-CD-8124
                                         BCD-16850
004 "The House down the Block"   Pep 106 / SLP-172 L/LS-8017 AUD-CD-8124
                                         BCD-16850; [alt.] AUD-CD-8124 BCD-16850
005 "Right After the Dance"   Pep 106 588 / L/LS-8017 AUD-CD-8124 BCD-
                                         16850; [alt.] AUD-CD-8124 BCD-16850

c. spring 1956, Lu-Tal Recording Studio, 601 E. 18th St., Bakersfield, CA: Buck Owens, as Corky Jones (Roy Nichols [guitar], Fuzzy Owen [bass], Red Butler [percussion], Ray Heath [drums], possibly Lawrence Williams [piano]; producer: Buck Owens)

006 "Hot Dog"   Pep 107 45-6418 / L/LS-8017 AUD-CD-8124
                                         BCD-16850
007 "Rhythm and Booze"   Pep 107 / L/LS-8017 AUD-CD-8124

c. July or August 1956, Lu-Tal Recording Studio: Buck Owens, as Corky Jones (Roy Nichols [guitar], Fuzzy Owen [bass], Ray Heath [drums], possibly Lawrence Williams [piano]; producer: Buck Owens)

008 "There Goes My Love"   Pep 109 45-571 / SLP-172 AUD-CD-8124
                                         BCD-16850

009 "Sweethearts in Heaven"   Pep 109 45-6418 7010 / SLP-172 AUD-CD-8124 BCD-16850

c. 1956, probably Lu-Tal Recording Studio: Buck Owens

010 "Honeysuckle"   Chesterfield 44223 / SLP-172 AUD-CD-8124 HSRD-931 BCD-16850
011 "Country Girl (Leavin' Dirty Tracks)"   Chesterfield 44223 / L/LS-8017 AUD-CD-8124 BCD-16850
012 "You're for Me"   L/LS-8017 AUD-CD-8124 BCD-16850
013 "Blue Love"   L/LS-8017 BCD-16850
014 "Please Don't Take Her from Me"   L/LS-8017 AUD-CD-8124 BCD-16850
015 "Three Dimension Love"   L/LS-8017 AUD-CD-8124 BCD-16850
016 "Why Don't My Mommy Stay with   L/LS-8017 AUD-CD-8124 BCD-16850
My Daddy and Me"
017 "I'm Gonna Blow"   L/LS-8017 AUD-CD-8124 BCD-16850

1950s [demos], possibly in Bakersfield, CA: Buck Owens

01701 "Above and Beyond"   L/LS-8017
01702 "That Ain't Right Baby"   HSRD-931
01703 "I Will Always Love You Darling"   L/LS-8017
01704 "When I Hold You"   L/LS-8017
01705 "Lighter and Lighter and Lighter"   L/LS-8017

August 30, 1957 [No. 6160, 2:00–5:00 P.M.], Capitol Tower Recording Studio, 1750 N. Vine St., Hollywood, CA: Buck Owens (Buck Owens [vocals/guitar], Gene Moles [guitar], Roy Nichols [guitar], Jelly Sanders [bass], Glen Ayers [drums]; producer: Ken Nelson)

018 17412 "I Only Know That I Love You"   F3957 BCD-16850
019 17413 "Sweet Thing"   F3957 BCD-16850
020 17414 "I Know What It Means"   F3824 BCD-16850
021 17415 "Come Back"   F3824 BCD-16850

October 9, 1958 [No. 7313, 6:00–9:00 P.M.], Capitol Tower Recording Studio: Buck Owens (Buck Owens [vocals/guitar], Ralph Mooney [steel], Allen Williams [bass], Pee Wee Adams [drums], Jelly Sanders [fiddle], George French [piano]; producer: Ken Nelson)

022 30318 "Walk the Floor"   F4090 / T-1489 BCD-16850
023 30319 "My Everlasting Love"   F4172 / T-1489 BCD-16850
024 30320 "Second Fiddle"   F4172 / T-1489 BCD-16850
025 30321 "I'll Take a Chance on   F4090 / T-1489 BCD-16850
Loving You"

June 16, 1959 [No. 7806, 1:00–4:00 P.M.], Capitol Tower Recording Studio: Buck Owens (Buck Owens [vocals/guitar], Ralph Mooney [steel], Allen Williams [bass], Pee Wee Adams [drums], Jelly Sanders [fiddle], George French [piano]; producer: Ken Nelson)

026 31895 "Tired of Livin'"   F4245 / T-1489 BCD-16850
027 31896 "Under Your Spell Again"   F4245 / T-1489 ST-2105 BCD-16850
028 31897 "I'll Give My Heart to You"   T-1489 BCD-16850
029 31898 "I've Got a Right to Know"   4412 / T-1489 BCD-16850

December 23, 1959 [No. 9160, 1:00–4:00 P.M.], Capitol Tower Recording Studio: Buck Owens (Buck Owens [vocals/guitar], Rollie Weber [guitar], Ralph Mooney [steel], Allen Williams [bass], Pee Wee Adams [drums], Don Rich [fiddle], George French [piano]; producer: Ken Nelson)

030 33000 "Above and Beyond"   4337 6075 / EAP-1-1550 / T-1489 BCD-16850; [alt. t. 23] BCD-16850
031 33001 "Excuse Me (I Think I've Got   4412 / EAP-1-1550 / T-1489 ST-2105 BCD-16850
a Heartache)"
032 33002 "Take Me Back Again"   T-1489 BCD-16850
033 33003 "Till These Dreams Come True"   4337 / T-1489 BCD-16850

December 3, 1960 [No. 9798, 12:00–3:00 P.M.], Capitol Tower Recording Studio: Buck Owens (Buck Owens [vocals/guitar], Ralph Mooney [steel], Allen Williams [bass], Pee Wee Adams [drums], Jelly Sanders [fiddle], George French [piano]; producer: Ken Nelson)

034 34968 "Think It Over"	ST-1482 BCD-16850	
035 34969 "Foolin' Around"	4496 / EAP-1-1550 / ST-1482 ST-2105	
	BCD-16850	
036 34970 "Nobody's Fool but Yours"	*ST-1912* ST-2105 BCD-16850	
037 34971 "High as the Mountains"	4496 / EAP-1-1550 / ST-2105 BCD-16850	

January 16, 1961 [No. 9885, 1:30–4:30 P.M.], Capitol Tower Recording Studio: Buck Owens & Rose Maddox (Buck Owens [vocals/guitar], Rose Maddox [vocals], Ralph Mooney [steel], Allen Williams [bass], Pee Wee Adams [drums], Don Rich [fiddle], George French [piano]; producer: Ken Nelson)

038 35214 "Loose Talk"*	4550 / *ST-1718* ST-2186 BCD-16850
039 35215 "Mental Cruelty"*	4550 / *ST-1654* BCD-16850
040 35216 "Under the Influence of Love"	unissued—lost
041 35217 "We're the Talk of the Town"	unissued—lost

* denotes duet with Rose Maddox

March 6, 1961 [No. 9969, 12:00–3:00 P.M.], Capitol Tower Recording Studio: Buck Owens (Buck Owens [vocals/guitar], Don Rich [guitar/fiddle], Ralph Mooney [steel], Bobby Austin [bass], Wayne Stone [drums], George French [piano]; producer: Ken Nelson)

042 35494 "I Don't Believe I'll Fall in Love Today"	ST-1482; [alt. t. 5] BCD-16850; [t. 5] BCD-16850
043 35495 "Pick Me Up on Your Way Down"	ST-1482 BCD-16850
044 35496 "Let's Agree to Disagree"	ST-1482 BCD-16850
045 35497 "Keeper of the Key"	ST-1482 BCD-16850
046 35498 "Lyin' Again"	ST-1482 BCD-16850; [t. 7] BCD-16850
047 35499 "Heartaches for a Dime"	ST-1482; [t. 1] BCD-16850

March 7, 1961 [No. 9970, 12:00–3:30 P.M.], Capitol Tower Recording Studio: Buck Owens (Buck Owens [vocals/guitar], Ralph Mooney [steel], Bobby Austin [bass], Wayne Stone [drums], Don Rich [fiddle], George French [piano]; producer: Ken Nelson)

048 35500 "Heartaches by the Number"	ST-1482 BCD-16850; [alt] BCD-16850
049 35501 "The One You Slip Around With"	ST-1482 BCD-16850; [alt.] BCD-16850
050 35502 "Key's in the Mailbox"	ST-1482 BCD-16850; [alt.] BCD-16850
051 35503 "I'll Catch You When You Fall"	ST-1482 BCD-16850; [alt.] BCD-16850
052 35504 "Save the Last Dance for Me"	unissued / BCD-16850

May 24, 1961 [No. 10118, 12:00–3:00 P.M.], Capitol Tower Recording Studio: Buck Owens (Buck Owens [vocals/guitar], Ralph Mooney [steel], Bobby Austin [bass], Wayne Stone [drums], Don Rich [fiddle], Jim Pierce [piano]; producer: Ken Nelson)

053 35216 [remake] "Under the Influence of Love"	4602 / ST-1777 ST-2105 BCD-16850
054 35955 "Nobody's Fool but Yours"	4679 / ST-1777 BCD-16850
055 35956 "Down to the River"	ST-1777 BCD-16850
056 35958 "Bad Bad Dream"	4602 / ST-1777 BCD-16850

September 26, 1961 [No. 10295, 1:00–5:00 P.M.], Capitol Tower Recording Studio: Buck Owens (Buck Owens [vocals/guitar], Ralph Mooney [steel], Bobby Austin [bass], Wayne Stone [drums], Don Rich [fiddle], George French [piano]; producer: Ken Nelson)

057 36507 "Down on the Corner of Love"	ST-1777 BCD-16850
058 36508 "The House Down the Block"	4872 / ST-1777 BCD-16850
059 36509 "Fool Me Again"	ST-1777 BCD-16850
060 36510 "You're for Me"	4872 6075 / ST-1777 BCD-16850
061 36511 "Blues for Life"	ST-1777 BCD-16850

September 27, 1961 [No. 10296, 1:00–4:00 P.M.], Capitol Tower Recording Studio: Buck Owens (Buck Owens [vocals/guitar], Ralph Mooney [steel], Bobby Austin [bass], Wayne Stone [drums], Don Rich [fiddle/guitar], George French [piano]; producer: Ken Nelson)

062 36512 "King of Fools"		unissued / BCD-16850; [alt.] BCD-16850
063 36513 "Bring It to Jesus"		ST-2497 BCD-16850; [t. 3] BCD-16850
064 36514 "All the Way with Jesus"		ST-2497 BCD-16850; [t. 3] BCD-16850; [alt.] BCD-16850
065 36515 "Mexican Polka" (instrumental)		ST-1777 BCD-16850
066 36516 "Country Polka" (instrumental)		ST-1777 BCD-16850

December 5, 1961 [No. 10390, 6:00–9:00 P.M.], Capitol Tower Recording Studio: Buck Owens (Buck Owens [vocals/guitar], Ralph Mooney [steel], Bobby Austin [bass], Wayne Stone [drums], Don Rich [fiddle/guitar], George French [piano]; producer: Ken Nelson)

067 36826 "Mirror, Mirror on the Wall"	4679 / ST-1777 BCD-16850
068 36827 "Storm of Love"	ST-2135 BCD-16850
069 36828 "One Way Love"	ST-1879 BCD-16850
070 36829 "Kickin' Our Hearts Around"	4826 / ST-1879 ST-2105 BCD-16850
071 36512 [remake] "King of Fools"	unissued—lost

April 18, 1962 [No. 10592, 12:00–3:00 P.M.], Capitol Tower Recording Studio: Buck Owens (Buck Owens [vocals/guitar], Ralph Mooney [steel], Bobby Austin [bass], Wayne Stone [drums], Don Rich [fiddle/lead acoustic guitar], George French [piano]; producer: Ken Nelson)

072 37538 "Save the Last Dance for Me"	4765 / ST-2135 BCD-16850; [t. 17] BCD-16850
073 37539 "King of Fools"	4765 / ST-1879 BCD-16850
074 37540 "I Can't Stop (My Lovin' You)"	4826 / ST-1879 ST-2105 BCD-16850

February 12, 1963 [No. 11050, 5:30–8:30 P.M.], Capitol Tower Recording Studio: Buck Owens (Buck Owens [vocals/guitar], Jelly Sanders [guitar], Jay McDonald [steel], Kenny Pierce [bass], Ken Presley [drums], Don Rich [fiddle/lead guitar]; producer: Ken Nelson)

075 39214 "Act Naturally"	4937 6093 / ST-2105 BCD-16850
076 39215 "Over and Over Again"	4937 6093 / ST-2135 BCD-16850
077 39216 "My Heart Skips a Beat"	unissued / BCD-16850

February 13, 1963 [No. 11054, 5:30–8:30 P.M.], Capitol Tower Recording Studio: Buck Owens & His Buckaroos (Buck Owens [vocals/guitar], Jelly Sanders [guitar], Jay McDonald [steel], Kenny Pierce [bass], Ken Presley [drums], Don Rich [fiddle/guitar]; producer: Ken Nelson)

078 39224 "There's a Gonna Come a Day"	ST-2353 BCD-16850
079 39225 "Diggy Liggy Lo"	ST-1879 BCD-16850
080 39226 "Orange Blossom Special" (instrumental)	ST-1879 *SC-11091* BCD-16850
081 39227 "Cotton Fields"*	ST-1879 BCD-16850
082 39237 "Touch Me"**	ST-1879 BCD-16850

denotes duet with Don Rich
**denotes vocal by Kenny Pierce*

February 14, 1963 [No.11055, 3:30–6:30 P.M.], Capitol Tower Recording Studio: Buck Owens (Buck Owens [vocals/guitar], Jelly Sanders [guitar], Jay McDonald [steel], Kenny Pierce [bass], Ken Presley [drums], Don Rich [fiddle/guitar/vocals]; producer: Ken Nelson)

083 39228 "Saw Mill"*	ST-1879 BCD-16850
084 39229 "Sweethearts in Heaven"*	ST-1879 BCD-16850
085 39230 "Sally Was a Good Old Girl"**	ST-1879 BCD-16850
086 39231 "Release Me"	ST-1879 BCD-16850

denotes duet with Don Rich
**denotes vocal by Don Rich*

March 19, 1963 [No. 11097, 1:00–4:00 P.M.], Capitol Tower Recording Studio: Rose Maddox & Buck Owens (Buck Owens [vocals/guitar], Cal Maddox [guitar], Don Rich [guitar/fiddle], Jay McDonald [steel], Kenny Pierce [bass], Ken Presley [drums], Jim Pierce [piano]; producer: Ken Nelson)

087	39382 "Sweethearts in Heaven"	4992 / BCD-16850
088	39383 "We're the Talk of the Town"	4992 / BCD-16850
089	39384 "Back Street Affair"	unissued / BCD-16850
090	39385 "No Fool Like an Old Fool"	unissued / BCD-16850

July 11, 1963 [No. 11331, 5:30–9:00 P.M.], Capitol Tower Recording Studio: Buck Owens (Buck Owens [vocals/guitar], Don Rich [vocals/lead guitar/fiddle], Jelly Sanders [rhythm guitar/fiddle], Jay McDonald [steel], Bob Morris [bass], Mel King [drums]; producer: Ken Nelson)

091	50123 "Love's Gonna Live Here"	5025 / ST-2105 BCD-16850
092	50124 "Getting Used to Losing You"	5025 / ST-2135 BCD-16850
093	50125 "Smooth Sailin'"	ST-1989 Hilltop JS-6071 BCD-16850
094	50126 "But I Do"	ST-1989 Hilltop JS-6071 BCD-16850
095	50127 "If You Ain't Lovin' (You Ain't Livin')"	ST-1989 Hilltop JS-6071 BCD-16850
096	50128 "My Last Chance with You"	ST-1989 Hilltop JS-6071 BCD-16850
097	50129 "Down, Down, Down"	ST-1989 BCD-16850

July 12, 1963 [No. 11332, 5:30–9:00 P.M.], Capitol Tower Recording Studio: Buck Owens (Buck Owens [vocals/guitar], Don Rich [vocals/guitar/fiddle], Jelly Sanders [guitar/fiddle], Jay McDonald [steel], Bob Morris [bass], Mel King [drums]; producer: Ken Nelson)

098	50130 "You Gotta Have a License"	ST-1989 Hilltop JS-6071 BCD-16850
099	50131 "High on a Hilltop"	ST-1989 Hilltop JS-6071 BCD-16850
100	50132 "It Tickles"	ST-1989 BCD-16850
101	50133 "Whatcha Gonna Do Now"	ST-1989 Hilltop JS-6071 BCD-16850
102	50134 "I Always Get a Souvenir"	ST-1989 Hilltop JS-6071 BCD-16850
103	50135 "There'll Be No Other"	ST-1989 Hilltop JS-6071 BCD-16850
104	50136 "No Love Have I"	ST-1989 Hilltop JS-6071 BCD-16850

October 22, 1963 [No. 11425/11426, live], Bakersfield Civic Auditorium, 1001 Truxtun Ave., Bakersfield, CA: various artists

10401	50746 104 "Act Naturally" (Buck Owens)	ST-2009

January 6, 1964 [No. 11623, 10:00 A.M.–1:00 P.M.], Capitol Tower Recording Studio: Buck Owens & His Buckaroos (Buck Owens [vocals/guitar], Don Rich [vocals/guitar/fiddle], Jelly Sanders [guitar/fiddle], Tom Brumley [steel], Doyle Holly [bass/vocals], Mel King [drums]; producer: Ken Nelson)

105	51075 "Louisiana Man"*	ST-2186 BCD-16850
106	51076 "Abilene"**	ST-2186 BCD-16850
107	51077 "A Maiden's Prayer" (instrumental)	ST-2283 BCD-16850
108	51078 "Bud's Bounce" (instrumental)	ST-2186 BCD-16850

denotes vocal by Don Rich
**denotes vocal by Doyle Holly

January 28, 1964 [No. 11688, 5:00–8:00 P.M.], Capitol Tower Recording Studio: Buck Owens & His Buckaroos (Buck Owens [vocals/guitar], Don Rich [harmony vocals/guitar/fiddle], Jelly Sanders [rhythm guitar/fiddle], Tom Brumley [steel], Doyle Holly [bass/harmony vocals], Mel Taylor [drums]; producer: Ken Nelson)

109	51330 "Ain't It Amazing, Gracie"	ST-2135 BCD-16850
110	51331 "Close Up the Honky Tonks"	unissued—lost
111	51332 "My Heart Skips a Beat"	5136 6074 / ST-2135 BCD-16850
112	51333 "Together Again"	5136 6074/ST-2135 BCD-16850

June 10, 1964 [No. 11907, 10:00 A.M.–2:00 P.M.], Capitol Tower Recording Studio: Buck Owens & His Buckaroos (Buck Owens [vocals/guitar], Don Rich [harmony vocals/guitar/fiddle], Doyle Holly [rhythm guitar], Tom Brumley [steel], Bob Morris [bass/vocals], Willie Cantu [drums]; producer: Ken Nelson)

113 51331 [remake] "Close Up the Honky Tonks"	ST-2135 BCD-16850	
114 52181 "Truck Drivin' Man"	ST-2135 BCD-16850	
115 52182 "I Don't Hear You"	ST-2135 BCD-16850	
116 52183 "Hello Trouble"	ST-2135 BCD-16850	
117 52184 "A-11"	ST-2135 BCD-16850	

June 10, 1964 [No. 11909, time unavailable], Capitol Tower Recording Studio: Don Rich & the Buckaroos (Don Rich [vocals/guitar/fiddle], Doyle Holly [rhythm guitar], Tom Brumley [steel], Bob Morris [bass/vocals], Willie Cantu [drums]; producer: Ken Nelson)

B01 52102 "Love's Gonna Live Here"	*ST-2128* ST-2436 BCD-16855	
B02 52103 "Together Again"	*ST-2128* BCD-16855	

July 8, 1964 [No. 11970, 10:00–1:00 P.M.], Capitol Tower Recording Studio: Buck Owens & His Buckaroos (Buck Owens [vocals/guitar], Don Rich [guitar/fiddle/vocals], Doyle Holly [rhythm guitar], Jelly Sanders [guitar/fiddle], Tom Brumley [steel], Bob Morris [bass], Mel Taylor [drums]; producer: Ken Nelson)

118 52400 "I Don't Care (Just as Long as You Love Me)"	5240 / ST-2186 BCD-16850	
119 52401 "Don't Let Her Know"	5240 / ST-2186 BCD-16850	
120 52402 "Dang Me"*	ST-2186 BCD-16850	
121 52403 "This Ol' Heart"	ST-2186 BCD-16850	

denotes duet with Don Rich

July 8, 1964 [No. 11971, 1:30–4:30 P.M.], Capitol Tower Recording Studio: Buck Owens & His Buckaroos (Buck Owens [vocals/guitar], Don Rich [vocals/rhythm guitar/fiddle], Doyle Holly [rhythm guitar/vocals], Jelly Sanders [rhythm guitar/fiddle], Tom Brumley [steel], Bob Morris [bass], Mel Taylor [drums]; producer: Ken Nelson)

122 52404 "Understand Your Man"*	ST-2186 BCD-16850	
123 52405 "You're Welcome Anytime"	ST-2186 BCD-16850	
124 52406 "Buck's Polka" (instrumental)	ST-2186 BCD-16850	
125 52407 "Playboy"	ST-2186 BCD-16850	

denotes vocal by Doyle Holly

December 1, 1964 [No. 12169, 1:00–4:30 P.M.], Capitol Tower Recording Studio: Buck Owens & His Buckaroos (Buck Owens [vocals/guitar], Don Rich [vocals/guitar/fiddle], Doyle Holly [rhythm guitar/vocals], Jelly Sanders [rhythm guitar/fiddle], Tom Brumley [steel], Bob Morris [bass], Willie Cantu [drums]; producer: Ken Nelson)

126 53106 "We're Gonna Let the Good Times Roll"	ST-2283 BCD-16850	
127 53107 "Cryin' Time"	5336 6112 / ST-2283 BCD-16850	
128 53108 "I've Got a Tiger by the Tail"	5336 6112 / ST-2283 BCD-16850	

December 28, 1964 [No. 12201, 1:00–4:30 P.M.], Capitol Tower Recording Studio: Buck Owens & His Buckaroos (Buck Owens [vocals/guitar], Don Rich [vocals/guitar/fiddle], Jelly Sanders [rhythm guitar/fiddle], Tom Brumley [steel], Doyle Holly [rhythm guitar/vocals], Bob Morris [bass], Willie Cantu [drums]; producer: Ken Nelson)

129 53237 "Trouble and Me"	ST-2283 BCD-16850	
130 53238 "If You Fall Out of Love with Me"	R-5446 / ST-2283 BCD-16850	

131 53239 "Fallin' for You"   R-5446 / ST-2283 BCD-16850
132 53240 "The Band Keeps Playin' On"   ST-2283 BCD-16850
133 53241 "Memphis"*   R-5446 / ST-2283 BCD-16850
134 53242 "Streets of Laredo"**   ST-2283 BCD-16850

*denotes vocal by Don Rich
**denotes vocal by Doyle Holly.

December 29, 1964 [No. 12204, 1:00–5:00 P.M.], Capitol Tower Recording Studio: Buck Owens & His Buckaroos (Buck Owens [vocals/guitar], Don Rich [vocals/guitar/fiddle], Jelly Sanders [rhythm guitar/fiddle], Tom Brumley [steel], Doyle Holly [rhythm guitar/vocals], Bob Morris [bass], Willie Cantu [drums]; producer: Ken Nelson)

135 53247 "Gonna Have Love"   5465 6111 / ST-2353 BCD-16850
136 53248 "Let the Sad Times Roll On"   R-5446 / ST-2283 BCD-16850
137 53249 "Wham Bam"*   ST-2283 BCD-16850

*denotes vocal by Don Rich

March 25, 1965 [No. 12310, 12:00–4:00 P.M.], Capitol Tower Recording Studio: Buck Owens & His Buckaroos (Buck Owens [vocals/guitar], Don Rich [duet vocals/lead guitar], Doyle Holly [rhythm guitar], Jimmy Seals [rhythm guitar], Tom Brumley [steel], Bob Morris [bass], Willie Cantu [drums]; producer: Ken Nelson)

138 53542 "Before You Go"   5410 / ST-2353 *SWBB-257* BCD-16855
139 53543 "Getting Used to Loving You"   ST-2353 *SWBB-257* *JS-6078* BCD-16855
140 53544 "(I Want) No One but You"   5410 / ST-2353 *SWBB-257* BCD-16855
141 53545 "Number One Heel"*   ST-2353 *SWBB-257* BCD-16855
142 53548 "Raz Ma-Taz Polka" (instrumental)   ST-2353 ST-2367 ST-2994 BCD-16855

*denotes duet with Don Rich

March 26, 1965 [No. 12313, 12:00–4:00 P.M.], Capitol Tower Recording Studio: Buck Owens & His Buckaroos (Buck Owens [vocals/guitar], Doyle Holly [guitar/harmony vocals], Don Rich [lead guitar/harmony vocals], Jimmy Seals [guitar], Tom Brumley [steel], Bob Morris [bass], Willie Cantu [drums]; producer: Ken Nelson)

143 53549 "I Betcha Didn't Know"   ST-2353 *SWBB-257* BCD-16855
144 53555 "No Fool Like an Old Fool"   ST-2353 *SWBB-257* BCD-16855
145 53556 "If You Want a Love"   5517 / ST-2353 *SWBB-257* BCD-16855
146 53557 "Charlie Brown"   ST-2353 *SWBB-257* BCD-16855
147 53558 "Steel Guitar Rag" (instrumental)   ST-2353 ST-2367 BCD-16855

May 4, 1965 [No. 12359, 12:00–3:00 P.M.], Capitol Tower Recording Studio: Buck Owens & His Buckaroos (Buck Owens [vocals/guitar], Don Rich [lead acoustic guitar/fiddle], Doyle Holly [rhythm guitar], Jelly Sanders [rhythm guitar /fiddle], Jimmy Seals [guitar], Tom Brumley [steel], Bob Morris [bass], Willie Cantu [drums]; producer: Ken Nelson)

148 53667 "Roll Out the Red Carpet"   ST-2443 BCD-16855
149 53668 "Only You (Can Break My Heart)"   5465 6111 / ST-2760 ST-2897 BCD-16855
150/B03 53669 "Country Rag" (instrumental)   ST-2367 BCD-16855
151/B04 53670 "Bile 'Em Cabbage Down"   ST-2367 BCD-16855
(instrumental)

May 5, 1965 [No. 12360, 12:00–4:30 P.M.], Capitol Tower Recording Studio: Buck Owens & His Buckaroos (Buck Owens [vocals/ guitar], Doyle Holly [rhythm guitar], Red Simpson [rhythm guitar], Don Rich [lead guitar /fiddle], Tom Brumley [steel], Bob Morris [bass], Willie Cantu [drums]; producer: Ken Nelson)

152 53671 "Hangin' On to What I Got"   ST-2443 BCD-16855
153 53672 "Someone with No One to Love"   ST-2760 BCD-16855
154/B05 53673 "Buckaroo" (instrumental)   5517 / ST-2367 *SC-11091* BCD-16855
155/B06 53674 "Faded Love" (instrumental)   ST-2367 BCD-16855

June 1, 1965 [No. 12392, 10:00 A.M.–2:00 P.M.], Capitol Tower Recording Studio: Buck Owens & His Buckaroos (Buck Owens [vocals/ guitar], Doyle Holly [guitar], Red Simpson [guitar], Don Rich [lead guitar/fiddle/harmony vocals], Tom Brumley [steel], Bob Morris [bass], Willie Cantu [drums]; producer: Ken Nelson)

156 53780 "Blue Christmas Tree"		ST-2396 BCD-16855	
157 53781 "Because It's Christmas Time"		ST-2396 BCD-16855	
158 53782 "All I Want for Christmas, Dear, Is You"		5537 / ST-2396 BCD-16855	
159 53783 "Santa Looked a Lot Like Daddy"		5537 / ST-2396 BCD-16855	
160 53785 "Christmas Ain't Christmas"*		ST-2396 BCD-16855	
161 53786 "Christmas Time's a Comin'"		ST-2396 BCD-16855	
162 53787 "It's Christmas Time for Everyone but Me"		ST-2396 BCD-16855	

denotes harmony vocal by Don Rich

July 21, 1965 [No. 12449, 11:00 A.M.–2:00 P.M.], Capitol Tower Recording Studio: Buck Owens & His Buckaroos (Buck Owens [vocals/guitar], Doyle Holly [guitar], Red Simpson [guitar], Don Rich [lead guitar], Tom Brumley [steel], Bob Morris [bass], Willie Cantu [drums]; producer: Ken Nelson)

163 53907 "Here Comes Santa Claus Again"	ST-2396 BCD-16855	
164 53908 "Blue Christmas Lights"	ST-2396 BCD-16855	
165 53909 "Santa's Gonna Come in a Stagecoach"	ST-2396 BCD-16855	
166 53910 "Christmas Morning"	ST-2396 BCD-16855	
167 53927 "Jingle Bells"	ST-2396 BCD-16855	

July 22, 1965 [No. 12458, 12:00–3:30 P.M.], Capitol Tower Recording Studio: Buck Owens & His Buckaroos (Buck Owens [vocals/guitar], Doyle Holly [guitar/vocals], Red Simpson [guitar], Don Rich [lead guitar/fiddle/harmony vocals], Tom Brumley [steel], Bob Morris [bass], Willie Cantu [drums]; producer: Ken Nelson)

168 53929 "We Split the Blanket"	ST-2443 STCL-574 BCD-16855	
169 53930 "He Don't Deserve You Anymore"	ST-2443 STCL-574 BCD-16855	
170 53931 "After You Leave Me"*	unissued—lost	
171 53932 "Tom Cattin'" (instrumental)	unissued—lost	

denotes vocal by Doyle Holly

August 23, 1965 [No. 12498, 12:00–3:30 P.M.], Capitol Tower Recording Studio: Buck Owens & His Buckaroos (Buck Owens [vocals/guitar], Don Rich [duet vocals/lead guitar], Doyle Holly [rhythm guitar], Red Simpson [rhythm guitar], Tom Brumley [steel], Bob Morris [bass], Willie Cantu [drums]; producer: Ken Nelson)

172 55059 "Sam's Place"	5865 6148 / ST-2640 ST-2760 SKAO-145 STCL-574 *ST-670* BCD-16855
173 55060 "Heart of Glass"	5647 / ST-2640 BCD-16855
174 55061 "(I'll Love You) Forever and Ever"	ST-2443 BCD-16855
175 55062 "I'm Layin' It on the Line"*	ST-2443 SCTL-574 *SC-11091* BCD-16855

denotes duet with Don Rich

August 24, 1965 [No. 12500, 12:00–3:30 P.M.], Capitol Tower Recording Studio: Buck Owens & His Buckaroos (Buck Owens [vocals/guitar], Doyle Holly [guitar], Don Rich [lead guitar/fiddle/harmony vocals], Tom Brumley [steel], Bob Morris [bass], Willie Cantu [drums]; producer: Ken Nelson)

176 55063 "Waitin' in Your Welfare Line"	5566 6148 / ST-2640 *ST-2739* ST-2897 BCD-16855
177 55064 "That's What I'm Like Without You"	ST-2443 BCD-16855

178 55065 "There Never Was a Fool"   ST-2443 BCD-16855
179 55066 "In the Palm of Your Hand"   5566 / ST-2640 BCD-16855

August 25, 1965 [No. 12501 (180–183)/12503 (184–185), 12:30–4:00 P.M.], Capitol Tower Recording Studio: Buck Owens & His Buckaroos (Buck Owens [vocals/guitar], Doyle Holly [vocals/guitar], Red Simpson [guitar], Don Rich [lead guitar/fiddle/harmony vocals], Tom Brumley [steel], Bob Morris [bass], Willie Cantu [drums]; producer: Ken Nelson)

180 53931 [remake] "After You Leave Me"*   ST-2443 BCD-16855
181 55067 "A Devil Like Me (Needs an   ST-2640 BCD-16855
    Angel Like You)"
182 55068 "Cinderella"   ST-2443 BCD-16855
183 55070 "Cajun Fiddle" (instrumental)   unissued—lost
184 55075 "I'll Go to Church Again   ST-2497 BCD-16855
    with Momma"
185 55076 "Pray Everyday"   ST-2497 BCD-16855

denotes vocal by Doyle Holly

November 8, 1965 [No. 12604, 12:30–4:00 P.M.], Capitol Tower Recording Studio: Don Rich & the Buckaroos (Don Rich [lead guitar/leader], Doyle Holly [rhythm guitar], Jelly Sanders [rhythm guitar], Red Simpson [rhythm guitar], Tom Brumley [steel], Bob Morris [bass], Willie Cantu [drums]; producer: Ken Nelson)

B07 55327 "Act Naturally"   ST-2436 BCD-16855
B08 55328 "I've Got a Tiger by the Tail"   ST-2436 BCD-16855
B09 55329 "My Heart Skips a Beat"   ST-2436 BCD-16855
B10 55330 "I Don't Care"   ST-2436 BCD-16855
B11 55335 "Foolin' Around"   ST-2436 BCD-16855

November 9, 1965 [No. 12607, 12:30–5:30 P.M.], Capitol Tower Recording Studio: Don Rich & the Buckaroos (Don Rich [lead guitar/leader], Doyle Holly [rhythm guitar], Jelly Sanders [rhythm guitar], Red Simpson [rhythm guitar], Tom Brumley [steel], Bob Morris [bass], Willie Cantu [drums]; producer: Ken Nelson)

B12 55337 "Before You Go"   ST-2436 BCD-16855
B13 55338 "Second Fiddle"   ST-2436 BCD-16855
B14 55339 "Under Your Spell Again"   ST-2436 BCD-16855
B15 55340 "Don't Let Her Know"   ST-2436 BCD-16855
B16 55345 "Together Again"   ST-2436 BCD-16855
B17 55346 "Only You (Can Break My Heart)"   ST-2436 BCD-16855

November 10, 1965 [No. 12610, 12:30–3:30 P.M.], Capitol Tower Recording Studio: Buck Owens & His Buckaroos (Buck Owens [vocals/guitar], Don Rich [lead guitar/fiddle/harmony vocals], Doyle Holly [rhythm guitar], Red Simpson [rhythm guitar], Tom Brumley [steel], Bob Morris [bass], Willie Cantu [drums]; producer: Ken Nelson),

186 55358 "When Jesus Calls All His   ST-2497 BCD-16855
    Children In"
187 55359 "It Was with Love"   ST-2497 BCD-16855
188 55360 "Would You Be Ready?"   ST-2497 BCD-16855
189 55361 "An Eternal Vacation"   ST-2497 BCD-16855
190 55362 "Jesus Saved Me"   ST-2497 BCD-16855

November 11, 1965 [Nos. 12611/12611A, 12:30–3:30 P.M.], Capitol Tower Recording Studio: Buck Owens & His Buckaroos (Buck Owens [vocals/guitar], Don Rich [lead guitar/fiddle], Doyle Holly [rhythm guitar], Red Simpson [rhythm guitar], Tom Brumley [steel], Bob Morris [bass], Willie Cantu [drums]; producer: Ken Nelson)

191 55364 "Where Would I Be   ST-2497 BCD-16855
    Without Jesus"
192 55365 "Dust on Mother's Bible"   ST-2497 BCD-16855

193 55366 "Satan's Gotta Get Along   ST-2497 BCD-16855
    Without Me"
194 53932 [remake] "'Tom Cattin'"   ST-2443 BCD-16855
    (instrumental)
195 55070 [remake] "Cajun Fiddle"   ST-2443 BCD-16855
    (instrumental)

February 14, 1966 [No. 12739, 12:30–4:00 P.M.], Capitol Tower Recording Studio: Buck Owens & His Buckaroos (Buck Owens [vocals/guitar], Doyle Holly [guitar], Red Simpson [guitar], Don Rich [lead guitar/fiddle/harmony vocal], Tom Brumley [steel], Bob Morris [bass], Willie Cantu [drums]; producer: Ken Nelson)

196 55643 "You Made a Monkey Out of Me"   ST-2760 BCD-16855
197 55644 "Congratulations, You're   ST-2640 STCL-574 BCD-16855
    Absolutely Right"
198 55645 "You, You, Only You"   ST-2640 BCD-16855
199 55646 "Where Does the Good Times Go"   unissued / BCD-16855; [t. 9] BCD-16855;
    [t. 13] BCD-16855
200 55657 "Goodbye, Good Luck, God   ST-2640 STCL-574 BCD-16855
    Bless You"

February 15, 1966 [No. 12742, 12:30–4:00 P.M.], Capitol Tower Recording Studio: Buck Owens & His Buckaroos (Buck Owens [vocals/guitar], Don Rich [lead guitar/fiddle/harmony vocals], Doyle Holly [rhythm guitar], Red Simpson [rhythm guitar], Tom Brumley [steel], Bob Morris [bass], Willie Cantu [drums]; producer: Ken Nelson)

201 55658 "Cadillac Lane"   ST-2640 STCL-574 BCD-16855;
    [t. 9] BCD-16855
202 55659 "A House of Memories"   ST-2640 BCD-16855
203 55660 "Think of Me"   5647 / ST-2640 ST-2897 STCL 574 BCD-16855
204 55661 "No More Me and You"   5705 / ST-2640 STCL-574 BCD-16855

March 25, 1966 [Session number unavailable, live], Carnegie Hall, New York City: Buck Owens & His Buckaroos (Buck Owens [vocals/guitar], Don Rich [guitar/harmony vocals], Tom Brumley [steel], Doyle Holly [bass/vocal], Willie Cantu [drums]; producer: Ken Nelson)

20401 26303 "Act Naturally"   ST-2556 CMF-012
20402 26304 "Together Again"   ST-2556 CMF-012
20403 26305 "Love's Gonna Live Here"   ST-2556 CMF-012
20404 26306 "In the Palm of Your Hand"/   ST-2556 CMF-012
    "Cryin' Time"/"Don't Let Her Know"/
    "Only You (Can Break My Heart)"
20405 26307 "I Don't Care (Just as Long as   ST-2556 CMF-012
    You Love Me)"/"My Heart Skips a Beat"/
    "Gonna Have Love"
20406 26308 "Waitin' in Your Welfare Line"   ST-2556 CMF-012
20407 26309 "Buckaroo"   ST-2556 CMF-012
20408 26310 "Streets of Laredo"*   ST-2556 CMF-012
20409 26311 "I've Got a Tiger by the Tail"   ST-2556 CMF-012
20410 26312 "Under Your Spell Again"/   ST-2556 CMF-012
    "Above and Beyond"/"Excuse Me . . ."
20411 none "Fun 'n' Games with Don   CMF-012
    & Doyle"
20412 none "Twist and Shout"   CMF-012

denotes vocal by Doyle Holly

April 6, 1966 [No. 12828, 12:30–3:30 P.M.], Capitol Tower Recording Studio: Buck Owens & His Buckaroos (Buck Owens [vocals/guitar], James Burton [lead guitar], Don Rich [lead guitar], Doyle Holly [rhythm guitar], Jelly Sanders [rhythm guitar], Tom Brumley [steel], Bob Morris [bass], Willie Cantu [drums], Richie Frost [percussion]; producer: Ken Nelson)

205 55912 "Where Does the Good Times Go"*   5811 / ST-2841 SKAO-145 BCD-16855; [overdubbed t. 8B] BCD-16855
206 55913 "Open Up Your Heart"**   5705 / ST-2640 ST-2897 STCL-574 BCD-16855

*denotes overdub session February 23, 1967, Capitol Tower Recording Studio, with David Gates (leader), Israel Baker (violin), Arnold Belnick (violin), James Getzoff (violin), Lou Klass (violin), Henry L. Roth (violin), Albert Steinberg (violin)
**denotes lead guitar by James Burton

November 7, 1966 [No. 14172, 11:00 A.M.–2:00 P.M.], Capitol Tower Recording Studio: Buck Owens & His Buckaroos (Buck Owens [vocals/guitar], Don Rich [lead guitar/harmony vocal], Bert Dodson [guitar], Wayne Wilson [guitar], Tom Brumley [steel], Bob Morris [bass], Willie Cantu [drums]; producer: Ken Nelson)

207 56801 "The Way That I Love You"   5811 / ST-2841 BCD-16855; [overdubbed t. 4B] unissued
208 56802 "Rocks in My Head"   ST-2760 BCD-16855; [overdubbed t. 5B] unissued

Overdub session February 23, 1967, Capitol Tower Recording Studio, with David Gates (leader), Israel Baker (violin), Arnold Belnick (violin), James Getzoff (violin), Lou Klass (violin), Henry L. Roth (violin), Albert Steinberg (violin)

November 8, 1966 [No. 14173, 10:00 A.M.–1:00 P.M.], Capitol Tower Recording Studio: Buck Owens & His Buckaroos (Buck Owens [vocals/guitar], Don Rich [lead acoustic guitar/fiddle/harmony vocal], Jelly Sanders [rhythm guitar], Bert Dodson [guitar], Wayne Wilson [bass/guitar], Tom Brumley [steel], Bob Morris [bass], Willie Cantu [drums]; producer: Ken Nelson)

209 56806 "Only You and You Alone"   ST-2760 BCD-16855
210 56807 "Don't Ever Tell Me Goodbye"   5865 / ST-2760 BCD-16855; [overdubbed t. 8B] unissued—lost
211 56808 "What a Liar Am I"   5942 / ST-2760 BCD-16855; [overdubbed t. 2B] unissued—lost
212 56809 "Your Tender Loving Care"   5942 / ST-2760 BCD-16855; [overdubbed t. 1B] unissued—lost; [overdubbed alt. take] unissued—lost

Overdub session February 23, 1967, Capitol Tower Recording Studio, with David Gates (leader), Israel Baker (violin), Arnold Belnick (violin), James Getzoff (violin), Lou Klass (violin), Henry L. Roth (violin), Albert Steinberg (violin)

November 9, 1966 [No. 14177, 10:00 A.M.–1:00 P.M.], Capitol Tower Recording Studio: Buck Owens & His Buckaroos (Buck Owens [vocals/guitar], Don Rich [lead guitar/fiddle/harmony vocal], Bert Dodson [guitar], Wayne Wilson [guitar], Tom Brumley [steel], Bob Morris [bass], Willie Cantu [drums]; producer: Ken Nelson)

213 56822 "Song and Dance" (overdubbed)   ST-2760 BCD-16855
214 56823 "If I Had You Back Again"   ST-2760 BCD-16855
215 56824 "Highway Man"   unissued—lost
216 56825 "The Way That I Love You" (instrumental)*   ST-2722 BCD-16855

* listed as "When a Woman Loves a Man" in artist file

Overdub session February 23, 1967, Capitol Tower Recording Studio, with David Gates (leader), Israel Baker (violin), Arnold Belnick (violin), James Getzoff (violin), Lou Klass (violin), Henry L. Roth (violin), Albert Steinberg (violin)

January 3, 1967 [No. 1, 8:00–11:00 p.m.], Capitol Tower Recording Studio: Don Rich & the Buckaroos(Don Rich [guitar/fiddle/vocals], Wayne Wilson [guitar], Jelly Sanders [guitar], Tom Brumley [steel], Bob Morris [bass], Willie Cantu [drums], Glen D. Hardin [piano]; producer: Ken Nelson)

B18 58131/B 101 "I'll Be Swingin' Too"	*ST-2828 SC-11091* BCD-16855
B19 57090-8A/B 102 "It Takes a Lot of Tenderness"	*ST-2722* BCD-16855
B20 57093-6A/B 103 "Round Hole Guitar"	*ST-2722* BCD-16855

January 4, 1967 [No. 2, 7:00–10:00 P.M.], Capitol Tower Recording Studio: Don Rich & the Buckaroos (Don Rich [guitar/fiddle/vocal], Wayne Wilson [guitar/vocal], Jelly Sanders [guitar], Tom Brumley [steel], Bob Morris [bass], Willie Cantu [drums], Glen D. Hardin [piano]; producer: Ken Nelson)

B21 57092/B 104 "You'll Never Miss the Water (till the Well Runs Dry)"*	*ST-2722* BCD-16855
B22 57096/B 105 "Something to Remember You By"**	*ST-2722* BCD-16855
B23 57089/B 106 "The Happy-Go-Lucky Guitar"	*ST-2722 SC-11091* BCD-16855
B24 57099/B 107 "Tumwater Breakdown"	*ST-2722 ST-643 SC-11091* BCD-16855

denotes vocals by Don Rich and Wayne Wilson
**denotes vocal by Wayne Wilson*

January 5, 1967 [No. 3, 7:00–11:00 P.M.], Capitol Tower Recording Studio: Don Rich & the Buckaroos (Don Rich [guitar/fiddle/vocals], Wayne Wilson [guitar], Jelly Sanders [guitar], Tom Brumley [steel], Bob Morris [bass], Willie Cantu [drums], Glen D. Hardin [piano]; producer: Ken Nelson)

B25 57091/B 108 "The Neosho Waltz"	*ST-2722* BCD-16855
B26 57095/B 109 "Steel Polka"	*ST-2722* BCD-16855

c. January 1967: Buck Owens & His Buckaroos (Buck Owens [guitar], Don Rich [vocals/guitar], Tom Brumley [steel])

B27 57094 "A Happy Son of a Gun"*	*ST-2722* BCD-16855; [t. 1-15] BCD-16855
B28 57097 "Seven Come Eleven" (instrumental)	*ST-2722* BCD-16855
B29 57098 "Out of My Mind"*	*ST-2722* BCD-16855

denotes vocal by Don Rich

February 6, 1967 [No. 14325, live], Koseinenkin Hall, Tokyo, Japan: Buck Owens & His Buckaroos (Buck Owens [vocals/guitar], Don Rich [guitar/fiddle/vocals], Tom Brumley [steel], Wayne Wilson [bass/vocals], Willie Cantu [drums]; producer: Ken Nelson)

21601 57322 "Opening Remarks by Tetsuo Otsuka"	ST-2715
21602 57323 "Buck Owens Introduces His Buckaroos"	ST-2715
21603 57302 "Adios, Farewell, Goodbye, Good Luck, So Long"	ST-2715
21604 57303 "I Was Born to Be in Love with You"	ST-2715
21605 57304 "Open Up Your Heart"	ST-2715
21606 57305 "Second Fiddle"	ST-2715
21607 57306 "Fiddle Polka"	ST-2715
21608 57307 "Fishin' on the Mississippi"	ST-2715
21609 57308 "The Way That I Love You"	ST-2715

February 6, 1967 [No. 14326, live], Koseinenkin Hall, Tokyo, Japan: Buck Owens & His Buckaroos (Buck Owens [vocals/guitar], Don Rich [guitar/fiddle/vocals], Tom Brumley [steel], Wayne Wilson [bass/vocals], Willie Cantu [drums]; producer: Ken Nelson)

21610 57369	"Opening Remarks by Buck Owens"	ST-2715
21611 57309	"Tokyo Polka"	ST-2715 ST-2994
21612 57310	"Where Does the Good Times Go"	ST-2715
21613 57311	"Steel Polka"	ST-2715
21614 57312	"Don't Wipe the Tears That You Cry"	ST-2715
21615 57313	"Drum So-Low"	ST-2715
21616 57314	"Roll Out the Red Carpet"	ST-2715
21617 57615	"We Were Made for Each Other"	ST-2715
21618 57370	"Closing Remarks"	ST-2715

April 24, 1967 [No. 14395, 10:30 A.M.–2:00 P.M.], Capitol Tower Recording Studio: Buck Owens & His Buckaroos (Buck Owens [vocals/guitar], Don Rich [lead guitar], Wayne Wilson [guitar], Tom Brumley [steel], Bob Morris [bass], Willie Cantu [drums]; producer: Ken Nelson)

217 57559	"I'm Gonna Live It Up"	rejected
218 57560	"I've Got It Bad for You"	rejected
219 57561	"If I Knew"	rejected

June 6, 1967 [No. 14446, 3:00–6:00 P.M.], Capitol Tower Recording Studio: Buck Owens & His Buckaroos (Buck Owens [vocals/guitar], Jelly Sanders [guitar], Don Rich [lead guitar], Wayne Wilson [guitar], Tom Brumley [steel], Bert Dodson [bass], Willie Cantu [drums]; producer: Ken Nelson)

220 57762	"I'm Gonna Live It Up"	ST-2841 BCD-16855
221 57763	"If I Knew"	ST-2841 BCD-16855
222 57764	"Everybody Needs Somebody"	2080 / ST-2962 BCD-16855
223 57765	"I've Got It Bad for You"	ST-2841 BCD-16855

June 7, 1967 [No. 14450, 3:00–6:00 P.M.], Capitol Tower Recording Studio: Buck Owens & His Buckaroos (Buck Owens [vocalsl/guitar], Jelly Sanders [guitar/fiddle], Don Rich [lead guitar/fiddle/harmony vocals], Wayne Wilson [guitar], Tom Brumley [steel], Bert Dodson [bass], Willie Cantu [drums]; producer: Ken Nelson)

224 57781	"You Left Her Lonely Too Long"	2001 / ST-2841 BCD-16855
225 57782	"That's How I Measure My Love for You"	ST-2841 BCD-16855
226 57783	"Heartbreak Mountain"*	ST-2841 BCD-16855

denotes vocal by Don Rich

June 8, 1967 [No. 14455, 3:00–6:00 P.M.], Capitol Tower Recording Studio: Buck Owens & His Buckaroos (Buck Owens [vocals/guitar], Don Rich [lead acoustic guitar], Jelly Sanders [rhythm guitar], Wayne Wilson [bass], Tom Brumley [steel], Bert Dodson [bass], Willie Cantu [drums]; producer: Ken Nelson)

227 57797	"It Takes People Like You (to Make People Like Me)"	2001 / ST-2841 SKAO-145 BCD-16855
228 57798	"Toys for Tots"	unissued / BCD-16855; [t. 6] BCD-16855

June 1967 [No. 14541, time unavailable], Capitol Tower Recording Studio: Don Rich & the Buckaroos (Don Rich [guitar/fiddle/vocals], Doyle Holly [guitar/vocals], possibly Jelly Sanders [harmony vocals], Tom Brumley [steel], possibly Bert Dodson [bass], Willie Cantu [drums], possibly Earl Poole Ball Jr. [piano]; producer: Ken Nelson) [purchased masters, registered June 30]

B30 58120	"Kern County Breakdown"	*ST-2828* BCD-16855
B31 58121	"My Baby's Comin' Home"*	*ST-2828* BCD-16855

B32 58122 "Chicken Pickin'"   *2010/ST-2828 SC-11091* BCD-16855
B33 58123 "Free and Easy"   *ST-2828* BCD-16855
B34 58124 "Tom's Waltz"   *ST-2828* BCD-16855
B35 58125 "Buckersfield Breakdown"   *ST-2828 SC-11091* BCD-16855
B36 58126 "Love's Gonna Come a Knockin'"*   *ST-2828 SC-11091* BCD-16855
B37 58127 "I'm a Comin' Back to You"*   *ST-2828* BCD-16855
B38 58128 "Apple Jack"   *2010/ST-2828* BCD-16855
B39 58129 "A Foolish Notion"**   *ST-2828* BCD-16855
B40 58130 "Night Time Is Cry Time"**   *ST-2828* BCD-16855

denotes vocal by Don Rich
**denotes vocal by Doyle Holly*

August 28, 1967 [No. 14561, 5:30–9:00 P.M.], Capitol Tower Recording Studio: Buck Owens & His Buckaroos (Buck Owens [vocals/guitar], Don Rich [lead acoustic guitar], Jelly Sanders [rhythm guitar], Jimmy Bryant [rhythm guitar], Tom Brumley [steel], Doyle Holly [bass], Willie Cantu [drums/tambourine]; producer: Ken Nelson)

229 58221 "How Long Will My Baby   2080 / ST-2962 *STBB-2969* SKAO-145 *STFL-295*
    Be Gone?"   *ST-437* BCD-16855; [t. 5A] BCD-16855;
                                  [t. 9A] BCD-16855
230 58222 "Swingin' Doors"   ST-2962 BCD-16855
231 58223 "Long, Long Ago"   ST-2841 BCD-16855
232 58224 "Sing a Happy Song"*   ST-131 STCL-574 BCD-16855

denotes overdub session August 31, 1967, with unidentified vocal chorus

August 29, 1967 [No. 14563, 5:30–8:30 P.M.], Capitol Tower Recording Studio: Buck Owens & His Buckaroos (Buck Owens [vocals/guitar], Jimmy Bryant [guitar], Jelly Sanders [guitar], Don Rich [lead guitar], Tom Brumley [steel], Doyle Holly [bass], Willie Cantu [drums]; producer: Ken Nelson)

233 58229 "Let the World Keep On   ST-2841 BCD-16855
    a Turnin'"
234 58230 "The Girl on Sugar Pie Lane" ST-2962 BCD-16855
235 58231 "We Were Made for Each Other" ST-2841 BCD-16855

December 5, 1967 [No. 14742, 1:00–4:00 P.M.], Capitol Tower Recording Studio: Buck Owens & His Buckaroos (Buck Owens [vocals/guitar], Don Rich [lead gut-string guitar/harmony vocals], Jelly Sanders [rhythm guitar], Doyle Holly [rhythm guitar], Tom Brumley [steel], Bob Morris [bass], Jerry Wiggins [drums]; producer: Ken Nelson)

236 58810 "Happy Times Are Here Again" 2142 / ST-2962 SKAO-145
237 58811 "Sweet Rosie Jones"   2142 / ST-2962 SKAO-145

December 6, 1967 [No. 14747, 1:00–4:00 P.M.], Capitol Tower Recording Studio: Buck Owens & His Buckaroos (Buck Owens [vocals/guitar], Don Rich [lead guitar], Doyle Holly [rhythm guitar], Jelly Sanders [rhythm guitar], Tom Brumley [steel], Bob Morris [bass], Jerry Wiggins [drums]; producer: Ken Nelson)

238 58812 "The Heartaches Have Just Started" ST-2962 BCD-16855
239 58813 "Your Mother's Prayer"   ST-439 BCD-16855
240 58827 "That Sunday Feeling"   ST-439 BCD-16855
241 58828 "Hurtin' Like I've Never   ST-212 BCD-16855
    Hurt Before"

December 7, 1967 [No. 14750, 1:00–4:30 P.M.], Capitol Tower Recording Studio: Buck Owens & His Buckaroos (Buck Owens [vocals/guitar], Don Rich [lead guitar/fiddle], Doyle Holly [rhythm guitar], Jelly Sanders [rhythm guitar/fiddle], Tom Brumley [steel], Bob Morris [bass], Jerry Wiggins [drums/tambourine]; producer: Ken Nelson)

242 58835 "You'll Never Miss the Water ST-2962 BCD-16855
    (till the Well Runs Dry)"*

243 58836 "There's Gonna Be Some   2377/ST-212 BCD-16855
     Changes Made"**
244 58837 "If I Had Three Wishes"   ST-2962 BCD-16855

*denotes overdub session January 8, 1968, with Earl Poole Ball Jr. (piano)
**denotes overdub session August 22, 1968, Nashville, TN, with the Jordanaires and Anita Kerr (background vocals)

**January 3, 1968 [No. 14797, 1:00–5:00 P.M.], Capitol Tower Recording Studio: Don Rich &
the Buckaroos (Don Rich [vocals/lead guitar], Doyle Holly [vocals/rhythm guitar], Jelly
Sanders [rhythm guitar], Tom Brumley [steel], Bob Morris [bass], Jerry Wiggins [drums],
Earl Poole Ball Jr. [piano]; producer: Ken Nelson)**

B41 58964 "Hello California"*   *ST-2902* BCD-16855
B42 58965 "Highway Man"**   *ST-2902* BCD-16855
B43 58966 "I Can't Stop (My Loving You)"**   *2173 / ST-2902* BCD-16855
B44 58967 "Chaparral"*   *ST-2902 SC-11091* BCD-16855

*denotes vocal by Don Rich
**denotes vocal by Doyle Holly

**January 4, 1968 [No. 14798, 1:00–5:00 P.M.], Capitol Tower Recording Studio: Don Rich &
the Buckaroos (Don Rich [vocals/lead guitar], Doyle Holly [rhythm guitar], Jelly Sanders
[rhythm guitar], Tom Brumley [steel], Bob Morris [bass], Jerry Wiggins [drums], Earl
Poole Ball Jr. [piano]; producer: Ken Nelson)**

B45 58980 "You Bring Out the Best in Me"*   *ST-2902* BCD-16855
B46 58981 "I'm Coming Back Home to Stay"*   *2173 / ST-2902 SC-11091* BCD-16855
B47 58982 "The Waltz of the Roses"   *ST-2902* BCD-16855
B48 58983 "Pedal Patter"   *ST-2902* BCD-16855

*denotes vocal by Don Rich

**January 5, 1968 [No. 14799, 1:00–4:00 P.M.], Capitol Tower Recording Studio: Don Rich &
the Buckaroos (Don Rich [lead guitar], Doyle Holly [rhythm guitar], Jelly Sanders [rhythm
guitar], Tom Brumley [steel], Bob Morris [bass], Jerry Wiggins [drums], Earl Poole Ball Jr.
[piano]; producer: Ken Nelson)**

B49 58984 "Down on the Bayou"   *ST-2902 ST-643* BCD-16855
B50 58985 "Pretty Girl Hoedown"   *ST-2902 ST-643 SC-11091* BCD-16855
B51 58986 "Sad Is the Lonely"   *ST-2902 SC-11091* BCD-16855
B52 58987 "Rattle Traps"   *ST-2902* BCD-16855

**January 8, 1968 [No. 14800, 1:00–4:00 P.M.], Capitol Tower Recording Studio: Buck Owens
& His Buckaroos (Buck Owens [vocals/guitar]. Don Rich [lead guitar], Doyle Holly
[rhythm guitar], Jelly Sanders [rhythm guitar], Tom Brumley [steel], Bob Morris [bass],
Jerry Wiggins [drums], Earl Poole Ball Jr. [piano]; producer: Ken Nelson)**

245 59004 "Leave Me Something to   ST-2962
     Remember You By"
246 59005 "That's All Right with Me (If It's   2300/ST-131 STCL-574
     All Right with You)"*
247 59006 "Wait a Little Longer Please Jesus"   ST-439
248 59007 "You'll Never Miss the Water"   unissued—lost

*denotes overdub session August 22, 1968, Nashville, TN, with the Jordanaires and Anita Kerr (background vocals)

**January 9, 1968 [No. 14804, 1:00–4:00 P.M.], Capitol Tower Recording Studio: Buck Owens
& His Buckaroos (Buck Owens [vocals/guitar]. Don Rich [lead guitar/harmony vocals],
Doyle Holly [rhythm guitar], Jelly Sanders [rhythm guitar], Tom Brumley [steel], Bob Mor-
ris [bass], Jerry Wiggins [drums], Earl Poole Ball Jr. [piano]; producer: Ken Nelson)**

249 59026 "Hello Happiness, Goodbye   ST-2962
     Loneliness"
250 59027 "Don't Let True Love Slip Away"*   ST-131 STCL-574
251 59028 "The Great Judgment Day"   ST-439

*denotes overdub session August 22, 1968, Nashville, TN, with the Jordanaires and Anita Kerr (background vocals)

January 10, 1968 [No. 14809, 1:00–4:00 P.M.], Capitol Tower Recording Studio: Buck Owens & His Buckaroos (Buck Owens [vocals/guitar]. Don Rich [lead acoustic guitar], Doyle Holly [rhythm guitar], Jelly Sanders [rhythm guitar], Tom Brumley [steel], Bob Morris [bass], Jerry Wiggins [drums], Earl Poole Ball Jr. [piano]; producer: Ken Nelson)

252	59046	"Sally, Mary and Jerry"	ST-2962
253	59047	"In God I Trust"	ST-439
254	59048	"Buckaroo Polka"	unissued

February 27, 1968 [No. 14897, 1:00–4:00 p.m.], Bakersfield, CA: Buck Owens & His Buckaroos Capitol Tower Recording Studio (Buck Owens [vocals/guitar]. Don Rich [lead guitar], Doyle Holly [rhythm guitar], Jelly Sanders [rhythm guitar], Tom Brumley [steel], Bob Morris [bass], Jerry Wiggins [drums], Earl Poole Ball Jr. [piano]; producer: Ken Nelson)

| 255 | 59314 | "All I Want for Christmas Is My Daddy" | ST-2977 |
| 256 | 59315 | "Christmas Shopping" | 2328 / ST-2977 *ST-11226* |

February 28, 1968 [No. 14899, 1:00–4:00 P.M.], Capitol Tower Recording Studio: Buck Owens & His Buckaroos (Buck Owens [vocals/guitar]. Don Rich [lead guitar], Doyle Holly [rhythm guitar], Jelly Sanders [rhythm guitar], Tom Brumley [steel], Bob Morris [bass], Jerry Wiggins [drums], Earl Poole Ball Jr. [piano]; producer: Ken Nelson)

257	59322	"One of Everything You Got"	2328 / ST-2977
258	59323	"Good Old Fashioned Country Christmas"	ST-2977
259	59324	"The Jolly Christmas Polka"	ST-2977

May 27, 1968 [No. 17140, 1:00–4:00 P.M.], Capitol Tower Recording Studio: Buck Owens & His Buckaroos (Buck Owens [vocals/guitar], Buddy Alan [vocals], Don Rich [lead guitar], Doyle Holly [rhythm guitar], Jelly Sanders [rhythm guitar], Tom Brumley [steel], Bob Morris [bass], Jerry Wiggins [drums], Earl Poole Ball Jr. [piano]; producer: Ken Nelson)

260	59826	"Let the World Keep On a Turnin'"*	2237 / ST-131 STCL-574 ST-874
261	59827	"I'll Love You Forever and Ever"*	2237 / ST-131 STCL-574 ST-874
262	59828	"A Very Merry Christmas"	ST-2977

denotes duet with Buddy Alan

May 28, 1968 [No. 17145, 1:00–4:00 P.M.], Capitol Tower Recording Studio: Buck Owens & His Buckaroos (Buck Owens [vocals/guitar], Don Rich [lead guitar], Doyle Holly [rhythm guitar], Jelly Sanders [rhythm guitar], Tom Brumley [steel], Bob Morris [bass], Jerry Wiggins [drums/bells], Earl Poole Ball Jr. [celesta/piano]; producer: Ken Nelson)

263	59832	"Christmas Time Is Near"	ST-2977 BCD-16855
264	59833	"Tomorrow Is Christmas Day"	ST-2977 BCD-16855
265	59834	"Christmas Schottische"	ST-2977 BCD-16855

June 17, 1968 [No. 17202, 1:00–4:00 P.M.], Capitol Tower Recording Studio: Buck Owens & His Buckaroos (Buck Owens [vocals/guitar], Don Rich [lead guitar], Doyle Holly [rhythm guitar], Jelly Sanders [rhythm guitar], Tom Brumley [steel], Bob Morris [bass], Jerry Wiggins [drums], Earl Poole Ball Jr. [piano]; producer: Ken Nelson)

266	70004	"Home on Christmas Day"	ST-2977 BCD-16855
267	70006	"Merry Christmas from Our House to Yours"	ST-2977 BCD-16855
268	70007	"It's Not What You Give"	unissued / BCD-16855

June 18, 1968 [No. 17203, 1:00–4:30 P.M.], Capitol Tower Recording Studio: Don Rich & the Buckaroos (Don Rich [vocals/lead guitar], Doyle Holly [vocals/ rhythm guitar], Jelly

Sanders [rhythm guitar], Tom Brumley [steel], Bob Morris [bass], Jerry Wiggins [drums], Earl Poole Ball Jr. [piano]; producers: Buck Owens & Ken Nelson)

B53 70018 "You Let Me Down"**	*ST-2973* BCD-16855
B54 70019 "Woman Truck Drivin' Fool"**	*ST-2973* BCD-16855
B55 70020 "I Got a Letter from Home"*	*ST-2973* BCD-16855
B56 70021 "Pitty Pitty Patter"*	*ST-2973* BCD-16855

denotes vocal by Don Rich
**denotes vocal by Doyle Holly*

June 19, 1968 [No. 17211, 1:00–4:00 P.M.], Capitol Tower Recording Studio: Don Rich & the Buckaroos (Don Rich [vocals/lead guitar], Doyle Holly [rhythm guitar], Jelly Sanders [rhythm guitar], Tom Brumley [steel], Bob Morris [bass], Jerry Wiggins [drums], Earl Poole Ball Jr. [piano]; producers: Buck Owens & Ken Nelson)

B57 70032 "I'm Goin' Back Home Where I Belong"*	*2264 / ST-2973 SC-11091* BCD-16855
B58 70033 "Meanwhile Back at the Ranch"	*ST-2973* BCD-16855
B59 70034 "Tracy's Waltz"	*ST-2973* BCD-16855
B60 70035 "Runnin' Short"	*ST-2973* BCD-16855

denotes vocal by Don Rich

June 20, 1968 [No. 17212, 1:00–4:00 P.M.], Capitol Tower Recording Studio: Don Rich & the Buckaroos (Don Rich [lead guitar], Doyle Holly [rhythm guitar], Jelly Sanders [rhythm guitar], Tom Brumley [steel], Bob Morris [bass], Jerry Wiggins [drums], Earl Poole Ball Jr. [piano]; producers: Buck Owens & Ken Nelson)

B61 70036 "Louisiana Waltz"	*ST-2973 ST-643* BCD-16855
B62 70037 "Saturday Night"	*ST-2973 SC-11091* BCD-16855
B63 70038 "Spanish Moonlight"	*ST-2973 SC-11091* BCD-16855
B64 70039 "Too Many Chiefs (Not Enough Indians)"	*2264 / ST-2973* BCD-16855

August 6, 1968 [No. 17324, time unavailable], Capitol Tower Recording Studio: Buck Owens & His Buckaroos (Buck Owens [lead acoustic guitar], Don Rich [guitar], Buddy Alan [guitar], Red Wooten [bass], Jerry Wiggins [drums], Earl Poole Ball Jr. [piano]; producer: Ken Nelson)

269 70321 "Guitar Fandango" (instrumental)	ST-2994 BCD-16855
270 70322 "Things I Saw Happening at the Fountain on the Plaza When I Was Visiting Rome or Amore" (instrumental)	2330 / ST-2994 BCD-16855
271 70323 "The Gaucho Came Riding" (instrumental)	ST-2994 BCD-16855

August 6, 1968 [No. 17325, 7:30–10:30 P.M.], Capitol Tower Recording Studio: Buck Owens & His Buckaroos (Buck Owens [lead acoustic guitar], Don Rich [guitar], Buddy Alan [guitar], Red Wooten [bass], Jerry Wiggins [drums], Earl Poole Ball Jr. [piano]; producer: Ken Nelson)

272 70324 "Mexican Jumping Bean" (instrumental)	ST-2994 BCD-16855
273 70325 "Turkish Holiday" (instrumental)	2330 / ST-2994 BCD-16855

August 7, 1968 [No. 17326, 3:00–6:00 P.M.], Capitol Tower Recording Studio: Buck Owens & His Buckaroos (Buck Owens [vocals/guitar], Don Rich [lead guitar], Buddy Alan [rhythm guitar], Doyle Holly [bass], Tom Brumley [steel], Jerry Wiggins [drums], Earl Poole Ball Jr. [piano], Larry Wooten [unknown]; producer: Ken Nelson)

274 70326 "I've Got You on My Mind Again"	2300 / ST-131 *STBB-217 STFL-295* STCL-574 BCD-16855

Overdub session August 22, 1968, Nashville, TN, with the Jordanaires and Anita Kerr (background vocals)

September 3, 1968 [No. 17378, 1:00–6:00 P.M.], Capitol Tower Recording Studio: Buck Owens & His Buckaroos (Buck Owens [vocals/guitar], Don Rich [lead guitar], Doyle Holly [rhythm guitar], Jelly Sanders [rhythm guitar], Tom Brumley [steel], Red Wooten [bass], Jerry Wiggins [drums], Earl Poole Ball Jr. [piano]; producer: Ken Nelson)

275 71000 "I Wanna Be Wild and Free"*   ST-131 BCD-16855
276 71001 "Where Has Our Love Gone?"*   ST-131 STCL-574 BCD-16855
277 71002 "I Ain't Gonna Be Treated This   ST-131 STCL-574 BCD-16855
  a Way"*
278 71003 "Darlin' You Can Depend on Me"**   ST-212 BCD-16855
279 71016 "Jesus, Jesus Hold Me"   ST-439 BCD-16855

*denotes overdub session October 16, 1968, Nashville, TN, with unidentified vocal chorus
**denotes overdub session February 12, 1969, Capitol Tower Recording Studio, with Walter Rowe (cello), Hyman Davidson (viola), Billy Armstrong (leader/violin),Chuck Andell (violin), Hixon Boranian (violin),Margie Warren (violin), Billy Wright (violin)

September 4, 1968 [No. 17379, 1:00–6:00 P.M.], Capitol Tower Recording Studio: Buck Owens & His Buckaroos (Buck Owens [vocals/guitar], Don Rich [lead guitar], Doyle Holly [rhythm guitar], Jelly Sanders [rhythm guitar], Tom Brumley [steel], Red Wooten [bass], Jerry Wiggins [drums], Earl Poole Ball Jr. [piano]; producer: Ken Nelson)

280 71004 "Sing That Kind of Song"*   2570 / ST-212 BCD-16855
281 71005 "Love Is Me"   ST-131 BCD-16855
282 71006 "Hurry, Come Running Back to Me"   ST-131 STCL-574 BCD-16855
283 71007 "Alabama, Louisiana or Maybe   ST-131 STCL-574 BCD-16855
  Tennessee"

Overdub session October 16, 1968, Nashville, TN, with the Jordanaires and members of the Anita Kerr Singers

*denotes overdub session February 12, 1969, Capitol Tower Recording Studio, with Walter Rowe (cello), Hyman Davidson (viola), Billy Armstrong (leader/violin),Chuck Andell (violin), Hixon Boranian (violin),Margie Warren (violin), Billy Wright (violin)

September 9, 1968 [No. 20077, live], White House, Washington, DC: Buck Owens & His Buckaroos [purchased masters, registered July 24, 1972]

28301 78933 "Introduction by Buck Owens"   ST-11105
28302 78934 "Act Naturally"/"Together   ST-11105
  Again"/"Love's Gonna Live Here"/"Cryin'
  Time"/"Happy Times Are Here Again"
28303 78935 "Streets of Laredo"/   ST-11105
  "Orange Blossom Special"/"Gentle on
  My Mind"/"When I Turn Twenty-One"/
  "I've Got a Tiger by the Tail"/"Truck
  Drivin' Man"

October 8, 1968 [No. 17459, 1:00–5:00 P.M.], Capitol Tower Recording Studio: Don Rich & the Buckaroos (Don Rich [lead guitar], Doyle Holly [vocals/ rhythm guitar], Bill Sampson [rhythm guitar], Tom Brumley [steel], Bob Morris [bass], Jerry Wiggins [drums], Earl Poole Ball Jr. [piano]; producer: Ken Nelson)

B65 71242 "Greensleeves"   ST-194 BCD-16855
B66 71243 "Gathering Dust"*   2420 / ST-194 BCD-16855
B67 71244 "The Price I'll Have to Pay"*   ST-194 BCD-16855
B68 71245 "Aw Heck"   ST-194 SC-11091 BCD-16855

*denotes vocal by Doyle Holly

October 9, 1968 [No. 17460, 2:00–5:00 P.M.], Capitol Tower Recording Studio: Don Rich & the Buckaroos (Don Rich [vocals/lead guitar], Doyle Holly [vocals/ rhythm guitar], Bill

Sampson [rhythm guitar], Tom Brumley [steel], Bob Morris [bass], Jerry Wiggins [drums], Earl Poole Ball Jr. [piano]; producer: Ken Nelson)

B69 71246 "Keep On Your Keepin' On"*	ST-194 BCD-16855
B70 71247 "Bad Luck and Bad Weather"**	ST-194 BCD-16855
B71 71248 "Anywhere U.S.A."**	2420 / ST-194 BCD-16855
B72 71249 "Tim-Buck-Too"	ST-194 SC-11091 BCD-16855

*denotes vocal by Don Rich
**denotes vocal by Doyle Holly

October 10, 1968 [No. 17461, 2:00–6:00 P.M.], Capitol Tower Recording Studio: Don Rich & the Buckaroos (Don Rich [lead guitar/fiddle], Doyle Holly [rhythm guitar], Bill Sampson [rhythm guitar], Tom Brumley [steel], Bob Morris [bass], Jerry Wiggins [drums], Earl Poole Ball Jr. [piano]; producer: Ken Nelson)

B73 71250 "Georgia Peach"	ST-194 ST-643 SC-11091 BCD-16855
B74 71251 "Highland Fling"	ST-194 BCD-16855
B75 71252 "Moonlight on the Desert"	ST-194 BCD-16855
B76 71253 "March of the McGregor"	ST-194 BCD-16855

November 9, 1968 [No. 17553], Capitol Tower Recording Studio: Don Rich & the Buckaroos (producer: Ken Nelson)

| B77 71483 unknown title | unissued |

December 4, 1968 [No. 17586, 1:00–4:30 P.M.], Capitol Tower Recording Studio: Buck Owens & His Buckaroos (Buck Owens [vocals/guitar], Susan Raye [duet vocals], Don Rich [lead fuzztone guitar/fiddle], Al Bruno [guitar/lead National guitar], Doyle Holly [rhythm guitar], Tom Brumley [steel], Bob Morris [bass], Jerry Wiggins [drums], Earl Poole Ball Jr. [electric harpsichord]; producer: Ken Nelson)

| 284 71558 "Who's Gonna Mow Your Grass" | 2377 / ST-830 |
| 285 71559 "We're Gonna Get Together"* | 2731 / ST-437 ST-448 ST-11084 |

*denotes duet with Susan Raye

December 5, 1968 [No. 17587, 1:00–4:30 P.M.], Capitol Tower Recording Studio: Buck Owens & His Buckaroos (Buck Owens [vocals/guitar], Don Rich [guitar], Al Bruno [guitar/lead National guitar], Doyle Holly [rhythm guitar], Tom Brumley [steel], Bob Morris [bass], Jerry Wiggins [drums], Earl Poole Ball Jr. [electric harpsichord/piano]; producer: Ken Nelson)

286 71560 "White Satin Bed"	2646 / ST-212
287 71561 "In the Middle of a Teardrop"	ST-212
288 71562 "You Can't Make Nothin' Out of That but Love"	ST-476

Overdub sessions: January 9, 1969, no details; February 12, 1969, Capitol Tower Recording Studio, with Walter Rowe (cello), Hyman Davidson (viola), Billy Armstrong (leader/violin),Chuck Andell (violin), Hixon Boranian (violin),Margie Warren (violin), Billy Wright (violin)

December 6, 1968 [No. 17588, 1:00–4:30 P.M.], Capitol Tower Recording Studio: Buck Owens & His Buckaroos (Buck Owens [vocals/guitar], Don Rich [lead guitar], Doyle Holly [rhythm guitar], Al Bruno [rhythm guitar], Tom Brumley [steel], Bob Morris [bass], Jerry Wiggins [drums], Earl Poole Ball Jr. [electric harpsichord/piano]; producer: Ken Nelson)

289 71563 "I Would Do Anything for You"	ST-212 BCD-16855
290 71564 "Maybe If I Close My Eyes"	2485 / ST-212 BCD-16855
291 71565 "Across This Town and Gone"	ST-212 BCD-16855

Overdub sessions: January 9, 1969, no details; February 12, 1969, Capitol Tower Recording Studio, with Walter Rowe (cello), Hyman Davidson (viola), Billy Armstrong (leader/violin),Chuck Andell (violin), Hixon Boranian (violin),Margie Warren (violin), Billy Wright (violin)

January 8, 1969 [No. 17625, 1:00–4:00 P.M.], Capitol Tower Recording Studio: Buck Owens & His Buckaroos (Buck Owens [vocals/guitar], Don Rich [lead gut-string guitar], Doyle Holly [rhythm guitar], Al Bruno [rhythm guitar], Tom Brumley [steel], Bob Morris [bass], Jerry Wiggins [drums], Earl Poole Ball Jr. [electric harpsichord/piano], the Jordanaires with Anita Kerr [background vocals]; producer: Ken Nelson)

292 71662 "Tall Dark Stranger"	2570 6189 / ST-212 *SWBB-562 SW-599* ST-830
293 71663 "I've Got a Happy Heart"	unissued
294 71664 "Somewhere Between"	ST-448

January 9, 1969 [No. 17626, time unavailable], Capitol Tower Recording Studio: Buck Owens & His Buckaroos (producer: Ken Nelson)

295 71666 "Just a Few More Days"	ST-439
296 71667 "Lonesome Valley"	ST-439
297 71668 "My Savior Leads the Way"	ST-439

March 9, 1969 [No. 17860, live, 7:00–10:00 P.M.], London Palladium, London, UK: Buck Owens & His Buckaroos (Buck Owens [guitar/vocals], Don Rich [lead guitar/fiddle/vocals], Jay Dee Maness [steel], Doyle Holly [bass], Jerry Wiggins [drums]; producer: Ken Nelson)

29701 72212 "Intro by David Allen"/ "Happy Times Are Here Again"	ST-232
29702 72213 "Act Naturally"/"Together Again"	ST-232
29703 72214 "A Happening in London Town"	ST-232
29704 72215 "Sweet Rosie Jones"	ST-232
29705 72216 "Sing Me Back Home"	ST-232
29706 72217 "Sam's Place"	ST-232
29707 72218 "It Takes People Like You"	ST-232

March 9, 1969 [No. 17861, live, 7:00–10:00 P.M.], London Palladium, London, UK: Buck Owens & His Buckaroos (Buck Owens [guitar/vocals], Don Rich [lead guitar/fiddle/vocals], Jay Dee Maness [steel], Doyle Holly [bass], Jerry Wiggins [drums]; producer: Ken Nelson)

29708 72211 "Johnny B. Goode	2485 / ST-232 ST-830
29709 72219 "Love's Gonna Live Here"/ "Cryin' Time"/"I've Got a Tiger by the Tail"/ "Open Up Your Heart"	ST-232
29710 72220 "Who's Gonna Mow Your Grass"	ST-232
29711 72221 "Diggy Liggy Lo/Louisiana Man"	ST-232
29712 72222 "Cajun Fiddle"	ST-232
29713 72223 "Dust on Mother's Bible"	ST-232

May 15, 1969 [No. 13314, time unavailable], Columbia Recording Studio, 804 16th Ave. S., Nashville, TN: Buck Owens

298 54922 "But You Know I Love You"	ST-212

July 1969 [No. 18043, time unavailable], Capitol Tower Recording Studio or Buck Owens Studios, 1215 N. Chester Ave., Oildale, CA: Buckaroos (producer: Ken Nelson) [registered August 15]

B78 72736 "I'm a Natural Loser"	*ST-320*
B79 72737 "The Biggest Storm of All"	*ST-320*
B80 72738 "If I Had You by My Side"	*ST-320*

July 1969 [No. 18047, time unavailable], Capitol Tower Recording Studio or Buck Owens Studios: Buckaroos (producer: Ken Nelson) [registered August 15]

B81 72754 "Down at the Corner Bar"	*ST-320*
B82 72755 "Nobody but You"	*ST-320*
B83 72756 "Lay a Little Light on Me"	*2630 / ST-320*

July 1969 [No. 18053, time unavailable], Capitol Tower Recording Studio or Buck Owens Studios: Buckaroos (producer: Ken Nelson) [registered August 15]

B84 72768 "Catfish Capers"	*ST-320 ST-643*	
B85 72769 "Bossanova Buckaroo Style"	*ST-320*	
B86 72770 "Sweet T-Pie"	*ST-320*	
B87 72771 "Pull Your Own"	*ST-320*	

July 14, 1969 [No. 18063, time unavailable], Capitol Tower Recording Studio or Buck Owens Studios: Buck Owens (producer: Ken Nelson) [registered August 15]

299 72804 "When the Roll Is Called Up Yonder" ST-439
300 72805 "That Old Time Religion" ST-439
301 72806 "Big in Vegas" unissued

July 25, 1969 [No. 18096, live], Las Vegas, NV: Buck Owens & His Buckaroos (vocals: Buck Owens, Buddy Alan, Sanland Brothers, Susan Raye, the Hagers; producer: Ken Nelson)

30101 73264 "Intro by Chris Lane" ST-413 Hilltop JS-6128
30102 73265 "Big in Vegas" ST-413 Hilltop JS-6128
30103 73266 "Lodi"* ST-413 Hilltop JS-6128
30104 73267 "Let Me Get My Message Thru"** ST-413
30105 73268 "Maybe If I Close My Eyes"*** ST-413 Hilltop JS-6128
30106 73269 "Goin' Home to Your ST-413 Hilltop JS-6128
    Mother"****
30107 73270 "With Lonely"**** ST-413

*denotes vocal by Buddy Alan
**denotes vocals by Sanland Brothers
***denotes vocal by Susan Raye
****denotes vocals by the Hagers

July 26, 1969 [No. 18097, live], Las Vegas, NV: Buck Owens & His Buckaroos (Doyle Holly, Don Rich, Ira Allen; producer: Ken Nelson)

30108 73271 "Opening Announcement by ST-413
    Mike Hoyer"
30109 73272 "Las Vegas Lament" ST-413 Hilltop JS-6128
30110 73273 "Together Again" ST-413
30111 73274 "I'm a Natural Loser"* ST-413
30112 73275 "Catfish Capers"** ST-413
30113 73276 "Roving Gambler" ST-413 Hilltop JS-6128
30114 73277 "Cold Cold Wind"*** ST-413 Hilltop JS-6128
30115 73278 "Along Came Jones" ST-413 Hilltop JS-6128
30116 73279 "We're Gonna Let the Good ST-413 Hilltop JS-6128
    Times Roll"

*denotes vocal by Doyle Holly
**denotes vocal by Don Rich
***denotes vocal by Ira Allen

August 19, 1969 [No. 18129, 6:00–9:00 P.M.], Capitol Tower Recording Studio or Buck Owens Studios: Buck Owens & His Buckaroos (Buck Owens [vocals/guitar], Don Rich [lead acoustic guitar], Buddy Alan [rhythm guitar/background vocal], Jay Dee Maness [steel], Doyle Holly [bass], Jerry Wiggins [drums], Billy Armstrong. [string arrangement], Susan Raye [duet vocals], Jim and Jon Hager [background vocals]; producer: Ken Nelson)

302 72992 "Big in Vegas" 2646 6189 / *SWBB-562 SW-598* ST-830
303 72993 "The Wind Blows Every Day unissued
    in Oklahoma"
304 72994 "Love Is Strange" ST-448

December 17, 1969 [No. 18331, time unavailable], Buck Owens Studios: Doyle Holly & Buckaroos

B88 73748 "Cinderella"	*2756 / ST-440*
B89 73749 "I'll Be All Right Tomorrow"	*2756 / ST-440*
B90 73750 "Hurry Come Running Back to Me"	*ST-440*
B91 73751 "Ensenada"	*ST-440*

Overdub sessions January 7, 1970

December 18, 1969 [No. 18332, time unavailable], Buck Owens Studios: Don Rich & Buckaroos

B92 73752 "The Night They Drove Old Dixie Down"	*ST-440*
B93 73753 "Take Care of You for Me in Kansas City"	*ST-440*
B94 73754 "One More Time"	*ST-440*

Overdub sessions January 7, 1970

December 19, 1969 [No. 18333, time unavailable], Buck Owens Studios: Buckaroos

B95 73756 "Goin' Home to the Bayou"	*ST-440*
B96 73757 "Country Pickin'"	*2810 / ST-440 ST-670 SC-11091*
B97 73758 "Rompin' and Stompin'"	*2810 / ST-440*

Overdub sessions January 7, 1970

December 29, 1969 [No. 18350, time unavailable], Buck Owens Studios: Buck Owens & Susan Raye (producer: Ken Nelson)

305 73797 "We Were Made for Each Other"	ST-448 ST-11084
306 73798 "Everybody Needs Somebody"	2731 / ST-448
307 73799 "Togetherness"	2791 / ST-448 ST-11084

February 2, 1970 [18388, 7:00–10 P.M.], Capitol Tower Recording Studio: Buck Owens & His Buckaroos (Buck Owens [vocals], Don Rich [lead electric guitar], Doyle Holly [rhythm guitar], Al Bruno [rhythm guitar] Buddy Emmons [steel], Earl Poole Ball Jr. [piano/organ], Doyle Singer [bass], Jerry Wiggins [drums], Billy Sampson [harmonica], the Blossoms [background vocals], Susan Raye [duet vocals]; producer: Ken Nelson)

308 73924 "The Kansas City Song"	2783 / ST-476 ST-830
309 73925 "I'd Love to Be Your Man"	2783 / ST-476 ST-830
310 73926 "Together Again"*	ST-448 ST-11084
311 73927 "Fallin' for You"*	2791 / ST-448 ST-11084

* denotes duet with Susan Raye

February 3, 1970 [18389, time unavailable], Buck Owens Studios: Buck Owens & Susan Raye (producer: Ken Nelson)

312 73955 "Cryin' Time"	3368 / ST-448 ST-11084
313 73956 "Foolin' Around"	ST-448 *ST-670*

April 9, 1970 [No. 18584, time unavailable], Buck Owens Studios: Buck Owens & Susan Raye (Buck Owens [vocals]; Susan Raye [duet vocals], Don Rich [lead guitar]; Doyle Holly [rhythm guitar]; Jeff Haskell [Moog synthesizer]; Red Simpson [electric harpsichord], Doyle Singer [bass], Jerry Wiggins [drums]; producer: Ken Nelson)

314 74599 "The Great White Horse"	2871 / ST-558 ST-11084 *SMAS-11111*

April 1970 [No. 18586, time unavailable], Buck Owens Studios: Buck Owens & His Buckaroos

315 74603 "Black Texas Dirt"	3314 / ST-476
316 74604 "Bring Back My Peace of Mind"	ST-476

April 17, 1970 [No. 18680, live], Oslo, Norway: Buck Owens & His Buckaroos (includes Bakersfield Brass, Buddy Alan, the Hagers)

31601 74974	"Opening Announcement by Gunnar Eide"	7C-80578 (Norway)
31602 74975	"Murray Kash Introduces Don Rich & the Buckaroos"	7C-80578 (Norway)
31603 74976	"Up on Cripple Creek"	7C-80578 (Norway)
31604 74977	"Okie from Muskogee"	7C-80578 (Norway)
31605 74978	"The Night They Drove Old Dixie Down"	7C-80578 (Norway)
31606 74979	"Buckaroo"	7C-80578 (Norway)
31607 74980	"Murray Kash Introduces Buddy Alan"	7C-80578 (Norway)
31608 74981	"Freeborn Man"	7C-80578 (Norway)
31609 74982	"Big Mama's Medicine Show"	7C-80578 (Norway)
31610 74983	"Murray Kash Introduces the Hagers"	7C-80578 (Norway)
31611 74984	"I'm Jesse James"	7C-80578 (Norway)
31612 74985	"Six Days on the Road"	7C-80578 (Norway)
31613 74986	"Murray Kash Introduces Buck Owens"	7C-80578 (Norway)
31614 74987	"Act Naturally"/"Together Again"	7C-80578 (Norway)
31615 74991	"Gunnar Eide Wishes Buck Owens Welcome"	7C-80578 (Norway)
31616 74992	"Love's Gonna Live Here"/ "Cryin' Time"/"Sam's Place"	7C-80578 (Norway)
31617 74993	"I've Got a Tiger by the Tail"/ "Open Up Your Heart"	7C-80578 (Norway)
31618 74994	"Orange Blossom Special"	7C-80578 (Norway)
31619 74995	"Let the World Keep On a Turnin'"	7C-80578 (Norway)
31620 74996	"Tall Dark Stranger"	7C-80578 (Norway)
31621 74997	"Johnny B. Goode"	7C-80578 (Norway)

May 11, 1970 [No. 18544, time unavailable], Buck Owens Studios: Don Rich & Buckaroos

B98 74479	"Guitar Pickin' Man"	*2861 / ST-550*
B99 74480	"Dublin Waltz"	*ST-550 ST-643*
B100 74481	"I'd Love to Be Your Man"	*ST-550*
B101 74482	"Cajun Steel"	*ST-550*

May 12, 1970 [No. 18545, time unavailable], Buck Owens Studios: Buckaroos

B102 74483	"Fishin' Reel"	*ST-550*
B103 74484	"Potter's Field"	*ST-550*
B104 74485	"When I'm with You"	*ST-550*

May 13, 1970 [No. 18546, time unavailable], Buck Owens Studios: Buckaroos

B105 74487	"Pick-Nickin'"	*ST-550 SC-11091*
B106 74488	"Boot Hill"	*ST-550 SLB-6721*
B107 74489	"Up on Cripple Creek"	*2861 / ST-550*

May 14, 1970 [No. 18542, time unavailable], Buck Owens Studios: Buck Owens & Buckaroos

317 74471	"Long Way to London Town"	ST-476
318 74472	"Scandinavian Polka" (instrumental)	ST-476

319 74473 "Amsterdam"   ST-476

May 21, 1970 [No. 18585, time unavailable], Buck Owens Studios: Buck Owens & Buckaroos
320 74600 "New Orleans"   unissued
321 74601 "The Wind Blows Every Day   ST-476
  in Oklahoma"
322 74602 "Full Time Daddy"   3262 / ST-476

May 22, 1970 [No. 18576, time unavailable], Buck Owens Studios: Buck Owens & Susan Raye (producer: Ken Nelson)
323 74571 "Let the World Keep On Turnin'"   unissued
324 74572 "High as the Mountains"   ST-558
325 74573 "Today I Started Loving You Again"   ST-558
326 74574 "I've Never Had a Dream Come   ST-558
  True Before"

May 1970 [No. 18577, time unavailable], Buck Owens Studios: Buck Owens & Susan Raye (producer: Ken Nelson)
327 74575 "Tennessee Bird Walk"   ST-558
328 74576 "Then Maybe I Can Get Some Sleep"   ST-558

May 1970 [No. 18583, time unavailable], Buck Owens Studios: Buck Owens & Susan Raye (producer: Ken Nelson)
329 74595 "Your Tender Loving Care"   2871 / ST-558
330 74596 "Think of Me"   ST-558
331 74597 "I Thank Him for Sending Me You"   ST-558
332 74598 "I Don't Care (Just As Long As   ST-558
  You Love Me)"

August 14, 1970 [No. 18718, 1:30 –4:30 P.M.], Buck Owens Studios: Buck Owens (Buck Owens [vocals], Don Rich [guitar], Jim Shaw [piano/harmonica], Doyle Singer [bass], Jerry Wiggins [drums]; producer: Ken Nelson)
333 75329/75332 "I Wouldn't Live in New   2947 / ST-628
  York City"
334 75330 "No Milk and Honey in Baltimore"   unissued
335 75331 "Reno Lament"   unissued

September 3, 1970 [No. 18748, time unavailable], Buck Owens Studios: Buck Owens & His Buckaroos
336 75441 "Houston-Town"   ST-628
337 75442 "Santo Domingo"   ST-628
338 75443 "Down in New Orleans"   ST-628
339 75444 "The Wind Blows Every Day   ST-628
  in Chicago"

September 4, 1970 [No. 18750, time unavailable], Buck Owens Studios: Buck Owens & His Buckaroos
340 75450 "(It's a Long Way to) Londontown"   ST-628
341 75451 "The Kansas City Song"   ST-628
342 75452 "Big in Vegas"   ST-628
343 75453 "Reno Lament"   ST-628
344 75454 "No Milk and Honey in Baltimore"   2947 / ST-628

November 30, 1970 [No. 19565, live], John Ascuaga's Nugget Hotel Casino Resort, 1100 Nugget Ave., Reno, NV: Buck Owens & His Buckaroos (vocals: Kenni Huskey, Bakersfield Brass, Susan Raye) [mastered February 14, 1972]
34401 78083 "Introduction"   ST-11039
34402 78084 "Good Ole Mountain Dew"   ST-11039

34403 78085 "Nugget Lament"	ST-11039
34404 78086 "Rollin' in My Sweet Baby's Arms"	ST-11039
34405 78087 "Ruby (Are You Mad)"	ST-11039
34406 78088 "Help Me Make It Through the Night"*	ST-11039
34407 78089 "Lookin' Out My Back Door"	ST-11039
34408 78090 "Fishin' on the Mississippi"	ST-11039
34409 78091 "Introduction"	ST-11039
34410 78092 "Sally Was a Good Old Girl"**	ST-11039
34411 78093 "Flint Hill Special"**	ST-11039
34412 78094 "Pitty Pitty Patter"***	ST-11039
34413 78095 "L.A. International Airport"***	ST-11039
34414 78096 "We're Gonna Get Together"***	ST-11039
34415 78097 "I'll Still Be Waiting for You"	ST-11039
34416 78098 "Johnny B. Goode"	ST-11039

*denotes vocal by Kenni Huskey
**denotes instrumental by Bakersfield Brass
***denotes vocal by Susan Raye

December 1970 [19266, time unavailable], Buck Owens Studios: Buck Owens (Buck Owens [vocals], Don Rich [gut-string guitar/harmony vocals] Jim Shaw [piano/organ], Doyle Singer [bass/harmony vocals], Jerry Wiggins [drums]) [purchased masters, registered February 1, 1971]

345 76007 "Bridge over Troubled Water"	3023 / ST-685 ST-830
346 76008 "I Am a Rock"	ST-685
347 76009 "Homeward Bound"	ST-685
348 76010 "The Devil Made Me Do That"	ST-685
349 76011 "Everything Reminds Me You're Gone"	ST-685
350 76012 "Try and Catch the Wind"	ST-685
351 76013 "San Francisco Town"	ST-685
352 76014 "Within My Loving Arms"	ST-685
353 76015 "(I'm Going) Home"	3023 / ST-685 ST-830
354 76016 "Love Minus Zero/No Limit"	ST-685

March 1, 1971 [No. 19373], Buck Owens Studios: Buckaroos [purchased masters]

B108 76316 "Ring of Fire"	ST-767
B109 76317 "Last Date"	ST-767
B110 76318 "El Paso"	ST-767
B111 76319 "King of the Road"	ST-767
B112 76320 "Orange Blossom Special"	ST-767
B113 76321 "Tall Dark Stranger"	ST-767
B114 76322 "Detroit City"	ST-767
B115 76323 "Gentle on My Mind"	ST-767
B116 76324 "It's Such a Pretty World Today"	ST-767
B117 76325 "Okie from Muskogee"	ST-767

March 23, 1971 [No. 19420, time unavailable], Buck Owens Studios: Buck Owens & His Buckaroos (Buck Owens [vocals], Don Rich [rhythm guitar/fiddle/vocals], Ronnie Jackson [banjo], Doyle Singer [bass/harmony vocals], Jerry Wiggins [drums/percussion], Jim Shaw [piano/organ])

355 76502 "Ruby (Are You Mad)"	3096 6221 / ST-795 ST-830
356 76503 "Heartbreak Mountain"	3096 / ST-795 ST-830
357 76504/76509 "Uncle Pen"	ST-795

May 4, 1971 [No. 19493, time unavailable], Buck Owens Studios: Buck Owens & His Buckaroos (Buck Owens [vocals], Don Rich [rhythm guitar/fiddle/harmony vocals], Ronnie Jackson [banjo], Doyle Singer [bass/harmony vocals], Jerry Wiggins [drums/percussion], Jim
Shaw [piano/organ])

358 76743 "Corn Liquor"	3164 / ST-795	
359 76744 "Rollin' in My Sweet Baby's Arms"	3164 / ST-795 *SMAS-11111* ST-11273	
360 76745 "I Know You're Married but I Love You Still"	ST-795	

May 5, 1971 [No. 19494, time unavailable], Buck Owens Studios: Buck Owens & His Buckaroos (Buck Owens [vocals/guitar], Don Rich [guitar/fiddle/vocals], Ronnie Jackson [banjo],
Doyle Singer [bass/vocals], Jerry Wiggins [drums/percussion], Jim Shaw [piano/organ])

361 76746 "Ashes of Love"	ST-795
362 76747 "Ole Slew Foot"	ST-795
363 76748 "Rocky Top"	ST-795
364 76749 "Salty Dog Blues"	ST-795

c. June 1971 [Session number, time unavailable], Buck Owens Studios: Buck Owens &
Susan Raye [purchased masters, registered August 20]

365 77188 "One of Everything You Got"	3225 / ST-837 *ST-11226*
366 77189 "Home on Christmas Day"	ST-837
367 77190 "All I Want for Christmas Is My Daddy"	ST-837
368 77191 "A Very Merry Christmas"	ST-837
369 77192 "It's Not What You Give"	ST-837
370 77193 "Good Old Fashioned Country Christmas"	ST-837
371 77194 "Christmas Ain't Christmas Dear Without You"	ST-837
372 77195 "Santa Looked a Lot Like Daddy"	ST-837 *ST-11226*
373 77196 "Santa's Gonna Come in a Stagecoach"	3225 / ST-837 *ST-11226*
374 77197 "Tomorrow Is a Christmas Day"	ST-837

August 13, 1971 [No. 19667, time unavailable], Buck Owens Studios: Buck Owens & Buddy
Alan [purchased masters, registered September 23]

375 77435 "Too Old to Cut the Mustard"	3215 / ST-874
376 77436 "Wham Bam"	3215 / ST-874

November 1, 1971 [No. 19742, time unavailable], Buck Owens Studios: Buck Owens &
Buddy Alan [purchased masters, logged November 16]

377 77692 "Pfft You Were Gone"	ST-874
378 77693 "You're a Real Good Friend"	ST-874
379 77694 "Tobacco White Lightning and Women Blues No. 2"	ST-874
380 77695 "I Won't Go Huntin' with You Jake (but I'll Go Chasin' Wimin)"	ST-874
381 77696 "Cigareets, Whuskey and Wild, Wild Women"	ST-874
382 77697 "Beautiful Morning Glory"	ST-874

December 23, 1971 [No. 19792, 9:30–11:30 A.M.], Buck Owens Studios: Buck Owens & His
Buckaroos [Buck Owens (vocals), Don Rich (acoustic guitar/harmony vocals), Jerry Brightman [steel], Jim Shaw [piano], Doyle Singer [bass/harmony vocals], Jerry Wiggins [drums])

383 77872 "I'll Still Be Waiting for You"	3262 / ST-11273

December 29, 1971 [No. 19805, time unavailable], Buck Owens Studios: Buckaroos

B118 77899	"Daddy Frank (The Guitar Man)"	*ST-860*
B119 77900	"Today I Started Loving You Again"	*ST-860*
B120 77901	"The Fightin' Side of Me"	*ST-860*
B121 77902	"Silver Wings"	*ST-860*
B122 77903	"Okie from Muskogee"	*ST-860*
B123 77904	"The Legend of Bonnie and Clyde"	*ST-860*
B124 77905	"Hungry Eyes"	*ST-860*
B125 77906	"Swinging Doors"	*ST-860*
B126 77907	"I Take a Lot of Pride in What I Am"	*ST-860*
B127 77908	"Mama Tried"	*ST-860*

March 7, 1972 [No. 19905, 1:00–4:00 P.M.], Buck Owens Studios: Buck Owens & His Buckaroos (Buck Owens (vocals), Don Rich (lead guitar/fiddle), Ronnie Jackson [rhythm guitar], Jerry Brightman [steel], Jim Shaw [Farfisa organ], Doyle Singer [bass/harmony vocals], Jerry Wiggins [drums])

384 78259 "Made in Japan" 3314 6221 / *ST-11111* ST-11136 ST-11273

April 26, 1972 [No. 11987, 09:00–12:00], Buck Owens Studios: Buck Owens & His Buckaroos [Buck Owens (vocals), Don Rich (lead guitar), Buddy Alan [rhythm guitar], Jerry Brightman [steel], Jim Shaw [piano], Doyle Singer [bass], Jerry Wiggins [drums])

385 78619 "Arms Full of Empty" 3688 / ST-11136 ST-11222 *ST-11238*
386 78620 "Ain't It Amazing, Gracie" 3563 / ST-11180 *ST-11238* ST-11273

April 30, 1972 [No. 11986, time unavailable], Buck Owens Studios: Buck Owens & Susan Raye

387 78618 "Looking Back to See" 3368 / ST-11084

June 20, 1972 [No. 20046, 10:00 A.M.–12:30 P.M.], Buck Owens Studios: Buck Owens & His Buckaroos [Buck Owens (vocals), Don Rich (lead guitar/harmony vocals), Buddy Alan [rhythm guitar], Jerry Brightman [steel], Jim Shaw [piano], Doyle Singer [bass], Jerry Wiggins [drums])

388 78804 "You Ain't Gonna Have Ol' Buck 3429 / ST-11105 ST-11136
to Kick Around No More"

c. July 1972 [No. 20069, time unavailable], Buck Owens Studios: Buck Owens & His Buckaroos [purchased masters, registered July 24]

389 78880 "I Love You So Much It Hurts" 3429 / ST-11136

Early October 1972 [No. 20162, time unavailable], Buck Owens Studios: Buck Owens [purchased masters, registered October 10]

390 79210	"There Goes My Love"	ST-11136
391 79211	"A Whole Lot of Somethin'"	ST-11136
392 79212	"Sweethearts in Heaven"	ST-11136
393 79213	"Get Out of Town Before Sundown"	ST-11136
394 79214	"Something's Wrong"	ST-11136

c. Late October 1972 [No. 20183, time unavailable], Buck Owens Studios: Buck Owens [purchased masters, registered November 3]

395 79293 "In the Palm of Your Hand" 3504 / ST-11136

November 6, 1972 [No. 20280, 1:00–4:00 P.M.], Buck Owens Studios: Buck Owens & His Buckaroos [Buck Owens (vocals), Don Rich (lead National guitar/harmony vocals), Ronnie Jackson [rhythm guitar], Jerry Brightman [steel], Jim Shaw [keyboards], Doyle Singer [bass], Jerry Wiggins [drums]) [purchased masters, registered February 9]

396 79712 "The Good Old Days (Are 3563 / ST-11180 ST-11273
Here Again) "

397 79713 "I Know That You Know   ST-11180
(That I Love You)"
398 79714 "When You Get Back from   ST-11180
Nashville"
399 79715 "When You Get to Heaven   ST-11180
(I'll Be There)"
400 79716 "Long Hot Summer"   ST-11180
401 79717 "Streets of Bakersfield"   ST-11180
402 79718 "She's Had All the Dreamin' She   ST-11180
Can Stand"
403 79719 "Your Monkey Won't Be   ST-11180
Home Tonight"

c. February 1973 [No. 20310, time unavailable], Buck Owens Studios: Buck Owens & Susan Raye [purchased masters, registered March 19]
404 79862 "The Good Old Days   3601 / ST-11204
(Are Here Again) "

March 1973 [No. 20331, time unavailable], Buck Owens Studios: Buck Owens & His Buckaroos [purchased masters, registered March 26]
405 79905 "Old Faithful"   ST-11180

March 1973 [No. 20337, time unavailable], Buck Owens Studios: Buck Owens & Susan Raye [purchased masters, registered March 22]
406 79937 "Take a Taste of My Wine"   ST-11204
407 79938 "I Think I'm Going to Like   ST-11204
Loving You"
408 79939 "Sweethearts in Heaven"   4100 / ST-11204
409 79940 "I've Got a Happy Heart"   ST-11204
410 79941 "Arms Full of Empty"   ST-11204 ST-11222 *ST-11238*
411 79942 "All the Dreamin' They Can Stand"   ST-11204
412 79943 "Honey . . . Let's Fall in Love"   ST-11204
413 79944 "When You Get to Heaven   3601 / ST-11204
(I'll Be There)"
414 79945 "Love Makes the World Go Round"   ST-11204

Early April 1973 [No. 20347, time unavailable], Buck Owens Studios: Buck Owens [purchased masters, registered April 4]
415 79967 "Love Makes the World Go Round"   ST-11222

Late June 1973 [No. 20475, time unavailable], Buck Owens Studios: Buck Owens & His Buckaroos [purchased masters, registered July 5]
416 90396 "Loving You"   ST-11222
417 90397 "I Won't Be Needing You"   ST-11222
418 90398 "Songwriter's Lament"   3688 / ST-11222
419 90399 "That Loving Feeling"   3769 / ST-11222
420 90400 "Someday I'm Gonna Go to Mexico"   ST-11222
421 90401 "Colors I'm Gonna Paint the Town"   ST-11222
422 90402 "It Never Will Be Over Me"   ST-11222
423 90403 "Happy Hour"   ST-11222

c. Late July 1973 [No. 20507, time unavailable], Buck Owens Studios: Buck Owens & His Buckaroos (producer: Bob Morris) [purchased masters, registered August 8]
424 90523 "Your Daddy Was a Preacher   ST-11390
(and Your Mama Was a Dancing Girl)"
425 90524 "Hello Trouble"   ST-11390

October 8, 1973 [No. 20576, 9:00 A.M.–12:00 P.M.], Buck Owens Studios: Buck Owens & His Buckaroos [Buck Owens (vocals), Don Rich (lead guitar), Buddy Alan [rhythm guitar], Jerry Brightman [steel], Jim Shaw [piano], Doyle Singer [bass], Jerry Wiggins [drums])
426 90763 "Big Game Hunter"   3769 / ST-11273

October 30, 1973 [No. 20780, 8:00–11:00 A.M.], Buck Owens Studios: Buck Owens & His Buckaroos (Buck Owens [vocals], Don Rich [lead guitar], Ronnie Jackson [rhythm guitar], Jerry Brightman [steel], Jim Shaw [keyboards/laughs], Doyle Singer [bass], Jerry Wiggins [drums], Sylvia Cariker [screams]) [purchased masters, registered May 23, 1974]
427 91342 "(It's a) Monster's Holiday"   3907 / ST-11332

November 1973 [Session number, time unavailable], Buck Owens Studios: Buck Owens & His Buckaroos [purchased masters, registered November 29]
428 90925 "I Wish I Was a Butterfly"   ST-11390
429 90926 "John Law"   unissued
430 90927 "Stony Mountain West Virginia"   3841 / ST-11332
431 90928 "Let the Fun Begin"   3976 / ST-11390
432 90929 "Holdin' On"   ST-11390
433 90930 "Great Expectations"   3907
434 90931 "All Around Cowboy of 1964"   ST-11390

c. Early January 1974[Session number, time unavailable], Buck Owens Studios: Buck Owens (producers: Buck Owens & Ken Nelson)[purchased masters, logged January 10, 1974]
435 91026 "Meanwhile Back at the Ranch"   4181 / ST-11332

0. 20691, 9:00 A.M.–12:00 P.M.], Buck Owens Studios: Buck Owens & Owens [vocals], Don Rich [lead guitar/harmony vocals], Ronnie Jack- Jerry Brightman [Dobro], Jim Shaw [piano, harmony vocals], Doyle ry vocals], Jerry Wiggins [drums])
over of the Music   3841 / ST-11332

4 [No. 20750, live], Tokyo, Japan: Buck Owens & Cast (vocals: Buck uddy Alan, Susan Raye) [purchased masters, registered May 1]
ome"   *STBB-23281*(Japan)
43602 91267 "Big in Vegas"   *STBB-23281*(Japan)
43603 91268 "Roll Over Beethoven"   *STBB-23281*(Japan)
43604 91269 "Rollin' in My Sweet   *STBB-23281*(Japan)
  Baby's Arms"
43605 91270 "Medley (Vobo): Act Naturally"/   *STBB-23281*(Japan)
  "Together Again"/"Love's Gonna Live Here"/
  "Waitin' in Your Welfare Line"/"Sam's Place"/
  "Cryin' Time"/"I've Got a Tiger by the Tail"
43606 91271 "Green Onions"   *STBB-23281*(Japan)
43607 91272 "Duelin' Banjos"   *STBB-23281*(Japan)
43608 91273 "Orange Blossom Special"   *STBB-23281*(Japan)
43609 91274 "Cajun Fiddle"*   *STBB-23281*(Japan)
43610 91275 "On the Cover of the   *STBB-23281*(Japan)
  Music City News"
43611 91277 "Georgia Pineywoods"   *STBB-23281*(Japan)
43612 91278 "Ramblin' Man"**   *STBB-23281*(Japan)
43613 91279 "I Never Had It So Good"   *STBB-23281*(Japan)
43614 91280 "Key's in the Mailbox"   *STBB-23281*(Japan)
43615 91281 "Lonely Street"   *STBB-23281*(Japan)
43616 91282 "Stop the World"***   *STBB-23281*(Japan)
43617 91283 "L.A. International Airport"***   *STBB-23281*(Japan)

43618 91284 "Jackson"***	*STBB-23281*(Japan)
43619 91285 "You're Gonna Love Yourself in the Morning"	*STBB-23281*(Japan)
43620 91286 "Johnny B. Goode"	*STBB-23281*(Japan)
43621 91287 "Good Ole Mountain Dew"	*STBB-23281*(Japan)
43622 91288 "Ruby (Are You Mad)"	*STBB-23281*(Japan)

* denotes vocal by Don Rich
** denotes vocal by Buddy Alan
*** denotes vocal by Susan Raye

c. Late February 1974 [No. 20784, live], Christchurch Town Hall, Christchurch, New Zealand: Buck Owens & Susan Raye [purchased masters, registered March 1]

43623 91360 "Y'all Come"	ST-23261 (New Zealand)
43624 91361 "Your Daddy Was a Preacher"	ST-23261 (New Zealand)
43625 91362 "Big in Vegas"	ST-23261 (New Zealand)
43626 91363 Medley: "Waiting in Your Welfare Line"/"Act Naturally"/"Together Again"/"Love's Gonna Live Here"/"Sam's Place"/"Cryin' Time"/"I've Got a Tiger by the Tail"	ST-23261 (New Zealand)
43627 91364 "Dueling Banjos"	ST-23261 (New Zealand)
43628 91365 Cajun Medley: "Diggy Liggy Lo"/"Louisiana Man"	ST-23261 (New Zealand)
43629 91366 "L.A. International Airport"	ST-23261 (New Zealand)
43630 91367 "Whatcha Gonna Do with a Dog Like That"	ST-23261 (New Zealand)
43631 91368 "Plastic Train, Paper Planes"	ST-23261 (New Zealand)
43632 91369 "Stop the World and Let Me Off"	ST-23261 (New Zealand)
43633 91370 "Jackson"	ST-23261 (New Zealand)
43634 91371 "Somewhere Between You and Me"	ST-23261 (New Zealand)
43635 91372 "Looking Back to See"	ST-23261 (New Zealand)
43636 91373 "Johnny B. Goode"	ST-23261 (New Zealand)

Early March 1974 [No. 20831, live], Sydney Opera House, Sydney, Australia: Buck Owens & His Buckaroos [purchased masters]

43637 91504 "Y'all Come"	ST-23372 (Australia)
43638 91505 "Big in Vegas"	ST-23372 (Australia)
43639 91506 "Roll Over Beethoven"	ST-23372 (Australia)
43640 91507 "Rollin' in My Sweet Baby's Arms"	ST-23372 (Australia)
43641 91508 "Made in Japan"	ST-23372 (Australia)
43642 91509 "Dueling Banjos"	ST-23372 (Australia)
43643 91510 "Dust on Mother's Bible"	ST-23372 (Australia)
43644 91511 "Move It on Over"	ST-23372 (Australia)
43645 91512 "Key's in the Mailbox"	ST-23372 (Australia)
43646 91513 "L.A. International Airport"	ST-23372 (Australia)
43647 91514 "Plastic Trains,Paper Planes"	ST-23372 (Australia)
43648 91515 "Jackson"	ST-23372 (Australia)
43649 91516 "Mountain Dew"	ST-23372 (Australia)

July 1974 [No. 20832, time unavailable], Buck Owens Studios: Buck Owens [purchased masters, registered August 2]

437 90930 [remake] "Great Expectations"	3976 / ST-11332
438 91517 "Amazing Love"	ST-11332
439 91518 "I Love"	ST-11332

440 91519 "You're Gonna Love Yourself   ST-11332
    in the Morning"
441 91520 "Kiss an Angel Good Mornin'"   ST-11332
442 91521 "Pass Me By (If You're Only   ST-11332
    Passing Through)"

November 20, 1974 [No. 20939, time unavailable], Buck Owens Studios: Buck Owens & His Buckaroos [purchased masters]

443 91877 "41st Street Lonely Heart's Club"   4043 / ST-11390
444 91878 "Weekend Daddy"   4043 / ST-11390

February 22, 1975 [No. 20956, time unavailable], Buck Owens Studios: Buck Owens & His Buckaroos

445 91921 "I Finally Gave Her Enough   *ST-11392*
    Rope to Hang"
446 91922 "Run Him to the Round   4138 / *ST-11392*
    House Nellie"

March 14, 1975 [Session number, time unavailable], Buck Owens Studios: Buck Owens & His Buckaroos[purchased masters]

447 92593 "Drifting Away"   *E-ST-11471* (UK)

March 31, 1975 [Session number, time unavailable], Buck Owens Studios: Buck Owens & His Buckaroos [purchased masters]

448 92592 "He Ain't Been Out Bowling with   *E-ST-11471* (UK)
    the Boys"

April 11, 1975 [No. 21026, time unavailable], Buck Owens Studios: Buck Owens & Susan Raye

449 92184 "Love Is Strange"*   4100 / ST-11471
450 92596 "A Different Kind of Sad"   *E-ST-11471* (UK)

denotes duet

April 17, 1975 [Session number, time unavailable], Buck Owens Studios: Buck Owens & His Buckaroos [purchased masters]

451 92591 "You Don't Find Work in Pool   *E-ST-11471* (UK)
    Rooms (and Love Don't Make the Bars)"
452 92598 "How's Everything"   *E-ST-11471* (UK)

June 20, 1975 [Session number, time unavailable], Buck Owens Studios: Buck Owens & His Buckaroos [purchased masters]

453 92590 "California Okie"   *E-ST-11471* (UK)

c. June 1975 [No. 21082, time unavailable], Buck Owens Studios: Buck Owens & His Buckaroos [purchased masters, registered July 30]

454 92388 "Battle of New Orleans"   4138 / ST-11471

September 29, 1975 [Session number, time unavailable], Buck Owens Studios: Buck Owens & His Buckaroos [purchased masters]

455 92594 "Country Singer's Prayer"   4181 / ST-11471 *E-ST-11471* (UK)
456 92595 "John Law"   *E-ST-11471* (UK)

c. March 1976 [Session number, time unavailable], Nashville, TN: Buck Owens (producer: Norro Wilson)

457 "Child Support"   Warner 8255 / BS-2952
458 "We're Gonna Build a Fire"   BS-2952
459 "It's Been a Long, Long Time"   Warner 8395 / BS-2952
460 "Lady Madonna"   BS-2952
461 "Hollywood Waltz"   Warner 8223 / BS-2952
462 "Rain on Your Parade"   Warner 8223 8395 / BS-2952

463 "John Law"	BS-2952
464 "Ozark Mountain Lullaby"	BS-2952
465 "Love Don't Make the Bars"	Warner 49651 / BS-2952
466 "California Okie"	Warner 8255 / BS-2952

c. October 1976 [Session number, time unavailable], Buck Owens Studios: Buck Owens (producer: Norro Wilson)

467 UCA6643 "World Famous Holiday Inn"	Warner 8316 / BS-3087
468 UCA6644 "He Don't Deserve You Anymore"	Warner 8316 / BS-3087
469 UCA6645 "Texas Tornado"	Warner 8486 / BS-3087
470 "Cinderella"	BS-3087
471 "Our Old Mansion"	Warner 8433 / BS-3087
472 "Let Me Touch You"	BS-3087
473 "Feel Good Again"	BS-3087
474 "Different Kind of Sad"	BS-3087
475 "How Come My Dog Don't Bark"	Warner 8433 / BS-3087

June 8, 1977 [Session number, time unavailable], Columbia Recording Studio: Buck Owens (producer: Norro Wilson)

| 476 VTN0867 "Let the Good Times Roll" | Warner 8486 / BS-3087 |
| 477 "You're Gonna Need No Doctor" | unissued |

April 5, 1978 [Session number, time unavailable], Columbia Recording Studio: Buck Owens (producer: Norro Wilson)

478 WTN0993 "Nights Are Forever Without You"	Warner 8614
479 "When I Need You"	Warner 8614
480 "I Just Want to See You Again"	unissued

September 26, 1978 [Session number, time unavailable], Columbia Recording Studio: Buck Owens (producer: Norro Wilson)

481 WTN1067 "Do You Wanna Make Love"	Warner 8701
482 WTN1068 "Without You"	Warner 49651
483 "Seasons of My Heart"	Warner 8701
484 "Massachusetts"	unissued

March 21, 1979 [Session number, time unavailable], Enactron Truck, Los Angeles, CA: Buck Owens & Emmylou Harris (Buck Owens [vocals/guitar], Emmylou Harris [harmony vocals/guitar], Herb Pedersen [guitar], Frank Reckard [guitar], Rick Cunha [guitar], Hank DeVito [steel], Glen D. Hardin [piano], Tony Brown [piano], Emory Gordy [bass], John Ware [drums], Norro Wilson [harmony vocals]; producer: Norro Wilson)

| 485 XCA8701 "Play Together Again Again"* | Warner 8830 |
| 486 XCA8703 "Moonlights and Magnolias" | Warner 49278 |

denotes duet

c. April 1979 [Session number, time unavailable], Columbia Recording Studio: Buck Owens (producer: Norro Wilson)

| 487 XTN1185? "Hangin' In and Hangin' On" | Warner 49046 |
| 488 "Sweet Molly Brown's" | Warner 49046 |

May 10, 1979 [Session number, time unavailable], Enactron Truck, Los Angeles, CA: Buck Owens (producer: Norro Wilson)

489 XCA8825 "Love Is a Warm Cowboy"	Warner 49200
490 "I Don't Want to Live in San Francisco"	Warner 49200
491 "Keep Me from Blowing Again"	unissued

c. September 1979 [Session number, time unavailable], Columbia Recording Studio: Buck Owens (producer: Norro Wilson)

492 XTN1240 "Let Jesse Rob the Train" Warner 49118
493 "The Victim of Life's Circumstances" Warner 49118

c. May 1980 [Session number, time unavailable], unknown: Buck Owens (producer: Norro Wilson)

494 "Nickels and Dimes" Warner 49278

October 19, 1982 [Session number, time unavailable], Soundshop Studio, 1307 Division St., Nashville, TN: Buck Owens (producer: Buddy Killen)

495 "I've Been Loving You Too Long" unissued
496 "There Must Be Something About Me unissued
 That She Loves"

April 4, 1988 [Session number, time unavailable], Capitol Tower Recording Studio: Dwight Yoakam & Buck Owens (Buck Owens [vocals], Dwight Yoakam [vocals/guitar], Pete Anderson [lead guitar], Don Reed [fiddle], Flaco Jimenez [accordion], Skip Edwards [piano], Taras Prodaniuk [bass], Jeff Donavan [drums]; producer: Pete Anderson)

497 GCA4260 "Streets of Bakersfield" Reprise 27964 / 25749-2

July 2, 1988 [Session number, time unavailable], Maximus Recording Studio, Fresno, CA: Buck Owens (producers: Jerry Crutchfield & Jim Shaw)

498 83159 "Take Me Back Again" C2-92893

August 3, 1988, [10:00 A.M.–1:00 P.M.] Capitol Tower Recording Studio: Buck Owens & His Buckaroos (Buck Owens [vocals], Terry Christofferson [lead guitar/steel], Doyle Singer [rhythm guitar], John Herrell [rhythm guitar], Jim Shaw [piano/harmony vocals], Dusty Wakeman [bass/vocals], Jim McCarty [drums], Charlie Paakkari [vocals]; producer: Jim Shaw)

499 82926 "Hot Dog" 44248 / C1-91132
500 82927 "Put Another Quarter in 44356 / C1-91132
 the Jukebox"
501 82928 "Don't Let Her Know" 44356 / C1-91132

August 3, 1988 [Session number, time unavailable], Nashville, TN: Buck Owens (producer: Jim Shaw)

502 82932 A-11 44295 / C1-91132
503 82933 "Second Fiddle" 44248 / C1-91132
504 82934 "Under Your Spell Again" C1-91132
505 82935 "Sweethearts in Heaven" 44295 / C1-91132

August 3, 1988, Nashville, TN: Buck Owens (producer: Jim Shaw)

506 82937 "Key's in the Mailbox" 44409 / C1-91132
507 82938 "Memphis" C1-91132
508 82939 unknown title unissued
509 82940 "Summertime Blues" C1-91132

August 4, 1988 [Session number, time unavailable], Nightingale Studio, 1815 Division St., Suite 115, Nashville, TN: Buck Owens (producers: Jerry Crutchfield & Jim Shaw)

510 83152 "Out There Chasing Rainbows" 44465 / C2-92893

October 23, 1988 [Session number unavailable, live] Austin City Limits, Austin, TX: Buck Owens (Buck Owens [vocals], Terry Christofferson [guitar/steel], Doyle Singer [bass], Jim McCarty [drums], Jim Shaw [keyboards], Dwight Yoakam [guest vocal])

51001 "Act Naturally" NW-6123
51002 "Together Again" NW-6123

51003 "Love's Gonna Live Here Again"	NW-6123	
51004 "Cryin' Time"	NW-6123	
51005 "I've Got a Tiger by the Tail"	NW-6123	
51006 "A-11"	NW-6123	
51007 "Hot Dog"	NW-6123	
51008 "Put a Quarter in the Jukebox"	NW-6123	
51009 "Memphis"	NW-6123	
51010 "Under Your Spell Again"*	NW-6123	
51011 "Johnny B. Goode"	NW-6123	

denotes duet with Dwight Yoakam

March 27, 1989 [10:00 A.M.–1:00 P.M.], EMI Recording Studio, 3 Abbey Road, St John's Wood, London, NW8 9AY, UK: Ringo Starr & Buck Owens (Buck Owens [vocals], Ringo Starr [vocals], Reggie Young [lead guitar], Terry Christofferson [rhythm guitar], Jim Shaw [piano], Doyle Singer [bass], Jim McCarty [drums]; producers: Jerry Crutchfield & Jim Shaw)

511 83096 "Act Naturally"	44409 / C2-92893

July 5, 1989 [Session number, time unavailable], Nightingale Studio: Buck Owens (producers: Jerry Crutchfield & Jim Shaw)

512 83150 "Tijuana Lady"	44504 / C2-92893
513 83155 "Playboy"	C2-92893
514 83156 "Rock Hard Love"	C2-92893

July 6, 1989 [Session number, time unavailable], Nightingale Studio: Buck Owens (producers: Jerry Crutchfield & Jim Shaw)

515 83153 "I Was There"	C2-92893
516 83154 unknown title	unissued

July 7, 1989 [Session number, time unavailable], Nightingale Studio: Buck Owens (producers: Jerry Crutchfield & Jim Shaw)

517 83151 "Gonna Have Love"	44465 / C2-92893
518 83157 "Cryin' Time"*	C2-92893
519 83158 "Brooklyn Bridge"	44504 / C2-92893

denotes duet with Emmylou Harris

January 1991 (finished January 7, 1991) [Session number, time unavailable], Nashville, TN: Buck Owens (producers: Jimmy Bowen & Buck Owens)

520 84329 "You and Me and Love"	CDP-7-95340
521 84330 "Kickin' In"	79396 / CDP-7-95340
522 84331 "On the Wings of Love"	CDP-7-95340
523 84332 "Did Anybody Get the License Number"	CDP-7-95340
524 84333 "Twice the Speed of Love"	CDP-7-95340
525 84334 "Forever Yours"	79896 / CDP-7-95340
526 84335 unknown title	release status unknown
527 84336 "They'd Have to Carry Me Away"	CDP-7-95340
528 84337 "We're Gonna Build a Fire"	CDP-7-95340
529 84338 "Never Never Land"	CDP-7-95340
530 84339 "All the Tea in China"	CDP-7-95340

August 12, 1995 [Session number unavailable, live], Continental Club: Buck Owens

53001 "Love's Gonna Live Here"	release status unknown

c. late 2000, Castle Recording Studio, 1393 Old Hillsboro Road, Franklin, TN: Brad Paisley (Brad Paisley [vocal/acoustic guitar/electric guitar/six-string tic-tac], Gary Hooker [electric guitar], Mike Johnson [steel], Bernie Herms [keyboards/Hammond B-3 organ], Glen Duncan [fiddle], Jim Heffernan [Dobro], Ron Block [banjo], Kevin "Swine" Grantt [upright bass], Eddie Bayers [drums], Mitch McMitchen [percussion], Wes Hightower [background vocals], Kenny Lewis [background vocals]; guest vocals by the Kung Pao Buckaroos: Buck Owens, Bill Anderson, George Jones; producer Frank Rogers)

000 "Too Country"*   Arista 07863-67008-2

denotes vocal by the Kung Pao Buckaroos

Recordings

Below is a partial listing of the official and unofficial recorded output of Buck Owens. Not all samplers, compilations, and reissued works, especially foreign releases, are listed. Singles and albums by Buckaroos are also not included. Where appropriate, the peak *Billboard* Country Singles or *Billboard* Country Albums position achieved by a recording is denoted by # before its title.

Singles
No./Title/Released

Pep (1956–1957)
105 "Down on the Corner of Love"/"It Don't Show on Me," 1956
106 "The House down the Block"/"Right After the Dance," 1956
107 "Hot Dog"/"Rhythm and Booze" (as Corky Jones), September 1956
109 "There Goes My Love"/"Sweethearts in Heaven," January 1957
45-6418 "Hot Dog"/"Sweethearts in Heaven," c. 1961 (reissue, released on New Star)
45-571 "There Goes My Love"/"It Don't Show on Me," December 1961 (reissue, released on Starday)
588 "Down on the Corner of Love"/"Right After the Dance," April 1962 (reissue, released on Starday)
7010 "Down on the Corner of Love"/"Sweethearts in Heaven," 1964 (reissue, released on Starday)

Chesterfield (1957)
44223 "Country Girl (Leavin' Dirty Tracks)"/"Honeysuckle," 1957

Capitol (1957–1976)
F3824 "Come Back"/"I Know What It Means," October 21, 1957
F3957 "Sweet Thing"/"I Only Know That I Love You," April 7, 1958
F4090 "I'll Take a Chance on Loving You"/"Walk the Floor," November 10, 1958
F4172 #24 "Second Fiddle"/"My Everlasting Love," March 23, 1959
F4245 #4 "Under Your Spell Again"/"Tired of Livin'," July 13, 1959
4337 #3 "Above and Beyond"/"Till These Dreams Come True," February 1, 1960
4412 #2 "Excuse Me (I Think I've Got a Heartache)"/#25 "I've Got a Right to Know," August 1, 1960
4496 #2 "Foolin' Around"/#27 "High as the Mountains," January 2, 1961
4550 #4 "Loose Talk"/#8 "Mental Cruelty" (w. Rose Maddox), April 10, 1961
4602 #2 "Under the Influence of Love"/"Bad Bad Dream," July 24, 1961
4679 #11 "Nobody's Fool but Yours"/"Mirror, Mirror on the Wall," January 2, 1962
4765 #11 "Save the Last Dance for Me"/"King of Fools," May 21, 1962
4826 #8 "Kickin' Our Hearts Around"/#17 "I Can't Stop (My Lovin' You)," August 20, 1962
4872 #10 "You're for Me"/#24 "The House down the Block," November 5, 1962
4937 #1 "Act Naturally"/"Over and Over Again," March 11, 1963
4992 #15 "We're the Talk of Town"/#19 "Sweethearts in Heaven" (w. Rose Maddox), June 24, 1963

5025 #1 "Love's Gonna Live Here"/"Getting Used to Losing You," August 19, 1963

5136 #1 "My Heart Skips a Beat"/#1 "Together Again," February 24, 1964

5240 #1 "I Don't Care (Just as Long as You Love Me)"/#33 "Don't Let Her Know," August 3, 1964

5336 #1 "I've Got a Tiger by the Tail"/"Cryin' Time," December 28, 1964

5410 #1 "Before You Go"/"(I Want) No One but You," April 19, 1965

5465 #1 "Only You (Can Break My Heart)"/#10 "Gonna Have Love," July 5, 1965

6074 "My Heart Skips a Beat"/"Together Again," 1965 (Star Line reissue)

6075 "Above and Beyond"/"You're for Me," 1965 (Star Line reissue)

5517 #1 "Buckaroo"/#24 "If You Want a Love," October 11, 1965

5537 "Santa Looked a Lot Like Daddy"/"All I Want for Christmas, Dear, Is You," November 8, 1965

5566 #1 "Waitin' in Your Welfare Line"/#43 "In the Palm of Your Hand," January 3, 1966

5647 #1 "Think of Me"/"Heart of Glass," May 2, 1966

5705 #1 "Open Up Your Heart"/"No More Me and You," August 15, 1966

6093 "Act Naturally"/"Over and Over Again," 1966 (Star Line reissue)

5811 #1 "Where Does the Good Times Go"/"The Way That I Love You," December 26, 1966

5865 #1 "Sam's Place"/"Don't Ever Tell Me Goodbye," March 13, 1967

5942 #1 "Your Tender Loving Care"/"What a Liar I Am," June 26, 1967

2001 #2 "It Takes People Like You (to Make People Like Me)"/"You Left Her Lonely Too Long," September 25, 1967

2080 #1 "How Long Will My Baby Be Gone"/"Everybody Needs Somebody," January 8, 1968

6111 "Only You (Can Break My Heart)"/"Gonna Have Love," 1968 (Star Line reissue)

6112 "Cryin' Time"/"I've Got a Tiger by the Tail," 1968 (Star Line reissue)

2142 #2 "Sweet Rosie Jones"/"Happy Times Are Here Again," April 1, 1968

2237 #7 "Let the World Keep On a Turnin'"/"I'll Love You Forever and Ever" (w. Buddy Alan), July 8, 1968

2300 #5 "I've Got You on My Mind Again"/"That's All Right with Me (If It's All Right with You)," September 30, 1968

2328 "Christmas Shopping"/"One of Everything You Got," November 4, 1968

2330 "Things I Saw Happening at the Fountain on the Plaza When I Was Visiting Rome or Amore"/"Turkish Holiday," November 4, 1968

2377 #1 "Who's Gonna Mow Your Grass?"/"There's Gonna Be Some Changes Made," January 13, 1969

2485 #1 "Johnny B. Goode" (live)/"Maybe If I Close My Eyes (It'll Go Away)," May 5, 1969

2570 #1 "Tall Dark Stranger"/"Sing That Kind of a Song," July 21, 1969

2646 #5 "Big in Vegas"/"White Satin Bed," October 20, 1969

2731 #13 "We're Gonna Get Together"/"Everybody Needs Somebody" (w. Susan Raye), February 2, 1970

6148 "Sam's Place"/"Waitin' in Your Welfare Line," 1970 (Star Line reissue)

2791 #12 "Togetherness"/"Fallin' for You" (w. Susan Raye), April 6, 1970

2783 #2 "The Kansas City Song"/"I'd Love to Be Your Man," May 18, 1970

2871 #8 "The Great White Horse"/"Your Tender Loving Care" (w. Susan Raye), July 27, 1970

2947 #9 "I Wouldn't Live in New York City (If They Gave Me the Whole Dang Town)"/"No Milk and Honey in Baltimore," October 5, 1970

3023 #9 "Bridge over Troubled Water"/"(I'm Goin') Home," January 11, 1971

3096 #3 "Ruby (Are You Mad)"/"Heartbreak Mountain," April 12, 1971

3164 #2 "Rollin' in My Sweet Baby's Arms"/"Corn Liquor," August 16, 1971

3215 #29 "Too Old to Cut the Mustard"/"Wham Bam" (w. Buddy Alan), November 8, 1971

3225 "Santa's Gonna Come in a Stagecoach"/"One of Everything You Got" (w. Susan Raye), November 22, 1971

3262 #8 "I'll Still Be Waiting for You"/"Full Time Daddy," January 17, 1972

3314 #1 "Made in Japan"/"Black Texas Dirt," April 3, 1972

3368 #13 "Looking Back to See"/"Cryin' Time" (w. Susan Raye), June 19, 1972

3429 #13 "You Ain't Gonna Have Ol' Buck to Kick Around No More"/"I Love You So Much It Hurts," August 28, 1972

3504 #23 "In the Palm of Your Hand"/"Get Out of Town Before Sun Goes Down," December 4, 1972

3563 #14 "Ain't It Amazing, Gracie"/"The Good Old Days (Are Here Again)," March 5, 1973

3601 #35 "The Good Old Days (Are Here Again)"/"When You Get to Heaven (I'll Be There)" (w. Susan Raye), May 21, 1973

3688 #27 "Arms Full of Empty"/"Songwriter's Lament," July 30, 1973

6189 "Big in Vegas"/"Tall Dark Stranger," 1973 (Star Line reissue)

6221 "Made in Japan"/"Ruby (Are You Mad)" (Star Line reissue)

3769 #8 "Big Game Hunter"/"That Loving Feeling," November 5, 1973

3841 #9 "On the Cover of the Music City News"/"Stony Mountain West Virginia," February 25, 1974

3907 #6 "(It's a) Monster's Holiday"/"Great Expectations," June 24, 1974

3976 #8 "Great Expectations"/"Let the Fun Begin," November 4, 1974

4043 #19 "Weekend Daddy"/#19 "41st Street Lonely Heart's Club," March 10, 1975

4100 "Sweethearts in Heaven"/#20 "Love Is Strange" (w. Susan Raye), June 16, 1975

4138 "Battle of New Orleans"/"Run Him to the Round House Nellie," September 8, 1975

4181 "Country Singer's Prayer"/"Meanwhile Back at the Ranch," November 10, 1975

Warner Brothers (1976–1981)

8223 "Hollywood Waltz"/"Rain on Your Parade," May 26, 1976

8255 "California Okie"/"Child Support," August 18, 1976

8316 "World Famous Holiday Inn"/"He Don't Deserve You Anymore," January 19, 1977

8395 "It's Been a Long, Long Time"/"Rain on Your Parade," May 1977

8433 "Our Old Mansion"/"How Come My Dog Don't Bark," August 3, 1977

8486 "Texas Tornado"/"Let the Good Times Roll," October 19, 1977

8614 #27 "Nights Are Forever Without You"/"When I Need You," July 5, 1978

8701 "Do You Wanna Make Love"/"Seasons of My Heart," November 8, 1978

8830 #11 "Play Together Again Again" (w. Emmylou Harris)/"He Don't Deserve You Anymore," April 18, 1979

49046 #30 "Hangin' In and Hangin' On"/"Sweet Molly Brown's," August 15, 1979

49118 #22 "Let Jesse Rob the Train"/"The Victim of Life's Circumstances," November 4, 1979

49200 "Love Is a Warm Cowboy"/"I Don't Want to Live in San Francisco," March 5, 1980

49278 "Moonlights and Magnolias"/"Nickels and Dimes," June 18, 1980

49651 "Without You"/"Love Don't Make the Bars," March 15, 1981

Reprise (1988)

27964 #1 "Streets of Bakersfield" (w. Dwight Yoakam)/"One More Name" (Dwight Yoakam), June 17, 1988

Capitol—Curb/Capitol (1988–1990)

44248 #46 "Hot Dog"/"Second Fiddle," September 28, 1988

44295 #54 "A-11"/"Sweethearts in Heaven," January 4, 1989

44356 "Put Another Quarter in the Jukebox"/"Don't Let Her Know," March 22, 1989

44409 #27 "Act Naturally" (w. Ringo Starr)/"Key's in the Mailbox," June 21, 1989

44465 "Gonna Have Love"/"Out There Chasing Rainbows," September 13, 1989

44504 "Tijuana Lady"/"Brooklyn Bridge," January 31, 1990

79396 "Kickin' In" (promotional CD), October 22, 1990

79896 "Forever Yours" (promotional CD), July 22, 1991

EPs
No./Title/Released

Capitol

EAP-1-1550 *Foolin' Around*, May 8, 1961

R-5446 *Four by Buck Owens*, June 14, 1965

LPs
No./Title/Released

La Brea
L/LS-8017 *Buck Owens*, 1961

Capitol
T-1489 *Buck Owens*, January 30, 1961 (rechanneled and reissued on DT-1489 *Under Your Spell Again*, and with bonus songs on Sundazed SC-6042)

ST-1482 *Buck Owens Sings Harlan Howard*, August 28, 1961 (reissued with bonus song on Sundazed SC-6101)

ST-1777 *You're for Me*, October 1, 1962 (reissued with bonus songs on Sundazed SC-6043 in 1995)

ST-1879 #2 *On the Bandstand*, April 29, 1963 (reissued with bonus song on Sundazed SC-6044 in 1995)

ST-1989 #1 *Buck Owens Sings Tommy Collins*, November 11, 1963 (reissued with two songs omitted on Hilltop JS-6071 *If You Ain't Lovin'* in 1970 and with bonus song on Sundazed SC-6102 in 1997)

ST-2009 *Country Music Hootenanny* (various Bakersfield artists), November 18, 1963

ST-2105 #2 *The Best of Buck Owens, Vol. 1*, June 1, 1964 (reissued on SM-11827 in 1977)

ST-2135 #1 *Together Again/My Heart Skips a Beat*, July 20, 1964 (reissued with two songs omitted on STBB-532 and with bonus songs on Sundazed SC-6045 in 1995)

ST-2186 #1 *I Don't Care*, November 2, 1964 (reissued with bonus song on Sundazed SC-6046 in 1995)

ST-2283 #1 *I've Got a Tiger by the Tail*, March 1, 1965 (reissued on STCL-355 and with bonus songs on Sundazed SC-6047 in 1995)

ST-2353 #1 *Before You Go/No One but You*, July 26, 1965 (reissued with two songs omitted on STBB-355 in 1969 and with bonus songs on Sundazed SC-6048 in 1995)

ST-2367 #4 *The Instrumental Hits of Buck Owens and His Buckaroos*, July 26, 1965 (reissued with bonus songs on Sundazed SC-6049 in 1995)

ST-2396 *Christmas with Buck Owens & His Buckaroos*, October 4, 1965

ST-2436 #10 *The Buck Owens Song Book*, 1966

ST-2443 #1 *Roll Out the Red Carpet*, February 7, 1966 (reissued with bonus songs on Sundazed SC-6050 in 1995)

ST-2497 #1 *Dust on Mother's Bible*, May 2, 1966

ST-2556 #1 *Carnegie Hall Concert*, July 25, 1966 (Reissued with bonus songs on Country Music Foundation CMF-012-D *Live at Carnegie Hall* in December 1988)

ST-2640 #1 *Open Up Your Heart*, December 27, 1966 (reissued with bonus songs on Sundazed SC-6051 in 1995)

ST-2715 #1 *Buck Owens and His Buckaroos in Japan*, May 1, 1967 (live, reissued with bonus songs on Sundazed SC-6103 in 1997)

ST-2760 #1 *Your Tender Loving Care*, August 7, 1967 (reissued with bonus songs on Sundazed SC-6104 in 1997)

ST-2841 #1 *It Takes People Like You to Make People Like Me*, January 2, 1968 (reissued with two songs omitted on STCL-355 deluxe three pack in 1969 and with bonus songs on Sundazed SC-6105 in 1997)

ST-2897 #5 *The Best of Buck Owens, Vol. 2* (sampler), April 1, 1968 (reissued on SM-11677 in 1977)

ST-2962 #2 *Sweet Rosie Jones*, July 1, 1968

ST-2977 *Christmas Shopping*, October 7, 1968 (reissued on STBB-486 *Merry Hee Haw Christmas* in October 1970)

ST-2994 #27 *Buck Owens the Guitar Player*, October 7, 1968

ST-131 #19 *I've Got You on My Mind Again* (w. Buddy Alan), December 30, 1968

SKAO-145 #12 *The Best of Buck Owens, Vol. 3* (sampler), January 13, 1969

ST-232 #5 *Buck Owens in London*, June 2, 1969

ST-212 #2 *Tall Dark Stranger*, September 29, 1969

STCL-355 De-Luxe 3-Pack (sampler: ST-2283, ST-2353, ST-232 with omitted songs), 1969

ST-413 #9 *The Buck Owens Show: Big in Vegas*, December 29, 1969 (reissued in 1973 on Hilltop JS-6128 *The Buck Owens Show Live in Las Vegas* with omitted songs)

ST-439 *Your Mother's Prayer*, March 2, 1970

ST-448 #10 *We're Gonna Get Together* (w. Susan Raye), April 6, 1970

ST-476 #10 *The Kansas City Song*, July 6, 1970

STCL-574 *Buck Owens and His Buckaroos* (sampler: ST-2640, ST-2443, ST-131 with omitted songs), August 1970 (3 LP set)

ST-558 #22 *The Great White Horse* (w. Susan Raye), September 8, 1970

ST-628 #12 *I Wouldn't Live in New York City*, November 2, 1970

7E-062-80578 *Buck Owens & the Buckaroos Live in Scandinavia*, 1970 (released in Norway)

ST-685 #11 *Bridge over Troubled Water*, February 15, 1971

ST-795 #9 *Buck Owens' Ruby & Other Bluegrass Specials*, June 21, 1971

ST-837 *Merry Christmas from Buck Owens and Susan Raye* (w. Susan Raye), September 20, 1971

ST-830 #17 *The Best of Buck Owens, Vol. 4*, October 4, 1971

ST-874 #35 *Too Old to Cut the Mustard* (w. Buddy Alan), January 1972

ST-11039 #3 *Buck Owens Live at the Nugget*, April 24, 1972

ST-11084 #15 *The Best of Buck Owens and Susan Raye* (w. Susan Raye), July 1972

ST-11105 #10 *Buck Owens Live at the White House*, September 5, 1972

ST-11136 #21 *In the Palm of Your Hand*, January 8, 1973

ST-11180 #17 *Ain't It Amazing, Gracie*, May 14, 1973

ST-11204 #29 *The Good Old Days (Are Here Again)* (w. Susan Raye), July 1973

ST-11222 #32 *Arms Full of Empty*, September 10, 1973

ST-23261 *Buck Owens Live in New Zealand*, 1974 (released in New Zealand)

ST-23372 *Buck Owens Live at the Sydney Opera House*, 1974 (released in Australia)

ST-11273 #35 *The Best of Buck Owens, Vol. 5*, February 1974

ST-11332 #10 *(It's a) Monster's Holiday*, September 1974

ST-11390 #21 *41st Street Lonely Heart's Club/Weekend Daddy*, May 5, 1975

ST-11471 #34 *The Best of Buck Owens, Vol. 6*, January 12, 1976

C1-91132 #37 *Hot Dog!* November 16, 1988

C2-92893 *Act Naturally*, October 4, 1989

Starday

SLP-172 *Fabulous Country Music Sound of Buck Owens*, April 1962 (reissued in 1965 on SLP-324 *Country Hitmaker No. 1* and in 1969 on SLP-446 *Sweethearts in Heaven* with two songs omitted)

Warner Brothers

BS-2952 #39 *Buck 'Em*, June 25, 1976

BS-3087 *Our Old Mansion*, September 30, 1977

Compact Discs

Audium

AUD-CD-8124 *Young Buck: The Complete Pre-Capitol Recordings of Buck Owens*, February 27, 2001

Bear Family (Germany)

BCD-16850 *Act Naturally*, August 2008 (five-CD box, 1953–1964)

BCD-16855 *Open Up Your Heart*, March 29, 2010 (seven-CD box, 1965–1968, plus a 120-page book)

Capitol—Curb/Capitol

CDP-7-91132-2 *Hot Dog!* November 16, 1988 (CD release of LP C1-91132)

CDP-7-92893-2 *Act Naturally*, October 4, 1989 (CD release of LP C2-92893)
D2-77342 *All-Time Greatest Hits, Vol. 1*, August 13, 1990
D2-77349 *Christmas with Buck Owens*, August 27, 1990
CDP-7-95340 *Kickin' In*, January 7, 1991
D2-77342 *All-Time Greatest Hits, Vol. 2*, 1992
D2-77342 *All-Time Greatest Hits, Vol. 3*, 1993

New West

NW-6123 *Buck Owens Live from Austin, TX*, July 10, 2007

Rhino

R2-71016 *The Buck Owens Collection (1959–1990)*, 1992 (three-CD boxed set)
R2-71816 *The Very Best of Buck Owens, Vol. 1*, 1994
R2-71817 *The Very Best of Buck Owens, Vol. 2*, 1994
R2-74093 #55 *Buck Owens 21 #1 Hits: The Ultimate Collection*, August 1, 2006
RHM2-7724 *The Warner Bros. Recordings*, March 2007 (two-CD set; limited edition of 5,000 copies)

Compiled by Frank Frantik and Eileen Sisk

Sources: AlbumLinerNotes.com; AllMusic.com; Amazon.com; Bakersfield Californian; Bear Family Records CD booklets; The Billboard Book of Top 40 Country Hits, 2nd ed., by Joel Whitburn (New York: Billboard Books, 2006); Billboard.com; Capitol Label Discography, CD-ROM, compiled by Michel Ruppli, Bill Daniels, and Ed Novitsky, with Michael Cuscuna (Names & Numbers, 2007); Crystal Palace official Web site (www.buckowens.com); Buckowensfan.com; LPDiscography.com; popculturefanboy (http://popculturefanboy.blogspot.com); Praguefrank's Country Music Discographies (http://countrydiscography.blogspot.com); Rockin' Country Style (http://rcs-discography.com); Rhino Records official Web site (www.rhino.com).

BIBLIOGRAPHY

Blumay, Carl, with Henry Edwards. *The Dark Side of Power*. New York: Simon & Schuster. 1992.
Bohemian Club. *Bohemian Club*. San Francisco: Bohemian Club, 1965.
Burke, Kathryn. *The Dust Bowl, Bakersfield Sound, and Buck*. North Charleston, SC: BookSurge Publishers, 2007.
Campbell, Glen, with Tom Carter. *Rhinestone Cowboy*. New York: Villard Books, 1994.
Carnes, Patrick, Ph.D. *Contrary to Love*. Center City, MN: Hazelden, 1989.
Clark, Roy, with Marc Eliot. *My Life in Spite of Myself!* New York: Simon & Schuster, 1994.
Cochran, Johnnie L., Jr. with Tim Rutten. *Journey to Justice*. New York: Ballantine Books, 1996.
Collins, Ace. *The Stories Behind Country Music's All-Time Greatest 100 Songs*. New York: Boulevard Books, 1996.
Cooper, Daniel. *Merle Haggard: Down Every Road*. Nashville: Capitol Nashville, 1996.
Country Music Foundation, ed. *Encyclopedia of Country Music*. New York: Oxford University Press, 1998.
Dawidoff, Nicholas. *In the Country of Country*. New York: Pantheon Books, 1997.
Emery, Ralph, with Patsi Bale Cox. *The View from Nashville: On the Record with Country Music's Greatest Stars*. New York: Quill, 1998.
Englehardt, Kristofer. *Beatles Undercover*. Canada: Collector's Guide Publishing. 1998.
Epstein, Edward Jay. *Dossier: The Secret History of Armand Hammer*. New York: Random House, 1996.
Escott, Colin. *Tattooed on Their Tongues*. New York: Schirmer Books, 1996.
Finstad, Suzanne. *Child Bride*. New York: Harmony Books, 1997.
Fredson, Michael. *Hood Canal*. Washington: Arcadia Publishing, 2007.
George-Warren, Holly, and Michelle Freedman. *How the West Was Worn*. New York: Harry N. Abrams, 2001.
Goldman, Albert. *Elvis*. New York: McGraw-Hill, 1981.
Golomb, Elan. *Trapped in the Mirror: Adult Children of Narcissists in Their Struggle for Self*. New York: William Morrow and Co., 1992.
Haggard, Merle, with Peggy Russell. *Sing Me Back Home*. New York: Times Books, 1981.
Haggard, Merle, with Tom Carter. *My House of Memories: For the Record*. New York: HarperCollins, 1999.
Hively, Kay, and Albert E. Brumley Jr. *I'll Fly Away*. Branson, MO: Mountaineer Books, 1990.
Jones, George, with Tom Carter. *I Lived to Tell It All*. New York: Villard, 1996.
Kienzle, Rich. *The Buck Owens Collection 1959–1990*. Santa Monica, CA: Rhino Records, 1992.
Killen, Buddy, with Tom Carter. *By the Seat of My Pants*. New York: Simon & Schuster, 1993.
La Chapelle, Peter. *Proud to Be an Okie*. Berkeley, CA: University of California Press, 2007.
Lovullo, Sam, and Marc Eliot. *Life in the Kornfield*. New York: Boulevard Books, 1996.
McCloud, Barry. *Definitive Country*. New York: Perigee Books, 1995.
Nash, Alanna. *The Colonel*. New York: Simon & Schuster, 2003.
Nelson, Ken. *My First 90 Years Plus 3*. Pittsburgh, PA: Dorrance Publishing Co., 2007.
O'Brien, Cathy, and Mark Phillips. *Tranceformation of America*. Las Vegas: Reality Marketing, 1995.

Oermann, Robert K. *America's Music*. Atlanta: Turner Publishing, 1996.

Reed Elsevier, Inc. *The Complete Who's Who Biographies*. New Providence, NJ: Reed Elsevier, 2000.

Reed Elsevier, Inc. *Who's Who in Entertainment*. Various eds. New Providence, NJ: Reed Elsevier, 1991–1999.

Rovin, Jeff. *Country Music Babylon*. New York: St. Martin's Paperbacks, 1993.

Schoeman, Amy. *Skeleton Coast*. Portland, OR: International Specialized Book Service, 1986.

Sisk, Eileen. *Honky-Tonks*. San Francisco, California: HarperCollins West, 1995.

Spitz, Werner U., M.D. and Russell S. Fisher, M.D., eds. *Medicolegal Investigation of Death*. Springfield, IL: Charles C. Thomas, 1973.

Stacey, Linda. *Freight Train Running*. Bakersfield, CA: Bear State Books, 2006.

Stambler, Irwin, and Grelun Landon. *The Encyclopedia of Folk, Country & Western Music*. New York: St. Martin's Press, 1984.

Stoneman, Roni, as told to Ellen Wright. *Pressing On*. Urbana, IL: University of Illinois Press, 2007.

Whitburn, Jewell. *Billboard's Top Country Singles 1944–1993*. Menomonee Falls, WI: Records Resources, 1994.

Wiener, Allen J. *The Beatles: The Ultimate Recording Guide*. Holbrook, MA: Bob Adams, 1994.

INDEX